GRAPHIC COMMUNICATIONS TODAY

GRAPHIC COMMUNICATIONS TODAY

THIRD EDITION

THEODORE E. CONOVER
University of Nevada, Reno

WEST PUBLISHING COMPANY

St. Paul/Minneapolis • New York • Los Angeles • San Francisco

Copyediting: Benjamin Shriver
Illustrations: Precision Graphics
Composition: Parkwood Composition
Index: Terry Casey

Cover Image by Ron Chan. Artist's statement: "This artwork was created using a combination of traditional and electronic techniques. Sketches were done by hand using markers and pencils on tracing paper. The final sketch was scanned into a Macintosh computer and opened in Adobe Illustrator as a template. The template was used to retrace the drawing in a new Illustrator file. Once this was accomplished, the color was added and rendered. The total process, from sketch to finish, took approximately six days to complete." (Courtesy the artist and Jim Lillie, artist representative.)

WEST'S COMMITMENT TO THE ENVIRONMENT

In 1906, West Publishing Company began recycling materials left over from the production of books. This began a tradition of efficient and responsible use of resources. Today, 100% of our legal bound volumes are printed on acid-free, recycled paper consisting of 50% new paper pulp and 50% paper that has undergone a de-inking process. We also use vegetable-based inks to print all of our books. West recycles nearly 27,700,000 pounds of scrap paper annually—the equivalent of 229,300 trees. Since the 1960s, West has devised ways to capture and recycle waste inks, solvents, oils, and vapors created in the printing process. We also recycle plastics of all kinds, wood, glass, corrugated cardboard, and batteries, and have eliminated the use of polystyrene book packaging. We at West are proud of the longevity and the scope of our commitment to the environment.

Production, Prepress, Printing and Binding by West Publishing Company.

Printed with **Printwise**
Environmentally Advanced Water Washable Ink   ∞

British Library Cataloguing-in-Publication Data. A catalogue record for this book is available from the British Library.

COPYRIGHT ©1985, 1990   By WEST PUBLISHING COMPANY
COPYRIGHT ©1995   By WEST PUBLISHING COMPANY
                         610 Opperman Drive
                         P.O. Box 64526
                         St. Paul, MN 55164-0526

Library of Congress Cataloging-in-Publication Data

Conover, Theodore E.
    Graphic communications today / Theodore E. Conover. — 3rd ed.
      p. cm.
    Includes bibliographical references and index.
    ISBN 0-314-04424-8
    1. Printing, Practical—Layout.   2. Newspaper layout and
typography.   3. Newsletters—Design.   4. Magazine design.
5. Graphic arts.   I. Title
Z246.C58   1995
686.2'252—dc20   94-35459
                                                          CIP

TO EDNA

CONTENTS

CHAPTER SIX
ART AND ILLUSTRATIONS   111

CHAPTER SEVEN
COLOR: A POWERFUL COMMUNICATION TOOL   137

CHAPTER EIGHT
PAPER AND INK   157

CHAPTER TWELVE
ADVERTISING DESIGN   249

CHAPTER THIRTEEN
DESIGNING FOR PUBLIC RELATIONS   271

CHAPTER FOURTEEN
DESIGNING THE MAGAZINE   281

PREFACE

This book is intended to be a beginning. A starting point. I hope that the book will open a door and the reader will go on from there to continuing, perhaps more complex studies of one of humanity's oldest—and at the same time newest—arts, the art of visual communication.

My hope is that this book will provide useful information for those who desire to produce effective and attractive communications intended for their selected target audiences. In addition, I hope this book will help designers to understand the communications philosophies of editors and editors to understand the philosophies of designers so they can work together in reaching common communication goals.

It should be mentioned, too, that the demarcation line that separated designers and editors in the past is disappearing. A new era of the visual communicator—the person with both design and writing skills—is upon us.

In addition, this book is intended for those who aspire to careers in communications and suddenly find themselves putting together publications. All at once they have to know layout, typography, and graphics, and know them fast. They have to put out a newsletter, a company magazine, a financial report, or a brochure. This book, hopefully, will help them, too. It is written for the writer who must now be an editor and layout person and for people who shift from one medium—such as the electronic—to another.

Finally, I hope that practicing professionals will find this book worthwhile. Even though busy communicators may know their fields thoroughly, a review from a different perspective may trigger new inspiration and enthusiasm. This book provides a chance for professionals to stand back and reexamine the way they do things, to break out of daily routines to consider improvements so that the messages they produce are more readable, more attractive, and more effective.

ACKNOWLEDGMENTS

➤ It would be impossible to list everyone who has had a part in making this third edition of *Graphic Communications Today* a reality. Since the first edition appeared in 1985, scores of students and professionals in every field of visual communication have responded to my requests for help. The response has been overwhelming; all have my everlasting gratitude.

Several people, though, must be cited for their special help with this new edition. They include those who read the second edition and offered many valuable suggestions for improvement:

Pat Sarraino, Lorain County Community College, Ohio; Robert Willett, The University of Georgia, Athens; Jessica Kimbrough, University of Alabama, Tuscaloosa; Priscilla Nash, Nashville State Technical Institute, Tennessee; Alfredo A. Marin-Carle, Ball State University, Indiana; W. A. West, Grant MacEwan Community College,

Edmonton, Alberta, Canada; Alma Mary Anderson, Indiana State University, Terre Haute, Indiana.

Alma Mary Anderson
Indiana State University

Laura Berthelot
Louisiana State University

Daniel Boyarski
Carnegie-Melon University, Pennsylvania

Alan Dennis
University of Alabama

Robert J. Fields
Virginia Polytechnic Institute and State University

Marie Freckleton
Rochester Institute of Technology, New York

Charlotte R. Hatfield
Ball State University, Indiana

Robert H. Hawlk
Ohio University

Kenneth F. Hird
California State University, Los Angeles

Jessica Kimbrough
University of Alabama

Tom Knights
Northern Arizona University

Alfredo A. Marin-Carle
Ball State University

Sean Morrison
Boston University

W. S. Mott
California Polytechnic State University, San Luis Obispo

Priscilla Nash
Nashville State Technical Institute

James F. Paschal
University of Oklahoma

Bob Pike
Syracuse University, New York

Roger Remington
Rochester Institute of Technology, New York

Jerry Richardson
North Dakota State University

David W. Richter
Ohio State University

Bill Ryan
University of Oregon

Pat Sarraino
Lorain County Community College

Thomas E. Schildgen
Arizona State University

Sexton Stewart
Moorpark College, California

Wally A. West
Grant MacEwan Community College

Terry Whistler
University of Houston, Texas

Robert Willett
University of Georgia, Athens

Harold W. Wilson
University of Minnesota

Karen F. Zuga
Kent State University, Ohio

Once again, Edna Conover read much of the manuscript, made suggestions, and helped with record keeping. I am also grateful to others: Lee Hawes of the *Tampa Tribune;* Michael Kennedy, designer; Michael J. Parman, publisher, *Press Democrat;* Dean Rae and William Ryan of the University of Oregon; Lee Cavin, former newspaper publisher; Daniela Birch, Aldus Corporation; Stephen Porter, The Pennsylvania State University; Brian Slawson, University of Florida; Christopher Burke, University of Michigan; Paul H. Conover; Dierck Casselman, *Detroit News* and University of Nevada; Tom Wixon, Eddy Street Agency; Eric Anderson, InnerWest; Janet Rash, Donrey Outdoor; Colleen Muller, Adobe Systems; Dennis Rudat, Michigan Farm Bureau; Richard Ebel, Promotional Products Association International; Dave Noel, Heidelberg Harris; Rich Johnson, Idaho Farm Bureau; and that outstanding electronic designer, Laurence M. Gartel.

Edmund C. Arnold, who has been my mentor since my weekly newspaper days of many years ago and who has contributed much to the world of visual communication, played a part in making this book possible; he will always have my sincere thanks.

Once again, Clyde Perlee and his fine staff at West Educational Publishing made me realize many times how fortunate I have been to have them guiding this project to completion. A special thanks to Jan Lamar, senior developmental editor, and Ann Rudrud, production editor. Ben Shriver edited the copy and made many helpful suggestions. And, my thanks to the designer, Janet Bollow.

In addition, I would like to thank my associates for many years in the American Amateur Press Association who encouraged my interest in the printed word for the pleasure it can bring, rather than for its profit potential.

Theodore E. Conover

INTRODUCTION

Visual Communication. It's a new term for a new age in the communication industry. As the information age progresses and more and more information is distributed to an overcommunicated society, each communication must be crafted with written and visual skill if it is to be received, understood, and used.

The flood of information threatens to bury us, making it increasingly difficult for pertinent and essential material to attract the attention of its intended audiences. The situation challenges us to find ways to present information even more dramatically and effectively.

Thus there is a clear need for a visual communicator—a communicator who understands the effective use of words and who also understands how to present information in a graphic manner. In the world of communications, the visual communicator and the graphic journalist are now filling important roles in publishing and printing offices as well as in the production facilities in public relations, advertising, and electronic media establishments. This role will increase in importance as time marches on.

Consider what editors in the magazine division of McGraw-Hill told me when I was working on three of their magazines under a program sponsored by the American Business Press. Again and again staffers on *Business Week, Chemical Week,* and *Engineering and Mining Journal,* emphasized the need for writers and editors who knew something about the mechanics of effective printed communication. They lamented that many journalism and design school graduates did not know how to select and arrange type, how to lay out pages, or even how to use white space effectively.

At the same time, designers and photographers complain that editors do not understand graphics, good design, and good visual display.

This need for understanding graphics has been accented in recent years for a number of reasons. One concerns the technological advances in the profession. Another has to do with the challenge to communications from competing forces such as changing lifestyles, the welter of activities that infringe on time for reading, and the declining emphasis on reading in our education system—a system wherein courses such as film and use of the video camera are substituted for English and literature.

As we trace the careers of our students in graphic design and journalism we find that there is an inclination for people in the communication industry to switch from one area to another. The person who is writing editorials today may be asked to plan and design a newsletter tomorrow. An eclectic background that includes design skills along with writing skills can pay dividends.

Then there is the new technology. It has made printing and duplication of printed messages easily available to everyone involved in the distribution of information. As a result we are being flooded with an incredible amount of poorly designed and poorly executed communications. A lot of wastebaskets are overflowing with unread communications, brochures, and newsletters because they are visually unattractive.

My hope is that this is a situation that is reversible. With the solid foundation in visual communication this text can provide you, your message will be the one that stands a better chance of actually being read and acted upon. That's the goal we both share.

WHY VISUAL COMMUNICATION?

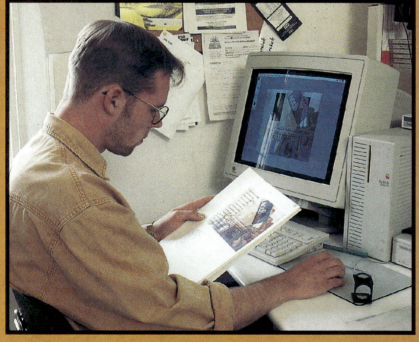

© Churchill & Klehr

1 It was the first day of fall semester. Louis and Tanya, Zack and Emilia met in the student union after class. They sat in a booth in the snack bar and considered what they'd been discussing in class that day. Louis and Emilia were journalism majors; he was in the editorial sequence, aiming towards a career as an editor in newspapers or magazines. She was a visual communication major who hoped one day to use her graphic skills in a major public relations agency. Zack saw himself as a future account executive in an advertising agency. Tanya wasn't really sure which career direction she would choose, but she did know her interests were centered on communications.

"We were discussing why we need to know so much more about the production end of communications now than they did when our instructor was in the business," Zack remarked. "Professor Kimbrough told us about what it was like back in the 1960s when she was a reporter. She said everytime she turned in a story, about 13 people worked on it in some way. All those people saw what she had written, and anyone of them might catch mistakes or make suggestions on how the story could be better. Now, most of those people are gone from the process."

The professor had told her class the following story.

BEFORE THE BIG CHANGE

➤ "I was a reporter on the *Daily Times,* over in Midland. One day I was banging out a story on my battered typewriter about an airplane crash I covered. When it was finished I took it to the city editor.

"He went over it and asked a few questions about some facts, made a note or two on the copy, and handed it to the copy editor.

"The copy editor was seated in the "slot." He was in the middle of a U-shaped desk, and four copy readers were on the "rim," or outside edges of the desk, busily making corrections and writing heads for stories.

Fig. 1-1 ■ Visual communicators today produce the vast majority of their work on sophisticated, high-speed imaging systems. But, it wasn't always like this. An understanding of the evolution of graphic design and reproduction systems can be a good base for building a satisfying career. (Photo by Churchill & Klehr)

Fig. 1-2 ■ A typical newsroom before the electronic era. This is the old *New York Journal-American* city room, about 1939. Some reporters are working at their desks with manual typewriters. The men grouped around the desk (center right) are laying out page "dummies" using rulers, pencils, paste jars, and scissors. The copy readers on the outside or "rim" of the u-shaped desk are checking copy for errors and writing headlines under the direction of the editor in the "slot." Now all this work is done on computers. (UPI/Bettmann newsphoto)

Fig. 1-3 ■ A pressman prepares assembled newspaper pages for printing in the days of "hot type" (below, left). He is brushing the type, rules, and plates to make sure they are clean and free of lint and dust. This ponderous process was replaced by "cold type" and the pasteup of pages (right). Note the dummy, or sketch of the page in the upper right corner. It is used as a guide for the pasteup artist. (Left, The Bettmann Archives; right, photo by Rick Gunn)

"The editor saw that one of the readers had just finished editing a story, so he tossed my story in that direction for a final going over before it was sent to the composing room.

"My day was over, so on my way to my car I walked through the composing room. It was bedlam. Linotype machines seven feet high were clashing and clanging as they cast lines of type from molten metal for the page forms. People were rushing about making proofs of galleys of type, sawing strips of metal for spaces between lines of type, mitering corners on other strips of metal borders to make boxes for some stories and advertisements, casting the headline type, and using routers to shave unwanted metal off castings for illustrations.

"Other people were putting all the metal pieces in proper order within chases, the metal frames that hold the pages together while they are put through a molding press to make mats, or molds, of the pages

▶ **IN THE NEWSROOM**

This from the Society of Newspaper Design.

The newspaper design and graphics field—which now includes artists and designers as well as content planners and new technology innovators—is one of the hottest career paths in the newspaper business today.

There are far more job openings than applicants to fill them. The problem is, newspapers are relying on graphics and typographic research from the 1970s and earlier to make visual decisions today. And, despite all the industry attention focused on newspaper graphics and design, only a handful of universities teach anything about it.

Newspaper graphics and design is a new fast track to the top jobs in the newsroom, if you've got the knowledge and experience to take advantage of it.

—Letter from George Benge, Chairman of the Society of Newspaper Design Foundation, to the author.

for casting in the foundry. The resulting castings (plates) would be locked on the press for printing.

"I remembered I wanted to leave a message in the advertising department to try not to put the story I had written about the airplane crash on the same page with an airline advertisement, just in case an editor overlooked that when he dummied pages.

"In the advertising department salespeople were turning in ad copy. Two graphic artists were sketching illustrations and making layouts on their drawing boards. The advertising layout people were "marking up" completed advertisements. They were adding instructions for the composing room workers who prepared the advertisements for printing.

"Drawing boards, T squares, pens and pencils, X-acto knives, and all kinds of other tools were being used to create the layouts.

"Others in the advertising department were marking the areas for advertising placement on dummies, miniature sketches of pages that would be used as "blueprints" by people making up the pages.

"I'm trying to list all the people who, typically, handled an advertisement or story before it appeared in print. I might say that whether you were a reporter, editor, graphic artist, designer, advertising or public relations person, the procedure was about the same.

"Look at the backup personnel we had back then, to catch errors and make suggestions on how we might improve what we had done:

- Editors to check our copy or layouts.
- Typesetters to watch for errors.
- Proofreaders to check for errors and make corrections when the material was set in type.
- Makeup people to handle the type and place it in the forms.
- Even the people who ran the presses would check things over.

"Why am I taking the time to tell you this? Because now most of those people are gone and all the responsibility is on your shoulders. In the world of computers there is a saying: What you see is what you get. That has become a cliche, but it is so true—and also true of publishing. What you produce is going to be what will see the light of day on the printed page."

"Well, in Intro to Vis Com, Dr. Wright told us that we have to know the printing business," Emilia chimed in. "After he got through telling us what vis com is all about—you know, combining all the communication tools, art, photos, copy, type, dingbats, borders, color, even paper, to make our communications as visually and psychologically effective as possible—he added that we need to know how to work with printers.

"He said, 'What if you have designed a brochure and you take it to a printer and he asks you: "Shall we set the body matter 8 on 10 or 9 on 11? Can I make a suggestion? I think an Oxford rule or star border would work better than the 6-point solid rule you indicate. What do you think? Also, would you like us to print it on 60-pound machine finish book, or do you think 70-pound would be better? Tell me, too, can you produce camera-ready pages in your shop? Or, would you expect us to do typesetting and page formatting on our computers?"'"

" 'You are going to have to work with printers,' Dr. Wright went on, 'and you should know how to tell them what you want. You should know what a particular printer is capable of producing. You should be familiar with the printers' trade customs, as well.' "

"Good grief," interrupted Tanya, "I wasn't sure what he was talking about. I guess design skills are just part of the job of being a good visual communicator.

"Dr. Wright said we would be jumping right into the big change."

THE BIG CHANGE

➤ Now a new century is approaching, and if we are to select one word to characterize the new ecology of visual communication it is *change*.

In Professor Kimbrough's *Daily Times* there have been a lot of changes. It is quiet. The clatter of typewriters and staccato beats of the teletypes are gone. Reporters are staring intently at video display screens as they type their stories on computers.

"Wire copy" is stored in a computer, ready to be called up on the wire editor's screen. Computer-enhanced wire service photographs are transmitted by satellite to give the editor a wide selection of sharper and more timely illustrations from around the world.

When the reporters finish their stories, they press code keys and the stories disappear from the screens to be stored in a computer until an editor wants to call them up to process them for printing.

The U-shaped copy desk is gone. So are the copy readers. But the editors are still there. They are seated in front of their computer work stations. When an editor wants a reporter's story she will type a code and the story will appear on her editing screen. She will scan the story and make changes—shift paragraphs, add or delete words, correct

Fig. 1-4 ■ The tools of the trade are changing rapidly. This is a typical newsroom today. Gone are the typewriters and disappearing are the pencils, rulers, and paste jars. Electronic equipment is now used for writing stories and designing pages. (Photo by Steve Johnson)

spelling or punctuation or facts—simply by sending instructions to the computer.

She also will tap out a headline and then instruct the computer as to the size and style of the head. She will store the edited story with others in her computer. Then she will switch to a page layout program. A grid will appear on the screen, and she will lay out the page—integrating the stories and illustrations—and then generate a hard copy of the page with the laser printer.

The advertising department, too, has been moved into the computer age. The graphic artist is creating most of his illustrations on a computer. He has access to a vast array of stock art through a software program. However, he often prefers to create his own art with a draw program. Also he can scan art from the original into his computer with a scanner.

The advertisements created on computers are placed in position on pages which are transferred to the editorial department by cables or modems that connect the computers in each department.

When a page is completed it will go to the "back shop"—or printing department—where a plate will be made to be clamped on the press for printing.

The same techniques are being applied in the creation of advertising, public relations materials, and all sorts of printed communications. Although computer technology is rapidly taking over the industry, there are still communications being produced using photo composition and pasteup to create pages for printing. And some graphic artists utilize pasteup skills along with their computer work.

Many people working in the world of communications have become not only writers, editors, and designers, but they have become

Fig. 1-5 ■ Public relations and advertising agency personnel, as well as others working in communications, are producing in their offices much of the material formerly turned over to commercial printers. Charly Palmer, of TP Design, Atlanta, is preparing material in his studio. It will go to a printer for production. (Photo by Ernest Washington)

the typesetter, proofreader, typographer, and makeup person as well. They are not only communicators—they are visual communicators who do the whole job from conception to execution.

A REVOLUTION IN COMMUNICATIONS

▶ A revolution is sweeping through editorial, public relations, and advertising offices as well as graphic design firms across America. Every form of visual communication has been affected.

As with all change, there was considerable resistance for awhile. There are still a few who are reluctant to come to terms with the new technology. But doubters are disappearing rapidly.

Many have found that the new technology has provided the tools to do a better and more satisfying job. However, they have also discovered that, in making the job easier, the new technology can make the end product of their profession—words and graphics on paper—less effective.

Not too long ago, the principal method of producing printed communications was with metal type, engravings, borders, ornaments, and the letterpress. Everything printed was composed and arranged to very precise dimensions. In the metal, or "hot type," method, rules and borders had to be cut by hand. Type, illustrations, and borders had to be fitted much as carpenters fit materials to produce a building that is straight and true. True craftsmanship was needed to produce satisfactory results on the printed page.

Fig. 1-6 ■ (Top) In days gone by copy written and edited in the front office passed through as many as ten stations where people could catch errors and back up the writer or editor. (Middle) In the recent past advanced technology eliminated many of these stations. (Bottom) Technology continues and even more stations are eliminated. Very soon the digital revolution will enable the visual communicator to send images directly to a printing press.

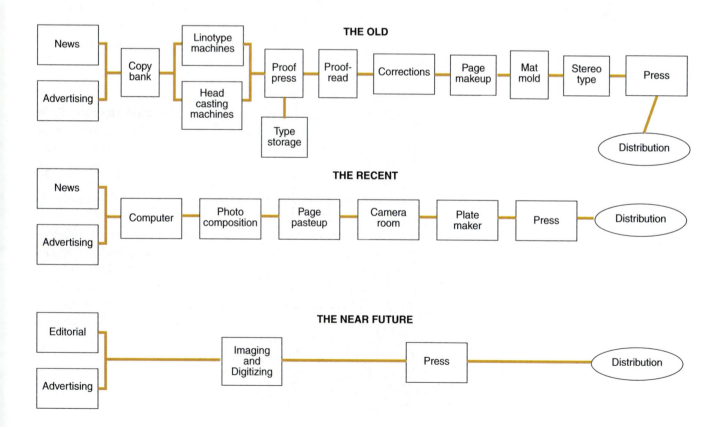

With the advent of cold type composition and the increased use of offset lithography, the process was simplified. It was possible to arrange words and illustrations on paper simply and easily. It was possible to produce excellent printed pieces with comparative ease. On the other hand, it was also possible to produce poorly conceived and executed work. Since the composition and printing processes have been simplified, there is a temptation to take the easy way out and be satisfied with work that does not quite measure up to its potential.

Another dramatic change occurred with the arrival of the computer and "desktop publishing" capabilities in the editorial, advertising, public relations, and graphic design offices. This, again, increases the potential for both good and poor communication. Many communicators now find that they are functioning as designers and compositors as well as writers and editors. They, like the staff at the *Daily Times,* are having to make decisions about type style and size, spacing, placement of elements, and all the graphic decisions handled by production departments not too long ago. Communicators are becoming compositors as well as designers as they operate the computers and electronic gear that have moved the composing room into the editorial offices and design studios. They are not only writers, editors, and designers—they are visual communicators.

BOMBARDED WITH COMMUNICATIONS

▶ The situation is further compounded by the nature of life today. Busy people may not have the time or inclination to decipher unattractive and difficult materials. Sloppy, poorly designed printed material will be tossed aside. There is too much that is interesting and attractive clamoring for our attention.

Competition among Media

We are bombarded with communications from the time our clock radios blare forth in the morning until we doze in front of the television set in the evening. You are exposed to approximately 3,000 commercial messages a day! Columnist George F. Will, who noted that figure, commented that the average American spends one and a half years of his life watching television commercials. The competition for our attention is awesome and it is getting worse.

In 1980 researchers estimated that the average person received between 1,500 and 1,800 messages a day. Today advertising messages alone have reached the 3,000 mark. There is no sign of a letup.

Try counting the number of messages that appeal for your attention during a prime-time hour on television. Counts can go as high as fifty. In the 1950s the sixty-second spot was the standard. Now there is a shift to fifteen-second formats, coupled with a further movement toward seven-and-a-half second commercials.

A study by John C. Schweitzer, of Indiana University, reported in the American Newspaper Publishers Association's "News Research for Better Newspapers" that the great majority of American newspaper readers spend less than thirty minutes a day with their newspapers. Many people surveyed said they only glance at the newspaper.

There is a growing reliance on television by many Americans. By 1963, television overtook newspapers as the source of most people's news about the world, and television became the most "reliable" medium in 1961. As early as 1972, 56 percent of the people surveyed by the Roper Organization said if they could keep only one medium it would be television. Newspapers would be retained by 22 percent and only 5 percent would give up the other media and keep magazines.[1]

And in spring 1981, a Gallup poll showed that 71 percent of the people believe that network television does a better job of providing accurate, unbiased news than anyone else.[2]

Competition within the Print Medium

It is not only competition from the electronic media that is challenging the visual communicator. Competition within the print medium is intensifying. We are all victims of the "stuffed mailbox", to take but one example. The number of pieces of direct mail handled by the Postal Service in 1986 was 55 billion. By 1992 it had climbed to 62 billion. Since then, responses to direct mail appeals indicate that this method of communication really works—hence the number of pieces that will stuff your mailbox even fuller will increase.[3]

Times have changed since the days when Will Rogers was quoted as saying, "All I know is what I read in the newspapers."

The point is, the person who works in communications has a challenge. Audiences are going to have to be lured away from other forms of communication. The "communicator" of today will have to use every tool available and become a creative "visual communicator" to entice the audience to select one message from the scores of others that are demanding attention. It just is not possible for everyone to examine every message. Some will be selected and some will be rejected.

Fig. 1-7 ■ Typographic devices such as lines set in all capital letters, lines too long for easy reading, lines with improper spacing, heavy rules, and reverses can hamper effective communication if not used with care and planning.

SIXTY ROWS OF VARIOUS GRASSES WILL PROVIDE A SITE FOR VO-AG TRAINING IN GRASS INDENTIFICATION. THE ROD-ROW PLANTING IS A COOPERATIVE PROJECT BETWEEN THE HIGH SCHOOL VO-AG PROGRAM AND SOIL CONSERVATION SERVICE. THE FFA CLUB PLOWED AND DISCED THE SHCOOL 924 SITE. THE CONSERVATION DISTRICT PROVIDED FUNDING. THE PLANTING INCLUDES BLOCKS OF BROME GRASSES, FESCUES, WHEATGRASSES, AND NATIVE RANGE GRASSES.

Extension efforts are also directed toward educating growers in the use of integrated pest management techniques. According to the university program coordinator, some 98 percent of all growers are using these techniques as a result of state-wide certification training program.

Pest Management

Extension efforts are also directed toward educating growers in the use of integrated pest management

Extension efforts are also directed toward educating growers in the use of integrated pest management techniques. According to the university program coordinator, some 98 percent of all growers are using these thecniques as a result of a state-wide certification training program. Extension efforts are also directed toward educating growers in the use of integrated pest management techniques. According to one official, integrated pest management is a proven method of preventing

The planting includes blocks of brome grasses, fescues, wheatgrasses, and native range grasses. Irrigated and dryland hay or pasture grasses are included along with rarely seen special purpose grasses. This project has attracted attention from local ranchers who are interested in observing how each grass will perform.

Many of the communications that threaten to suffocate people in a torrent of paper are hardly worth pursuing. They can be fired directly into the wastebasket. On the other hand, much significant information may be thrown out simply because it is poorly written, poorly designed, and poorly presented.

Some communications miss their targets because they are not attractively packaged. Effective content needs effective design to reach its maximum potential.

Getting an Edge on the Competition

Many communicators have turned to design specialists to help them produce presentable printed material. If the communicator can afford it, the help of a professional designer can be a valuable investment—a designer, that is, who understands how to communicate effectively and does not design simply for design's sake.

Many communicator's, however, especially those on tight budgets, do not have the luxury of access to a professional designer. They must become their own visual communicators.

Donna Valenti Weiss, publications manager for the National Rehabilitation Association, tells of arriving at work one day to find a Macintosh computer being installed in her workplace. She learned that she was expected to produce the association's monthly newsletter from that day on. She would take her camera-ready pages to the commercial printer who had done the whole job in the past.

Donna, along with many others in similar positions, had a lot to learn about type and how to use it in a hurry. For example, she had to learn that some type styles present a psychological image to create a mood but are, alas, unreadable. Bold, heavy borders alongside lightface reading matter may create contrast but cause readers to rub their eyes with fatigue. Lines of all capital letters set in Black Letter (also called Text type and more commonly by the misnomer Old English) must be deciphered a letter at a time before they make sense. Full columns or pages of reverse type (white letters on a black background) can be found in magazines. More often than not, readers will skip such messages rather than take the trouble to try to figure them out.

Improper spacing between letters and words turn headlines into globs of black rather than crisp, hard-hitting messages. Vertical lines of type make pleasing arrangements but require the reader to twist and turn to figure them out. Borders used for design effects sometimes become walls over which eyes must climb—but too often don't—to get at the message.

This list of visual offenses could go on and on. However, rather than spend too much time belaboring the point, let's concentrate on creating the most effective communication possible.

But where to begin?

The starting point for any journey through the world of visual communication is an understanding of the complete communication process. Graphics and typography are only parts of the whole. Effective communicators must understand all of the elements that make up communication.

Consider, as a related example, an auto mechanic setting out to rebuild a carburetor. The mechanic cannot begin without knowing how the part fits into the whole automotive system, or the working machinery of an automobile engine. That is, the mechanic needs to know how all the parts of the motor fit together to make the car go before beginning to rebuild the carburetor. The same is true with communications. A knowledge of how everything fits together to deliver a message is needed before a communication can be made to "go."

COMPLETE COMMUNICATION

A complete communication consists of five parts: the sender, the message, the delivery system (medium), the audience, or receiver, and, finally, some way to indicate that the communication was received and understood. The communicator calls this latter part *feedback*. Leave out any of these and communication might miss its mark. The process is outlined in Fig. 1–8.

With this model in mind, let's see how graphics and typography fit in. No matter what sort of printed communication is planned, it will not do its job unless each element in the complete communication model is doing its job.

So let's take a close look at that model and then zero in on our particular concern.

Consider the Sender

First of all, we must consider the sender. What does the sender need to know to put together effective printed communications? The answer is, several things. For instance, the sender needs to know the reason for communicating. Is it to sell something? Is it to keep people informed? Is it to try to change their minds or rally their support behind a cause? Is it to create a particular image for an organization? Or is it to get action and get it fast?

Before you do anything else, brainstorm the reason *why* you are communicating. Then, write it down on paper. Know exactly what is to

Fig. 1-8 ■ The Five Elements of a Complete Communication

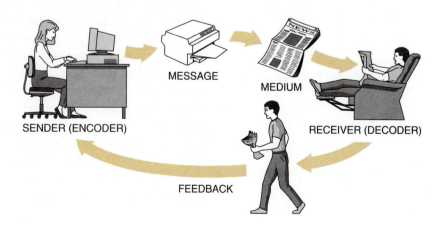

MESSAGE

MEDIUM

SENDER (ENCODER)

RECEIVER (DECODER)

FEEDBACK

be accomplished. Know exactly what is expected of the person who reads the message. If the message has no specific purpose, you can waste time and money. No one will pay attention.

Then consider what words and visuals will cause the audience to stop and look and read.

Words are needed that the audience will understand. Graphics and typography cannot cover up inadequate copy. Sometimes a poorly conceived message is dressed up with attractive typography and impressive graphics. But it still will not work. If words cannot be put together in a way that will attract attention, arouse interest, create curiosity, and convince the audience that what is said is worthwhile, the effort to communicate has failed.

Robert E. Huchingson, owner of a public relations counseling firm in St. Louis and former vice president, public relations, of a major corporation, likes to relate how he approached the problem of writing advertising copy for chicken feed early in his career. He didn't know anything about chickens and chicken feed. What did he do? Before he wrote a line, he bought some chicks and raised them in his kitchen while researching chickens and feed.

The visual communicator, too, must know the subject of his or her concern to do as effective a job as possible with this part of the communication process.

Of course, this is a rather superficial examination of the first element of a complete communication. However, it does put our concern, the purpose of the sender, into perspective.

Media Deliver the Message

The media—newspapers, magazines, brochures, and so on—can be considered channels for delivering a message. Communicators need to know which channels are best for a particular message. And they need to know how to prepare the message so it will be in its most effective physical form for each channel.

Here it is time to clarify something about the audience. In the past the audience, or receiver, of the message was often referred to as "all those people out there." In the days when communicators emphasized the "mass media" and "mass communications," one philosophy of communication was that there was a vast audience of people "out there" and that communications were designed to reach them all. Messages were aimed at the "common denominator," or the largest numbers of people, through the mass media—the media that reached the masses.

Now communicators are becoming convinced that messages aimed at the largest numbers are not always the messages that are the most effective. Many mass circulation newspapers and magazines are on the decline. Media tailored to specialized audiences are on the rise. The *Wall Street Journal,* aimed at an audience with a specific interest, business, continues as the newspaper with the largest circulation in the United States. Even *USA Today,* which has moved into second place in the circulation race, was carefully tailored to a specific audience after considerable research.

National Geographic, another specialized publication, has the fourth largest circulation in the United States. *Modern Maturity,* also aimed at one specific group, attained the largest periodical circulation in the country in fall 1988 and has widened its lead since then. It grew by 3 million subscribers in a three-year span. Nearly 23 million copies of each issue of *Modern Maturity* are distributed monthly. It tops *Reader's Digest* by 6 million. *Smithsonian,* a special interest magazine, is growing rapidly; it tops such well-known publications as *Popular Mechanics* and *Money. TV Guide,* about as specialized as a magazine can get, draws more than 15 million readers a week.[4]

Saturday Evening Post, Collier's, Life, Look, and *American,* circulation leaders of the past are gone. The *Post* and *Life* have been revived but on a very limited basis.

So, from now on, when we discuss the audience, we mean a "target audience." This is an audience that has been carefully defined and its interests and concerns clearly identified.

Let us return now to the medium or channel. The channel is the means of transmitting the message to the target audience. It could be radio, television, postcards, billboards, newspapers, newsletters, handbills, magazines, and so on.

Communicators usually devise a *communications mix* that will use several media because repetition and reinforcement are vital if a message is to be seen and remembered. *Repetition* is a key word in successful communication. This includes sufficient repetition of the message in a single medium as well as repetition through more than one channel. The successful communicator does this all the time.

The communicator must also deal with two kinds of "noise" that can affect the message. Noise is anything that interferes with the message as it moves toward its target. There are two kinds of noise in communication: semantic noise and channel noise.

Semantic noise refers to the words chosen for the message. When the communicator uses words that the target audience does not understand, semantic noise is created. When words are used that have different meanings for the target audience than for the communicator, semantic noise distorts the message. For instance, a soft drink is called a "soda" in the South; there most people would know what is meant. But it is called a "pop" in the Midwest. Messages about "sodas" there would not be clear. (People would think of an ice-cream confection.) Semantic noise would interfere. And, to compound the problem, people in New York still associate the word "soda" with soda water, a seltzer drink.

Channel noise occurs when there are problems with the medium itself. When there is static on the radio or a fuzzy picture on the television, channel noise is present. When there are typographical errors, borders that block a reader's eyes, a poorly printed page, or hard-to-read type, then print media channel noise is interfering with the communication. Channel noise occurs when a fine-screen plate of a photograph is used on textured paper and the details do not print sharply. It

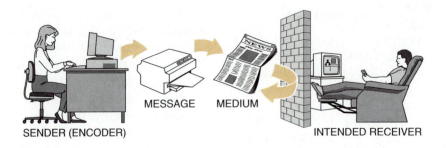

Fig. 1-9 ■ Channel noise and semantic noise can build a brick wall between you and your target audience. Channel noise includes wrong type style, wrong type size, lines too long, printing problems, and reproduction problems, to mention just a few. Semantic noise refers to poor syntax and word choice and even mistakes in spelling. The visual communicator must eliminate "noise" if the message is to be effective.

SENDER (ENCODER)   MESSAGE   MEDIUM   INTENDED RECEIVER

occurs when the harmony of a layout is destroyed by a mixture of bold, sans serif type with old-style Roman types.

A knowledge of typography and the proper use of design elements will help communicators eliminate channel noise and thus communicate more effectively.

Consider the Receiver

One of the secrets of effective communication is the realization on the part of the message sender that we are a civilization composed of diverse interests, increased specialization, and groups brought together because of common interests.

Thus there is much we should know about the target audience. What are its interests and concerns? What are its demographic characteristics—age, income level, and the like? What are its physical and psychological characteristics? What is its life-style?

If the target audience, for instance, is the outdoor type, certain typefaces and illustrations can be chosen to say "this is for you." If the target audience is highly artistic and appreciates excellence in esthetics, typefaces, illustrations, and borders can be arranged to appeal to this audience.

The communicator also needs to know what media or channels the target audience reads, views, and trusts. The channels it does not trust must be recognized as well. If the target audience does not trust a channel you absolutely must use, you may need to change the current typography and graphics to change the channel's image so that trust can be developed.

However, if the receiver does not trust the communicator's client, no amount of distinctive or impressive typography will make the message acceptable.

It is possible, though, that a careful choice of words and arrangement of type and art on pages, and even the proper choice of paper, backed by quality performance on the part of the source, can begin to turn a poor image around.

Feedback Is Vital

Finally, a complete communication must have a way of letting the sender know the word is out, that it was received and understood by the target audience, that the message hit the target. A complete communication must be read, understood, and acted on.

A newspaper publisher, for example, needs to know if the readers are actually reading. Feedback is a must. It can be obtained by watching circulation figures and those of the competition. It can be obtained by the communicator going out and talking to readers. And it can be obtained with scientific research.

Feedback is important for typography and design, too. For years it was an unwritten law that publications should be arranged so that all the advertisements are placed next to editorial matter. Or, at least it was thought that every effort should be made to do this. The theory was that people reading the content of the magazine or newspaper would more likely see the advertisements if they were immediately adjacent to articles. This led to many unattractive inside pages of publications, especially newspapers.

Research, or feedback, then revealed that the proximity of editorial material to advertisements has little or no effect on the pulling power of advertisements.

There are many ways to obtain feedback, but obtain it we must. It must be obtained each and every time communication is attempted if communications are going to work.

Most of the design techniques and suggestions you will find in the chapters of this book are based on years and years of feedback concerning the most attractive and effective ways of putting messages on paper.

In the early 1800s, Thomas Codben-Sanderson, a British publisher and typographer, explained what typography was all about. His explanation is as valuable today as it was more than 175 years ago. In this "age of graphics" it can be applied to all the elements that are included in a visual communication. He wrote: "The whole duty of typography . . . is to communicate to the imagination without loss by the way the thought or image intended to be communicated by the author."[5]

We might take Codben-Sanderson's quote and modify it slightly for today's world:

The whole duty of visual communication is to communicate to the imagination without loss along the way the thought or image intended to be communicated by the designer.

If this goal is to be reached, communicators need to know something about type, printing processes, paper, illustrations, color, and design. Each of these elements is examined in subsequent chapters. Then we will see how to put them all together to produce better-read newspapers, lively and attractive magazines and newsletters, result-getting advertisements, and public relations communications that make people stop, read, and act.

Fig. 1-10 ■ This poster by Royal Design, Memphis, for the Arcade Restaurant commemorates its 75th anniversary. It demonstrates many of the attributes of an effective visual communication. The designer used art, color, typefaces, and overall arrangement to create an attention-getting and memorable production. (Courtesy Royal Design)

GRAPHICS IN ACTION

(*Note:* Starting with Chapter 2 the Graphics in Action assignments can be completed by using either the computer or traditional methods.)

1. Examine a copy of a newspaper and see how many instances of channel noise you can find. Analyze them, try to determine the cause of each, and, if possible, tell what you would do to remedy the situation. *Example:* Narrow columns of type running around a photo, thus causing awkward spacing between words. *Solution:* Enlarge photo to eliminate necessity to use narrow legs of type around a photo, or crop the edge of the photo in closer (depending on the content of the photo).

2. Examine a magazine, brochure, or direct mail piece and analyze it for channel noise. Discuss your findings in a small group and then report to the entire class. If your group is made up of family or friends, just get their feedback on what they like or don't like about the printed piece. Consider the intended target audience. You might save the results of this Action assignment to use later on to redesign the piece.

3. Assume you are planning a printed communication for a small target audience (such as an organization to which you belong). Analyze that audience. Prepare a profile of the audience's characteristics. File for future reference in planning printed communications.

4. Refer to the information you collected in Number 3. What sort of printed communication might appeal to your target audience? What type style and type of art do you think would appeal to this audience? (Refer to the type styles in Appendix B. Or, if you are working in a vis com lab that has computer capabilities, use the typefaces available on your computer for this exercise.)

5. Take a look at the communications you receive from an organization to which you belong or from the firm for which you work. Do you think they are generally effective? Is there a good communications mix in place? What are the shortcomings of the communications and how do you think they could be improved?

NOTES

[1] Ernest C. Hynds, *American Newspapers in the 1970s* (New York: Hastings House, 1975), pp. 18–19.

[2] *Reader's Digest 1989 Almanac and Yearbook* (Pleasantville, N.Y.: Reader's Digest Association, Inc., 1989), p. 695.

[3] *Nevada Weekly,* Dec. 8–14, 1993, p. 24.

[4] *The World Almanac* (New York: Pharos Books, 1994), p. 300.

[5] Daniel B. Updike, *Printing Types,* Vol. 2 (Cambridge, Mass.: Harvard University Press, 1937), p. 212.

FROM CAVE WALLS
TO MODERN VISUAL COMMUNICATION

© Churchill & Klehr

2 Although the term "visual communication" is a fairly new one in the lexicon of those whose profession it is to create effective messages, visual communication has been a means of accomplishing this for thousands of years. Ever since humans first scratched and painted messages on cave walls they have used visual arts to communicate.

The goal of communications now, as then, is the same: to get the message across. The goal of visual communication is to help get the message across as effectively as possible. Advertisers have put together a formula for effective communication that goes something like this:

Our communication should be delivered by the right medium to reach the right audience at the right time and at the most reasonable cost.

Visual communicators, working in the reality of the "real world," should keep this definition in mind, as it applies to all communications, not just advertising messages. As we noted in the previous chapter, to accomplish this goal the professional must understand each step in the communication process. In addition, the communicator should have:

■ A knowledge of the development of visual design.

■ An understanding of what follows the creative process.

■ Well developed skills in the use of the tools of the craft.

DESIGN THROUGH THE AGES

➤ In this chapter we will take a look at the methods used to reproduce what we have created and how the approach to visual communication has been developed through the ages. Consider this chapter an opening of the doors to areas that you should study in depth all during your career.

Thousands of Years Ago

Thousands of years before the development of printing, humans were creating rudimentary forms of visual communications. From as long ago as 25,000 B.C. nomadic hunters of the Paleolithic Age and lake dwellers and growers of crops of the Neolithic Age who succeeded them were covering cave walls and other surfaces with crude drawings of animals and events as well as a variety of shapes and patterns. Petroglyphs, or crude drawings of ages past, have been found on rocks throughout much of the world from Africa to North America to New Zealand.[1]

Visual communications were taken a step further in a number of areas in the years before the birth of Christ. One of the most notable developments came in Egypt. In about 1500 B.C. the Egyptians were laying down a foundation for our profession. They developed hieroglyphics, a writing system that used pictographs to represent words and sounds. In addition, they developed papyrus, a form of paper. Not only that, but they are believed to be the first people to produce manuscripts in which words and pictures were combined to communicate information.

Fig. 2-1 ■ Evidences of early man's efforts to communicate visually have been found in many areas of Europe and the Americas. These petroglyphs illustrate a hunter and arrows and record the killing of a deer with spears. They were found at Newspaper Rock, Utah and date from 1050–1250. (Photo © 1992 Navaswan, FPG)

Fig. 2-2 ■ Progress in visual communication from cave drawings to symbols that represent events or thoughts is illustrated by these ancient Egyptian hieroglyphs, from *The Book of the Dead*. (Scala/Art Resource, New York)

More Recent History of Design

Although many other efforts at creating visual communications can be found in antiquity, we can jump ahead in this brief overview to the Gothic period of design. In medieval Europe, from the tenth to the fifteenth centuries, illuminated manuscripts were being produced, mostly in monasteries. The illumination, which consisted of bright colors as

Fig. 2-3 ■ This page from the Lindisfarne Gospels illustrates an early effort at incorporating visuals with words in the Western world. Books of the times were written and illustrated by hand. The Lindisfarne Gospels, it is estimated, were written in the seventh century. They were discovered on Lindisfarne Island (now Holy Island) in Great Britain. (Bridgeman/ Art Resource, New York)

Fig. 2-4 ■ Before the invention of movable type, books and playing cards were produced in the Western world that consisted of prints from woodcuts. This is an example from the early 1400s.

well as the use of precious metals such as gold leaf, gave brilliance to pages of manuscript in hand-copied and hand-bound books. The pages of these books were not made of paper but of vellum, a very thin sheet made from refined calf or sheep skin. These books were very costly. They were objects made primarily for the nobility, for wealthy merchants, or for the monasteries themselves.

During the twelfth century, the art of paper making from cotton rags came to Spain from China. As this industry grew, paper began to be widely used in books as a cheaper substitute for vellum. By the early fifteenth century, crude picture books and playing cards printed from hand-carved wooden blocks began to be produced in Europe. These books and games were intended for the common people, the vast majority of whom could not read.

As Europe emerged from the Middle Ages to the Renaissance, Johann Gutenberg of Mainz, Germany, was hard at work refining a process of printing books from movable type. His 42-line Bible, published about 1455, was printed in multiple copies from type cast in metal. Within fifty years, the typesetting and printing technology he developed spread all over Europe. Printing and typesetting revolutionized the world of visual communication in much the same way the computer has done in the late twentieth century. Now books could be pur-

Fig. 2-5 ■ The first page of the book of Genesis from the famous Gutenberg 42-line Bible, printed about 1455. Gutenberg designed his typeface after a manuscript style that was popular in Germany. As printing spread across Europe, many new typefaces were designed, based on the preferred styles of France or Italy or England, for example. (From Library of Congress copy in facsimile.)

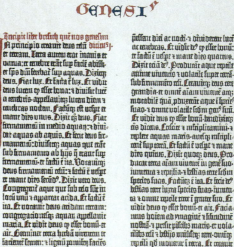

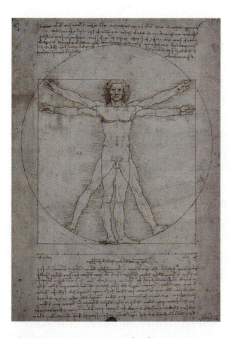

Fig. 2-6 ■ Leonardo da Vinci's Study of Human Proportions According to Vitruvius. c. 1485-90. Ink. (Cameraphoto/Art Resource, New York)

chased by the growing middle class, and scholars and students could more easily pursue research and attain knowledge. As this new technology traveled from one country to another, new typeface designs were developed to reflect regional tastes. Typefaces such as Bembo and Garamond date from this period.

In the Renaissance (which means "rebirth") of the late fifteenth and early sixteenth centuries, painters such as Leonardo da Vinci, Michelangelo, Raphael, and others perfected some of the principles of design still used today. These principles, which had their origins in the art of classical Greece and Rome, included the use of balance, proportion, and harmony. Renaissance artists combined these design principles with color to produce works of art that continue to be inspirations for designers.

Baroque is a design form that was popular in the seventeenth and eighteenth centuries. Baroque style features curvilinear, or curved-line, forms, dramatic lighting and brilliant colors. The style projects an image of luxurious elegance. Rococo, a French variation of Baroque, was even more elaborately ornamental.

Towards the end of the eighteenth century and well into the next, life started to speed up. Cities were developing and industries were

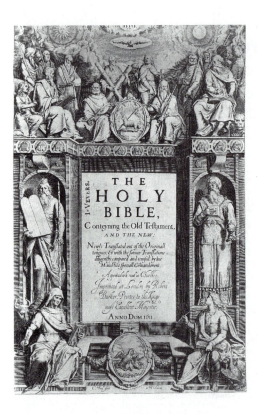

Fig. 2-7 ■ This title page from the original King James Bible is a typical example of Baroque graphic design. This Bible was published in London in 1611. (The Pierpont Morgan Library, New York, PML 5460)

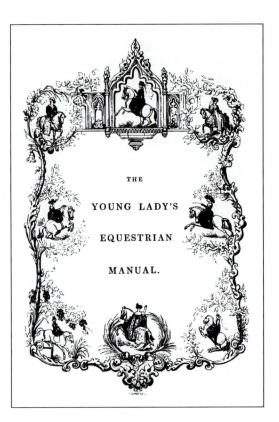

Fig. 2-8 ■ The graphic designers of the Victorian era used many approaches from the past—everything from Gothic to Baroque—as exemplified by this title page from a book published in London in 1838.

being established. This era of growth saw a rapid expansion of printing and advertising. Posters became a popular form of communication. In the second half of the nineteenth century a design form known as Victorian became popular. The name, of course, comes from the reign of Victoria, queen of England from 1837 to 1901. Victorian design appeared in architecture and virtually all forms of visual communication. It was an eclectic form. Everything from Gothic to Baroque to geometric designs can be found in the visuals of the era.

Then in 1880 another process was developed that would change the world of visual communication forever. In that year the *New York Graphic* printed the first reproduction of a photograph with a full tonal range in a newspaper. The use of this splendid tool will be discussed in detail in Chapter 6; the technique will be used extensively in all we do from that chapter on.

Among the many changes in visual design that occurred in the nineteenth century was the arrival of a style known as Art Nouveau. It came from France and was popular during the decade preceding and the decade after 1900. Art Nouveau might be called the bridge from the past to the future in design. Until this time, it had been the tendency of many designers to rely heavily on styles of the past in making layouts.

Fig. 2-9 ■ Art Nouveau, which was popular from about 1890 until 1910, has been called the design bridge from the past to the future. It is an ornamental style characterized by curved-line patterns, often tied to nature. This poster by Alphonse Mucha illustrates features of the Art Nouveau style. (Giraudon/Art Resource, New York)

Art Nouveau was an original, ornamental style characterized by curved-line patterns tied to nature. Emphasis was on energy and restless movement. Art Nouveau designs often incorporate features of Japanese art and often depict scenes from everyday life.

Towards Modern Design Concepts

The first twenty years of the twentieth century was a time of incredible ferment and change. Airplanes, motion pictures, radio—the list goes on—radically changed all aspects of life. The visual arts experienced a series of creative revolutions. A number of art forms emerged. These included:

■ Cubism, which expressed form in terms of lines, simplified planes, and elementary geometric forms.

■ Dada, which emphasized the absurd in life to protest war and a materialist society.

■ Futurism, which rejected traditional forms and tried to express the machine age with its energy and speed.

More important in the lasting development of visual communication, though, are the influences of the Bauhaus, an art school established in Weimar, Germany in 1919 by an illustrious group of artists from many disciplines. The school's curriculum centered on the systematic study of visual elements and their application. The Bauhaus philosophy held that designers were too isolated from the times and should

Fig. 2-10 ■ (Above) This 1929 poster by Walter Dexel is an example of the International Typographical Style. Note the absence of any decoration, the functional simplicity of the style, and the prominence of the message. (Courtesy Walter Dexel)

Fig. 2-11 ■ (Above, right) This 1929 poster for a French railroad line illustrates the features of Art Deco design. (Giraudon/Art Resource, New York)

create in the real world rather than in their imaginations.[2] The resulting work in architecture, household furnishings, and graphic design was simple, unornamented, and functional.

One of the longest-lasting design movements of the twentieth century, which was influenced by the Bauhaus artists, came out of Switzerland. It has been called the International Typographic Style. Its characteristics include:

■ Use of a grid for making layouts.

■ Asymmetrical placement of elements.

■ Use of sans serif types.

■ Clear, simple arrangement.

■ Straightforward, no nonsense presentation.

■ Use of ragged right in setting type.

The style emphasized presentation of the message rather than the personal expression of the creator. The International Typographic Style incorporated many of the design techniques that we have come to think of as "modern."

Art Deco emerged in the 1920s and dominated graphic design between the two world wars. It was characterized by streamlined objects and diagonal lines, as well as decorative geometric elements. Art Deco designers drew from cubism, Art Nouveau, and even in some cases, the Egyptians. Because of the current trend among some visual communicators to capture the elegance and sophistication of this style, we frequently see Art Deco influences in contemporary design.

Throughout the history of art and typography, designers have added much to help us develop techniques that will make our work more effective and fun. We will be expanding our knowledge of these techniques throughout the chapters ahead. Today technology has allowed us to have control over the elements that go into a visual communication that we never had in the past. We can use this control to create outstanding work that will make communication more effective than ever.

AFTER THE DESIGN—PRINTING

➤ Once you have created your visual communication on your drawing board or computer the next step is to produce it. Although most of the visual communicator's time is devoted to designing, the work often includes writing, editing, and preparing material for duplication. Therefore, it is important to know what happens in the "back shop." *Back shop* is a term used in industry to refer to the production end of the business.

Much of the work formerly done in the back shop now has been moved to the "front office" where writers, editors, and designers exercise their creativity. In many instances, designers and other communicators are performing all the tasks involved in production except actually running the printing press.

Most of the printing you will be concerned with is produced by one of three methods—letterpress, offset, and gravure. However, new methods are developing such as laser printing, ink-jet printing, and high-speed copying.

When we think of printing we think of Gutenberg. For Johann Gensfleisch zum Gutenberg, of Mainz, Germany, brought it all together. Gutenberg did not invent printing. His contribution was to devise a method of casting individual letters and composing type and combining all of the necessary printing components into a workable system.*

Printing had existed long before Gutenberg's marvelous achievement. Printing from movable type was used in China and Korea in the eleventh century. However, because of the fragility of the materials used and the enormous number of individual pictographs used in the Chinese alphabet, it remained an obscure practice.

---

*(*Note:* Scientists at the University of California, Davis, have discovered further evidence of Gutenberg's genius. They have broken down his formula for making ink and found that his ink included lead and copper. That is the reason his famous Bible remains fresh, glossy, and black after more than 500 years.)

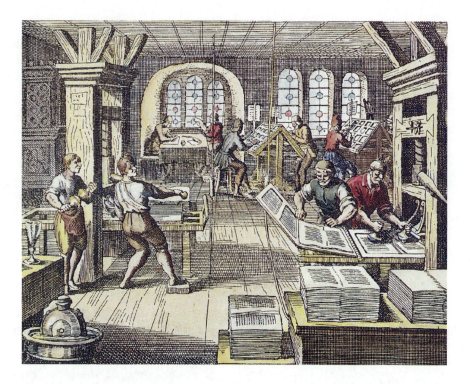

Fig. 2-12 ◼ A typical printing shop in the seventeenth century. (The Granger Collection)

LETTERPRESS PRINTING

➤ These early attempts at printing—both Chinese and German—were based on the letterpress principle. Letterpress is printing from a raised surface. The image to be printed is raised above the base on which it rests. This image is inked and paper is pressed against it to transfer the image to the paper. If the image is a letter, then it is pressed to form a print; thus, *letterpress*.

Letterpress printing is also called relief printing. Letterpress printing today is but a refinement of the way it was done 500 years ago. Letterpress was the principal method of commercial printing until quite recent times.

In the beginning it was a slow, laborious process, as all the type used was set by hand, a letter at a time. The press was a crude affair. But this same press was used for more than 300 years, even though it had been improved somewhat through the years. It would continue to be the basic printing press for 20 or 30 more years, and it would continue to see service in some parts of the world for another 100 years.

Two men working one of these presses, made of wood or iron, could turn out about 500 or 600 impressions a day. Today a simple offset press can produce 5,000 to 9,000 impressions an hour.

The letterpress, which evolved from the simple wine press, can be found in commercial printing plants, but its use is limited. There are three types of letterpress printing presses: the platen, the flatbed cylinder, and the rotary.

Platen Press

The platen press was the faithful "job press." It was used to produce everything from letterheads to tickets, handbills, and the general line of printed materials needed by society. Today the platen press is used mainly for short runs such as imprinting Christmas cards and for paper processing such as die cutting, creasing, and perforating.

The press is called a platen because it operates by having a platen, or flat surface, on which the paper is placed, move against the stationary type, which is locked in a chase, which in turn is locked in the bed of a press.

Flatbed Cylinder Press

In 1841, Friedrich Koenig sold the first power-driven press to *The Times* of London. He was able to devise a press operated by power, in this case steam, that continuously rotated a round impression cylinder. It was called a flatbed cylinder because the forms to be printed were placed on a flat surface in the press. This cylinder press was hailed as "the greatest improvement connected with printing since the discovery of the art itself." Later improvements to the flatbed cylinder press included the installation of automatic feeders and folders to fold the sheets as they emerged from the press.

Rotary Press

The basic shortcoming of the flatbed cylinder press was overcome when the web perfecting press was developed. This press is fast and efficient and can be used for long runs of magazines, newspapers, advertising brochures, and other publications with many pages. It uses a rotary impression (or platen) cylinder and a rotary type bed as well, plus a continuous roll of paper, rather than single sheets. It prints both sides of the sheet as it travels through the press. The rotary press uses forms cast into curved metal or plastic plates, which can be locked onto the cylinder. As many duplicates of the form as are desired can be made, and a number of presses can turn out the same product simultaneously.

It was *The Times* of London that again scored a triumph in printing when in 1869 their newspaper was printed on a continuous roll of paper from curved stereotype plates on a rotary press. During the next ten years Robert Hoe, the American printing press manufacturer, improved and developed newspaper printing by making it possible to deliver a complete newspaper—folded, counted, and ready for sale—

Fig. 2-13 ■ Three methods of letterpress (raised image) printing: platen, or flat surfaces (left); flatbed cylinder (middle); rotary (right).

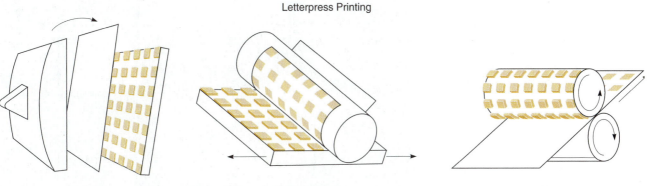

Letterpress Printing

platen   flatbed cylinder   rotary

from a roll of blank paper. Today web-fed presses can run so fast production is measured in feet per minute (fpm) of paper running through the press rather than the number of sheets that are printed.

Although other printing methods have taken center stage in the world of visual communication, letterpress is not dead. A new development, flexography, has revived the basic letterpress principle. We will consider flexo, as it is called, later in this chapter.

OFFSET PRINTING

▶ In recent years letterpress has been abandoned, and offset has become the method of choice in printing. Offset is actually a modification of lithography, or printing from a flat surface. Lithography is also referred to as planographic printing. This method of printing did not come to us through centuries of evolution. It was invented—almost by accident.

Beginning of Lithography

One day in Munich, Bavaria, a twenty-five-year-old artist who lived with his mother and who dabbled in the theater, playwriting, sketching, and drawing, was busy in his workshop. The year was 1796. He was Alois Senefelder.

Senefelder was seeking a way to duplicate plays he had written. He experimented with copper plates and practiced on limestone slabs. His idea was that he could etch his copy into plates and then print from them. This would be quicker and cheaper than the complicated and costly letterpress task of setting them into type by hand.

Fig. 2-14 ■ Alois Senefelder at work in his lithographic shop in the late eighteenth century. (Courtesy Rochester Institute of Technology)

He was working on this when his mother came in and asked him to write a list of items to hand to the waiting laundress. He reached for whatever was handy and picked up a piece of limestone and some correction fluid he had concocted to fill in the errors he made on the engraving plates.[3]

Senefelder wrote the laundry list with the correction fluid, which had a greasy base, on the flat limestone slab. Later he noticed that ink would stick to the words he had written, whereas water would wash off the ink on the blank areas of the stone. Senefelder had hit upon the chemical fact that is the basis of lithographic printing—oil and water do not mix!

How do we know so much about Senefelder's achievement? He wrote it all down in his *Invention of Lithography,* which was published in New York in 1911. In addition, he wrote *A Complete Course of Lithography,* which was translated from the original German and published in London in 1819.[4]

Lithographic Process

As mentioned, the central principle of lithography is the fact that oil and water do not mix but repel each other. All procedures of lithography observe this basic tenet. The stone is the carrier of the printing form. The design to be printed is applied to this stone's surface by various techniques. Drawing pens, brushes, or grease crayons are used. Although lithographers have complete control over their creations, they must prepare the design so that it reads backwards, as a mirror image. Then, when a print is made the lefts and rights will be in their proper positions.

After the design is completed, the stone is covered with a watery and slightly acidic gum arabis solution. This "seasons" the stone. There are some additional steps in preparing the stone, but for our purposes it is enough to say that the design on the stone is "prepared for printing." The stone is dampened and rolled with an ink roller. The grease-receptive design areas will accept the ink while the areas that have been moistened will not pick up the ink. After a series of inkings and moistenings, the paper is pressed against the stone and the reverse or mirror image of the original sketch will be printed on the paper. The press and method used by Senefelder are still used today to make artistic lithographic prints.

Improvements were made over the years and in 1889 the first lithographic press to print with zinc plates went on line. This greatly increased the printing speed.

Modern Offset Techniques

Offset was discovered quite by accident, and we do not know for sure just when and how. If the lithographic press missed a sheet, an impression would be made on the paper carrier (platen or cylinder). The next sheet through the press would pick up this impression in reverse (it would be backwards) on its back. Someone noticed that the quality of the reverse was quite good.

Fig. 2-15 ■ A schematic drawing of the offset lithography printing process. The printing plate with the planographic image is clamped on the plate cylinder; the dampening rollers coat the plate with water; the ink rollers ink the plate (the ink adheres to the image area but not to the area not to be printed); the image is offset to the offset cylinder and then transferred by impressions onto the paper.

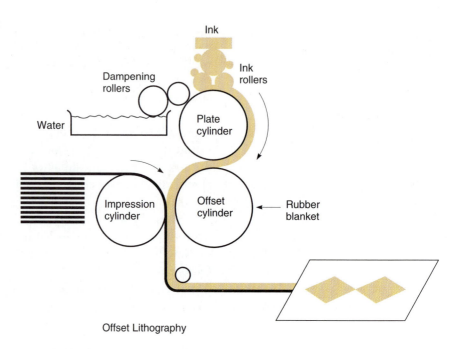

Offset Lithography

We can visualize the principle of offset by thinking of the letter E carved in relief, inked, and pressed against a sheet of paper. The image will appear in reverse Ǝ . But if another sheet of paper is pressed against this image before the ink dries, the image on the second sheet will be in the correct position—E.

The final product is obtained from an image of what is to be printed. This image is printed on a cylinder covered with a rubber blanket. The rubber blanket then becomes the printing plate and the image is printed (or offset) on the paper.

In 1906 the first offset press as we know it today began rolling out printed sheets in Nutley, New Jersey. Although some offset printing had been done in Europe well before this, the press developed by Ira. A. Rubel, a paper manufacturer, is considered the one that started the offset revolution.

A new development in offset printing was still being perfected as this book goes to press. It is an offset press that does not use water—the waterless offset press.

GRAVURE PRINTING

➤ Gravure, or intaglio as it is also called, is simply printing from a recessed surface. Just as letterpress printing evolved through the centuries until Gutenberg put the elements together in a manageable fashion, so gravure printing also has a long and sometimes murky history. Its beginnings can be traced to the fifteenth century. A finely detailed print of the Madonna enthroned with eight angels is considered the earliest known engraving. It was produced by an unknown German artist with the initials E. S. and is dated 1467.

Fig. 2-16 ■ A New Jersey native, Ira Rubel, designed the offset press in which a rubber cover is used on the cylinder of a lithographic press to produce a vivid image on paper. (Courtesy Rochester Institute of Technology)

Fig. 2-17 ■ (Above) A press operator attaches an offset plate to a cylinder of a Goss Colorliner press. (Courtesy Graphic Systems Division, Rockwell International Corporation)

Fig. 2-18 ■ A giant Goss Colorliner offset press. Part of the color revolution in newspaper design, this press enables a newspaper to place process color on any and every page of up to 160 pages. The presses cost more than $250 million each. (Courtesy Graphic Systems Division, Rockwell International Corporation)

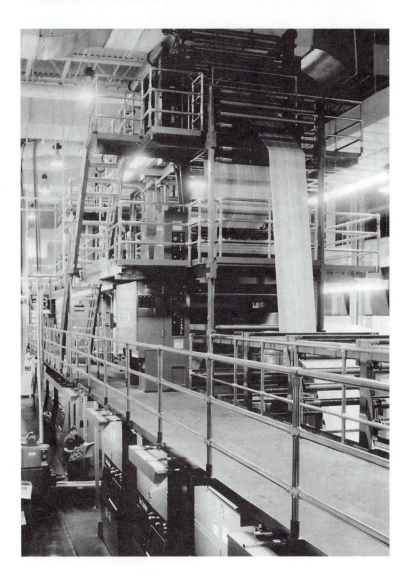

Fig. 2-19 ■ A schematic drawing of the gravure process. The image to be printed is engraved or carved into the impression surface. The entire area is inked, and the ink is removed from the nonprinting area. Pressure of paper on the plate pulls the ink out of the recessed areas.

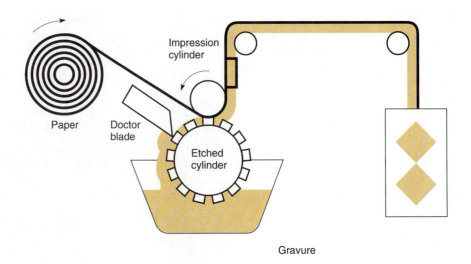

Paper   Doctor blade   Impression cylinder   Etched cylinder

Gravure

Gravure is a simple method of printing but is quite important today. It is called intaglio from the Italian word *intagliare,* which means "to carve." And that is what the gravure printer does, engraving the design into the printing surface.

This surface, or plate, is covered with ink, and the ink is wiped off the surface. But because of the "carving," the ink remains in the letters and designs that are sunk below the surface. A sheet of paper or other material is pressed against the plate and an impression is made.

The Rotogravure Method

The development of rotogravure printing has been one of the "hottest" advances in the communications industry. Many of the magazines, Sunday newspaper supplements, and catalogs we see today are the result of this method, which was invented by an Austrian, Karl Kleitsch. He developed a rotary method of printing gravure plates in Lancaster, England, in 1894. The *New York Times* installed a rotogravure plant in 1914. A rotogravure plate is capable of a million impressions, far more than plates made for letterpress or lithography.

Gravure printing is considered excellent for reproducing pictures. A distinct feature that makes it easy to recognize is that the entire image must be screened—type and line art as well as halftones of photographs. Many of our largest magazines are printed by rotogravure. These include *National Geographic, Family Circle, Reader's Digest,* and *Redbook,* to name but a few.

The *National Enquirer* is printed in Buffalo, New York, on rotogravure presses. Each press can reach speeds of 35,000 copies of a ninety-six-page newspaper per hour. The *Los Angeles Times* Sunday magazine, with a press run of about 2 million copies, is printed in Reno, Nevada, on rotogravure presses by R. R. Donnelley, the mammoth commercial printing company.

Our exploding technology is making great changes in the way we produce duplicate images of a visual communication. New methods as

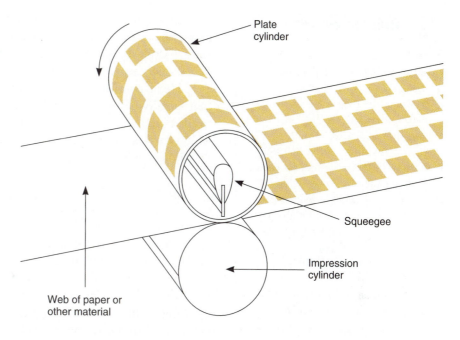

Fig. 2-20 ■ Diagram of a rotogravure press that uses the gravure process. Many of the largest magazines in the United States are printed by this method.

- Plate cylinder
- Squeegee
- Impression cylinder
- Web of paper or other material

well as new features of the basic printing processes are being developed constantly.

OTHER PRINTING METHODS

Not long ago experienced communicators could distinguish among products of the letterpress, offset press, and the gravure press. Now each method is capable of producing excellent quality, and the advantage of one over the others has largely disappeared. It is more the skill of the printer than the method used that should be the concern of the communicator.

Of course, most small visual communications operations will almost exclusively use offset and perhaps letterpress. But startling advances are being made each year in printing processes, and you should be familiar with what is happening.

Flexographic Printing

The future of flexography (flexo) looks bright. During the past fifteen years it has been the fastest-growing printing process in the world of communication and currently accounts for 25 percent of the total output of the printing industry. In the past the flexographic method was considered practical only for specialized uses such as printing paperback books, packaging materials, and plastic bags. Today flexography is used to print Sunday comics, newspaper inserts, television news magazines, business forms (the Internal Revenue tax forms are printed by flexography), telephone books, point-of-purchase material, and magazines.[5]

Fig. 2-21 ■ A pressman attaches flexographic plates to the press at the Modesto, California, Bee. Flexo uses the letterpress principle and water-base ink. (Courtesy Publishers Equipment Corporation)

Newspapers, too, are installing flexography presses. Among the newspapers that are using flexo are those in Portland and Bangor, Maine; Modesto and Monterey, California; Buffalo, New York; Knoxville, Tennessee; and Trenton and Atlantic City, New Jersey to name a few.

Flexo printing is a comparatively simple process. It uses an ink that usually is water based. The ink comes in contact with an engraved "anilox" cylinder. This cylinder distributes the ink to another cylinder which carries a flexible letterpress-type plate that is made out of rubber or photopolymer (a plastic material). This inked plate makes the impression on the paper.

Anilox cylinders have a hard surface with millions of tiny cells of equal size and shape. The ink fills these cells and the excess is scraped off by doctor blades, much as the ink is scraped off a gravure printing plate. However, the function of the anilox cylinder is to distribute the ink on the printing plate. This gives an even, reliable distribution of ink.

Flexo advocates cite a number of advantages of the method. It can print on very light paper with no show-through. Full-color illustrations with fine definition can be printed with excellent results. Since water-based inks are used, the problem of rub-off (ink from the printed sheet imprinting on adjacent printed material or on the hands of people handling the sheet) is virtually eliminated. There is little waste of paper compared with offset. Vibrant colors are possible with flexo, and it can print large solids without "ghosting" (the appearance of light areas in large areas printed in color).

As more and more flexo presses move into the publication and commercial printing fields, advertisers, editors, and graphics people will need to become familiar with this method of printing.

Laser Printing

Laser printers are playing an ever larger role in the world of printed communications, and most people who enter public relations, advertising, or editorial positions will sooner or later use a laser printer.

Laser printers are used for creating mechanicals. These are completed pages of newsletters, flyers, magazine pages, and so on that can be used for making printing plates. Laser printers are also good for making proofs and for producing limited copies of printed materials.[6] Another important use of the laser printer is to produce copy directly from a computer. It can merge type and graphics.

The laser printer uses a tiny pinpoint of light that passes through a finely tuned and complex optical system and lands on a light-sensitive drum. As the drum revolves, a strong charge is applied to its surface. The laser beam pulses on and off at amazing speed as it scans the surface of the drum. Wherever it strikes, a different charge appears and dots are formed at these points on the drum. A series of dots forms the letters or illustrations on the drum. When toner is applied, an image appears. As the drum rotates, this image is attracted to an oppositely charged sheet of paper. Heat and pressure fuse the toner to the paper, creating a permanent image.

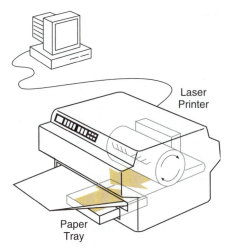

Laser
Printer

Paper
Tray

Fig. 2-22 ■ A laser printer. The printer receives a page that has been created on a computer. The page is formed into a bit-map image, and a laser beam "etches" the image on the rotating drum with an electrostatic charge. After toner is applied to the image, the image is printed when the toner is fused onto blank paper.

Fig. 2-23 ■ In the screen printing process, the ink is squeezed through a stencil and a screen onto the surface to be printed.

The quality of the printing produced by a laser printer is determined by the density of the dots. The more dots per inch, the greater the quality or clearness of the image to be printed. For instance, a printer that uses 300 dots per inch (dpi) is considered at the low end of the quality scale. The 600 dpi printer is the standard for budget-minded operations. Laser printers with 1200 dpi resolution can produce high-quality press proofs and camera-ready mechanicals.[7]

The computer and the laser printer have moved everything but the printing press into the office. The plate-making equipment has been moving into the office as well. As a result more and more businesses and organizations are producing their printing "in house."

Screen Printing

Screen printing, also called silk screen or screen process printing, uses a fine, porous screen made of silk, nylon, Dacron, or even stainless steel mounted on a frame. A stencil is cut either manually or photomechanically with the lettering or design to be reproduced and then placed over the screen. Printing is done on a press by feeding paper under the screen, applying paintlike ink to the screen, and spreading and forcing it through the fine mesh openings with a rubber squeegee.

The use of the stencil to produce images can be traced back to 1000 B.C. in China, but screen printing did not become an important part of the printing industry until after World War II. Today automatic screen presses, four- and five-color screen presses, and rotary screen presses are used to turn out posters, sheets for billboards, menu covers, and bumper stickers.

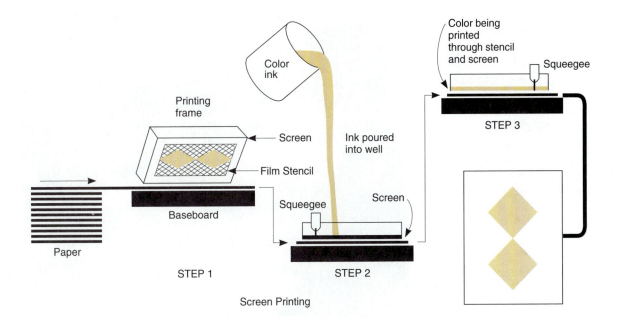

Screen Printing

ADVANCES IN PUTTING WORDS ON PAPER

In recent years we have seen the introduction of ink-jet printers that produce excellent color work. In addition, ink-jet typewriters are coming on the market.

Universally used in the business world is xerography. *Xero* is a Greek word meaning "dry"; thus, dry printing. Xerography is used for copying text and graphic material, and improvements are constantly being made in these copying devices. The Xerox uses reflective light to expose a photoconducting surface. A negatively charged toner on this surface is transferred to a positively charged sheet of paper and fused through the use of heat and a pressure roller. It produces an exact copy of the original.

Another printer that has come on the scene is the ion deposition printer. *Ion* means "atom" or "group of atoms." An ion cartridge creates an image on a rotating drum by shooting charged particles on it in dot matrix format. Then toner is employed to develop an image which is fused to a sheet of paper. Cold roll pressure is used to make the image stick, rather than heat and pressure as is used in a laser printer.

Ion printing produces a very high-quality product that can sustain long runs on a printing press.

Many new advances in science, such as the laser beam, the computer, and the cathode ray tube, are a part of the printing industry. However, it is safe to say that no matter how we place words on paper, the basic theme of this book will not become obsolete. That is, no matter how we print our message, no matter whether we arrange the elements of our printed message with a pagination device that puts those elements in place on a video screen or with a pencil on a piece of paper, we must still make basic typographic decisions.

Those decisions involve the choice of type styles and sizes; the width of the printed lines; the amount of spacing between letters, words,

Fig. 2-24 ■ A visual communicator works at a modern composition system. But even though technological advances are made constantly, the basic principles of letterpress, gravure, and lithography are still applied in printing most communications. The system shown here is the Crosfield TM9700R, which uses high-speed RISC technology to dramatically increase the productivity of stripping and page assembly. (Courtesy DuPont Printing & Publishing)

CREATIVE COMMUNICATION

"Creativity . . . it's elusive.

"It's this emotionally charged thing that comes from the depths. You can't define it. I find that creative people need motivation. Some do it for money.

"What motivates me now is not money. Now it's what my peers are going to think. I have two or three people in mind that I hope will be impressed with my work.

"I work for that ideal. Sometimes I can shoot 6 or 7 photographs that will get into *National Geographic,* then go six weeks and won't have a thing.

"Stress helps. The general public perceives artists and photographers as sitting around waiting for that creative inspiration, but most of the time it's the pressure that delivers. I do my worst work when I'm most peaceful. I'm at my best when I'm in a foreign country and I don't know when the sniper's bullet might hit."

—Jim Brandenburg, *National Geographic* photographer, in *Design,* the Journal of the Society of Newspaper Design, No. 29

and lines of type; and the size and composition of pieces of art. All these decisions are still critical to the effectiveness of a message.

The starting place in creating effective printed communications is deciding on the basic ingredient of any recipe for effective printed communication. That is *type,* and type is what we consider next, after a short excursion into the technology that's changing everything—desktop publishing.

▶ GRAPHICS IN ACTION

1. Study carefully the illustrations of the design techniques that are covered in this chapter (Art Deco, Victorian, Art Nouveau, and so on). Select one or more of them. See if you can find evidences of the techniques in use in current issues of publications, advertisements, direct mail pieces, and so on. Clip the examples and then explain the techniques used and evaluate them for their effectiveness in the context of the image the designer seems to be seeking to convey.

2. The best way to acquire an understanding of the basic printing methods is to see the actual processes in action. Plan a trip to a local printing plant. Join a team of classmates to visit a printing plant. Obtains samples of printed work from the plant you visit. If this is a group assignment, some members of the group might visit a letterpress facility, some an offset plant, and so on, and then report to the group on their experiences. (*Note:* It might be even more worthwhile to plan a visit to a printing plant after learning about layout and preparation for production.)

3. Prepare an essay that updates trends in printing methods. Consult trade publications such as *American Printer* and *Graphic Arts Monthly* and interview plant managers, if possible.

NOTES

[1] *Encyclopedia Americana* (Danbury, Conn.: Grolier Incorporated, 1991), vol. 22 pp. 75–76.

[2] Philip B. Meggs, *A History of Graphic Design* (New York: Von Nostrand Reinhold, 1983), p. 379.

[3] Alois Senefelder, *A Complete Course in Lithography* (New York: Da Capo Press, 1977, reprint of original published in London in 1819), p. 22.

[4] Warren A. Chappell, *A Short History of the Printed Word* (New York: Alfred A. Knoff, 1970), pp. 171–173.

[5] *American Printer,* "Bullish on Flexography," March, 1989, p. 26.

[6] White Paper, Lasers in Graphic Arts (Wilmington, Mass.: Compugraphic Corporation, 1987), p. 6.

[7] "Laser Printers: Beyond 300 dpi," *Journal of the National Association of Desktop Publishers,* July, 1993, pp. 12–13.

INTRODUCTION TO DESKTOP PUBLISHING

CONTENTS

© Churchill & Klehr

3 While national interest centers on the all-encompassing information superhighway, another superhighway arrives in the world of visual communication. It is the digital superhighway. The digital superhighway will start at your desk and end at the printing press—or in some cases at the terminals of your target audience.

Significant digital technology was introduced in the fall of 1993 that made possible an electronic path that winds from the creative mind through prepress operations, into the pressroom, and even on to the bindary.[1]

But wait just a minute. We are getting ahead of ourselves. First, we have to understand just what our role will be as communicators in the world of the information superhighway. We will be the "message senders," and our tool, at least for the present, will be the computer and its supporting equipment in our studio or office. In short, we will be desktop publishers.

WHAT IS DESKTOP PUBLISHING?

Many visual communicators believe the term *desktop publishing* is trite and an oversimplification; they prefer the term *electronic publishing.* Students and others wonder if it is a device for amateurs that will turn them into professional publishers, or is it a tool for professionals to produce better and more effective work?

The answer lies at both ends of the spectrum. The matter was summed up by Jeffrey Parnau in his book, *Desktop Publishing: The Awful Truth:* "Professional designers and writers have always been able to work with or without sophisticated tools. Certain desktop publishing equipment and software make the professional's job easier, but does not make the professional. Design is in the head. Creativity is in the soul. And like an X-acto knife or scissors, desktop publishing is on the desk."[2]

Roger Black, designer of many magazines and editorial art director of the *New York Times,* sees desktop publishing as an enchanting world in which communicators can "sit down, write, lay out, and print whatever they want, whether it's poetry, recipes, a book, or a newsletter."

"You are in control," he adds. "Completely. It's also immediate. You can proof and refine and correct things instantly. It's like having your own printing press and type house. In fact, it's not *like that* at all. That's exactly what you have to do."[3]

If you are planning to work in communications (and most likely you wouldn't be reading this book if you weren't), you are sure to become involved in desktop publishing. The graphic skills you are acquiring here and now can help.

Although some equipment manufacturers tend to oversimplify the ease with which a person can become a desktop publisher, it takes a little more work than they suggest. In desktop publishing "you just don't pop in the software and away you go," says Robert Chishold, art director for a Hewlett Packard facility in San Diego. "In the hands of the right person desktop publishing can be incredible. In the wrong hands, it can become a nightmare."[4] However, don't let these cautions intimidate you, because *desktop publishing is fun!* So, let's take a trip through the world of desktop publishing and see what it is all about.

Let's start off by defining just what it is and how it came about. Then we will consider the equipment needed in the process. We will take a look at how we can learn to operate this equipment and how we can put it to work for us. Throughout this chapter we will attempt to provide hints and pointers so that those who enter the desktop world can enter it as quickly and easily as possible.

HOW DOES DESKTOP PUBLISHING WORK?

▶ How did desktop get such a toehold in the world of communication? It was not too long ago that designers, reporters, or copywriters wrote material and made layouts on typewriters and drawing boards. With desktop publishing all this work is done on a computer. The communicator can create, proofread, make corrections, designate type styles, draw pictures, design newspaper and magazine pages, brochures, and most printed communications without getting up from the workstation.

One person can now do what it formerly would take several people to accomplish. Desktop publishing systems can save time and money, and, ultimately, produce finished camera-ready ads and pages. At least such is the case at this time.

In the late 1970s considerable research on the subject was conducted in the San Francisco area at the Xerox Palo Alto Research Center and other facilities.[4] But desktop publishing really got its start in 1984 when Apple introduced its Macintosh computer. The Mac was aimed at being "user friendly" and easy to operate. It included a

Fig. 3-1 ■ A desktop publisher at his workstation. (Photo © Churchill & Klehr)

Quality

Lorem ipsum dolor sit amet, consectetuer adipiscing elit, sed diam nonummy nibh euismod tincidunt ut laoreet dolore magna aliquam erat volutpat. Ut wisi enim ad minim veniam, quis nostrud exerci tation ullamcorper suscipit lobortis nisl ut aliquip ex ea commodo consequat. Duis autem vel eum iriure dolor in hendrerit in vulputate velit esse molestie consequat, vel illum dolore eu feugiat nulla facilisis at vero eros et accumsan et iusto odio dignissim qui blandit praesent luptatum zzril delenit augue duis dolore te feugait nulla facilisi. Lorem ipsum dolor sit amet, consectetuer adipiscing elit, sed diam nonummy nibh euismod tincidunt ut laoreet dolore magna aliquam erat volutpat. Ut wisi enim ad minim veniam, quis nostrud exerci tation ullamcorper

Fig. 3-2 ■ Effects that can enhance a layout are easy to create with desktop publishing capabilities. Interest and elegance can be added to bland text documents by enlarging a single character and filling it with a light screen. This would be very difficult and it would require a lot of work if traditional methods were used. (© Image Club Graphics, 1–800–387–9193)

"mouse," that little device the user can control by hand so as to move an arrow (curser) around the computer screen and perform various tasks.

The Mac also featured pull-down menus to offer you on-screen displays of what the computer can do next, as well as a simple way of storing and retrieving information.

Key players in the development of desktop publishing were Dr. John Warnock, of Adobe Systems, Steven Jobs and his partner, Steve Wozniak founders of Apple Computer (and the whole team at Apple that developed the Mac), and Paul Brainard, of Aldus. Warnock is credited with coining the word "PostScript." PostScript is a computer programming language—or, strictly speaking, an operating system—that might be called the little guy in the computer who tells it what to do. For instance it is used by software to tell the output device, such as a typesetting machine, the tiny steps necessary to generate type and images in the correct position on a page. It is the bridge between the actual software an individual who is sitting in front of a computer screen uses to create a page layout and the complex instructions that make the computer driving the output device do what is wanted.

For instance, take the case of when you compose a layout on your computer and want to make a copy of it. You instruct the printer to print through a command entered on the keyboard, and Postscript takes it from there and passes all the necessary instructions on to the printer.

It was in 1984, too, that the word "desktop" came into use. Paul Brainard, president of the Aldus Corporation, had a goal of creating a program that would combine the functions of low-cost microcomputers and laser printers to produce camera-ready mechanicals. Mechanicals are completed layouts that are camera-ready, that is, ready for the making of page plates which are clamped on the press for the actual printing.

Brainard coined the word "desktop," and Aldus produced a software program—PageMaker—that brought writing, editing, designing, and production into the world of personal computers. Since then newspapers, books, newsletters, manuals, reports, and even magazines have been designed with PageMaker. Since then, too, many more desktop publishing programs have entered the market. Many new features have been added to them.

Brainard did not claim this new method of producing printed communications would eliminate the skills of the professional designer. "The need for people who understand visual design isn't diminished," he said. "The software is simply another tool of the designer, an addition to the toolbox already loaded with T squares, triangles, rules, and rubber cement. PageMaker might be a substitute for some of those tools, but it is not a substitute for creativity."[5]

EQUIPMENT FOR DESKTOP PUBLISHING

➤ A desktop publishing system consists of hardware and software. The hardware includes the machinery—basically a computer, printer, and scanner. Software includes the entities needed to run the

Fig. 3-3 ■ Desktop publishing is accomplished with a computer (the larger the screen the better), keyboard, and a mouse. This plus a printer and scanner and you are in business. (© Churchill & Klehr)

hardware—the programs. A program (on a disk) contains a sequence of instructions that tells the computer how to do a task. It operates the system.

A word processing program would be used to compose copy. Another program might turn the computer into a page layout system, and another might enable the operator to create art on the screen.

So the equipment needed for a typical desktop publishing system usually includes a personal computer, a printer, a scanner, and perhaps a modem, and the software needed to create copy and graphics and blend them to produce a camera-ready mechanical.

The Computer

In the pasteup days of design and layout, the communicator used scissors, X-acto knives, waxers, T squares, right triangles, cropping Ls, and so on to create mechanicals. The computer contains all these tools packaged in one convenient machine. Although there are many computers on the market, the choice for desktop publishing narrows down to one of two types. These are the Macintosh by Apple and the IBM PC and its compatibles. (Compatible means that the computer and its hardware and software are interchangeable with those of the IBM PC. Everything that can be used with the IBM can be used with the compatible.)

The Macintosh became the desktop publishing leader when it entered the market in 1984. Before the appearance of the Mac, computer design was limited to firms that could afford to invest as much as $100,000 or more for equipment.

Not only did the Mac enable communicators with limited budgets to become desktop publishers, but also it was "user friendly," that is, relatively easy to learn and use. In addition, the Mac offered a mouse. The mouse allowed users to "point and shoot," and thus activate every tool the computer contained to set type, create art, and combine elements in a page layout.

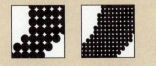
Apple's innovations made it the clear-cut leader in producing computers for desktop publishing in the early years. Today the competition is producing computers that are equally satisfactory. But the Mac continues to be a leader in the field.

Experienced desktop publishers have a few suggestions to help you select the right computer. They start by suggesting you read books and magazines on the subject, talk to computer dealers, and attend workshops and seminars.

Select a computer that can produce the types of communications you need. The minimum amount of power for desktop publishing is considered to be 2 to 5 MB (megabytes) of RAM.[6]

The computer should have a hard drive, or hard disk. A hard disk is a rigid disk used for storing rather large quantities of data.

The graphic ability of the computer—as well as its flexibility—is an important consideration. This includes the scope of communications it is capable of handling. For instance, you would not need a computer with the capacity to compose multipage manuals or books if you are going to use it mainly for flyers and newsletters.

The Printer

The second key piece of equipment for desktop publishing is the printer. Actually, a computer and a printer are all the hardware you absolutely must have to get started in desktop publishing.

There are three basic types of printers. One operates with a dot matrix system; the others are ink-jet and laser printers.

A dot matrix printer forms images by arranging a series of dots. Their quality varies, but the resulting print is really not suitable for quality work.

Laser and ink-jet printers can produce type and art with more detail and resolution. Most provide 300 or more dots per inch (dpi). The Apple LaserWriter was introduced in 1985; it opened the door to quality desktop production. It proved to be suitable for newsletters, small publications, and reports, although not for quality commercial work.

Generally, commercial-quality work requires a much higher resolution such as that produced by phototypesetting machines that provide resolutions of up to 2,540 dpi. This compares with all but the very highest quality professional typesetting equipment.

While the cost of advanced equipment may be beyond the reach of many communicators, capabilities of such equipment can be obtained through the use of a service bureau. A service bureau is an independent business that provides help in layout, graphics, and production. Often material created on economy equipment can be taken to a service bureau where it can be made camera ready for a reasonable cost. The service bureaus also will provide instruction and use of their equipment on an hourly basis.

When discussing desktop equipment and costs, we must realize that the technology is changing constantly. Ever new manufacturing methods are being developed to reduce costs, so the situation can change almost overnight.

Fig. 3-4 ■ An example of digitized type, left. It is made up of dot patterns similar to an arrangement for a mosaic. Digitized type also could be compared to letters formed in needlepoint, as in this example from a turn-of-the-century textbook for cross-stitching, right.

Fig. 3-5 ■ For years personal computers have stored type as a pattern of dots, as in the diagram on the left. In the outline font system, the curves and lines that outline the letter are stored as mathematical formulas.

An example is the development of outline type fonts. These new fonts will allow the desktop publisher who is limited to digital type to produce type rivaling that generated on expensive laser printers.

Companies are offering software that produces outline fonts, enabling a computer to generate letters in a wide variety of type styles in virtually any size. Instead of bit maps, in which the character is represented by a letter design made up of dots, the outline-font approach uses mathematical curves and lines to produce the letter. This eliminates the rough edges that characterize bit-mapped letters.

The Scanner

A device that enables you to copy a photograph or line art or text and transfer it to a page layout on a computer is becoming increasingly useful and economical. That device is a scanner, which reads, or scans, the image and converts it into a series of dots that can be accepted by the computer.

Fig. 3-6 ■ A drum scanner used in high-quality imaging for commercial production. This scanner has a direct connection with a computer. It is a DuPont Crosfield Magnascan Plus that is fully digital and can scan in full color. (Courtesy DuPont Printing & Publishing)

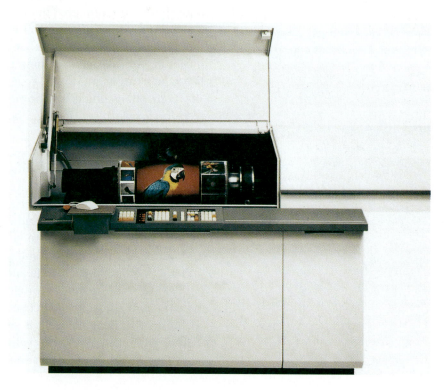

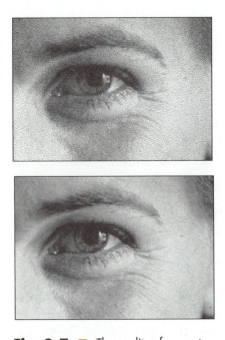

Fig. 3-7 ■ The quality of computer-generated art depends on which mode is used for the final output. For example, black and white images can be converted to either bitmap or grayscale mode. Bitmap images, as in the example at the top, consist of one bit of color (black or white) per pixel and require the least amount of memory of all image types. Grayscale uses up to 256 shades of gray to represent the image and, as you can see in the lower example, compares well with the continuous tone original.

There are economical small hand scanners, but they are limited to scanning areas about 2 to 4 inches wide. They are also limited in their resolution capabilities. Most hand scanners are 200- to 400-dpi models, which are useful for scanning small images, such as signatures and corporate logos. They also provide a good low-cost introduction to scanner applications.

Moving up the scanner ladder, the designer has a wide choice of more sophisticated scanners that are rated by their gray-scale or color capabilities, ranging from 4-, 6-, 8- and 24-bit gray-scale or color. For example, four-bit scanners can produce 16 levels of gray or color, compared with 64 levels for 6-bit scanners and 256 levels for 8-bit devices.

The Modem

A modem is an electronic device that permits one computer to talk to another or to a network of computers over telephone lines. This enables the desktop publisher to send files to service bureaus, other offices, and clients who have modems to receive them. Modems are rated by bauds. A *baud* is a measurement of the rate of speed at which modems can transmit data. Most data sent to a service bureau is sent at 4800 to 9000 bauds.

SOFTWARE FOR DESKTOP PUBLISHING

➤ An instructor of introductory computer courses likes to build the confidence of her beginning students by impressing on them the fact that computers are "dumb." They can only do what you tell them to do. And you tell them what to do by selecting the right software.

There are a great number of programs already on the market for desktop publishing, with new programs being introduced constantly. With such an array it may appear difficult to select the right programs for your publishing goals. However, only three are needed to get started: one for word processing, one for graphics, and one for page layout.

Word Processing Software

Word processing is used to enter and edit written copy which will be incorporated with graphics to form the basis of a layout created with the page layout program. Word processing programs give the communicators the capability to write and edit on the screen. Such programs have features that enable them to search through copy and replace words, cut out copy, bring in copy and insert it where desired, and to put headers and footers on each page automatically.

Most word processing programs can check spelling, justify columns of type, and adjust space between lines. Just about anything needed to be done with copy before it is sent to the printer can be accomplished. These programs should be evaluated in terms of the features they contain that would be useful for the type of work you wish to do.

Graphics Programs

Graphics programs are used to prepare and edit illustrations and decorative graphics and to produce diagrams, drawings, charts and graphs, and digitized line art and photographs. Many graphics programs are bit-mapped. A bit-mapped graphic is composed of a pattern of individual pixels which form the images on the screen, as is done in composing bit-mapped letters.

Graphics programs are draw (called *vector*) or paint (*raster*). You can usually tell which is which, as they will have *draw* or *paint* in their titles. Draw programs store your creations as collections of vectors, or lines, rather than dots. They are good for creating things like charts and graphs.

Paint programs, on the other hand, store what you create in the form of clusters of dots. They are good for creating free-form graphics.

It is important to see graphics programs demonstrated, as well as to know if the software and your hardware are compatible, before making a purchase decision.

Page Layout Software

Page layout software lets the communicator combine the text from the word processing programs with the images produced by the graphics programs. A page layout program can enable you to produce complete mechanicals for the ink-jet or laser printer. A good quality laser printer is capable of producing mechanicals that can be taken to the printer for plate making and printing. Sometimes short runs of copies can even be made on the laser printer or other duplicating equipment.

These programs vary greatly in price and in the features they contain. Some programs are better suited for certain types of desktop publishing than others. In selecting a page layout program the communicator should consider the results he or she is hoping to achieve and go from there. Refreshers on updates of programs are important. As we have emphasized, the field is one of constant change. For instance, *Personal Computer* magazine, which monitors changes in software packages, lists as many as thirteen changes in popular programs in one 30-day period.

Some features to look for in selecting a page layout program include:

- The page size on the computer screen, the bigger the better.
- The ability to create grids that are standardized from one page to the next for use in designing publications.
- The ability to select and bring up to the screen grids with a standard set of column widths per page.
- The ability to run copy through a number of pages and adjust it automatically throughout the newsletter or other type of publication.
- The assortment of tools contained in the program such as fill patterns, screens, rules, and tools that let you create ovals, boxes, and so on.

Life on the Mississippi

Life on the Mississippi

Life on the Mississippi

Fig. 3-8 ■ Over-tight kerning, as in the top example, is seen all too frequently in the world of desktop publishing. The middle example shows more proper kerning, while the bottom line is the type set in normal letter spacing. The middle and bottom examples are acceptable; the top line is not.

Fig. 3-9 ■ This page was composed on a Macintosh computer, using Aldus Freehand 4.0 software. The large ampersand was made by typing a 72-point Goudy Old Style ampersand into a text block, selecting the text block with the selection arrow, enlarging it by 300%, then scaling it minus 60%. (adapted from a page designed by Roger Black, for *Publish!* magazine.)

❷

This caption and the box, right, are both good ways to add supplemental information to the page. They stand out from the rest of the text because of their different shapes, placement, and especially textures. Texture in type is the result of a combination of size, weight, and line spacing. You can make a block of type look light and airy, like the type in the box, or dark and dense, like the Franklin Gothic Heavy in this caption.

14-Pt Franklin Bold
and a few other indispensable faces

Goudy *or Galliard or Garamond—an "old style" serif face for readable body text*

Franklin *or Helvetica, Futura, or Univers—a "contemporary" sans serif face for weight contrast in heads and captions*

Baskerville *or Century or Times—a refined "transitional period" face substantial enough for either text or display type*

Bodoni*—an elegant "modern" face for decorative accents or classic-looking text*

Effective typography comes not so much from the *variety* of typefaces used, as from the imagination employed in their use. Using fewer faces is simpler, costs less, and, frankly, usually makes for better design.

So what faces should make up your basic type library? The chart above lists four categories of typefaces and their most common uses. Owning one or two faces from each category will give you a good selection to start with; more will expand the range of looks you can achieve.

With a repertoire of classics like these, and by using the basic design techniques of layout, contrast, and details, you'll be able to use just a few good typefaces over and over again while keeping your newsletter fresh and exciting looking.

Layout: tactic two
Layout is the art of placing text, art, and other elements on the page. You should base your newsletter layout on an underlying grid to provide structure and consistent placement from page to page. The illustration at the lower left show how the grid for this page appears on screen as the page is being designed. The rows and columns serve as guidelines for placing the text, art, elements, and captions.

Grid structure
Grid structure can consist of simple vertical columns or can incorporate more complex combinations of both vertical columns and horizontal rows. At first glance, this newsletter seems to have a simple three-column structure, but that structure is actually based on a six-by-ten modular grid. The three text columns are each two modules wide, and the half-column captions are one module wide. The horizontal rows help provide guidelines for placing the art elements.

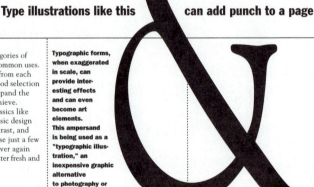

Type illustrations like this   **can add punch to a page**

Typographic forms, when exaggerated in scale, can provide interesting effects and can even become art elements. This ampersand is being used as a "typographic illustration," an inexpensive graphic alternative to photography or illustration.

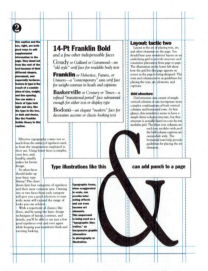

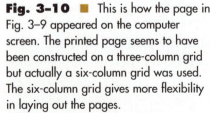

Fig. 3-10 ■ This is how the page in Fig. 3–9 appeared on the computer screen. The printed page seems to have been constructed on a three-column grid but actually a six-column grid was used. The six-column grid gives more flexibility in laying out the pages.

- ■ The cropping and scaling capabilities for processing art.
- ■ The type of kerning program. Some are automatic and some are manual.
- ■ Hyphenation and justification ability.
- ■ Ability to import text from the word processing program and graphics from the graphic program.

Supporting Programs
Many supporting programs can be obtained to augment the basic word processing, graphics, and page layout process. An example is a hyphenation program. One way to destroy readability in desktop publishing is

to write copy and then simply tell the computer to justify this copy. You could end up with something like this:

> Hyphenation programs can help you turn out copy with much more realistic word spacing. These programs can read text and check all the words against a comprehensive dictionary. Words of as few as five letters are matched with the dictionary and broken into proper divisions for hyphenation. The result is a neat appearance that eliminates rivers of white and unsightly gaps between words.

Hyphenation programs can help you turn out copy with much more realistic word spacing. These programs can read text and check all the words against a comprehensive dictionary. Words of as few as five letters are matched with the dictionary and broken into proper divisions for hyphenation. The result is a neat appearance that eliminates rivers of white and unsightly gaps between words.

The same copy properly spaced is seen in the following example:

> Hyphenation programs can help you turn out copy with much more realistic word spacing. These programs can read text and check all the words against a comprehensive dictionary. Words of as few as five letters are matched with the dictionary and broken into proper divisions for hyphenation. The result is a neat appearance that eliminates rivers of white and unsightly gaps between words.

A wide variety of clip art software is available, some of which is excellent. But don't rely on clip art for all your needs. Sometimes professional designers prefer to originate the art themselves. Cost can be an important factor here.

Type fonts for laser printers as well as fonts for the computer screen can be purchased very reasonably. Criteria for selecting fonts for desktop and other publishing are discussed in Chapters 4 and 5.

THE COMPLETE DESKTOP PUBLISHING SHOP

▶ What do you need to get into desktop publishing and how much will it cost? That's the question most communicators soon ask.

Learning to be a desktop publisher is simplified because the manufacturers of the hardware and software use everyday terms to designate commands and functions. Page makeup programs use terms such as "cut," "paste," "clipboard," and "scrapbook" to make the programs understandable. For instance, the term "cut and paste" means just what it says: you "cut" copy and "paste" it in place on a page just as you

Fig. 3-11 ■ Logo design made easy. These examples were created by the firm of Galarneau & Sinn, using Adobe Illustrator. (a) Once the type was set in Italia Bold, the house and roof were drawn with the pen and box tools. To cover some of the serifs in the typeface, they used the box tool to create white shapes. They also elongated some of the strokes in the letterforms using the same tools. (b) In this example, they set the words in Futura Extra Bold Condensed. White rules were placed over the *E,* which was effortlessly flopped using the reflection tool and placed in front of *xchange.* (c) After the type was set in Futura Bold Condensed, they used the pen tool to draw a wrench. Then it was a simple matter of placing the illustration over the ampersand and coloring it white. (Courtesy Adobe)

(a)

(b)

(c)

would in the traditional method, except you do it on a computer monitor instead of a drawing board (and thus take far less time).

In working with a page design system, the designer—to repeat—runs a program like PageMaker which takes information that has been generated with word processing software and stored in digital form on disk and converts it into type displayed on a "page" on the computer screen. It is quite helpful at this stage to have done some preliminary work, such as creating thumbnails and roughs with pencil and paper, to visualize how the page will look when assembled on the screen.

Various kinds of illustrations, then, obtained from a clip art program (stored on hard disk or introduced via a floppy) or created by the designer on the screen with a draw or print program, can be incorporated in the layout. All this is done on a grid that has been designed on the screen before the type and art are imported.

Once the information is assembled, the computer allows the designer to manipulate the material on the screen in almost every imaginable way, with far more speed and accuracy than any traditional method permitted. You can change page size or typeface size and posture—regular to bold or italic—at the press of a key. Line length and leading, position of columns and margins, and location, size, and shape of illustrations can be manipulated with ease. You can even reverse type in seconds.

After the designer is satisfied with the layout, it is printed on a laser printer. Laser output may be used for the mechanical. It can then be handled just as a mechanical is traditionally handled. A flap can be

Fig. 3-12 ■ Examples of electronic art from a computer art program. These were created using Digitart clip art, Volume 30, Art Jam. (Courtesy Image Club Graphics, Inc.)

attached and instructions for the printer added. One final advantage of desktop publishing at this stage of the production process is that last-minute changes can be made simply and quickly.

Another advantage is that, quite often, once the mechanical is ready for the printer it can be sent on a disk or transferred by a modem to a service bureau or a commercial printer. There the digital information from the designer's computer can be translated by a typesetting machine that produces either film or paper output. In many association and business offices these days, however, the product of the laser printer is printed in house; that is, the organization has its own production facilities.

But before all these benefits can be reaped, those who have not mastered desktop techniques have to learn to turn on the machine and start from the beginning. Often a big barrier in the path of the neophyte desktop student is the manual that is produced by the manufacturers of the hardware and software. Many such manuals are written by technicians and contain a maze of information that is baffling and frightening. There are supplemental books that simplify desktop publishing procedures for most programs. However, one way to really understand what you're doing might be to write a personal manual in your own words.

Just start with the first thing you do and continue to jot down each step you take as you learn your computer and its programs. Here are the beginning steps one student wrote as she started to learn a particular desktop publishing system.

Step 1: To get into the program, go to the hard drive, then place the arrow on the program's symbol and click the mouse twice.

Step 2: When the program symbol appears on the screen, place arrow on the symbol and click twice again. Move the arrow to

Fig. 3-13 ■ A graphic created by a student for his desktop publishing manual. The student moved the arrow to File and clicked the button on the mouse. The various icons and names of the programs appeared on the menu screen of the Macintosh. If the student wishes to work in a program, he will move the arrow to the proper icon and click the button on the mouse twice. The program will appear on the screen.

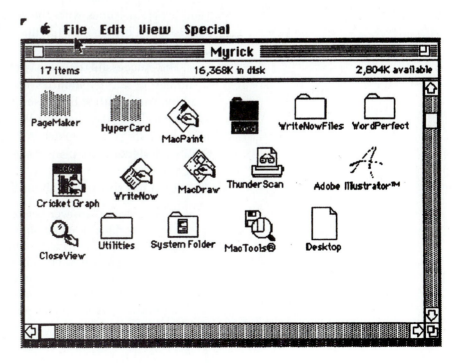

"File" and hold the button down, then pull down to "New" to open a new file.

Step 3: The page setup will appear. Here you can select the page size, number of pages, options, and margins. After you have done this, click once on "OK."

Step 4: Your screen should show a blank page (or grid) and you are ready to go to work.

The steps continue, covering such things as bringing in copy from a word processing program, wrapping text around art, enlarging and reducing art, many further design functions. Of course, the steps you write will be determined by the program you are using.

THE FUTURE OF DESKTOP PUBLISHING

➤ "It is fun being part of the revolution in electronic graphic design and publishing. If I had to give up my computer and software, I think I'd have to find something else to do for a living. I don't even want to ponder it. I'd never go back to using a drawing table, waxer, and T square. I'm completely spoiled," is the way Fletcher H. Maffett, Jr., a professional designer, expresses his enthusiasm for the computer as a design tool.[7]

Desktop publishing has changed graphic communication and it will continue to change it in the future. The hardware and software necessary to create color separations on the computer are now available. Magazines are discovering that desktop publishing can be professional publishing when a competent designer is at the computer controls.

Desktop publishing "has made people rethink the way they put words on paper," says Serge Timacheff, associate editor of *Infoworld*. "The problem comes with the realization that you can give someone a palette and a brush, but that doesn't guarantee they can paint the Mona Lisa."[8]

The successful desktop publisher is the person who can take advantage of the capabilities of electronic publishing equipment and combine them with skillful use of graphics and typography. Two people who have done just that are William E. Ryan, visual communications and advertising design instructor at the University of Oregon, and David Cundy, designer and principal of David Cundy, Inc., a Connecticut design firm.

Ryan has this to say about the future of desktop publishing:

"Today, more than ever before, it is important—even critical—that the person working in communications has a basic understanding of type, design, composition and production.

Desktop publishing has imposed responsibilities in these areas on those who may know very little about them. And so along with writing, writers need to be able to make intelligent decisions about design and type. Editors, copywriters, public relations directors and other communication

Fig. 3-14 ■ Jarrett Jester designed this striking piece and co-authored it with Michele Tarnow. Designing this advertisement began on the computer via a series of thumbnails. Eventually all the typography (including construction of the logotype) was carefully figured, set and positioned in the ad on a Macintosh. Jester's airbrushed art was painted to the ad's specifications and the typography was then overlaid atop the art and shot.

Fig. 3-15 ■ Debbie Hardy worked as the designer/artist for this piece and Leslie Jones was the typographer/copywriter. In this instance, the students designed black borders for the art and reversed copy to give it a dramatic flair. Care was taken to improve the readout of the reverse block by increased point size and leading to 14/17. Helvetica, also 14/17, was used for the signature and identification of Clean Ocean Action because it nicely contrasted with the serif face used for the headline and copy. The tag, "Until the coast is clear," was set in a bold, oblique Helvetica. Artwork was executed to fit the designed format exactly and dropped in one-to-one.

professionals also must be educated beyond their fields because computers and desktop publishing are central to their work. Like it or not, that is today's technology, and if you expect to work effectively (or even land a job, for that matter), you'd better know it."[9]

Cundy adds a word of advice and caution:

"But the computer, like the paintbrush or pen, is only a tool, and must be regarded as such. Design education must continue to emphasize

aesthetics (imagery), typography (structure), communication skills (content), and experimentation (objectivity/risk). Students with a broad understanding of art, craft and culture, as well as an eagerness to explore, will find it easier to adapt to the methods—and mindset—the future will surely require."[10]

A NEW VOCABULARY

➤ Desktop publishing uses a new vocabulary for a new world of design. Here, trimmed to the bones, are the essential words needed for working with electronic design tools.

■ *bit (binary digit):* the smallest unit of information making up the digital or dot image of a character or graphic; small parts of a letter; just little dots.

■ *bit-map graphic:* a graphic image document formed by a series of dots, with a specific number of dots per inch. Also called a "paint-type" graphic.

■ *boot:* getting your computer going; getting it started up and into the program you're going to use.

■ *byte:* eight bits make a byte and a byte can store one character; a unit of measurement.

■ *card:* a printed circuit board; computer systems are made up of these boards.

■ *clipboard:* a temporary holding place for material, in the computer. You can store text, graphics, or a group selection on a clipboard for later use.

■ *cursor:* a blinking, movable marker or position indicator on the screen to show you where you are.

■ *data base:* a collection of information that is organized and stored so that an application program can access individual items.

■ *download:* to transfer data from one electronic device to another. You could download information from one computer to another with a modem, for instance, or you could download information from a hard disk to a floppy disk.

■ *downloadable fonts:* fonts that you can buy separately and install so as to expand the variety of fonts available on your printer.

■ *dpi:* dots per inch.

■ *DTP:* desktop publishing.

- *fax:* facsimile, a machine used to transmit a copy of a file over telephone lines.
- *fax modem:* a modem that permits a computer operator to send and receive facsimile messages.
- *file:* a collection of stored information with matching formats, the computer version of a filing cabinet.
- *finder:* the file that manages all the other files; the finder is like an index; it saves, names, renames and deletes things in a file.
- *footer:* one or more lines of text that appear at the bottom of every page, similar to folio lines or running feet.
- *header:* same as a footer, but at the top of each page, like a running head.
- *H & J:* hyphenation and justification; programs will do the hyphenation of text for you following a standard dictionary.
- *icon:* a small graphic image that identifies a tool, file, or command displayed on a computer screen.
- *kerning:* to decrease the space between letters, by moving them closer together; if you are not careful you may move them so they overlap and become illegible.
- *kilobyte:* 1,024 bytes of 1K; 1 3½ inch floppy disk holds 800 kilobytes (800K) or about 400 double-spaced typewritten pages (a rough estimate).
- *megabyte:* 1,048,576 bytes of information, shortened to 1 million bytes in general conversation about storage capacity.
- *menu:* a list of commands that appears when you point to and press the menu title in the menu bar.
- *menu bar:* the area at the top of the publication window that lists the menus.
- *modem:* a telecommunications device that translates computer signals into electronic signals that can be sent over a telephone line; a way to get information from one computer to another or from your computer to a print shop, and so on.
- *object-oriented graphic:* an illustration created in an object-oriented, or draw-type application. An object-oriented graphic is created with geometric elements. Also called a "draw-type" graphic.
- *pixel (picture element):* the smallest part of a graphic that can be controlled through a program. You could think of it as a building block used to construct type and images. The resolution of text and graphics on your screen depends on the density of your screen's pixels.
- *RAM:* random access memory; the temporary memory inside the computer that allows you to find stored text and graphics.
- *resolution:* the number of dots per inch (dpi) used to represent a character or graphic image. The higher the resolution the more dots per inch and the clearer the image looks.
- *scanner:* a hardware device that reads information from a photograph, image, or text, converting it into a bit-map graphic.

PHOTO CD: A NEW DESKTOP TOOL

When Eastman Kodak introduced the photo CD it wasn't targeting desktop publishers. It was aiming at the American family with a new device to take the place of slides and prints. However, the compact disc has become a powerful production tool for electronic publishing.

A photo CD is a compact disc that can be used to store information or art in digital form. This information—even presentations that include visuals and sound—can be played on a television or a computer.

Many business concerns are marketing discs that include stock photographs and clip art. Further uses of compact discs for desktop are being developed constantly.

- *text wrap:* to run text around an illustration on a page layout. Some programs have an automatic text-wrap feature that will shorten lines of text when a graphic is encountered; in other systems you need to change the length of lines to go around a graphic.
- *vertical justification:* automatic adjustment of leading, or the space between lines, in very small amount so columns on a page can all be made with the same depth.
- *WYSIWYG:* an acronym for "what you see is what you get."

COMPUTER DESIGN HELPS TELL THE STORY

Visual communicators in just about every field one can imagine can use illustrations to tell the story. These excellent illustrations are examples of computer design work by students in the Graduate Program in Medical and Biological Illustration at the School of Art, University of Michigan.

Instructor for these computer graphics projects was Christopher Burke, adjunct assistant professor.

The illustration in Fig. A of *Giardia lamblia,* an intestinal parasite, was created using Adobe Illustrator and Photoshop by Matthew Bohan.

The simple shapes of the intestine wall and individual parasites were drawn in Illustrator, and then brought into Photoshop where they were kept as separate files. Textures, highlights, and small details were added using the filters and channels. The individual portions were then composited using channels, paste into, and paste behind commands.

Gene Therapy (Fig. B) was drawn in Adobe Illustrator and was colored in Adobe Photoshop. This is the second half of a two-part series on the subject. It was created by Michael Austin.

In the upper center, a section of an altered DNA strand is being spliced back into the DNA. The small slice is colored purple and red. That corresponds to the larger section of DNA. The messenger RNA is coming out of the nucleus and the problem that is being fixed will be fixed in the RNA. The ribosome is in yellow with the transfer RNA coming off that. The amino acid chain is going back in space.

Lisa Petkun created the illustration in Fig. C of a small incision cataract surgery. She used Adobe Illustrator 5.0 for creating an outline over a drawing that was scanned. It was imported to Adobe Photoshop for finishing.

GRAPHICS IN ACTION

1. This exercise is intended for those who are just learning desktop publishing. You will need the three basic software programs: word processing, graphics, and page layout. Find a news story in a newspaper. The story should be about 10 to 15 column inches long.

Fig. 3-17 ■ Examples of computer design and illustration by students in the Graduate Program in Medical and Biological Illustration at the School of Art, University of Michigan.

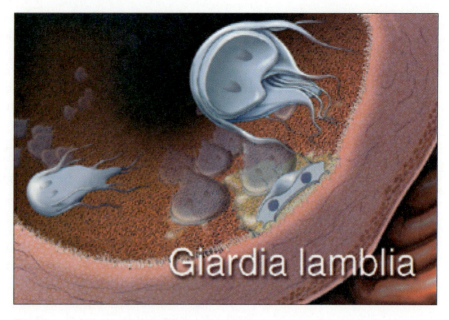

Fig. A

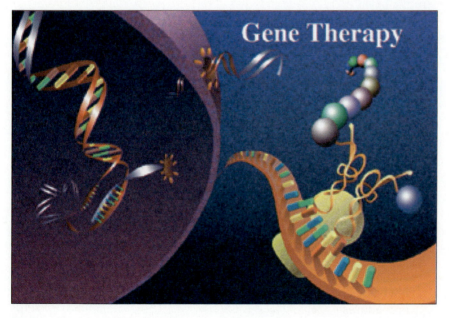

Fig. B

Fig. C

Copy the story with your word processor. Write a head for the story to fit in a three-column width on a page grid of your page layout program. Create a drawing or find a graphic in your graphics clip art program, if you have one. Combine all three elements into a layout with the page layout program and print the results.

(*Note:* A similar project has been devised by William Ryan, University of Oregon, whose students attempt to duplicate information found in newspapers. Many students are surprised to discover they can reproduce graphics very similar to the originals.)

2. Assume you are going to produce a monthly newsletter for an organization or business. Plan a desktop publishing workstation to produce the newsletter. Obtain literature and visit computer stores to obtain information and prices of hardware and software. Your goal is to create a camera-ready four-page newsletter. Work out a prospectus for the proposed newsletter that would include a budget for the equipment purchases.

3. If you have a draw program, practice by attempting to duplicate a simple illustration similar to the one included here. You will often be surprised at the results, especially if you can print your drawing with a laser printer.

4. Write your own manual for your particular needs (see the beginning of the manual written by a student in this chapter). Use a looseleaf notebook and organize it as your permanent reference book. For instance, one section could contain an alphabetical listing of all the material you have filed with the identifying file name. Another could contain ideas for graphics and layouts clipped from various sources. The most important part of your manual would likely be step-by-step instructions in your own words for various procedures.

5. Plan a newsletter as in exercise 2, but build your plan around the capabilities of the hardware and software already available to you rather than the purchase of new equipment. It might include a "wish list" of hardware and software you would like to add in order of the priority of purchase when funds would become available.

NOTES

[1]"Digital Bridges," *American Printer,* January 1994, pp. 30–31.

[2]"Doc, will I be able . . .," *Typeworld,* second March issue 1989, p. 4.

[3]"Pandora's Desktop," *Adweek* Special Report, October 3, 1988, p. 4.

[4]"Time for a Change," *Publish!* February 1989, p. 77.

[5]Mike Blum, *Understanding and Evaluating Desktop Publishing Systems* (San Luis Obispo, Calif.: Graphic Services Publications, 1992), pp. 5–6.

[6]Ibid.

[7]"Desktop Publishing: An Ode to Joy," *Magazine Design & Production,* January 1989, p. 22.

[8]"The '90s Skill Set," *Art & Design News,* March/April 1993, p. 12.

[9]Interview with the author, April 10, 1994.

[10]Interview with the author, April 12, 1994.

CHAPTER 4

TYPE: THE BASIC INGREDIENT

4 The recipe for building an effective printed communication includes a number of ingredients. But the basic ingredient is type. No matter what sort of communication is planned—newspaper, magazine, brochure, letterhead, or business card—it should be designed to accomplish five things.

1. *It should attract the reader.* If a printed piece does not attract the reader at the very beginning, it may not work. And it must attract a reader who is a member of the target audience—that particular segment of the population out there we specifically want to reach.

2. *It should be easy to read.* People simply will pass up material that appears difficult, unless they know it contains information they really want so badly they are willing to overcome any barrier to get to it. Busy people today avoid unattractive and difficult-looking reading material.

3. *It should emphasize important information.* One of the secrets of effective communication is to make sure the arrangement of type on the page and the size and styles of type employed make the heart of the message—the points we want to make—easy to recognize as important and easy to absorb.

4. *It should be expressive.* Everything in the message—the paper used, type, art, and ink—should provide a unified whole to reinforce the message and make it clear to the target audience. The reader should never say of the communication or any element in it, "I wonder what *that* means?"

5. *It should create recognition.* Printed messages can make a communications program more effective and can help build a permanent identity for our organization, our position, even our can of beans in the minds of the target audience, not just once, but time after time. Publications achieve this visual identity, for instance, by using the same type style for the nameplate, the masthead, or as a logo for house advertisements. The identity is extended by using that type style on everything from their trucks to the T-shirts of any teams they sponsor.

The starting place in planning a visual communication that will accomplish all this is with type—the basic ingredient. Proper selection and use of type can support the message. Improper selection and use can interfere with message transmission; channel noise strikes again.

All visual communicators can increase the effectiveness of their efforts if they acquire a basic knowledge of type and how to use it. This understanding can make work easier and faster, and it can help cut printing costs. It will enable communicators to give explicit instructions to printers and to communicate with them so that all involved can work together to produce the best possible product.

A CONFUSION OF TERMS

➤ Before we proceed we need to recognize that there is a problem concerning terms. With the universal acceptance of the computer as the basic tool of visual communication there has arrived a confusion of terms. Many people in the business who have not been grounded in the tradition of typography, design, and printing use different terms for the same thing. This has led to confusion and contradiction.

There are some efforts afoot to try to reach a consensus on what name to call what. The traditional terms evolved through centuries of working with type. The confusion of terms is a relatively new phenomenon. Perhaps, until a consensus emerges, those working in visual communication should be aware of these variations.

Let's take the basic letter design groups. These have always been referred to as races or species. Today some working in the field refer to them as categories, a very confusing and ambiguous term. As a further example, Clifton Karnes, writing in *Compute,* calls the basic races "groups."[1] In this confusing situation perhaps the best course to follow is just to make sure that you and those with whom you work agree on the terms you are using.

Understanding type and its uses involves some basic concepts.

First of all, communicators need to know how type is designed, the various typeface patterns available, and the suitability of each for specific messages.

Then, we must know how type is measured and how it is set and spaced. In addition, it is helpful to know basic typographic principles that have been established through practice and testing.

This chapter attempts to sort all this out, and the chapters that follow add the various ingredients needed to make sound decisions concerning printed communications.

Fig. 4-1 ■ Is it an A or an a? Letters are available in all shapes and sizes. The designer selects the best for the situation.

SOME ESSENTIAL TERMS

➤ We need to begin with an agreement on terms. These will be kept to a minimum, but the terms included in this chapter are considered by many professionals as essential for anyone who works with words, type, and printing. Our discussion starts off with some basic concepts concerning typefaces and how they came into existence.

When you look at a letter what do you see?

Is it an *a* or a *B?* This little squiggle might be any one of fifty-two different ones. A designer or typographer sees a squiggle that will create a sound that will create an image in someone's mind. The professional also notes the ascenders and descenders. Are they too long or too short, or just right? Do the serifs make the letter easier to read? Do the thick and thin letter strokes create an interesting contrast? Are the letters the right size on the body for maximum readability or legibility? Do the letters appear modern or old-fashioned?

In picking just the right type for a publication, the communicator needs to consider all these variations in letters and more. But before deciding on one of the more than 6,000 different designs of letters available in America today, the communicator needs to know what a serif is, what strokes are, and how big on the body a particular type might be.

So, in beginning to work with type, we need to know the anatomy of letter forms.

The basic elements of a letter are the *strokes,* or lines that are drawn to form the design. These can be *monotonal* (all the same width) or they can vary from *hairline* to quite *thick.*

Some designers have finished off the strokes that form the letters with rounded or straight lines called *serifs.* There are *rounded serifs* and *flat serifs.* Serifs that are filled in are called *bracketed serifs.*

Fig. 4–2 ■ Characteristics that differentiate modern and old style Roman types.

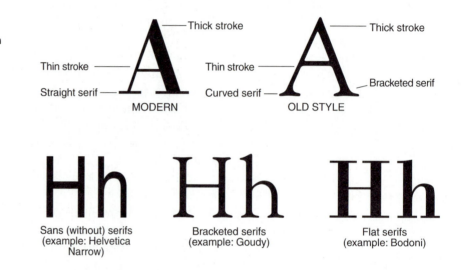

Fig. 4–3 ■ Serif treatments vary with type styles. Sans Serif typefaces have no serifs, old style Romans have bracketed serifs, and modern Romans have flat, straight-line serifs.

An alphabet of a certain design will be drawn to a consistent size for all letters. This size is determined by the *x* height of the letters. This is the height of the lowercase *x.*

Some letters have a stroke, or stem, which extends above the *x* height. This stroke is known as an *ascender.* The letters *g, j, y, p,* and *q* all have a tail or *descender* that drops below the x height.

Fig. 4–4 ■ The x height (the height of the lowercase x) is a critical basic measurement in the design of letters.

Fig. 4–5 ■ The letter stroke that extends above the x height is called the ascender. If the stroke extends below the x height, it is a descender.

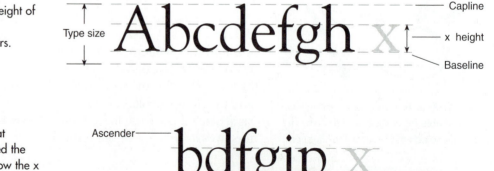

In the capital alphabet only the *Q* has a descender. There are no ascenders in capital letters.

Now that we are acquainted with a few terms, we can start our consideration of type and its use. As mentioned, there are more than 6,000 type designs in the Western world. In the days when printing was done from metal type cast by foundries, the letter designs were fairly consistent. The Caslon design, for example, which first was cast by William Caslon in England in 1734, was and still is one of the basic types. Caslon 224 is the typeface used for the text of this book.

With the advent of *photocomposition* and digital composition there has been a proliferation of type designs of various names. Many of these designs have characteristics of long-established and recognized styles but each manufacturer has made slight changes.

In addition, new faces are constantly being produced by the hundreds of new companies that have entered the printing market during the past two decades of the technological explosion.

Communicators can no longer rely solely on old family names for type styles. It is necessary to compare types on the specimen sheets of the various printing establishments with the styles that have become basic types through the years.

As far as learning about the correct use of types, we can start our discussion with the letter designs that are traditional and recognized by all good printers and graphic designers.

To create an effective communication, we need to decide which typeface would be easiest to read and give the best "image" to go with the message. We need to be acquainted with enough designs to understand the strengths and weaknesses of each.

ABC abc
ABC abc

Fig. 4-6 ■ Goudy (top line) and Bodoni are both members of the Roman race, but there are differences in the letter structures. Goudy is an old style Roman and Bodoni is a modern Roman.

TYPEFACES

➤ Type is classified in a way that makes differentiation among the designs easy. It is sorted rather like humans have been sorted by anthropologists. Just as there are various races of people, there are various *races* of types. Some communicators refer to these basic divisions as "species" of types.

Within these races are *families* of types. Each family has the basic characteristics of its race but in addition it has slight differences in letter design from the other families of the same race.

The Goudy family and the Bodoni family are both members of the *Roman* race of types. They have certain basic similarities, but they also have subtle differences.

An inspection of the Goudy and Bodoni types reveals their similarities and differences. They both have serifs, and they both have variations in the letter strokes. However, the Goudy serifs are rounded and bracketed, and the Bodoni serifs are straight-lined. The letter strokes of the Goudy letters do not have as pronounced a variation between thick and thin strokes. The Bodoni strokes are very thick and very thin. Note also the different treatment of the juncture of the thick and thin strokes at the top of the letters.

Once such differences and their effects on the printability, legibility, and suitability of a printed piece are mastered, the effective selection of letter styles becomes quite easy.

Many typographers and graphic artists recognize six races of typefaces. There isn't full agreement on this, but the majority usually classify all the thousands and thousands of letter styles within six categories. These races are the Romans, the Sans Serifs, the Square Serifs (or Egyptians), the Text types (or Black Letter), the Scripts and Cursives, and a catch-all category for those designs that defy specific identification called Miscellaneous (or Novelty).

No matter how the letters selected for a printed communication are imposed on the printing surface—by using the foundry types of the letterpress process, or letters produced from film by the photocompositor, or strike-on letters of an electric typewriter—they all will exhibit characteristics of the various races. They can all be discussed within the framework of this race-and-family system of classification.

Let's examine the characteristics of each of these six races.

Text or Black Letter

The first printing produced from movable type was, of course, the product of Johan Gutenberg's shop in Mainz, Germany. It is interesting to note that Gutenberg's most lasting achievement in printing was his famous forty-two-line Bible. Each page contained two columns, and each column was forty-two lines long. Nearly five hundred years later this Bible is still considered by typographers to be a superb example of printing and layout. (See Fig. 2–5, page 23.)

The letters that Gutenberg designed, cast, and printed, which are the letters used in the Gutenberg Bible, were copies of the heavy black letters of the northern European hand. They are thought of today as "Old English." Actually Old English is a family of the Text or Black

Fig. 4-7 ◼ The six races of type in lowercase letters for comparison.

Blackletter

Roman (Old Style)

Sans serif

Square serif

Script

Novelty

Castle
abcdefghijklmnopqrstuvwxyz
ABCDEFGHIJKLMNOPQRST
UVWXYZ

The New York Times

Letter race and is not a race itself. Black Letter types are ornate with a great variation in the strokes. They can be difficult to read.

These Text or Black Letter types do have a place in modern graphic design, however. What better way to say "medieval banquet," or "ye olde gift shoppe"? Although these types may remind you of Gothic cathedrals, don't call them "Gothic." Gothic is another name for an entirely different race of types.

Some more confusion can arise about this race of types. The name Text was attached to these designs because they were the "text" or reading matter types of the medieval northern Europeans. But today the term *text* is used to designate any reading matter. So from now on, to avoid this confusion, this race is referred to only as Black Letter.

Use Black Letter when you want to emphasize tradition and solemnity and when you want to give the image of strength and efficiency. Many newspapers adopted Black Letter types for their nameplates for these reasons. Avoid using Black Letter in all-capital lines; the letters are difficult, if not impossible, to read when set in all caps. Use them sparingly for title lines, logos, and subheads, where they are suitable. They are useful for formal invitations and stationery.

Roman

The birthplace of printing in the Western world was northern Europe. From there it spread south and west. Venice became a center for printing in the late fifteenth century. However, the people in southern Europe did not like the heavy type used in the north. They preferred the simpler and more open letters of the Romans. So typefaces developed in Venice, Paris, and elsewhere followed Roman letter forms and became known as the Roman race.

Caslon
abcdefghijklmnopqrstuvwxyz
ABCDEFGHIJKLMNOPQRSTUVWXYZ

Fig. 4-11 ■ The development of some modern letter forms can be traced back to the hieroglyphics of the Egyptians.

EGYPTIAN HIERATIC	SEMITIC PHOENICIAN	HELLENIC EARLY GREEK	ROMAN EARLY LATIN	TODAY F.W.G.
ς	⪡ ⪢	△ △ △	∧ ∧	A
⪡	⪡ ⪡ ⪡ ⪢	⪡ B ⪡	⪡ B	B
⪡	△ △	△ ⪡ △	▷ D	D
⌒	⪡ ⪡	⪡ ⪡ R	P R	R

25TH CENTURY B.C.	10TH TO 9TH CENTURY B.C.	7TH TO 4TH CENTURY B.C.	A.D. 200 TO 300	20TH CENTURY

The ancient Romans developed their alphabet from the Greeks and the other early civilizations of the eastern Mediterranean area. In fact, some letters of the Roman alphabet and thus of our alphabet can be traced back to the picture writing, or hieroglyphics, of the Egyptians.

Historians believe that the Phoenicians adopted and modified Egyptian letters and then the Greeks took some letter forms from the Phoenicians, rearranged their constructions, and used them to form the Greek alphabet. These forms passed from the Greeks to the Romans.

The tool most used by the Romans in writing inscriptions on their buildings was the brush. They painted inscriptions on the masonry and then stonemasons carved over the painted outline. The Romans could turn a brush to make curves and continuous lines, and thus they developed letter strokes of varying widths for their letters. They also finished off long broad strokes with a narrow stroke using the side of the brush. These endings became the serifs on our letters, one of the distinguishing features of the Roman race of types. All Romans have serifs and letter strokes that vary in width from thick to thin.

Roman types are classified as old style, transitional, and modern.

A typeface is classified as *old style* if it has little contrast between the thick and thin lines, if the strokes are sloping or round, and if the serifs are slanting or curved and extended outward at the top of the capital T and the bottom of the capital E.

Fig. 4–12 ■ Characteristics of old style Roman types. (Example: Goudy)

There is some contrast between thick and thin strokes.

There is a slight tilt to the angle of the swells of the round letters.

Tops of ascenders have a distinctly oblique serif.

The serif angles out from the stem and terminates in a crisp point (called a bracketed serif).

In 1773 Giambattista Bodoni, an Italian type designer and a contemporary and friend of Benjamin Franklin, introduced the so-called *modern* Roman types. These types are distinguished by strong contrast between thick and thin strokes and straight, thin, unbracketed serifs. Any type with these characteristics, even if a century and a half old, or if designed only yesterday, is classified as a modern Roman.

Type that falls between the (a) sloping or rounded strokes, little contrast between thick and thin lines, and slanting or curved serifs of the old style Roman and (b) contrasting thick and thin strokes and straight thin and unbracketed serifs of the modern Roman is considered a *transitional* Roman face. It is said to be half-way out of the old style Roman design and half-way into the modern Roman configuration.

In the transitional types the angle of the thin strokes is not as pronounced as in the old style Roman, and the variation between thick and thin strokes is more pronounced.

Romans are considered the basic types. They come in all weights and sizes. There are Romans available to help communicate virtually any message esthetically and effectively.

Fig. 4–13 ■ Examples of the three subgroups within the Roman race.

Goudy (old style)
ABCDEFGHIJKLMNOPQRSTUVWXYZ
abcdefghijklmnopqrstuvwxyz

ITC New Baskerville (transitional)
ABCDEFGHIJKLMNOPQRSTUVWXYZ
abcdefghijklmnopqrstuvwxyz

Bodoni (modern)
ABCDEFGHIJKLMNOPQRSTUVWXYZ
abcdefghijklmnopqrstuvwxyz

Fig. 4-14 ■ Characteristics of transitional Roman types. Transitionals are basically old style with modifications that move them toward modern Romans. (Example: New Baskerville)

There is greater contrast between thick and thin strokes.

There is almost no tilt to the angle of the swells of the round letters.

Ascenders have slightly less oblique angles on the serifs.

Serif feet are bracketed, but they terminate in a squared-off point.

Fig. 4-15 ■ Characteristics of modern Roman types. The contrast between thick and thin strokes is carried to the extreme and there is a vertical emphasis as shown by the thin strokes in the letter bowls, such as the top and bottom of the o. (Example: Bodoni)

There is a strong and abrupt contrast between thick and thin strokes.

The overall stress is clearly vertical.

All serifs are horizontal and end in squared-off points.

Serifs are usually unbracketed, but they can be slightly bracketed.

Sans Serif

The third broad category, Sans Serif, is comparatively new in name but it also has an ancient *derivation,* probably from the flat, even-bodied lines of the Greek and early Roman letters. Sans Serifs are called Gothics by some typographers, and in Europe they are known as the Grotesque types.

As the name implies (*sans* means "without" in French), Sans Serif types have no serifs. They are geometric, precise, and open. Some forms of Sans Serif types have slight variations in the letter strokes but most are monotonal.

Sans Serifs are excellent all-purpose types. Some of our newest designs, such as the Avant Garde Gothic, are renderings of the sans serif style of lettering. Sans Serifs are suitable for every purpose. They print well and have a modern look with good punch. And they probably will continue to be among the most popular faces for years to come. They are especially good for cold type production and offset printing methods as they stand up exceptionally well in photographic reproduction.

Fig. 4-16 ■ An example of the Sans Serif race, this type is a member of the Avant Garde Gothic family designed for the International Typeface Corporation.

Avant Garde
ABCDEFGHIJKLMNOPQRSTUVWXYZ
abcdefghijklmnopqrstuvwxyz

The Sans Serifs became especially popular in the 1920s when the Bauhaus movement in Germany, which emphasized functional design, made its influence felt in the world of typography. Sans Serifs may be rather monotonous when printed in mass. However, they are being used more and more, especially in newsletters and in-house magazines.

Square Serif

The fourth race of type is the Square Serifs. These have the general characteristics of the Sans Serifs except that a precise square or straight-line serif is added. Some typographers refer to the Square Serifs as Slab Serifs or Egyptians. They were called Egyptians when they first appeared.

In the early nineteenth century there was great interest in Egypt, most likely because of the discovery of the Rosetta stone in 1799. (The Rosetta stone contained an inscription in three languages—that of the rulers, that of the common people, and Greek. The Greek was used to unlock the secrets of Egyptian hieroglyphics and of ancient Egyptian history.)

About the same time, Vincent Figgins, a British type designer and founder, produced a typeface characterized by thick slab serifs and a general evenness of weight. The face had a certain quality reminiscent of Egyptian architecture in its capital letters. So it was only natural for it to be dubbed "Egyptian."

Today there are many versions of Square Serif types, many with Egyptian family names or with names that are descriptive of the type style. There are Memphis, Cairo, Karnak, and Luxor. And there are Stymies, Girders, and Towers.

Today Square Serifs are more logically associated with modern buildings than Egyptian architecture. They are sturdy and square. The capital letters look like steel girders, and the design gives the reader a feeling of strength, stability, and ruggedness.

The Square Serifs were not meant to be used in mass. They are excellent for headlines, headings in advertisements, and posters. They are monotonous and tiring when used in long columns of reading matter.

Fig. 4-17 ■ This example of the Square Serif race is a member of the Lubalin Graphic family produced by the International Typeface Corporation.

Lubalin Graph
ABCDEFGHIJKLMNOPQRSTUVWXYZ
abcdefghijklmnopqrstuvwxyz

Scripts and Cursives

The fifth race includes letter styles that resemble handwriting. The typographer calls them Scripts or Cursives. Since Scripts and Cursives are so similar, we can group them together in the Scripts and Cursives race.

But, why Scripts and Cursives? Why not just call them one or the other?

Fig. 4-18 ■ This is Shelley Allegro Script.

Shelley Allegro Script

A B C D E F G H I J K L M N O P 2 R S T U V W X Y Z

abcdefghijklmnopqrstuvwxyz

A little explanation is needed here. Some typographers classify *italic* types (Roman types with slanted letters) as a separate race. The slanted letters that we refer to as italics were actually a style all their own when they first appeared in the 1500s.

A printer and letter designer, Aldus Manutius, who established his famous Aldine press in Venice in 1490, wanted to publish small books of significant works. They might be called the first "everyone's library" books. Manutius sought a letter style for his type that would permit as many words as possible on a page.

He devised a cursive letter style that was the first italic typeface. A cursive letter (from the Latin *currere,* which means "run") is free flowing like handwriting.

When the Aldine books appeared in the original italic face, other printers quickly copied it and the design spread throughout Europe. (However, slanted letters in the Sans Serif and Square Serif races are called *obliques* and not italics.)

In some books on type the authors insist that Scripts are letters resembling handwriting and are connected, while Cursives have a noticeable gap between the letters. On the other hand, just the opposite is cited as the distinguishing feature of the two types (that Scripts have

Fig. 4-19 ■ The first italic type appeared in Virgil's *Opera,* printed by Aldus Manutius in 1501. (Courtesy The Pierpont Morgan Library, New York. PML 1664)

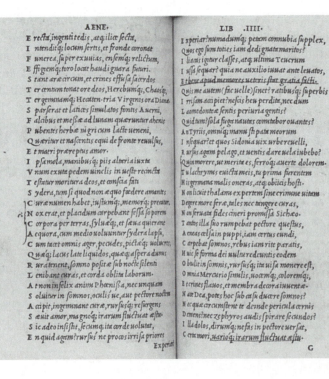

Fig. 4-20 ■ A comparison between script, italic and oblique type.

This is a script, called Freestyle, not to be confused with an italic type face.

This is Garamond italic, not to be confused with scripts and cursives.

And this is an oblique, a slanted version of the sans serif type face, Futura.

Fig. 4-21 ■ Some Scripts or Cursives are designed so that the letters appear to join (left); others have noticeable gaps between the letters.

Shelley Allegro *Ribbon*

gaps between the letters and Cursives do not) in other texts on typography and graphics. It is usually sufficient, however, to recognize and define the letter styles that resemble handwriting as either Scripts or Cursives. The safest way to approach these types is to select the style you want to use and refer to it by its family name.

Scripts and Cursives play an important role in good design. They can give a special "tone" to a printed piece. They are excellent for announcements and invitations and they can be used for titles, headings, and subheads. They can also add interest, contrast, and life to a

Fig. 4-22 ■ A traditional wedding invitation set in Shelley Allegro script. Note how this typeface helps create the image of a formal occasion.

Mr. and Mrs. Reginald Harper
request the honor of your company
at the marriage of their daughter

Jacqueline Marie
to
Mr. Alfred Bruce Taylor

on the evening of
Friday the first of October
at half after seven o'clock
Six hundred and ten Richelieu Place
Kingsland, Wyoming

printed page. But because they have a low readability rating, they (and italics, too, for that matter) should be used sparingly—only for a line or two or three—not for many sentences or paragraphs.

Miscellaneous or Novelty

The sixth race is not actually a race. It is a catchall category for all those unusual designs that do not have the clear-cut characteristics of the other races. These can include hand-designed types and types designed for special effects, logos, trademarks, and novelty arrangements. They are "display" types and most are unsuitable for use in blocks of reading matter. They also are called Decorative.

Selection and use of these types should be governed by the same criteria we would use in selecting and using a Script or Cursive.

Fig. 4-23 ■ Types of unusual or decorative design that cannot be clearly classified by race are placed in the Miscellaneous or Novelty category. This typeface is called Paisley, designed by Image Club Graphics.

Paisley
ABCDEFGHIJKLMNOPQRSTUVWXYZ
abcdefghijklmnopqrstuvwxyz

Families of Type

Roman, Black Letter, Sans Serif, Square Serif, Scripts and Cursives, and Miscellaneous—these are the basic races of types. But not only can each letter design be identified by its race, each has a name as well. Quite often, the name of the designer is used. There is Bodoni, named after the designer of this popular modern Roman type, Giambattista Bodoni. There is (Nicholas) Jenson, (William) Caslon, (Claude) Garamond, and (Frederic) Goudy, to mention a few faces that are in use today.

Sometimes the type name may be descriptive of its design or function. There is Cloister, a Black Letter type reminiscent of the cloisters of medieval monks; the gaudy Lilith, named for the female demon of Jewish folklore; and there is Bankers Gothic, a no-nonsense type often used for business forms and letterheads.

Or, the type names may reflect a geographical area, such as the Square Serifs called Cairo, Memphis, and Karnak.

Within these families there are further divisions that are called series. A series of type within a family consists of all the sizes of a structure, or variation, within that family. Such variations might be letters that are bold, letters that are condensed or extended, and so on. Each one of these variations in all the sizes available is a series.

Finally, there is the font. A font consists of all the characters available in one size of a particular type style.

MEASUREMENT OF TYPE

➤ Graphic design and printing have unique units of measurement. These units are quite simple, but anyone working with printing should understand them thoroughly. It will be difficult to function with

Fig. 4–24 ■ Variations of type designs within a family are called a series. These are members of the Caslon family.

Caslon Book
Caslon Medium
Caslon Bold
Caslon Black
Caslon Book Italic
Caslon Medium Italic
Caslon Bold Italic
Caslon Black Italic

Fig. 4–25 ■ Here is a series of the Helvetica family, medium weight, from 6 to 36 point.

Point Size

6 abcdefghijklmnopqrstuvwxyz
7 abcdefghijklmnopqrstuvwxyz
8 abcdefghijklmnopqrstuvwxyz
9 abcdefghijklmnopqrstuvwxyz
10 abcdefghijklmnopqrstuvwxyz
11 abcdefghijklmnopqrstuvwxyz
12 abcdefghijklmnopqrstuvwxyz
14 abcdefghijklmnopqrstuvwxyz
16 abcdefghijklmnopqrstuvwxyz
18 abcdefghijklmnopqrstuvwxyz
24 abcdefghijklmnopqrstuvw
30 abcdefghijklmnopqrs
36 abcdefghijklmnop

Fig. 4–26 ■ A font of type. Many more than 26 characters are needed to set type. The usual bare minimum of characters in a font is about 125. This typeface is ITC Fenice.

abcdefghijkjlmnopqrstuvwxyz
ABCDEFGHIJKLMNOPQRSTUVWXYZ
1234567890&$¢%#@*(:;.!?-——/""'')
[¡™£¢§¶•ªºœ´®†¥¨ˆ°¬…æç˜µ÷≠¤◊fifl‡°]

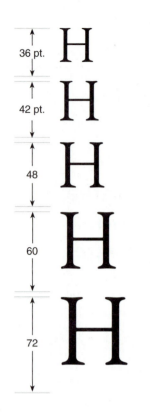

36 pt.

42 pt.

48

60

72

Fig. 4-27 ■ The body of type is large enough to accommodate the descending lowercase letters, such as g, p, y and the ascending letters such as b, h, d. The vertical line indicates the true body size. The typeface shown is Goudy.

any sort of efficiency as a visual communicator if you do not understand and know this measurement system.

For about 300 years after Gutenberg there was no standard system of measurement for printers. Typecasters gave names to the various sizes of types they produced. Usually the types of one foundry could not be used with those of another. The problem was further compounded because the names given to types of certain sizes by one foundry might be used to designate entirely different sizes by another. One foundry might have called a type "nonpareil," while another used nonpareil for a different size type. (*Note:* The term *nonpareil* became accepted later as referring to type now called 6 point.)

A system of sizing type by units of measurements called *points* was devised in the mid-eighteenth century by a French typographer, Pierre Simon Fournier, and further refined by his countryman Francois Ambroise Didot. In 1886, under the sponsorship of the U.S. Type Founders Association, a point system was adopted as the official uniform measurement of types in the United States. England adopted it in 1898.

The point is the smallest unit of measurement in the printer's and graphic designer's world. It is commonly defined as being $\frac{1}{72}$ of an inch. (Actually, the point is slightly less than that. Specifically, it is 0.0138-plus of an inch. But for all practical purposes communicators consider 72 points as equalling an inch.)

The thickness of spaces such as the space between lines of type, thickness of rules and borders (rules are straight lines of various thicknesses, and borders are decorative "frames" around graphics) and the height of type are all measured in points. If type is 36 points high it is approximately $\frac{1}{2}$ inch high. Type that is 72 points is approximately 1 inch high.

Some of the old typographical terms have made their way down into the world of graphics today. Pica and agate are the most common type terms still in use. A pica is a unit of measurement that is 12 points in width. Pica type is type that is 12 points in height. Agate refers to type or a unit of measurement that is 5½ points in size. Printers and advertisers use the agate type size for measuring advertisements and consider 14 agate lines as equalling 1 inch in measuring the depth of an advertisement.

Pica is used to designate 12 points of space. Thus there are 12 points in a pica and 6 picas in 1 inch. The type on a pica typewriter (or pica type on a word processor) is 12-point type.

Points and picas are the heart of the printer's and the communicator's measurement system, just as inches and feet are used to measure most things in our daily lives.

Sometimes the word *em* is used as a synonym for pica. This is erroneous usage, but it has become so prevalent that only a purist would object now. A pica is linear measure. That is, it measures height, width, or depth. An em is the measurement of the square of an area.

The em is an important unit of measurement in graphic design. Formally it is the square of the type size in question. For example, a 36-point em measures 36 points, or ½ inch, on all four sides. An em that measures 12 points, or a pica, on each side is referred to as a *pica em*.

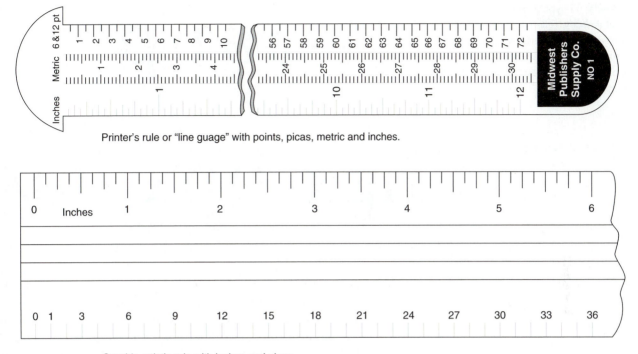

Printer's rule or "line guage" with points, picas, metric and inches.

Graphic artist's rule with inches and picas.

Fig. 4-28 ■ Units of measure (actual size).

Another measure of area, but not a square area, is the *en*. An en is half the width of an em. An en in 36-point type is 36 points, or ½ inch high—the same height as the type. However, it is only 18 points, or half the 36-point measure, wide. Thus, a 36-point en would be 36 points high and 18 points wide.

Old-timers, to keep the two terms from being confused, referred to an em as a mutton or mut, and an en as a nut.

Ems and ens are still used quite often to indicate indentation. Many video display terminal keyboards have an em and an en key. If copy for 9-point type is marked for an em indent, it will be indented 9 points when the operator hits the em key on the keyboard. If copy set in 12 points is marked for an en indentation, it will be indented 6 points. The compositor does not have to stop and figure out spacing if copy is properly marked by the communicator.

Once we understand the classification of types and type measurements, we can put this information to work. However, there are a few more points to keep in mind that apply to all the styles of types.

For instance, two typefaces may have the same point-size designation, but the body of the letters in one may be considerably larger than those of the other. This is referred to as being "big on the body" or "small on the body." The *body* is the actual base size or true point size of the type.

It is possible for types that have, say, 48 points as their size designations to be quite different in appearance. The *x* height of the letter forms may be different even though the total point sizes of the types are the same.

EM   EN

Fig. 4-29 ■ An em is a unit of measurement that is the square of the type size being used. An en is one-half the width of an em. The square on the left illustrates the area of a 48-point em. The rectangle on the right illustrates the dimensions of a 48-point en.

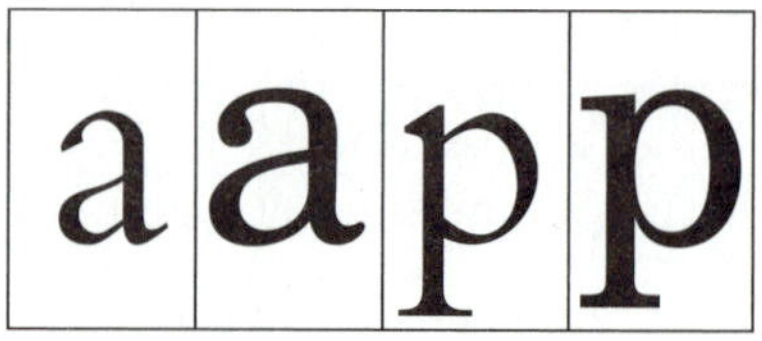

Fig. 4–30 ■ Type is measured by the height of its body. Letters that vary in appearance still can be considered the same size. The a on the left is "small on the body" and the largest a is "large on the body."

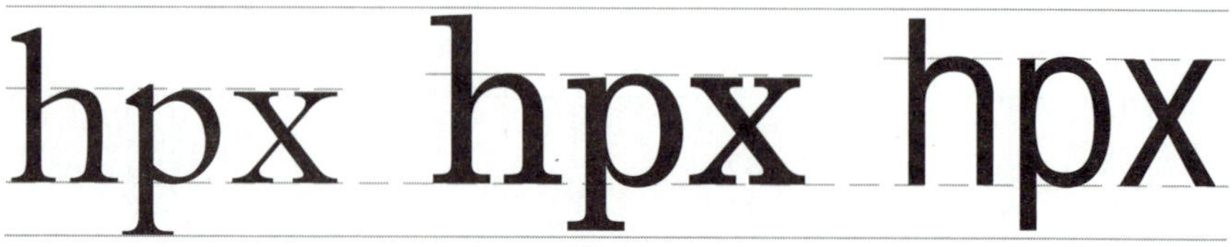

Fig. 4–31 ■ Even though these letters appear to be different sizes, they are all 72-point.

Notice how the lowercase *h*'s in Fig. 4–31 are actually in three different sizes, even though all are called 72-point types.

The size of letters cannot be measured accurately by placing a line gauge or graphic arts ruler on the letters themselves. To be perfectly accurate the base has to be measured. However, we can get a close reading, or workable reading, of the point size of a certain type. We can do this by measuring from the top of the ascender to the bottom of the descender of sample letters.

This is useful when we spot a type that is just the right size for the purpose in mind but the point size is not known. We can measure the letters and find the size. We can then proceed to make a layout and specify the size of type, or we can tell the printer, "Set it in 48 point" or whatever.

➤ IMPORTANT POINTS TO REMEMBER

■ Type size is measured in points. There are 72 points in 1 inch.

■ Line length is measured in picas. There are 6 picas in 1 inch.

■ The pica is used to express overall width or depth as well as the length of a line. There are 12 points in 1 pica.

■ The most common use of the em is to indicate indentation of blocks of copy or to indicate the indentation at the start of a paragraph. The em is the square of the type size being used.

■ The agate line is used to measure the depth of advertising space. There are 14 agate lines in 1 inch.

➤ EFFECTIVE DESIGN CHECKLIST

■ There is a Roman type to fit nearly every need. Old-time printers said, "When in doubt, use Caslon."

Fig. 4-32 ■ You are in control when generating type on the computer. This is a command image from Ventura Publisher. Note the use of terms such as *kerning, letter spacing, justification,* and *ens.* The technology has changed but many practices and terms from the past continue to be the basis of good typography.

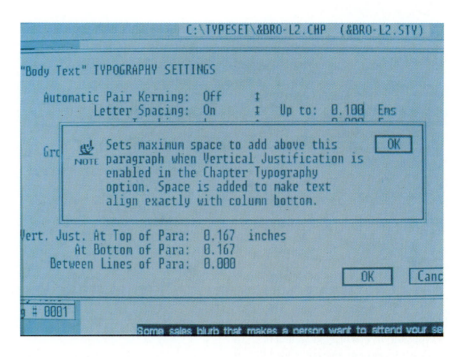

- Square Serifs print well and are good for "no-nonsense" messages.
- Black Letters emphasize tradition. They give the feeling of Gothic cathedrals, medieval castles, institutions. They are, however, rarely used in today's designs. They, and Scripts and Cursives, are also difficult, if not impossible, to read in all capital letters.
- Scripts and Cursives are like spices and seasonings. They can add interest, contrast, and life to a printed page. However, they have low readability and should be used sparingly.
- Miscellaneous or Novelty faces should be selected and used sparingly, like Scripts and Cursives.
- It is considered better to have a wide range or series of a few families rather than a wide variety of families with limited series.
- In selecting a font of type, consider the characters it contains in addition to the letters, numerals, and punctuation marks.
- Compare the x heights of letters, the lengths of ascenders and descenders of the various families, as well as the letter designs when selecting types.

➤ GRAPHICS IN ACTION

1. Collect examples of types representing each of the races. Mount them on plain white paper and indicate the widths of the lines in inches and picas. If you are working on a computer, this exercise can be done on the computer with the typefaces available to you.
2. Explain how type is classified according to race, family, and series. Illustrate your explanation with examples clipped from publica-

CREATIVE COMMUNICATION

Are you the creative type?

A number of personality studies have been made in efforts to identify the characteristics of creative people. But there has been little consistency in the findings.

One study indicated that individualism and social nonconformity were correlated with problem-solving ability. Fluency, flexibility, and the ability to elaborate also seemed to be important.

Some investigators have found that creative people often have immature personality traits, such as dependency, defiance of convention or authority, a feeling of destiny or omnipotence, and gullibility.

Psychologists have made some progress in attempting to describe the process of creative thinking, but they admit that they haven't found a magic key to creativity. The evidence does indicate that training, knowledge, and hard work are vital. In addition, it is important for the creative person to take time to mull over ideas and let them percolate in the mind.

tions. This assignment could be done in its entirety on a computer with enough fonts.

3. Identify the following types by race and give the reasons for your choices:

POWERFUL

Professional

Jazzy

Stylish

Playful

Distinguished

Mechanical

4. If you are working on a computer, or if you have typefaces available from another source, make a printout or copy on an 8½ × 11 sheet of paper of all the typefaces at your disposal. Make them at least 24-point. Label them by race and family. Keep this in your notebook as it will prove to be valuable when you start selecting types for design projects.

NOTES

[1] "Truetype and Beyond," *Compute*, May 1993, p. 58.

CREATIVE TYPOGRAPHY

Courtesy Storter Childs Printing Company, Inc.

5 The proper selection and use of the hundreds of type designs available is the second step in creating an effective printed communication. The first step is a look at one word in that sentence: *creating.*

All the work done by the visual communicator is the result of creativity. We start with little more than an idea. But even before that we have to come up with the idea—originate it, consider it, examine it, revise it, try it. We have to be creative.

Among professional communicators more and more attention is being paid to effective creativity. There are some important reasons for this. We have the tools to expand our ability to execute what we create. We have computers, laser printers, scanners, and other tools that are capable of producing highly refined work. At the same time, we are working in an overcommunicated environment. If we want our communication to penetrate the consciousness of our target audience, we have to come up with new and novel and creative ways to get our message to do its job.

"But," you say, "I am not the creative type. I have to work and struggle. I have a hard time getting started. How do I begin? How did people like Einstein and Galileo and Thomas Edison come up with their ideas? I wish I could get ideas that work, too."

So, before we take a look at how we can select and work with type and art to create the most effective communication possible, let's listen to the experts for a minute or two.

"Human creativity uses what is already existing and available and changes it in unpredictable ways," explains noted psychiatrist Silvano Arieti.[1] As we shall see, we can take words, experiences, pieces of art, even a scrap of paper in the street, and use them to trigger creative ideas of all sorts.

Writer Arthur Koestler has an idea to get us started thinking about creativity. Koestler notes that children are instinctively creative. They all create without restraint. They sing, dance, draw, fantasize, play, all in a world of their own creation.[2]

But then, as children get older something happens. Their lives become increasingly structured in a mass of rules and regulations imposed by mother, father, and teacher. The creativity of their early days is restricted and repetition replaces creativity.

Now, to unleash our abilities and come up with ideas that are unique and different we have to break out of the restraints, if only for a while, that have ordered our lives. We have to bring the right brain into action and tap the creativity that exists in us all.

Psychologists tell us we have two brains. The left brain orders our talking, walking, and all our mechanical actions. The right brain is the repository of our imagination, intuition, and creative thinking. We use our left brain in much of our day-to-day living; to be creative we need to unlock the right brain—the home of our creative abilities.

We need to call up our right brain and let it work with the left to develop creative problem solving. This starts the whole brain operating—using things we have learned about the fundamentals of effective communication that are stored in our left brain with the innovative and creative potential of the right brain.

Fig. 5-1 ■ Type talks. Note how the design of the typeface and its arrangement help to create the image intended by the word used. (Courtesy Celestial Seasonings)

The advertisement or brochure layout or the magazine cover design start with an effort to solve a problem; for example, how to get our target audience to buy a product or idea or how to get it to select our magazine from the scores in the rack.

One approach suggested by Edward de Bono, author, physician, and psychologist, is first to list every possible solution to the problem. Come up with as many as you can. If you get stuck, de Bono says, use the random input technique. In this technique the designer selects a word or an object completely at random and adds it to what he or she has already worked out. Then the designer works backward and often comes up with a fresh idea.

Fig. 5-2 ■ Type can be selected to reinforce the message, as in the title and initial letter for this magazine article about Gothic cathedrals. The use of Black Letter for the title and for the initial letter aids unity. The subhead and byline in Roman are subordinated to the title and illustrate proper mixing of the races—there should be definite contrast and one should dominate. (Reprinted by permission of *Sciences*, copyright, The America Association for the Advancement of Science. Cathedral photo by R. Mark, Princeton University)

Suppose you have to create a cover idea for a promotional brochure for a computer company. You don't want a boring image of a person just sitting and looking at the computer. You're looking for a fresh way to get at the problem. What can you do?

One approach would be to start with a word picked at random from a dictionary. It has to be random. If it isn't you are choosing it and that won't work, de Bono says. Let's try it. Let's take the first word, left-hand column, on page 869 of *Webster's Ninth New Collegiate Dictionary*. The word is pen. Can you play with this word and come up with a fresh idea of how this word could be used to illustrate a promotional brochure for a new computer?

Andy Hertzfeld, who headed the team that built the Macintosh computer, says about creativity and ideas: "I get inspired by the chance to make a difference in the world. An idea has to be able to help people in some fashion to make it worth pursuing."[3]

Hertzfeld believes the best way to fight creative blocks is to work on two or three problems at once. "When you're blocked on one thing you can go work on something else. Often a nice solution to your former problem will occur when you're working on something else," he notes.

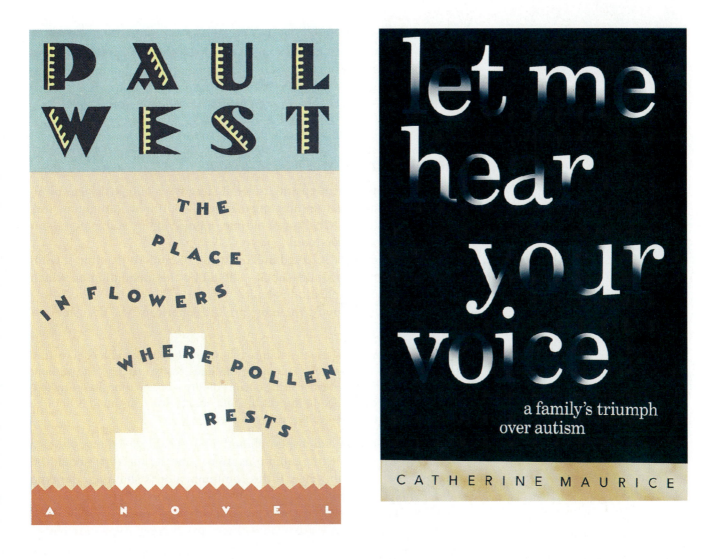

Fig. 5–3 ■ Carin Goldberg's striking book jackets reflect her strong sense of design history. In the example on the left, Goldberg redesigned and improved Max Salzman's eccentric 1922 typeface, Zierdolmen. On the right is a book jacket designed by Michael Bierut of Pentagram Design. His manipulation of the type in the title conveys a sense of the halting speech patterns of autism. (Courtesy Carin Goldberg and Michael Bierux)

Quite often success comes from "something old, something new." This is the approach of four graphic designers in New York. Paula Scher, Louise Fili, Carin Goldberg, and Lorraine Louie say they obtain their creative ideas from such approaches as the study of European design going back to the first fifty years of the twentieth century, unorthodox typefaces, and a flagrant disregard for the rules of proper typography.[4]

Unorthodox attitudes about the rules of proper design and typography permit them to take risks and experiment.

Goldberg says the study of design history is important for anyone seeking new and creative ways to tackle graphic problems. "Without a sense of design history graphic designers are lost in space," she comments. A striking image is needed in today's overcommunicated environment, and art and design history provide her with an important source.[5]

Developing a sense of creativity should be a continuing process. Browsing through magazines can trigger ideas. So can looking at objects as you stroll around your community or take a relaxing hike. Ideas are everywhere. All it takes to find them is putting the right side of your brain to work.

Many creative ideas develop by ignoring accepted procedures. In this chapter we attempt to examine some rules and accepted practices and then some examples of creative typography that might bend or break some of these rules. Perhaps we can get both sides of our brains working to help us become more effective communicators.

READABILITY IS THE FOUNDATION

The proper selection and use of the hundreds of type designs available is important in creating an effective printed communication. A production is a terrible waste of time, money, effort, and material if it is not read and understood.

Type should be selected and arranged to achieve maximum readability of the message. Readability should be the foundation on which the printed communication is built.

Frederic W. Goudy, the most prolific American type designer, put it this way:

> Letters must be of such a nature that when they are combined into lines of words the eye may run along the lines easily, quickly, and without obstruction, the reader being occupied only with the thought presented. If one is compelled to inspect the individual letters, his mind is not free to grasp the ideas conveyed by the type[6]

Type selection and display should not only aid readability but also reinforce the goal of the communication. That is, the type should be appropriate to the message. If the communicator is shouting, the type should help. If the communicator is trying to reason with the reader, the type should reflect this goal, and it can. There are "stern" types for stern and remonstrative messages, and there are "happy" types for happy messages.

An effective message must first gain attention. That is one reason why newspapers use headlines. The type is selected and arranged to get

Fig. 5-4 ■ Text matter set in a slightly bold Sans Serif (middle) is considered to have greater readability than the light Sans Serif (top). Roman (bottom) is the preference of most readers.

Four score and seven years ago our fathers brought forth on this continent, a new nation, conceived in Liberty, and dedicated to the proposition that all men are created equal.

Four score and seven years ago our fathers brought forth on this continent, a new nation, conceived in Liberty, and dedicated to the proposition that all men are created equal.

Four score and seven years ago our fathers brought forth on this continent, a new nation, conceived in Liberty, and dedicated to the proposition that all men are created equal.

Fig. 5-5 ◼ Type talks. Notice how the letter designs help create the image the words transmit.

1. Type can be light or **heavy**
2. Type can be unassuming or graceful
3. Type can *whisper* or **shout**
4. Type can be monotonous or sparkle
5. Type can be **UGLY** or BEAUTIFUL
6. Type can be **MECHANICAL** or Formal
7. Type can be *Social* or **ecclesiastical**
8. Type can be **fat** or thin
9. Type can be playful or **SERIOUS**
10. Type can be easy to read or hard to read

Key to the type faces listed above, left to right in order:
1. 18 pt. Avant Garde Extra LIght; 18 pt. Futura Extrabold.
2. 18 pt. Times;18 pt. Trump Mediaeval.
3. 10 pt. Cochin italic; 18 pt. Lubalin Graph Demibold.
4. 18 pt. Helvetica Narrow; 18 pt. Tiffany.
5. 18 pt. Lithos Black; 18 pt. Charlemagne.
6. 18 pt. Machine Bold; 18 pt. Caslon Open Face.
7. 18 pt. Shelley Allegro Script; 18 pt. Castle.
8. 18 pt. Avant Garde Bold; 18 pt. Arcadia.
9. 18 pt. Paisley; 18 pt. Copperplate Gothic 33.
10. 18 pt. New Century Schoolbook; 6 pt. Bembo.

the attention of the potential reader. Proper selection and arrangement make a publication stand out from other publications.

Proper selection and use of type can also help create identification. *Time* magazine, for instance, can be spotted quickly because of its consistent use of certain graphics and types. There is no mistaking which newspaper is the *New York Times*. Harlequin books are easily spotted among the paperbacks because their typography says "light, romantic novel" and helps define this particular publisher's audience.

It should be kept in mind that the proper use and arrangement of type is both an art and a science. It is an art in that within limitations there is wide freedom of action. To begin with, there is only a blank page. The designer has comparative freedom in designing the elements that will occupy this page. The communicator is an artist using type, borders, illustrations, and color to create a physical environment for the written message.

CHARLEMAGNE
Baskerville
Hiroshige
Bodoni Poster

Fig. 5-6 ■ Examples of Roman types that might be used for display purposes. They suggest dignity, stability, and integrity, and they rate high in legibility. Many Romans have their own personalities and individuality. They can help establish an image for an organization or product.

Helvetica

Eras

Futura

Optima

Fig. 5-7 ■ Although Sans Serifs are basically versions of a style introduced in the nineteenth century, they are considered by many designers the most modern of type designs. Their precise, simple lines give high legibility to titles and headings. Optima especially, with its Roman appearance, seems warm and human.

Typography is a science as well. It is a science in that it uses rules that have been proven by research and testing. These rules must be understood and applied with creative freshness to produce the most effective printed pieces possible. So, the communicator who desires to produce the most effective printed communication must apply a mixture of art and science.

Let us consider the science of typographic design first and then look at the art of using type.

Below are ten suggestions based on experimentation, research, and testing that have proved to be effective in working with type:

1. Use the right type style.
2. Set the type on the proper measure.
3. Watch the spacing.
4. Remember the margins.
5. Select the proper type size.
6. Mix type styles carefully.
7. Use all-cap lines sparingly.
8. Do not be boring.
9. Avoid oddball placement.
10. Spell it out.

If we keep these ten rules in mind, they will help us produce an end product that is suitable, readable, and legible. These suggestions are quite easy to apply and can be summed up as: Keep the reader (or target audience) in mind when making layouts or giving instructions to the compositor or printer.

USE THE RIGHT TYPE STYLE

➤ The first step in selecting the right type is to divide the content of the message into words that speak out in short, crisp phrases and words that must be read in mass.

The short phrases (headings, titles, subheads) should be set in large type for emphasis. This type is called *display* as contrasted with *text* or *body* types for masses of words, or reading matter. The headline of a news story, for example, will be set in display type and the story itself in body type.

Types in the range of 8 to 12 point are considered suitable for reading matter. However, much depends on the design of the typeface selected. Types larger than 14 point are considered display types.

Both classifications of type must be considered, initially, as separate entities. Remember, however, that for unity the two must work together and harmonize. Sometimes the most effective choice for display is a larger size of the same design used for the body type, or a larger size from another series of the same family as the body type.

The second step in selecting the most effective type design for a message is to read the copy. What sort of message is this? If it is a hard-

Lubalin Graph
American
Typewriter

Fig. 5-8 ■ Square Serifs, or Egyptians, are hard-hitting, bold, no-nonsense typefaces.

Balmoral

Ribbon

Shelley Allegro

Fig. 5-9 ■ Scripts and Cursives try to capture handwriting. They can give an image of austere formality or casual informality, create an effect of graciousness or rugged individualism. They should be used sparingly.

Fig. 5-10 ■ Miscellaneous or Novelty types can be effective if used sparingly for display lines. They run the gamut from dainty to solid. They are unsuitable for more than a line or two.

sell advertisement, then display type in a heavy-hitting design is the obvious choice. Clean-lined, bold Sans Serifs would be a good choice. A bold Square Serif has a forceful voice.

Suppose we want to say "Here is a long-established organization that has become an institution in our city"—what type should we select? The *New York Times* and many other newspapers say this by using Black Letter types for their nameplates. An old-style Roman, such as Caslon or Goudy, would help get the idea across, too.

If the message is crisp and modern but dignified as well, a modern Roman might be a good face to choose. Bodoni or Craw Modern would do the job.

High fashion dictates a Script or Cursive or perhaps a light-faced Sans Serif. Vogue is a family that speaks to high society. It was designed especially for the audience of *Vogue* magazine.

The improper type design can sabotage the message. A newspaper would look ridiculous setting a banner head concerning an exposé at city hall in Black Letter type. Yet Black Letter would be a fine choice to say "Merry Christmas."

When it comes to body or text type for reading matter, there is controversy. Some designers maintain that Sans Serif is the modern type and those who eschew it are old-fashioned. Others stick by the Romans that have been used since printing was introduced in England.

The argument in favor of Romans is twofold. First, we are used to it because so much of what we read—books, magazines, newspapers—is set in Roman types and always have been. Second, the thick and thin strokes of Romans and the rounded shapes of the letters cause less eye fatigue and make reading more pleasant.

SET THE TYPE ON THE PROPER MEASURE

➤ How wide should the columns in a publication be? If we have a block of copy we want to include in an advertisement layout, what width is best? Can we just arbitrarily select a width that looks nice? Does width make a difference? It certainly does. If columns of type are too wide, reading will be slow and difficult. Readers will tire easily, and they can lose their places in the message as their eyes shift from one line to the next. They may become discouraged and stop reading.

If, on the other hand, type is set in columns that are too short, the constant eye motion from left to right and back to left again will slow reading and make it a tiring chore. In addition, type set too narrow causes many awkward between-word spacing situations. Words must also be divided between lines more frequently and this can disfigure a printed piece.

Setting type on the proper measure is easy, and there are several rules of thumb that can be used. The proper measure (or line width) is, of course, determined by the type size and style selected. For small type sizes, say, 6 or 8 point, narrow columns are suitable. But larger type requires wider columns.

Some typographers have developed a theory of *optimum line length*. This refers to the width of a line that is considered ideal for greatest reading ease. It has been found that a good way to determine the optimum width for lines of any typeface and size is to measure the lowercase alphabet (all the letters lined up from *a* to *z*) and add one-half to this.

For instance, if the lowercase alphabet measures 18 picas, the optimum line-width for that type would be 27 picas.

Fig. 5-11 ■ The ideal line width (1½ times the lowercase alphabet).

---

abcdefghijklmnopqrstuvwxyzabcdefghijklm

(Ideal line width: 11/2 times the lowercase alphabet)

Typographers using this theory believe the minimum width any type should be set is the width of one lowercase alphabet, and the maximum width should never exceed the width of two lowercase alphabets.

Another rule of thumb that works out to approximately the same measure is to double in picas the point size of the type being used. For instance, 18-point type would ideally be set about 36 picas wide and 6-point type would be set no more than 12 picas wide.

The thing to remember is, the smaller the type used, the shorter the lines in which it should be set. As the size of type is increased, the width of the lines should be increased, but never to more than double the lowercase alphabet.

Type set on an improper measure can detract from the good looks of a printed communication. But, more important, it can be a definite deterrent to easy, pleasant reading.

Fig. 5-12 ■ Examples of 8-point type set on three different measures. [Adapted from Ralph W. and Edwin Polk, *Practice of Printing* (Peoria, Ill.: Bennett Publishing Company, © 1971.) Used with permission of the publishers. All rights reserved.]

The width of a column of reading matter influences its legibility. The ideal width for any piece of composition is based on the breadth of focus of the eye upon the page. For small types the focus will be narrow, and it will widen out as the type faces increase in size. If the column is set in too wide a measure, as is the case with this paragraph, the lines will be scanned with somewhat of effort, and it will be found harder to "keep one's place" as one reads. Also, it will require some effort to locate the starting point of each new line. A large amount of reading matter set like this would be tedious to read.

On the other hand, if the column is too narrow, fewer words may be grasped at a time, and thus, too frequent adjustments must be made for the numerous shortlines of the type, seriously hindering the steady, even flow of the message. In addition, a greater proportion of words must be divided at the ends of the lines, and the spacing of the lines is necessarily un-even and awkward, also affecting the legibility.

This group is set the proper width for the comfortable, easy reading of 8 point type. The eye may easily take in a line at a time, and in this way the messsage may be read without any mechanical encumberances. Larger types set to this width will present the same difficulties to the reader that are experienced in the 8 point example, set in the narrow measure, above. There is a suitable width for each size and style of type.

abcdefghijklmnopqrstuvwxyz

15 picas
(minimum width)

abcdefghijklmnopqrstuvwxyzabcdefghijklmnopqrstuvwxyz

30 picas
(maximum width)

Fig. 5-13 ■ This 12-point Square Serif type should not be set in lines narrower than 15 picas or wider than 30 picas for ordinary composition.

WATCH THE SPACING

➤ Too much spacing can make the message unattractive and difficult to read; too little can jam the words and lines together so that the message's appearance is destroyed and reading is a real task. Most people will skip over poorly spaced printed matter unless the content of the message is so overpowering that they will put up with unnecessary channel noise (in this case poor spacing) to get at the information.

White space, when applied to type masses, is the space between words and the space between lines. Words that are crowded too closely together are difficult to read. Words that are spread too far apart can create gaps of ugly white within the printed block. Lines that are too close together also cause problems. The reader must sort out where a new line starts. When lines are packed too tightly the reader may start to reread the same line. When lines are too far apart there are time-consuming gaps as the eye travels from one line to another.

Thus we need to decide how much space to use between lines of a printed piece. Printers call this *leading* (pronounced *ledding*). The term originated when thin strips of lead were used between lines of metal type as spacing material. When a printer suggests a paragraph should be leaded out, it means that more space is needed between the lines.

For reading matter, the 2-point lead (or space) to separate the lines of type has been considered standard.

Spacing between lines depends on several things. One is the size of the type being used. Another is the design of the type, whether it is

Fig. 5-14 ■ Some examples of appropriate word spacing.

A line of 8 pt. Garamond is difficult to read with only a thin space.
Its legibility is greatly improved when the words are separated.

A narrow type needs much less space between the words.
A wide type needs much more space.

A type with a small x-height requires only a thin space.
A type with a large x-height needs a thick space.

❶

It may be said of all printers that their job is to re-produce on paper the exact face of the letters which they have set into pages. This face is of a definite, constant and measurable size and shape; with any one press and any one paper there is a right and exact quan-

❷

It may be said of all printers that their job is to reproduce on paper the eact face of the letters which they have set in-to pages. This face is of a definite, constant and measurable size and shape; with any one press and any one paper there is a right and exact quantity of ink and pressure necessary to

❸

It may be said of all printers that their job is to reproduce on paper the exact face of the letters which they have set in-to pages. This face is of a definite, constant and measurable size and shape; with any one press and any one paper there is a right and exact quantity of ink and pressure necessary to

❹

It may be said of all printers that their job is to reproduce on paper the exact face of the letters which they have set into pages. This face is of a definite, constant and measurable size and shape; with any one press and any one paper there is a right and exact quantity of ink and pressure necessary to

❺

It may be said of all printers that their job is to reproduce on paper the exact face of the letters which they have set into pages. This face is of a definite, constant and measurable size and shape; with any one press and any one paper there is a right and exact quantity of ink and pressure necessary to

❶ Improper word spacing;   ❷ No extra leading;   ❸ 1 point leading;   ❹ 2 points leading;   ❺ 3 points leading.

Fig. 5-15 ■ Space for readability has two aspects: space between words and space between lines. The first copy block illustrates improper space between words. The other examples show the effects of various amounts of space between lines.

big or small on the body. Type that is small on the body—that is, type that has a rather small x height for its point size—has more natural leading between lines than type that is big on the body, that has a large x height. Type styles that have large x heights need more spacing between lines.

Here, again, there isn't exact scientific data to prove the ideal. However, experimentation and practice have given some clues. In a general way, the longer the type line, the more spacing is needed between lines. For example, say an 8-point type is selected for a 12-pica-wide line and 1 point of space is designated between lines. If the width of the line is increased to 18 picas, the message would be easier to read if the space between the lines would be increased to about 2 points. So a "sub-hint" for this general suggestion might be, when the line width is increased the space between lines should be increased, too.

This is even truer of display type, though we need to restate the rule as, the larger the type, the more space needed between lines. While 1 or 2 points of space between lines is fine for reading matter, when it comes to display type (type between 14 and 36 points and larger), as such as 6 points between lines will be needed.

We need to be aware, however, that too much space between lines creates islands of black in a sea of white. If the lines of a head are too far apart, unity will be destroyed. The reader can become confused or waste time figuring out what the head is trying to say. The lines need to be properly spaced and also kept together so that they can be seen as a unit.

Space between lines is just about right in this headline

There's too much space between lines in this headline

Spacing in this headline illustrates negative leading

Fig. 5-16 ■ The traditional approach of line spacing is illustrated by the first headline. The last arrangement illustrates minus or negative leading, in which lines are overlapped. This approach can create an effective design unit, but care must be taken so that ascenders and descenders do not collide and destroy readability.

REMEMBER THE MARGINS

➤ The *margins* (the white space) that surround a printed product are important elements for creating an attractive and effective communication. Margins act as frames for the page. If the margins are too small, the framing effect can be destroyed. The page will look cramped and crowded. Reading will be more difficult. If the margins are large enough to be strong frames for the page, they help unify the page, hold the layout together, and make reading easier and more pleasant.

Try this. Take a column of type and trim the margins as close to the type as you can. Read it. Now read a column with the margins intact. See how much easier it is to read? Although the margins are nothing but white space they hold the column together.

Margins can help set the mood of a printed communication. The traditional book margin is known as the *progressive margin*. This means that the smallest margin on the page is the *gutter* margin (the area between two adjacent pages). The top-of-the-page margin is larger. The outside margin is larger than the top, and, finally, the bottom-of-the-page margin is the largest of all. In other words, the margins are progressively larger around the page.

Progressive margins help give a look of careful consideration that denotes quality to the reader. Some "class" magazines use progressive

Fig. 5-17 ■ Margins are too small on the left and the page looks crowded and unattractive. The larger margins on the right frame the type and give it light, at the same time unifying the page.

Fig. 5-18 ■ Progressive margins. The margins increase in size counterclockwise on the left-hand page and clockwise on the right-hand page. The margins in the middle between the two pages are known as the gutter.

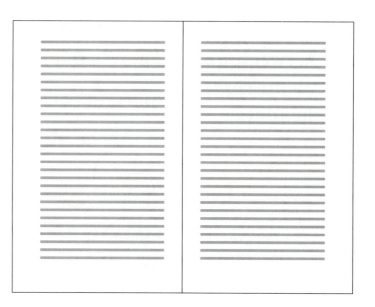

Fig. 5-19 ■ Proper use of margins with a border. The outside rectangle indicates the page, the inner is a border around the type. On the left, the margins between the type and border and the border and edge of page are the same. They should be unequal. On the right, the border is closer to the type for greater unity of type and border—it is better to have smaller margins inside than outside.

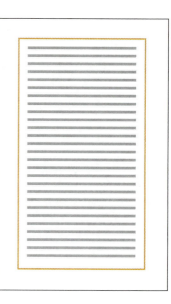

margins for this quality look. Progressive margins are also suitable for brochures describing museums, art festivals, cultural events, or menus of exclusive restaurants.

How much space on the page should be devoted to margins? A good rule of thumb is: about 50 percent of the printed page. At first glance that seems excessive—half a page for margins! But look. Suppose we are designing a layout for a 9 by 12 page. That means there are 108 square inches of space on the page. If the 50 percent rule is followed, 54 square inches will be devoted to margins. On a 9 by 12 page that works out to a margin of less than 1½ inches around the printed part of the page—not excessive at all for a 9 by 12 page.

SELECT THE PROPER TYPE SIZE

➤ So far, we have picked out a type style for our message, determined that the columns of type will be one and a half times the lowercase alphabet in width, designated 2 points of space between the lines of body copy, and have designated the printed area to be about 50 percent of the page. Now, what size type should we select?

As with all decisions regarding the most effective way to produce the best possible piece of printing, the decision as to what size of type to use depends on other factors. These include such decisions as the type design, the line width, the amount of leading, and the type of audience. The decision about type size cannot be made alone but must be coordinated with other legibility factors.

However, there are some general rules that are worth considering.

Remember being cautioned to "read the fine print" in contracts and legal documents? It is not just to save paper that some printed pieces contain much small print. It is a fact that the smaller the type the less likely it is to be read carefully. This is not to imply that small print means something devious is afoot. It is just to point out a truism of printing—the smaller the type, the more difficult it is to read. Rather than tackle the formidable task of reading small print, many people will skip it.

At the other end of the scale, reading matter set in too large type takes longer to read. It occupies a larger area and simply requires more time to cover.

Fig. 5-20 ■ Legibility of reading matter increases as the size of type is increased, but 12 point is the maximum size for legibility. [Adapted from Ralph W. and Edwin Polk, *Practice of Printing* (Peoria, Ill.: Bennett Publishing Company, © 1971). Used with the permission of the publisher. All rights reserved.]

The small sizes of body type are not as legible as larger ones. This paragraph is set in 6 point type, and it is far too small for ordinary reading matter, for it causes undue eye strain to make out the letter forms. Many of the ads now appearing in newspapers and periodicals contain types no larger than this and some are even harder to read than this paragraph is. Whenever possible, the use of such type should be avoided.

This paragraph appears in 8 point, and as you read it you are impressed with the greater ease with which it may be read. One may read it faster than the 6 point and with much less eye strain. However, it is still somewhat small for perfect ease in reading, as will be seen by a comparison with the following two examples.

When we get into 10 point type, we begin to get a sense of more comfortable, easy reading. The letters now are large enough that the eye can take them in at a rapid glance, without any strain or tension. This is a size of type found in many books and other reading matter, and we are quite familiar with it. consequently, we read it with ease and speed. 10 1/2 point type, with 13-point leading, is used for the body of this book.

We come to the highest degree of legibility when we consider the 12 point size of body type. A great number of authorities designate this size of type, leaded adequately, as offering the maximum of legibility in the mass, and being the most inviting to the eye of the reader. At any rate, the range of sizes for most satisfactory reading is around 10 and 12 point type.

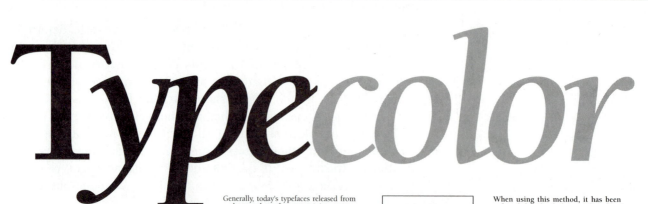

The copy has been written, the artwork is finished, the layout has taken shape, the headline typeface has been chosen. Now for the body text. In addition to the typeface that will be chosen, what color will it be? Color?

You could choose to have it printed in any color imaginable to go with the design. In fact, there's been a trend for printing the text in one color, with the sentences that are to stand out printed in another color, and it can look great.

But the color referred to at the outset is the type that is to be printed in black.

Generally, today's typefaces released from the noted typeface companies are released in four or five different weights: light, book, medium, bold, and black. In type specimen books, there are blocks of body text settings in these various weights. A good type specimen book will show the typefaces set solid and with added leading (extra space between the lines). This can have an effect on the color.

When looking at these blocks of text, one begins to see various shades of grey, ranging from very light grey to almost solid black. The shade of grey will depend upon the design of the typeface.

Now, getting back to the question: which color will you choose?

Designers and art directors who are concerned about the typecolor have various reasons for choosing different weights of body text.

One way that has been used with success is to compare the art and body text with the different percentage values found in a screen tint scale. This works best when the scale is placed on a clear piece of film.

Lay the scale next to the artwork, headline type, or photographs (color or black and white halftones), and see what shade works best. Then, in a type specimen book, find the typeface to be used, and choose the weight that matches the screen value that looked best.

When using this method, it has been found that the darker weights of body text look better with line drawings and lighter halftones. (Light line drawings get lost next to very thin, light weight body text.) On the other hand, lighter body text looks best next to darker artwork and halftones.

Those who design magazine formats generally use a medium weight typeface for the body text, because they deal with all kinds of artwork and photographs.

The secret is to get viewers so involved in reading the material and enjoying the layouts that they don't mind the pieces being in black and white. This, of course, is important when the budget does not allow for color. Color?

The body text. What color will it be?

Fig. 5-21 ■ Type comes in various weights—bold, medium, light, and so on—the weight you specify for the body text creates a "color" or shade of gray when the type is printed in black ink. Which weight or typecolor is best? In selecting a typeface for body text, designer Robert Wakeman suggests laying a tint scale—see illustration above—next to the artwork, headline type, or photographs to see what shade works best. Then, select the typeface with the weight that harmonizes with the other elements in the layout.(Adapted from a poster designed by Robert Wakeman)

As always, there are no fixed rules. However, in a general way it has been found that the most legible size for type in newspapers, magazines, and books is between 9 and 12 points. Reading matter set in smaller or larger type is more difficult to read. A number of tests made by researchers through the years, some of them back in the late 1800s, have indicated that 11-point type is the most legible size for constant reading.

There are, however, situations in which a larger type should be selected. Reverses (white letters on a black background) require larger sizes as well as clear letter designs (such as sans serifs or clean-line Romans) for easier reading. Children and older people find larger type sizes more pleasant to read. Thus the audience should be kept in mind.

Type style should also be considered when specifying type size. Most decorative and novelty faces and Scripts and Cursives should be set in larger sizes. The unfamiliar letter forms make reading and comprehension more difficult. Larger sizes help overcome these problems.

Condensed types, except in short messages, should be set in larger sizes than the easier-to-read regular widths.

Sometimes it is a temptation to cram as much material as possible into the space available by using smaller type sizes. Text type set in 10 point will take up about 25 percent less space than text set in 12 point. It is tempting to take advantage of this obvious economy. But remember that the objective is to have the message read and understood. If 12-point type will make the message easier to read and understand, it should be considered. If economy is important, the copy can be edited a little more tightly to preserve readability.

MIX TYPE STYLES CAREFULLY

➤ Old-time printers knew what they were doing. They said, "If you start a job with Bookman, finish it with Bookman." They knew that the most attractive printed product was one with the least amount of mixing of typefaces. Modern typographers call this the rule of monotypographic harmony.

Monotypographic harmony means that a harmonious layout will result if one family of type, or one design, is used throughout. Contrast and emphasis can be obtained by using type from different series of the same family. An attractive printed product will be produced with a minimum of typographic noise.

But there are times when faces must be mixed. Perhaps a certain emphasis or contrast is desired and a boldface or italic of another family will do the job better. Or we may decide a change of face is needed for contrast or to punch up our design.

When families are mixed, care should be taken to avoid mixing families of the same race unless they are of a strongly contrasting design. For instance, the basic racial structures of Caslon and Garamond letters are the same: limited variation in the widths of letter strokes, slight diagonal slant at the thin point in bowls, and generally rounded serifs. However, each treats these basic characteristics differently. Confusion can thus result if these similar but different types are used together.

When faces are mixed, some means of contrast should be used to separate the two. One can be used for headlines and the other for body copy, for example. Or, one can be used in boldface or italic and the other in its regular form.

When two inharmonious types are used, one should be small. If a line of 24-point Black Letter is mixed with several lines of Sans Serif on the title page of a booklet, the Sans Serif lines should not be more than 10 or 12 point. The Black Letter, then, will dominate, and dissonance will be reduced to a minimum. This technique can often result in a very pleasing arrangement.

This is Clarendon Bold
This is Franklin Gothic

This is Clarendon Bold
This is Franklin Gothic

Fig. 5-22 ■ The Sans Serif at top is subordinated so that the two races are harmonious. When the Sans Serif is increased in size as in the bottom example, the two races begin to compete and harmony breaks down.

cg CG

Fig. 5-23 ■ Lowercase letters have more character and are less likely to be confused than capital letters.

Fig. 5-24 ■ The creative person can enhance the beauty of type set in all caps by the proper use of the negative space— or the space in, around, and between letters. Lowercase letters are carefully designed to fit together properly in any combination and almost never need any letterspacing. Capital letters, however, will naturally have inconsistent spaces between them when they are set into words. Proper letterspacing requires study and a little practice. (Courtesy Robert Wakeman)

USE ALL-CAP LINES SPARINGLY

➤ There was a time when printers and typographers believed that the most legible letters were the old Roman capitals. It has since been found, without question, that lowercase letters are more legible than capitals.

Use capital letters, but use them sparingly. The reasons for this can be summarized by two points: Lowercase letters have more character and they speed reading.

"Lowercase letters have more character" means that the letter forms of each letter in the lowercase alphabet are distinctive and not as easily confused as capitals, which have many similarities. Contrast, for example, the lowercase c and g with the capital C and G. There is less likelihood of the reader confusing the letter forms in the lowercase line than in the all-capital line.

Research has shown that lowercase letters increase reading speed and are more pleasing to the reader. They do not tire the eye as easily as all-capital letters. However, words or lines set in all caps can be important design elements in headlines, headings, title pages. They can also be used to emphasize points in a layout.

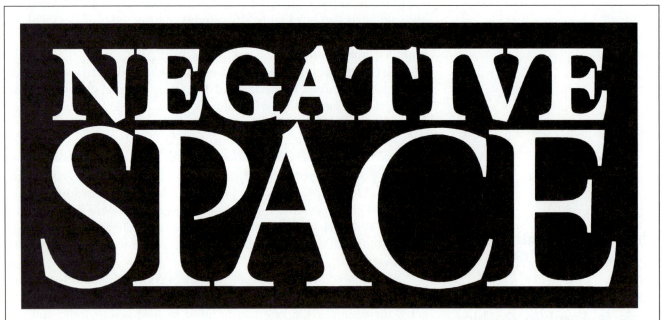

Look at the space in, and around, and in between the letters above. This is called the negative space. But good negative space does not come about simply by spacing out each letter equally, or by doing so mechanically. This creates irregular space between letters. The negative space must be given some uniformity of visual weight around the letter, in order to be balanced and pleasing to the eye.

Good designers and typographers gain, over the years, experience in knowing how much negative space to put between each two letters This means more than just putting letters next to each other. Capital letters are more difficult to do than the lowercase letters. The same holds true for the thinner weights. The larger the letter, the more important the negative space. The negative spaces between the serif typefaces are more graceful and easier to accomplish, design-wise, than the sans-serif typefaces. The latter almost require the skill at geometry of an architects.

Certain fundamental principles should be taken into consideration when dealing with negative spaces. Letter combinations that have almost no space at all between them. Vertical stroke against vertical stroke. This includes such combinations as AW, AV, IM, IN, IL, etc. These are often put too close together, especially when setting sans-serif typefaces. The trained eye will allow enough space in such combinations to complement the other letters in the word.

Again, there are certain letter combinations with unavoidably large negative spaces. For example, LA, TT, IT, TY, LL, TE, and the like. They can be overlapped slightly, or altered, to cut down on the negative space between letters, and the rest of the word can be spaced out visually to please the eye. This does not mean, however, that all other letters in that word are to have the same amount of space between them as the examples above. But one has to take into consideration the space inside and around each letter to get the proper negative space.

Other letter combinations to watch carefully would be verticals next to curves; curves next to curves; and open curves next to verticals.

One well-known designer and art director in the New York City area always looks at the negative space first, before looking at the positive areas.

So, when taking all of the above into consideration, the creative person can enhance the beauty of the typeface design by the proper use of the negative space. The result? Typographical masterpieces!

BLACK LETTER
SCRIPT

Fig. 5-25 ■ Lines of Black Letter or ornamental types should never be set in all-capital letters: They can be virtually unreadable.

In the instances where all caps would enhance a layout, designers suggest that they should be limited to two or three lines at a time and the lines should be short. The lines should also have ample leading.

Lines set in all caps must always be used with care. You will find that, unlike lowercase letters, capitals will naturally have inconsistent letterspacing when they are set into words. Often you will need to make very subtle changes in the letterspacing so that the space between the letters appears consistent and equal. It may help to imagine that you are filling the spaces between letters with grains of sand. The goal of proper letterspacing is to place an equal amount of sand between each letter. This may require reducing space in some cases and increasing—always slightly—in other cases.

CHAPTER TWELVE

Sometimes designers will use capitals with extreme letterspacing. If you want to try this, remember to adjust letterspacing optically first, then mechanically add equal space between the letters. You will also need to increase word spacing to keep the type legible. Legibility is always the goal.

C H A P T E R   T W E L V E

DON'T BE BORING

▶ It is getting harder and harder to grab and hold the reader's attention. People are bombarded by efforts to make them listen or read. People are becoming more conditioned to receiving information in bits and short takes. The average television news item is from 90 to 110 seconds long—barely 100 to 150 words. A half-hour television drama packs a complete story line from introduction to climax into about 22 minutes.

When readers are confronted with columns of reading matter, many will rebel. The reading matter looks forbidding and boring—there's nothing to catch the eye but line after line of type similar in size and tone. There is a temptation to skip it.

Here are some ways to make long body matter more attractive:

■ Use that old standby, white space. For instance, if fairly narrow columns are used on a page (say, ones that do not exceed about 12 picas), three columns can be used in a four-column space or five columns in a six-column space.

■ Occasional indented paragraphs can help.

■ An extra lead between paragraphs can be used.

■ Shorter paragraphs can help, especially when type is set on narrow columns.

■ Subheads with a contrasting face or boldface or a larger size of type than the body type can help break up the gray flow of type.

Lorem ipsum dolor sit amet, consectetuer adipiscing elit, sed diam nonummy nibh euismod tincidunt ut laoreet dolore magna aliquam erat volutpat. Ut wisi enim ad minim veniam, quis nostrud exerci tation ullamcorper suscipit lobortis nisl ut aliquip ex ea commodo consequat. Duis autem vel eum iriure dolor in hendrerit in vulputate velit esse molestie consequat, vel illum dolore eu feugiat nulla facilisis at vero eros et accumsan et iusto odio dignissim qui blandit praesent luptatum zzril delenit augue duis dolore te feugait nulla facilisi. Lorem ipsum dolor sit amet, consectetuer adipiscing elit, sed diam nonummy nibh euismod tincidunt ut laoreet dolore magna aliquam erat volutpat.

Lorem ipsum dolor sit amet, consectetuer adipiscing elit, sed diam nonummy nibh euismod tincidunt ut laoreet dolore magna aliquam erat volutpat. Ut wisi enim ad minim veniam, quis nostrud exerci tation ullamcorper suscipit lobortis nisl ut aliquip ex ea commodo consequat. Duis autem vel eum iriure dolor in hendrerit in vulputate velit esse molestie consequat, vel illum dolore eu feugiat nulla facilisis at vero eros et accumsan et iusto odio dignissim qui blandit praesent luptatum zzril delenit augue duis dolore te feugait nulla facilisi. Lorem ipsum dolor sit amet, consectetuer adipiscing elit, sed diam nonummy nibh euismod tincidunt ut laoreet dolore magna aliquam erat volutpat.

Lorem ipsum dolor sit amet, consectetuer adipiscing elit, sed diam nonummy nibh euismod tincidunt ut laoreet dolore magna aliquam erat volutpat. Ut wisi enim ad minim veniam, quis nostrud exerci tation ullamcorper suscipit lobortis nisl ut aliquip ex ea commodo consequat. Duis autem vel eum iriure dolor in hendrerit in vulputate velit esse molestie consequat, vel illum dolore eu feugiat nulla facilisis at vero eros et accumsan et iusto odio dignissim qui blandit praesent luptatum zzril delenit augue duis dolore te feugait nulla facilisi. Lorem ipsum dolor sit amet, consectetuer adipiscing elit, sed diam nonummy nibh euismod tincidunt ut laoreet dolore magna aliquam erat volutpat.

Fig. 5-26 ■ Type set ragged left (above, left) should be avoided except in short sections because it slows reading. Type set ragged right (center) has the same reading ease as justified type, type with even margins both left and right sides (right).

■ Sometimes typographic devices can be used—bullets, stars, dashes, and other dingbats. But they should be used cautiously. When overdone they can disfigure the page and make the layout look amateurish.

Sometimes variety can be obtained on a page if a sidebar or boxed material is set ragged right. This means setting the left lines even but allowing the lines to end at natural breaks instead of justifying them. Studies have shown that ragged right does not slow reading. But ragged left should be used with caution. It is fine for limited use such as in the cutlines that identify illustrations, but it does slow reading, and most readers will skip long messages set in ragged left.

Initial letters can add spice to a page. These large letters at the start of paragraphs are a valuable typographic device. They can brighten up the page and they can help guide the reader.

Designers have a few suggestions for using initial letters. Initials should never be used at the top of a column except at the beginning of an article. When an initial is used at the top of a column it is a signal to the reader that this is the point where reading should begin. If an initial is used at the top of a column that does not begin the article, the reader might still think it is the beginning point and be confused.

Also, care should be used in placing initials so they do not appear side by side in adjacent columns when the copy is set in type. Initials should be scattered so they can create unity and balance and their weights serve a design purpose.

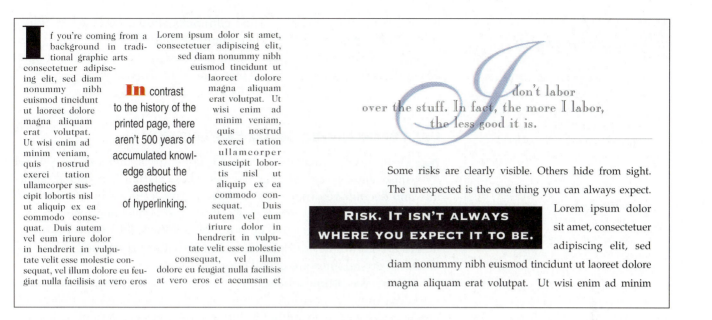

If you're coming from a background in traditional graphic arts consectetuer adipiscing elit, sed diam nonummy nibh euismod tincidunt ut laoreet dolore magna aliquam erat volutpat. Ut wisi enim ad minim veniam, quis nostrud exerci tation ullamcorper suscipit lobortis nisl ut aliquip ex ea commodo consequat. Duis autem vel eum iriure dolor in hendrerit in vulputate velit esse molestie consequat, vel illum dolore eu feugiat nulla facilisis at vero eros

In contrast to the history of the printed page, there aren't 500 years of accumulated knowledge about the aesthetics of hyperlinking.

Lorem ipsum dolor sit amet, consectetuer adipiscing elit, sed diam nonummy nibh euismod tincidunt ut laoreet dolore magna aliquam erat volutpat. Ut wisi enim ad minim veniam, quis nostrud exerci tation ullamcorper suscipit lobortis nisl ut aliquip ex ea commodo consequat. Duis autem vel eum iriure dolor in hendrerit in vulputate velit esse molestie consequat, vel illum dolore eu feugiat nulla facilisis at vero eros et accumsan et

I don't labor over the stuff. In fact, the more I labor, the less good it is.

Some risks are clearly visible. Others hide from sight. The unexpected is the one thing you can always expect.

RISK. IT ISN'T ALWAYS WHERE YOU EXPECT IT TO BE.

Lorem ipsum dolor sit amet, consectetuer adipiscing elit, sed diam nonummy nibh euismod tincidunt ut laoreet dolore magna aliquam erat volutpat. Ut wisi enim ad minim

Fig. 5-27 ■ Some examples of ways to break the flow of type to make a page look more inviting.

Fig. 5-28 ■ Curved lines, vertical lines, and lines on an angle should be avoided. (Ad produced by Fallon McElligot. © Ergodyne. reprinted with permission.)

AVOID ODDBALL PLACEMENT

➤ This is the easiest rule of all to follow. All this recommendation means is that types were meant to be read from left to right in straight lines. Curved lines, vertical lines, and lines on an angle should be avoided. Of course, there are times when it can be effective to set type in a curve or on an angle to create a special effect or in certain situations such as designating logos and seals.

Oddball placement should not be done just to be different. And it should be done with caution. Lines of type in curves or on an angle should be kept to a minimum—no more than a few words, if possible.

It is a good idea to avoid typographic affectations. Of course, Edward Estlin Cummings (e. e. cummings) used eccentricities of language, typography, and punctuation as a trademark for his works of poetry, and he became famous. But for straight forward professional

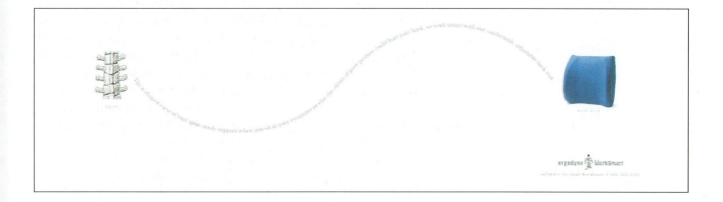

CREATIVE COMMUNICATION

The creative communicator can be frustrated by accumulating either too little or too much information.

Effective creative solutions require adequate information. Superficial research results in superficial design.

On the other hand, too much information that is not relevant to the goal of the layout can muddy the waters and cause confusion.

The creative communicator should make an effort to gather enough information to understand the design problem thoroughly. Irrelevant information, however, should be eliminated.

Creativity is aided by concentrating on information pertinent to the solution of the problem.

printed communications, unusual gimmicks should be avoided unless such devices will really improve communication. If they are used, they should be limited and considered, as one designer points out, like jewelry for the typographic dress. They can be easily overdone.

USE TYPOGRAPHIC COLOR TASTEFULLY

Decorative elements that can add "color" to layouts include several miscellaneous typographic devices. These are borders, both straight-line and decorative ornaments, and decorative letters. The straight-line borders, whether they are a single line or several lines together, are called *rules.* Rules with three or more lines of the same or varying thicknesses are known as *multiple rules.* Rules that are composed of a series of short vertical lines are called *coin-edge rules.*

There was a time when flowery ornaments and borders were considered a must in printing. The monks who illuminated hand-lettered manuscripts with colorful initial letters and curlicues produced beautiful pieces of art. Their skills were carried over into the early days of printing when letterpress-printed pages were often embellished with hand-drawn colorful ornamentation.

Fancy ornaments and borders in printing went along with ornamentation in other art forms. During the age of gingerbread turrets and scroll work in buildings, fancy letterings and ornamentation were popular in printing. But today the trend is toward simplicity, boldness, and functionalism. We are told to keep it simple, but give it punch. If it doesn't serve a function, leave the rule or ornament out.

Ornaments should not be discarded out of hand, however. Proper use, which is to say restraint, in adding borders and ornaments can add decorative relief to a printed page that might otherwise be mechanical and deadly severe.

The fancy curlicues and shaded borders of another era have been replaced with a simpler decorativeness that better fits today's design techniques and typography. A little added ornamentation can be much like a dash of spice in a cooking recipe—it can make the typographic production zesty.

Borders should extend the basic design of the art and type selected. An *Oxford rule* (parallel thick and thin straight lines), for instance, goes very well with the thick and thin lines of Bodoni or other modern Roman types with good contrast between thick and thin strokes and straight-line serifs. Single-line solid rules go well with the monotonal and simple Sans Serifs. A simple line drawing requires a simple straight-line rule. A decorative illustration can require a decorative border. The design and size of ornaments and borders should be in harmony with the design and size of the types and illustrations in the layout.

When borders and decorations are printed in color, the color value should be in tune with all the other elements in the layout. Decoration that may appear harmonious printed in black ink might appear weak and ineffective if printed in pastel or light colors. Also, if solid or screened backgrounds in color are used, care should be taken to be sure

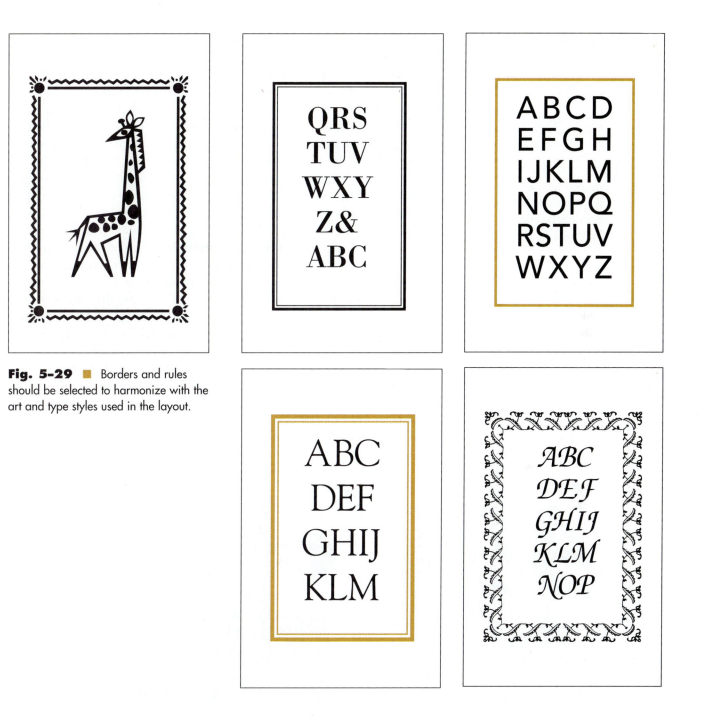

Fig. 5-29 ■ Borders and rules should be selected to harmonize with the art and type styles used in the layout.

the colors are light. Deep color for tint blocks or screened backgrounds will overshadow the type and make it difficult to read.

Generally, borders and decorations printed in color should be specified in a little heavier weight than if they are to be printed in black. This will give them more body and they will harmonize better with the black type.

When borders are placed around type masses, the borders should be closer to the type than to the margins of the page. But borders and rules should not butt up against type. A good rule of thumb is to leave

ABCDEL MN
OPQ STUVW
Notice We Lad

Fig 5–30 ■ The swash letters (above) are members of the Caslon family, in italic posture. Note how these decorative letters can be integrated with the regular Caslon italic letters.

Fig 5–31 ■ Considered one of the greatest typographic designers of all time, the late Herb Lubalin won many awards for his designs. These are some examples of his creativity with type. (Courtesy Rhoda Sparber Lubalin)

at least a pica of white space between type and borders. Borders and type should be handled as one unified typographic element.

Swash letters are usually "stretched-out" versions of regular letter forms that end in an ornamental flourish. Swash letters are used to add a touch of distinction to a logo or a company name or to create a graceful image for an invitation, an announcement, or a column heading.

Other exaggerated letter forms, such as abnormal extensions of ascenders and descenders or decorative initials, are also available.

But all of these ornamental letter forms should be used sparingly. They should be used only for the first or last letter of a word and not for letters within words. Letters with extended ascenders or descenders are an exception to this rule. However, they, too, must be placed very carefully in the layout so that they add to the unity of the whole arrangement.

The opportunity to be creative with type is almost limitless. For example, modern typesetting equipment makes it possible to reduce spacing between words and lines to the point where the letters overlap and leading doesn't exist between the lines. When spacing is reduced to the point where lines overlap beyond the normal baseline of the letters, the procedure is called *minus leading*. When spacing is reduced between the words or letters to the point where they butt against each other or overlap, the technique is called *minus spacing*.

In addition, type can be elongated, obliqued, shaded, expanded, placed in circles, and shaped in an almost limitless number of variations with electronic typesetting equipment.

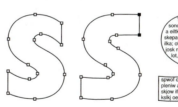

Fig 5-32 ■ (above) The designer may use creativity in type arrangement to transmit an idea by form as well as by meaningful words.

Fig 5-33 ■ (right) In today's design world the key word is creativity. Here are some examples of possibilities in type manipulation that can be achieved with a computer illustration program. It takes just a little practice. The S is converted to an outline and then the anchor points are extended. The S thus created can be filled with letter forms, text can be wrapped around, or you can even enter text on a curve. This demonstration was made using Adobe Illustrator.

Fig. 5-34 ■ Here is another effective book jacket design by Carin Goldberg. The arrangement of the title type conveys a sense of the book's content, a collection of stories about life in post-Cultural Revolution China, where a deeply rooted inertia ensures that "as long as nothing happens, nothing will." (Copyright © 1994 Grove/Atlantic, Inc.)

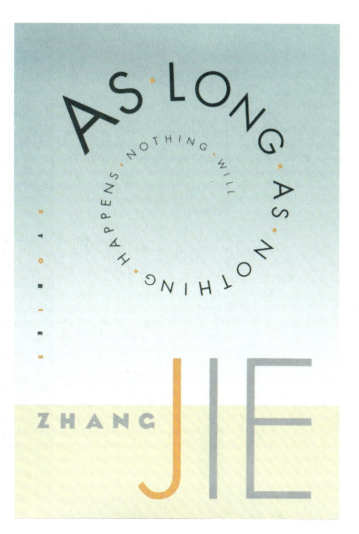

► EFFECTIVE DESIGN CHECKLIST

■ The design of a single letter of type can "talk" to the reader. Select a type style that will reinforce the message.

■ In general, Romans are preferred for body type.

■ One and a half times the width of the lowercase alphabet is considered the proper line width for easy reading.

■ One or two points of leading or spaces between lines is about right for reading matter (body type).

■ As the length of the line is increased, the space between the lines should be increased.

■ Generally, the larger sizes of body types are the easiest to read. Stick to between (and including) 9 and 12 point for body type.

■ Margins that occupy about 50 percent of the area of the page, in the aggregate, are considered about right.

■ Use a larger size type for reverses. Reverses are more effective if the types are simple in design. Fine serifs should be avoided.

■ Most Miscellaneous, Novelty, decorative, and condensed types should be set in larger sizes for better legibility.

■ Type styles should be mixed with care. When two very different styles are used, one should dominate.

■ In most cases, families of the same race of types should not be mixed.

■ All-capital lines are difficult to read and their use should be limited.

■ Long amounts of body copy should be broken up for easier reading. Subheads, indented paragraphs, and other devices can help.

■ Ragged right does not seem to reduce readability, but ragged left does and should be used sparingly.

➤ GRAPHICS IN ACTION

1. Find examples in publications of improper use of type and explain what is wrong with them. If you have enough experience and are working on a computer, see if you can produce improved versions.

2. Explain the points to keep in mind for selecting and arranging type. Illustrate the points with examples clipped from publications or generated on your computer.

3. Select typefaces from those in the appendix or other sources (or those available on your computer) that seem best suited to printing the following (or similar) phrases:

Country Barn Dance

Paris in the Spring

Trans-Siberian Express

Notre Dame Cathedral

Going Out of Business Sale

4. Build an idea file of creative uses of typographic color from examples found in publications. (Remember typographic color involves much more than color, per se.) Include a section for poor examples or techniques to be avoided.

NOTES

[1] Silvano Arieti, *Creativity, The Magic Synthesis* (New York: Basic Books, 1976), p. 4.

[2] "The 15-Second Course in Creativity," *Step-by-Step Graphics,* November/December, 1987, p. 108.

[3] "How Designers Create," *Design, the Magazine of the Society of Newspaper Design,* May, 1988, p. 6.

[4] "The Woman Who Saved New York," *Print,* January/February, 1989, p. 61.

[5] Ibid, p. 71.

[6] Frederic W. Goudy, *Typologia* (Berkeley: University of California Press, 1940), p. 80.

ART AND ILLUSTRATIONS

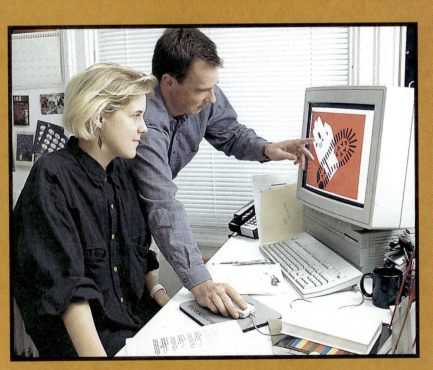

Richard Pasley, Stock Boston

6 It takes more than type printed on paper to make a successful communication. A number of other elements, or tools, can be used to make a message more attractive and effective. These include art, ornaments and borders, rules, paper, color, and even the ink used in printing. Each can add a dimension to the final product.

Conversely, these elements can ruin the effectiveness of a printed piece if applied haphazardly or used improperly. The visual communicator who works with type, much like an artist, interior decorator, architect, or any other creative person, must know the characteristics of all the elements and what each can contribute to the finished product. And the visual communicator must know how to use them.

That is not to say you need to know the technology of making these various elements. It is not necessary to know the circuitry inside your computer, or the properties of the chemicals used in making an offset printing plate. But it is necessary to know what can be done to a photograph to make it printable. The visual communicator must know how to prepare material for production.

Quite often art, illustrations, and photographs can be obtained and used effectively at a relatively low cost. We consider a number of

Fig. 6-1 ■ The key to effective use of art, as in all design, is creativity. This poster announces a five-play season for TheaterWorks. The designer created a collage illustration that expresses the unique qualities of each play. This is an excellent demonstration of ingenuity and creativity coming together to solve a design problem and save money. (Courtesy Peter Good Graphic Design, Chester, CT)

Fig. 6-2 ■ This dramatic image was created by Daniel Duch, a student in Professor Stephen Porter's art class at The Pennsylvania State University. The work was done on a computer using the Aldus FreeHand program.

sources in this chapter such as suppliers of stock photographs, clip art services, and computer illustration programs. Proper use of art requires knowledge more than money, in many cases. A photograph that reinforces and amplifies the message costs no more than those used simply as decorations.

A VISUAL AGE

➤ We live in a visual age. Greater attention is being paid to the role of graphics in printed communications. Designers and artists are moving into the editorial rooms of newspapers and the offices of advertising and public relations firms. News services are supplying more graphics to their clients.

Visuals have many functions. They can improve readability; they can clarify, attract attention, and add realism to writing. They can explain complicated information and provide data in an easy-to-understand way. They can give the reader or viewer a sense of place. They can not only amplify information, but also set a mood, and they can help create a pleasing design. Of course, visuals can entertain. How often have you leafed through a magazine and read the cartoons before settling down to the serious articles?

How can we take advantage of the types of graphics available to us in our quest to become professional visual communicators? First of all, we must understand how art and illustrations get from an idea to the printed page. We need to learn ways to make art and photographs more effective. In addition, we need to know how to crop and size art, the various ways cutlines can be handled, and how to pass along instructions to the printers so that we obtain the results we want. Finally, communicators need to know how to use a computer or, as the case may be, traditional methods (or a combination of the two) to produce finished layouts.

Where to start? Let's take the whole process a step at a time and concentrate in this chapter on what we can do graphically to enhance our communications. To get down to basics, this means how to obtain, process, and place art in a layout so that it will be affordable and effective.

Do not forget this is a visual age. Children are propped in front of a continuous electronic visual parade before they can read or write. More people watch television than read books. This can work to our advantage. Since people are oriented toward the visual, we can use this orientation to make them want to read. Our use of art that amplifies words can help us achieve this goal.

Printed communications must be powerful indeed to hold readers without the use of art. People will usually avoid words alone, unless those words really tell them what they want to hear. For instance, studies by the Gallup Applied Science Partnership, using a device called Eye-Trac, indicate readers use photos and graphic images as entry points into a printed page.[1]

But if art is used, it must be of high quality. It must be simple, well done, and get to the point quickly. Superfluous art can be worse than no art at all. It can distract the reader and dominate the layout. It can com-

Fig. 6-3 ■ An illustration delivers the message. Camera, design, and creative skills were used to produce this advertisement. Designer Dylan Coulter and photographer Michael Shindler created a simulated surface of the moon using a mixture of flour and cement on Shindler's garage floor. Then Shindler shot it in 35mm Kodachrome. The set was lighted with one strobe, no umbrella. Later the slide was scanned on a Nikon Coolscan at 300 dpi as a TIFF (Tag Image File Format) and imported to Photoshop, where it was converted to black and white and resized. The contrast was steeped and the shadow density adjusted. The Nike tag was also cleaned up, sized, and colored in Photoshop. The ad was assembled in PageMaker 5.0. Coulter ran a color proof of the ad on a Tektronics Phaser IIIPXi. Final output was achieved using a fiery interface connected to a Cannon color printer. The ad was transported to the fiery using a 135 megabyte optical disc. Client: Nike. Art direction and Creative Director: Dylan Coulter; photography: Michael Shindler. Both are advertising students at the University of Oregon's School of Journalism and Communication. (Courtesy Prof. William Ryan)

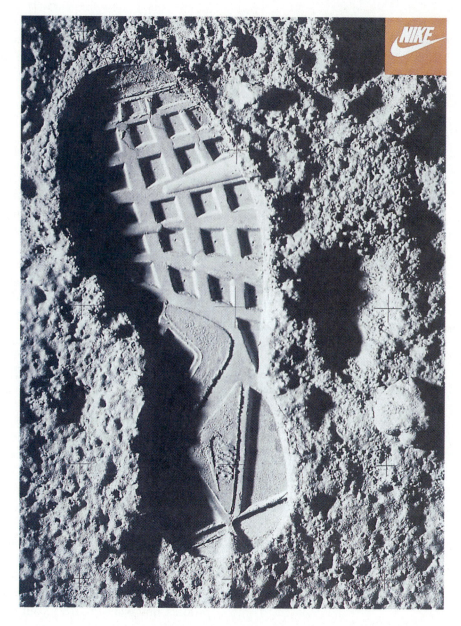

municate the message "Here's a sensational picture, look at it and don't bother to read the words on this page."

Art can help the communicator do a number of things. It can help set the mood for the message. For instance, it can promote a feeling of peace and contentment. It can say "Sit back, relax, and enjoy," or "Sit up and pay attention to this."

Want peace and serenity? How better to portray it than with a scene of a couple observing a quiet lake at sunrise or a calm sea at sunset?

Want to show discontent? A picture can create this mood more effectively than perhaps the legendary 1,000 words. But the picture must be selected carefully and properly cropped and processed and unified with the other elements in the layout. An improperly selected and presented piece of art can be as ineffective as 1,000 poorly written words. Also remember that these mood pieces of art must tie in with the

Fig. 6-4 ■ Graphics can translate complicated information quickly and create high reader interest. This pie-chart visual by Rose Zgodzinski tells the story graphically. Interest is increased by the addition of art to highlight the various "pieces" of the pie. (Courtesy Three-in-a-Box, Toronto)

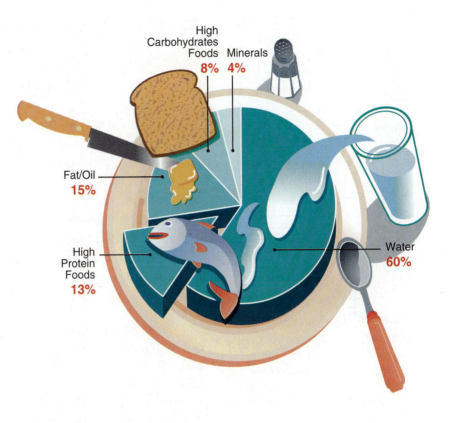

message being printed. They must not just be thrown in because they are attractive and the communicator believes readers will like them.

Art can also be effective in showing a situation or explaining a situation in sequence. And it can be used to establish identity. Most people are familiar with a number of trademark characters that have been used effectively by corporations. This identity value can be extended to printed communications, too. For example, the *Minneapolis Tribune*, when it was redesigned, adopted a simple symbol of a web-fed press and used it in nameplate, masthead, section pages, and column headings to create continuity and identity.

The first step in working with art, then, is to evaluate the message we want to tell. Can graphics do it better? Can art help the audience understand what we are trying to say? Will art attract attention? Will it make the layout more interesting, more entertaining? Will art help guide the reader through the message in proper sequence? Will it help create identity? Will the layout be improved with art?

If the answer is yes to any of these questions, the next step is deciding on the right piece of art and obtaining it.

Fig. 6-5 ■ Simplicity is the key to effective symbol design. The *Minneapolis Tribune* used this simple symbol of a roll of paper going through the press to give immediate recognition to its publication. (Courtesy *Minneapolis Tribune*)

ESSENTIALS OF AN EFFECTIVE GRAPHIC

➤ Graphics serve two purposes: to restate the main point of a story visually or to serve as a stand-alone visual to accompany an article and elaborate on a point related to but not included in the article.

Fig. 6-6 ■ Direction of art is important. In the layout on the left, directional art is used correctly. The motion, and therefore the reader's eye movement, will be into the copy. On the right, the direction of the art moves the reader's eye out of the layout.

The essentials of an effective graphic are listed by Bill Dunn, graphics editor, who has traveled the country making presentations to graphic seminars. They include:

- *Selection.* What is the proper type of graphic? Should it be a chart, a diagram, or a map, for instance?
- *Headline.* An easy-to-read explanation, the shorter the better.
- *Explainer.* All graphics must contain a short paragraph that explains not only what the graphic is about but also why the information is important to the reader.
- *Body.* The "meat" of a graphic. This element transforms data into visuals that explain information clearly.
- *Source.* All graphics must carry a source line that identifies the primary origin of the information.
- *Credit.* All graphics must have credit lines. They should be included as part of the finished artwork by the artist.

Approaches to Using Visuals

On large publications and in big advertising and public relations agencies, the editors and writers do not have to worry about obtaining the right art; that's an art director's job. But even though editors and writers may not be involved in the technical side of this part of the layout process, they do need to understand art and illustrations and the people who produce them.

Too often editors and writers are oriented toward words, whereas artists and graphics persons think "design" first and communication of the message last. It is not unusual for differing opinions to arise and for all to view the finished product from their individual perspectives.

This situation is changing as each develops a greater understanding of the value of teamwork in producing effective printed communications. Editors are becoming more knowledgeable about art and design, and designers are developing a greater understanding of how words are used and arranged for readability. This spirit of teamwork can go far in providing effective and attractive publications.

There are about 9,000 business and trade publications in the United States. Many of these are company papers and magazines aimed at employees or other special audiences. In addition, scores of newsletters are issued by various organizations and interest groups. Add to this small daily newspapers and the more than 8,000 weekly newspapers and you have a vast number of lesser-known publications.

Many entry jobs in communications are in these small publications, and many successful and satisfying lifetime careers can be had in editorial and production positions with these publications.

There are giant publications with their large editorial and design staffs and small publications with a single person performing all the editorial and design functions. There are firms and publications that can afford to hire free-lance artists and designers to assist them on a limited basis. And in all these situations the editor must know something about selecting and processing art.

Fig. 6-7 ■ An effective graphic includes five critical parts. The **headline** is an easy-to-read label (use as few words as possible); the **explainer** is a short paragraph that explains what the graphic is about and why the information is important; the **body** is the meat of a graphic; a **source** line must be included to give attribution of the information; the **credit** tells who produced the graphic. (Courtesy *Orange County Register*)

Fig. 6-8 ■ (Below) Three basic types of graphics are: charts, diagrams, and maps. A bar chart is used to compare different items on a common scale. A pie chart is a visual presentation of separate portions that fit together to make 100 percent. (Courtesy *Orange County Register*)

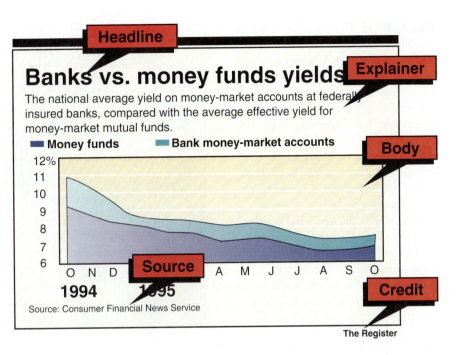

Headline · Explainer · Body · Source · Credit

Banks vs. money funds yields

The national average yield on money-market accounts at federally insured banks, compared with the average effective yield for money-market mutual funds.

■ Money funds   ■ Bank money-market accounts

1994   1995

Source: Consumer Financial News Service

The Register

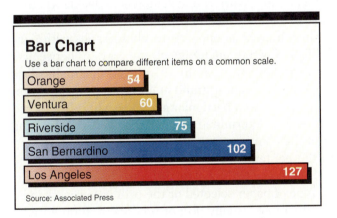

Bar Chart

Use a bar chart to compare different items on a common scale.

Orange	54
Ventura	60
Riverside	75
San Bernardino	102
Los Angeles	127

Source: Associated Press

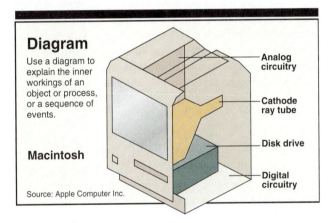

Diagram

Use a diagram to explain the inner workings of an object or process, or a sequence of events.

Macintosh

Analog circuitry · Cathode ray tube · Disk drive · Digital circuitry

Source: Apple Computer Inc.

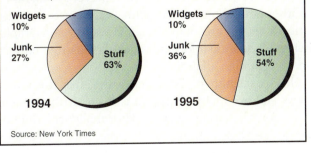

Pie Chart

Use a pie chart to compare different portions of a whole and show their relationship to that whole.

Widgets 10% · Junk 27% · Stuff 63% — 1994

Widgets 10% · Junk 36% · Stuff 54% — 1995

Source: New York Times

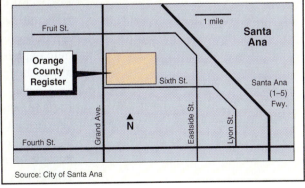

Map

Use a map to locate an event, trace a path and/or show relative distances between areas.

Fruit St. · Sixth St. · Fourth St. · Grand Ave. · Eastside St. · Lyon St. · 1 mile · N · Santa Ana · Santa Ana (1–5) Fwy. · Orange County Register

Source: City of Santa Ana

Fig. 6-9 ■ The old cliche "a picture is worth a thousand words" doesn't hold true any longer. It would take more than 1,000 words to communicate the message that a modern communicator with the needed skills and tools can create. Here is an example. This illustration was created by Tanya Leonello, a student in the graduate program in Medical and Biological Illustration at the University of Michigan School of Art. A black and white photograph of a dog skull was scanned at 300 dpi, then tinted a pale yellow in Adode Photoshop. The muscles were drawn in Adobe Illustrator and saved. A muscle was selected and darkened using the pen tool in the area of desired transparency. Then the muscle was copied and pasted onto the scull. Shadows underneath the muscle were airbrushed in. The drop shadow of the skull was applied by tracing the skull with the pen tool and distorting the selection. The edges were blurred out in the areas which are further away from the skull. The selection was filled with a 30 percent opacity. Instructor was Christopher Burke, adjunct assistant professor, University of Michigan School of Art.

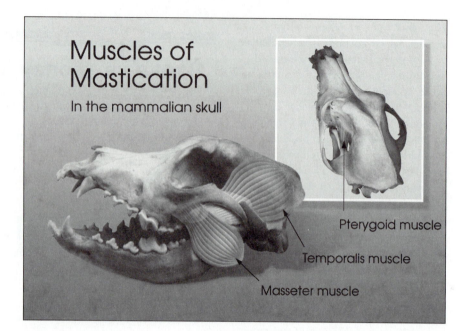

Which Art to Use?

Once the decision is made to use art, the next step is to decide whether a photograph or line art will be most effective. *Line art* is a term for straight black-and-white images as opposed to photographs with continuous tones from black to white, including all the grays in between.

In selecting art, the key word, as in all things typographical, is *reader.* The audience must be kept in mind at all times. Consideration should be given to the sort of art a particular audience will relate to and find appealing. (This can be determined by research carried out during the planning stages of the communication.)

In addition to the content questions regarding the most suitable art for a layout, there are some technical qualities to check. Will the art produce well on the type of paper selected or the printing process to be used for the job? Photographs usually do not produce well on antique or coarse finished paper. They need paper with a smooth, even high gloss finish to bring out all of their definition and contrast. (Paper is discussed in Chapter 8.)

One approach to selecting the proper art is to consider the content of the message. Some art directors like to use photographs for nonfiction to reinforce the sense of realism they wish to achieve. Photographs transmit a sense of authenticity. Some art directors like to use drawings for fiction. Schematic drawings are often helpful. Charts and graphs help explain complicated economic information. Maps illustrate national weather conditions and foreign affairs.

Nigel Holmes, chart designer for *Time* magazine, has the job of reducing complex news and events involving statistics to attractive and easy-to-understand art forms, mainly charts. The challenge, Holmes says, is "to present statistics as a visual idea rather than a tedious parade of numbers. Without being frivolous, I want to entertain the reader as well as inform him."

Sources of Art

Today about the only restricting factor is the limit of the imagination of the communicator. Those who do not have an art director to do the job or the funds to hire a professional artist, photographer, or photo researcher should learn to locate art themselves.

A number of firms supply *stock art.* This is art that is prepared and sold in a variety of sizes, shapes, and subjects. The firms usually offer *clip art* books or catalogs. These are available in scores of subjects from seasonal topics to special events. Each book contains art of various sizes that can be cut out and placed in a layout. They are camera ready and simple to use.

Then there are numerous clip art programs for computers, and communicators using desktop publishing programs can add a graphics program that will provide scores of illustrations.

Communicators who have professional designers and artists to produce what they need are fortunate. However, art is becoming increasingly costly, and in some cases the ideal of using the services of a professional designer or artist may not be the reality. And the facts of life may not include an unlimited budget.

These are alternatives. The quality of much stock art is excellent and clip art of top notch quality is available in proof books as well as on the computer disk. Good sources of illustrations, often at no cost at all, include public relations firms, chambers of commerce, state departments of tourism and economic development, and museums and historical societies. Quite often art can be borrowed from other publications; usually they ask only a modest fee or that a credit line be given.

Fig. 6-10 ■ Clip art is available in proof books for actual clipping and placing in layouts or in computer programs for integrating into a layout created on the screen. (Line art courtesy Image Club Graphics; photos and fine art courtesy PhotoDisc.)

THE TWO BASIC TYPES OF ART

▶ Art comes in two basic forms—*illustrations* and *photographs*. *Line art,* such as pen-and-ink drawings, consists of definable lines of black laid down upon white space. There are a number of techniques that the artist can employ to give a shaded effect to these drawings, but basically line art consists of just black lines or dots and white space.

A photograph consists of black and white and all the tones between—thus the term *continuous tone* art. The difference between continuous tone art and line art is important to understand because each requires different treatment.

No matter what printing method is used, continuous tone art must be converted to line art, or art that gives the illusion of continuous tone. This is done by photographing the image through a finely ruled screen. This produces a negative that consists of tones reduced to a dot formation. Since it is believed that half of the original image is lost in this process and half of the full tone remains, the resulting printing plate is called a *halftone.*

Fig. 6-11 ■ One of the first art decisions to be made is whether to use line art, as in the illustration above, or continuous tone art, as in the black and white photograph, above right, or in the color illustration, below right. Line art can give the illusion of continuous tone through shading but it is made up of only blacks and whites. Unlike continuous tone images, line art does not need to be screened for printing. (Line art and tropical fish illustrations by Tracy Turner; photograph by Richard Anderson)

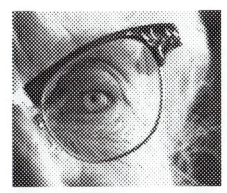

Fig. 6-12 ■ When this photograph is processed for printing it will be rephotographed through a screen and the resulting negative used to produce a printing plate. The enlarged area shows the configuration of dots that gives the illusion of continuous tone. (Photography: Richard Anderson)

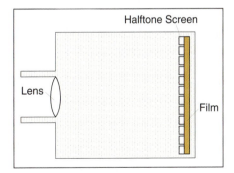

Fig. 6-13 ■ To make a halftone (or a line conversion), a screen is placed in front of the film in the camera and then the continuous tone art is photographed to produce a screened negative.

In the world of desktop publishing advances are being made in scanners and digital printing that can simplify continuous tone art production. These are discussed in chapter 3.

Screens used for making halftones come in a variety of numbers of lines per inch, ranging from about 65 to 200. The greater the number of lines per inch, the finer the detail of the printing plate. For high-quality reproduction, a fine screen and a high-gloss, smooth-finish paper is used. A plate made with a screen of about 135 lines per inch will produce an excellent result.

If a fine-screen halftone is printed on coarse paper, such as newsprint, the resulting print will look muddy. Most newspaper halftones are made with about an 85 screen for best results.

In making plates from line art no screen is used and the resulting plate is an exact duplicate of the art.

Photography is playing an increasingly important role in printed communications. It is a major tool in converting art to printing plates, and it can be used to produce a vast array of special effects for presenting this art on the printed page.

One example is called *line conversion.* In this process, continuous tone art is converted to line art for printing. Examples include reproducing a photograph so it looks like a drawing; making various finishes that look like antique matting; exaggerating dot structures to make the art look as if it is constructed of all sorts of circles, lines, squares, and shaded effects.

All this is done by placing a screen or film between the lens and the unexposed film and taking a picture to produce a negative for plate making, just as you would to make a halftone.

Although such special effects have surprise value or help set a special mood, they should be used sparingly. An example of how these special effects can be useful is the conversion of a photograph to line art for

85-line screen

100-line screen

150-line screen

175-line screen

Fig. 6-14 ■ The prints above illustrate the effects of various halftone screens. The 85-line screen is used for printing on rough paper such as newsprint, and the very fine 175-line screen is used for very smooth-finished or high-gloss papers. 150-line screens were used to print the half-tones in this text. (Photography: Richard Anderson)

printing on antique or very coarse paper that might not print the photograph well. Also, it is usually a good design principle to avoid mixing line and halftone art in the same layout. If, for instance, "mug shots" (head-and-shoulder photographs of people) are to be used in a brochure along with some line drawings, it might be much more attractive to do a line conversion of the photos.

Communicators should be familiar with the capabilities of the photographer, production department, or printer to produce these special effects and take advantage of them when they will result in more effective layouts.

A New Breed of Visual Communicator

In the world of publications a new breed of visual communicator is invading the editorial office. The breed is called "graphic journalists." A knowledge of how these graphic journalists operate could be valuable to those working in advertising and public relations as well in newspapers and magazines.

85-line halftone

Edge Exposure

Vertical line

Line tone

Posterization

Random grain screen

Fig. 6-15 ■ Some of the possibilities for handling black and white photographs. These were created by using various types of screens in the scanning process. (Photography: Richard Anderson)

Let's take a look at a day in the life of the graphic journalist. Her first step is to do some creative brainstorming about a project or idea. The planned project is discussed with editors and others who might be involved. Then serious research begins. The graphic journalist does on-site observing and collects visual resources. Sometimes she works with an artist outside the office to get a better understanding of a complex project.

Once information has been collected, the graphic journalist goes over it, evaluates it, and lists questions that might require further information gathering or clarification.

The graphic journalist writes the words to be used in the graphic. It is her job to see to it that all words are clear and conform to the style of the publication. Often the graphic will be gone over by the editor or whoever is responsible for the production. After this, the graphic is completed and a final rendition is made for production.

Michele Fecht was the first person to hold the position of graphic reporter/researcher at the *Detroit News.* She explains her role: "Primarily, I work in the same way that a news reporter works. I gather information and bring it back and work it out with an artist and a graphics editor. Research is a big part of it—making phone calls from the office to find visual resources."

Pam Reasner, graphics coordinator for the *San Francisco Chronicle,* says, "My primary responsibility is to work with editors who want graphics to make sure that what they're asking for is 'doable.' I hone the idea and work with an artist to get it done on time, make sure that it's good. I'm really a liaison between the artists and the editors."[2]

OBTAINING PHOTOGRAPHS

▶ There are two things to consider in obtaining effective photographs for publication: the creativity of the photographer and the quality of the image the photographer captures.

Perhaps a good way to consider creativity in photography is to go back to the Greek origin of the word *photography. Photos* means "light" and *graphos* means "writing." Thus, the photographer "writes" with light, whereas the writer records images with words. Both are the techniques of creative communication.

Philip C. Geraci, writing in *Photojournalism: Making Pictures for Publication,* has this to say about the role of photographs in communication:

> Editorially, photographs help to tell the publication's story, not better than words, for both words and pictures are essential to give the reader full understanding. But pictures generally say it first. That's the purpose of a photograph: to sum up in a rectangular frame the mood and essence of the story.[3]

Detailed advance planning is an important part of obtaining a quality photograph. If you are selecting a photographer for an assignment, write out exactly what you desire, look over his portfolio to see if it includes the types of illustrations you have in mind. If permissions are needed, secure them in advance as well. Often, you will need permission to restrict the place to be photographed, such as roping off an area. If all this is taken care of in advance, things will go smoothly and you will save money.

Here are a few hints on how to obtain good photographs for printing:

■ Even lighting is best, without extreme highlights or extreme shadows.

■ Dark shadows do not print well on course paper, such as newsprint.

■ A light source on or near the camera, if it is the only light source, can make the subject appear flat and shapeless.

■ Generally speaking, the outdoor photograph that will reproduce best is one taken in the evenly lit hours of the day—especially for printing on newsprint.

■ For reproduction on smooth and glossy paper outdoor photographs are often planned for early morning or late afternoon hours specifically to get shadows.

An ideal photograph for printing is one in which details are clearly visible in both highlight and shadow areas, there is good contrast within the mid-tone range, and shadow is held to an absolute minimum. Prints that are very contrasty or very flat and light should be avoided.

For black-and-white printing, photographs taken with black and white film are best. Prints made from color transparencies tend to have too much contrast and often they are not as sharp as original black-and-white prints.

Professional graphic designers who work with photographs learn to tell at a glance whether a print will reproduce well. Contrast quality is

Fig. 6-16 ■ Duotones are halftones printed using two screens—often using 2 colors. They work best with photographs that have a wide range of grays. This example is a black and yellow duotone. See more detailed discussion of duotones in Chapter 7. (Photography: Richard Anderson)

evaluated. The density range is also considered. Density is the lightness or darkness of a photograph.

A densitometer is a photoelectric device that measures density by recording the density range, which is the difference between the density of the lightest highlight in a photo and the darkest shadow. For optimum printed reproduction on newsprint, for instance, the recommended densitometer reading is 1.4 to 1.8 for a black-and-white print and 2.5 to 2.8 for a color transparency.

The size of the print is a factor to consider in ordering a photograph. In general, the larger the film format, the sharper the final photograph will be. Ideally, the size of the photographic print should be as close as possible to the size of the image to be printed. For instance, an 8 by 10 inch photograph should be ordered for a full page that is larger than 8½ by 11 inches. If the original is too small the photograph may become grainy and blurred when enlarged. Also, a large print is easier to retouch than a small one.

Here are some hints for the most satisfactory photograph:

■ Light- and medium-colored subjects are best when shot against a dark background for black-and-white photography.

■ Dark subjects are best photographed against a background that is just moderately light.

COLOR, GRAYSCALE, OR B&W?

Here are three examples of electronic art treatment available to the designer. Sometimes it helps to be able to see what an illustration will look like before a decision is made on which treatment to use.

At the top is line art in black and white. The middle example illustrates the addition of grayscale. The bottom example is in full color.

—Courtesy Dynamic Graphics

■ If a background is too light it may merge into the page it is printed on.

■ If there are dark and light subjects in the same photograph, select an intermediate-tone background that will give both fairly good contrast.

■ More contrast is obtained in color photography even though the subject and background are of similar tones.

■ Try to obtain several originals of different exposures to select the one best suited to your purposes and the paper and printing method to be used.

PREPARING ART FOR PRINTING

▶ Regardless of whether a photograph or a drawing is selected, there are certain steps that must be taken to prepare the art for printing. These include cropping, sizing (or scaling), and retouching.

Cropping Art

Cropping is the process of removing unwanted material or content or changing the size or direction of the art. It isn't just haphazard chopping away at a photograph or drawing. It is judicious editing with an eye toward enhancing the effectiveness and design characteristics of the art.

Art is usually cropped:

■ To emphasize the center of interest.

■ To eliminate an unwanted portion.

■ To compensate for technical errors.

■ To adjust the shape to fit a given layout.

Skillful cropping can be used to alter the proportions of the background and foreground. For instance, the horizon line can be raised or lowered to change the emphasis. The center of interest can be moved to a better location. If the art has motion in a certain direction, the center of interest should be given "elbow room" to move in that direction. For example, imagine a photograph of a sailboat moving across the sea. If the boat is moved out of the exact center of the photograph, the feeling of movement is increased and the illustration becomes more dynamic.

It isn't often that a photograph or drawing can be used in the form in which it is received. By careful and thoughtful cropping it is possible, for example, to convert a picture containing several people into one showing a single character, two characters, or whatever number is desired. Quite often a very dramatic head-and-shoulder shot of an individual can be obtained by cropping the person out of a group picture. This is especially true if the photograph is an informal action shot rather than a stiff group picture.

One illustration can serve many purposes if creative thought is given to cropping. For instance, in an illustration of a family group, a child can be isolated if a picture of a single child is needed. A person's

Fig. 6-17 ◼ Cropping can eliminate distracting influences and strengthen the art's impact. The colored lines show a few of many ways this photograph might be cropped. (Photo by Richard Anderson)

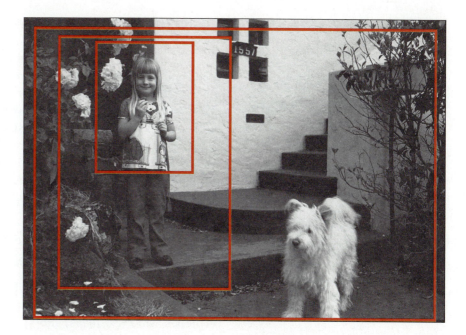

hand pointing might be isolated from the rest of the body if a hand pointing is needed. Legs and feet can be separated from the bodies if art just showing people's legs and feet is needed. The creative possibilities are limitless.

Most desktop publishing programs have cropping Ls in the computer "tool box"; cropping and sizing (or scaling) can be done on the computer screen. Even though you are working on a computer and you have cropping capabilities, it is a good idea to start off examining an illustration the traditional way—with cropping Ls. You can make your own cropping Ls. Just cut two right angles out of heavy paper or light cardboard. The Ls should be about 1½ inches wide, and each leg should be 8 or 10 inches long. Satisfactory Ls can be cut from a manila file folder. They are used to frame the various parts of an illustration.

If you are using traditional production methods, the desired cropping must be recorded so that whoever processes the art for printing will know exactly how you want it changed. The two most often used methods for doing this are with a marker or an overlay. Grease pencils or felt markers can be used to make crop marks, arrows or lines, in the margins. Marking should not be made on the face of the art. Grease pencils, also called china markers, can be purchased at most stationery or art supply stores. An overlay is a sheet of tracing paper taped to the illustration on which cropping and sizing can be indicated.

Scaling or Sizing Art

Once art has been cropped it must be scaled (or sized), that is, reduced or enlarged, to fit the desired spot in a layout. For instance, most photographs used in publication work are either 5 by 7 or 8 by 10 inches. But it is quite unusual for those sizes to be exactly right for the spot where the photograph is to be used in the layout. Therefore art must be reduced or enlarged. Also, sometimes the dimensions of the art piece

Fig. 6-18 ◼ Cropping Ls are an important tool for editors or designers working with art. They can be used to emphasize elements, to isolate parts of an illustration, and to determine where crop marks should be made.

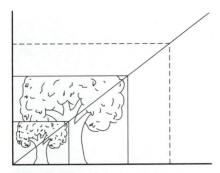

Fig. 6-19 ■ Art can be sized by using a simple proportion formula or by placing a straight edge to create the diagonal and the new width.

must be altered. A rectangle that is 5 by 7 might be cropped so it can be used in a space 6 by 4.

There is a general mathematical process that can be used to determine how much must be cropped from the width or depth to change the proportions so the art can be sized to fit the available space. This involves the principle of *proportion*. That is, when a four-sided area is reduced or enlarged, the sizes of the sides remain in direct relationship with each other. If we enlarge a 3 by 3 area to 5 inches wide, for instance, it will be 5 by 5 or 5 inches deep as well. If an 8 by 10 photo is reduced to half its original size, the width will be 4 inches and the depth will be 5 inches. This principle can be stated in an equation that is simple to calculate:

$$\frac{\text{New width}}{\text{Old width}} = \frac{\text{New depth}}{\text{Old depth}}$$

The unknown, or the dimension being sought, is indicated by x.

Suppose the designer has a photograph that is 8 by 10 and a space 6 inches wide (36 picas) has been allocated for it in the layout. The depth of the new, or "sized," art is not known, so it is x in the equation. The formula will look like this:

$$\frac{6 \text{ (new width)}}{8 \text{ (old width)}} = \frac{x \text{ (new depth)}}{10 \text{ (old depth)}}$$

To solve the equation, the algebra instructor tells us, we use cross-multiplication. That is, 6 times 10 equals 60 and 8 times x equals $8x$.

The equation now becomes $8x = 60$. We continue by dividing 60 by 8 to get the new depth of 7½ inches.*

There is another simpler, but more cumbersome, way to work proportions.

First, draw a diagonal line from the upper left to the lower right or from the upper right to the lower left corner of the original art. (Don't draw on the art, of course.) Any straight edge can be placed in this position. A ruler is best as it will give the depth in inches or picas (see Fig. 6–23).

Next, measure the width of the new art across the top of the original art. Indicate the width on the bottom of the original art as well. Now line up another ruler at these two points. The point where the two rulers intersect is the depth of the new art. If the art is to be enlarged rather than reduced, both proportion lines should be extended beyond the art until they intersect.

A little more challenging situation is when we have a rectangular piece of art that has a depth greater than the width and we want to use this art in an area that has a width greater than its depth. How can this art be cropped to change the shape?

---

*Note: Some designers state the proportion formula slightly differently. However, the results are exactly the same. They use:

$$\frac{\text{Old width}}{\text{Old depth}} = \frac{\text{New width}}{\text{New depth}}$$

Fig. 6-20 ■ The correct way to cut one illustration into another is shown on the left. The smaller illustration should be placed over the larger in a spot where it will not interfere with the center of interest.

Fig. 6-21 ■ When cutting one illustration into another, a common edge, as on the right, should be avoided, as the reader may not notice that two illustrations are involved.

First of all, since the depth must be changed to be shorter than the width, we have to crop the original depth. But how much?

We can use the proportional equation again. Let us assume that an 8 by 10 photograph must be used in an area 6 by 4 inches. Portions must be cropped from the original depth, which we will designate as x (the unknown) in the proportion formula:

$$\frac{6 \text{ (new width)}}{8 \text{ (old width)}} = \frac{4 \text{ (new depth)}}{x \text{ (old depth)}}$$

If we solve this formula, $6x$ will equal 32, and x will equal 5⅓. However, and here is the tricky part, since the original depth was 10 inches and the new depth must be 5⅓ inches, the difference must be subtracted from 10. That is, 4⅔ inches must be cropped from the original depth of the illustration. This cropping can be done from either the top or bottom, or parts of each, depending on the composition of the illustration. The result is an illustration that is now 8 by 5⅓.

These sizing results can be checked by working the equation using the solution (in this case, 8 by 5⅓) for the new "original" art by substituting x for either the new width or the new depth. If, in our example, the new width works out to 6 or the new depth to 4, we know the problem was solved correctly.

Quite often instructions for sizing art are given in percentages of enlargement or reduction. A communicator might crop the art and then write "reduce to 80 percent" on the instructions. It is easy to find the percentage of reduction or enlargement. Just take the original width of the art or photograph and divide it into the desired width for the layout. That is, if a photo is 5 by 7 and it is to be placed in an area that is

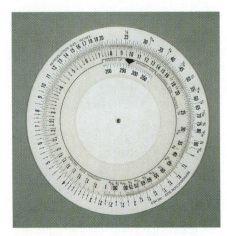

Fig. 6-22 ■ A proportion wheel can be mastered in minutes. It can be used to size art and calculate the percentage of enlargement or reduction.

3 inches wide, we simply divide 5 into 3 to find the percentage of reduction. In this case we would write "60% of original" on our instructions. If, on the other hand, this 5-inch-wide photo is to be used in an area that is 8 inches wide, we would divide 8 by 5 and write "160% of original."

Some communicators find it simpler to size art using picas rather than inches for the dimensions.

There are tools that help with these sizing problems. They are simple to use and can be mastered in a minute or two. The most common is a *proportion wheel,* which can be purchased at a reasonable cost from most art and graphic supply firms. There are *proportion slide rules,* too. One or the other should be in every editor's or designer's tool kit.

Always keep in mind that it is better to reduce than enlarge. Reduction makes flaws and imperfections less discernible and helps to make the definition of tones sharper and more contrasty. A good rule of thumb is to try to reduce most art at least 50 percent.

Retouching Art

Retouching is the process of eliminating unwanted material or flaws in artwork. It can be used to emphasize details or repair defects. However, it takes a skilled artist to do effective retouching.

Usually an airbrush is used for retouching. This is an atomizer that uses compressed air to spray watercolor paint on art. The retoucher masks the areas to be retained and sprays the areas to be eliminated or makes the background a uniform shade or tone. Bleaches are often used to remove unwanted portions of photographs.

Sometimes it is more economical, and possibly more effective, to correct photographs in the darkroom rather than to use the services of a retouch artist.

A photographer can alter the image by using different types of photographic paper to change the contrast. Techniques such as dodging and burning can also be used. *Dodging* is a method of lightening areas of a photograph by reducing the light reaching certain areas of the print.

Fig. 6-23 ■ The editing of photos for publication can be done on the computer, where photo manipulation has become a standard process for the experienced desktop publisher. There are programs to store, call up, and integrate photos into publishing programs. These programs manipulate the photos in many ways—you can adjust color, size, and crop. On the left above is a computer screen with a photograph about to be imported into a page layout. In the middle is a display of a file of photos imported from a compact disk. On the right is an image that has been imported from a CD and is ready for the designer to process. (Courtesy Aldus Corporation)

Fig. 6-24 ■ Software programs such as Adobe's Photoshop make it possible to retouch and enhance photogrpahs in amazing ways. This advertisement shows how seamlessly a photo can be altered. The aerial view of Minnesota lakes was cleverly transformed to mimic a figure from one of Matisse's paintings. (Courtesy Target Stores. Agency: Martin Williams)

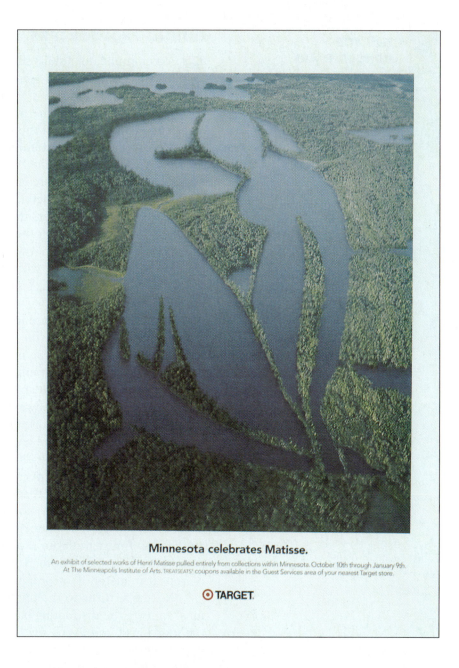

Minnesota celebrates Matisse.

An exhibit of selected works of Henri Matisse pulled entirely from collections within Minnesota. October 10th through January 9th. At The Minneapolis Institute of Arts. TREATSEATS¹ coupons available in the Guest Services area of your nearest Target store.

⊙ **TARGET.**

Burning is used to darken areas by allowing more light to reach areas of the print.

And now the computer has moved into the darkroom to take over many of the retouching and enhancement tasks. With the use of digital transformation through software programs such as Photoshop, graphic communicators can do amazing things to photographs.

Through electronic retouching the *National Geographic* slightly moved one of the great pyramids at Giza to fit the art into the shape of its cover. The *Asbury Park Press* removed a man from the middle of a news photo and filled in the space by copying part of an adjoining wall.

This ability to make changes in photographs that cannot be detected has created a twenty-first century ethical problem for the communicator.

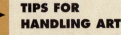

TIPS FOR HANDLING ART

- Don't use sharp pencils or ball-point pens to mark instructions on art. You might make impressions that will show up in the finished plate and in the printing.

- Avoid using paper clips and other devices to hold art and instructions together. They can cause creases that might show up in the printing. Use masking tape or write instructions on a protective flap.

- Keep art flat. Don't roll up or fold.

- Use a *slip sheet* to protect art. This is a cover made of tracing or light paper. It is attached to the underside of the art with tape or rubber cement and folded over the top. It acts as both a cover for the art and a frame, if an area is drawn on it to indicate cropping.

EDITING PHOTOGRAPHS

A communicator's skills should include editing photographs as well as editing the written word. Here is a typical photo-editing problem. The editor of a newsletter has received three mug shots. Two of them are slightly flawed. The editor wants to correct the flaws and also make the people's heads all the same size.

The first step is to examine the photographs. Photograph A is a good likeness of the individual. The head size is appropriate and there is good contrast. There are adequate tonal values—good color and bright whites with ample detail in the middle tones. This photo needs no additional work. In fact, the editor will use this as the model to match as she works on the other two.

Photograph B presents two obvious problems. The editor needs a photo of the woman alone, without her daughter. Plus, the head size is small compared with photo A. Otherwise, the color and general quality are excellent.

Photograph C also presents several problems—a distracting background must be removed, the individual must be enlarged to match photo A, and the glare on the man's glasses must be reduced.

First, all three photographs are scanned into Photoshop at a resolution of 330 pixels per inch and saved as CMYK files. Then, each photo is duplicated so the editor always has a backup copy of the original.

She then begins to work on Photo B. She uses the rubber stamp tool, selects the background color at various points, and "stamps" that color over the image of the daughter until she is completely covered. Likewise, where the daughter overlaps the mother's dress, the editor stamps the color of the mother's dress over the daughter, carefully following even the line of the mother's shoulder, so that the daughter is, apparently, erased. The editor then opens up the file for photograph A and places it next to Photo B on the screen, so she can determine the proper head size for Photo B. She enlarges Photo B accordingly and recrops it to match Photograph A as closely as possible.

Next, she turns to the file for Photograph C. First, she knows she must remove the distracting background. She begins by zooming in on the individual, and, using the lasso tool, carefully outlines the individual in sections, then loops around to take in the surrounding background, and deletes it. After she has accomplished this, she zooms back out and deletes the remaining background using the rectangular selection tool.

Now, to soften the edges of the individual, she selects the Feather option from the Select menu. She then zooms back in on the individual's eyes, and, working again with the rubber stamp tool, stamps flesh tones around his eyes to remove the glare from his glasses. Finally, she uses the lasso tool to select the area just around his eyes and chooses the Sharpen filter. Now this image of the individual against a white background is saved to a layer.

Next, she opens up the file for Photo A and makes another copy of it. This time she rubber stamps the background over the individual, so that the background completely fills the image. She copies and pastes

Here are the original photographs:

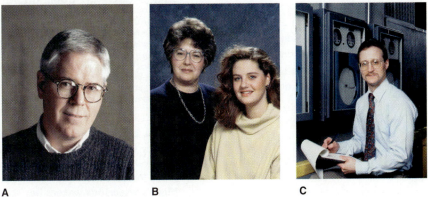

A   B   C

Here are the results:

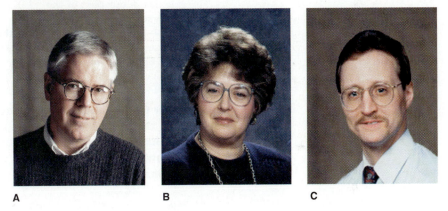

A   B   C

this image onto another layer in photo C. Then, going back to Photo C, she turns on both layers and the individual appears against the tan background of Photo A. She enlarges and crops this photo to match the other two photos and her work is finished.

Once upon a time, this kind of photo retouching was accomplished with masking paper and rubber cement, with fine artist's brushes and inks and a very steady hand. And even then, only the most skillful artist could do a convincing job. Now, with electronic photo programs such as Photoshop, this work can be mastered much more quickly, with nearly seamless results.

CAPTIONS AND CUTLINES FOR ART

Are they captions or cutlines? In newspaper design they are cutlines in the United States. In magazine design and in newspaper design in England they are captions. Regardless of what they are called, there are a number of ways to handle cutlines or captions when planning printed communications. Some are more suitable for newspapers, and others work better for magazines and brochures.

Fig. 6-25 ■ Captions for art. A caption style should be chosen that is compatible with the design of the publication or brochure. Consistency in caption style is important, and caption lines should not exceed the limits for readability of the typeface and its size chosen.

Opposite page: A Saudi mechanical engineer, on a year-long assignment to a Pensylvania turbo-machinery company as part of his career-development program, discusses a turbine with his American supervisor.

COME ON IN! Our tour hosts often welcome you with fresh-baked pastries and home cooking!

AS IF FOR PROTRECTION, a juvenile scarlet takes a friend under its wing. If human efforts to protect them and their rain forest home are successful, they may yet live out their years free and safe.

A SEA OF SUNS bound together by gravity fills the view when an infrared telescope aims toward the Milky Way's center (opposite). More mysterious waters lie beyond: the Great Attractor, discovered by the Carnegie Institution's Alan Dressler (above) and six other astronomers. All galaxies in our part of the universe—shown in the chart he holds—are being drawn toward this immense mass. One is the galaxy NGC 6861, shown behind him.

Laundry room recess lowers washing machine to comfortable height, while stand elevates dryer door to seat level. Dryer controls were moved forward for easier access.

LAUNDRY ROOM RECESS lowers washing machine to comfortable height, while stand elevates dryer door to seat level. Dryer controls were moved forward for easier access.

Our Golden Gate, one Chinese booster calls the new Yangpu Bridge spanning the Huangpu River, one of several huge government projects aimed at modernizing Shanghai's infrastructure.

OPPOSITE PAGE: A SAUDI MECHANICAL ENGINEER, ON A YEAR-LONG ASSIGNMENT TO A PENNSYLVANIA TURBO-MACHINERY COMPANY AS PART OF HIS CAREER-DEVELOPMENT PROGRAM, DISCUSSES A TURBINE WITH HIS AMERICAN SUPERVISOR.

Flying Colors: Larry Williamson's whirligigs, like "Shaman Lady in Star Dress" (above), evolved because he wanted to give his unique sculptures a sense of movement. "I flashed on the idea because clay is so stoic," he says.

*V*iew of the Grand Staircase. From an eighteenth-century engraving.

The basic design criterion is to select the arrangement believed best suited for the job and to stick to it. Also, cutline and caption styles should not be mixed within one publication.

Newspapers consider cutlines (in newspaper parlance a caption is a head *above* an illustration) a must. Some insist that a cutline accompany every illustration. There are several ways these cutlines are handled:

■ The cutline is boldface with the first two or three words in all caps.

■ The cutline is in the same face as the body matter but in a different point size.

■ The cutline is in an entirely different style of type, but one that harmonizes with the headline type.

■ The cutline has a sideline head. This is a line or two of display type placed together with the cutline but to its left.

■ The cutline has a catchline. A catchline is a display line placed between the illustration and the cutline. The catchline can be set flush left to line up the cutline or it can be centered. Most newspaper designers seem to prefer the centered catchline.

Whatever arrangement seems to harmonize best with the whole graphic design of the newspaper should be used consistently. Cutline styles should not be changed from illustration to illustration, though a single centered line might be used for mug shots and another arrangement used for all the other illustrations. The point is to be consistent.

Many designers in the magazine world prefer not to use captions. They see them as an annoyance that clutters up a layout. Many believe that a good illustration needs no caption, that it tells the story by its composition and content.

When captions are used, they appear in two basic design formats. One is adjacent to the illustration and the other is a combination caption that serves several adjacent illustrations on a page or in a layout.

The arrangement of the caption and its placement should be based on two criteria. First, the caption should not just be "thrown in." It should be part of the overall design and treated as an important element. That is, the caption should add something to the design and should be unified with all the other elements in the layout. Second, the caption should not be written or located in a way that confuses the reader. Numbers, arrows, and other devices should not be used in captions. They clutter and disfigure a layout.

Art that is carefully selected, prepared, and presented can be as important an element in a layout as the words. In this visual age it is a vital tool of the communicator.

➤ EFFECTIVE DESIGN CHECKLIST

■ Have a specific function in mind—do not use art just for decoration.

■ Remember the reader; try to select art from the reader's perspective.

■ Avoid art clichés. These are things like people shaking hands, speakers at the rostrum. They are dull, dull, dull!

■ Crop carefully and with a purpose. Don't crop unnecessarily and ruin a well-composed illustration.

■ Avoid unusual shapes in art. Circles, stars, and other decorations should be avoided unless there is a strong design reason for using them. Straightforward rectangles and squares are best.

■ Select art for its content. Do not select it for its shape. The shape can be altered but poor content is hard to improve.

■ Use mortises only after careful consideration. (Mortises are cut-out areas in art in which type or graphic elements are inserted.) Usually all mortises do is disfigure art.

■ Use silhouettes for a change of pace. In the silhouette the figure or center of interest is in outline form.

■ Use tricky treatment with caution. Mortises, surprints (type over art) and combination plates (line and halftone art together) should be used with great caution. The trend today is straightforward, simple, close-cropped art.

▶ GRAPHICS IN ACTION

1. Let's start off with a creative communication project. Try this: On a blank piece of paper or on your computer screen, using only your imagination, sketch a trademark that says: Made in (use your city or state).

Now try this: Select a concrete item such as a desk or a tree and see how many ideas you can come up with for its use in a layout.

Or this: Select an abstract word such as *love, kindness,* or *wealth* and see how many ideas you can come up with for illustrations to "say" this word.

Or this: Select a saying such as "A penny saved is a penny earned" and see how many possibilities you can come up with for illustrations that might accompany that saying in a layout and help communicate the message.

You've been creative! Try to analyze how you arrived at your solutions to these problems.

2. Select three articles from magazines or newspapers that have no illustrations. Decide if the articles could have been presented with more impact, more reader interest, or clearer understanding with art or an informational graphic. Create the art yourself, or give a detailed description of what it would be, or find a source for the art to be used.

3. Select an illustration. Make and use cropping Ls or scan it onto your computer screen. Use cropping Ls or your cropping tool and see how many uses you can find for variations of this one illustration. List these layout possibilities. If possible, make duplicates of the art so each possibility can be marked for cropping. Or crop and print them out via your computer.

4. Once photos have been cropped, size them to fit areas that are 4 inches (24 picas), 6 inches (36 picas), and 8 inches (48 picas) wide. Or, crop for content and size to change the dimensions. For instance, crop an 8 by 10 photo to fit a 7 by 5 area in a layout. When sizing is complete, calculate the new dimensions in both inches (or picas) and percentages of reduction or enlargement.

NOTES

[1] *The Louisville Chronicles,* Society of Newspaper Design, October 15, 1988, p. 3.

[2] *Design,* May 1988, p. 34.

[3] Philip C. Geraci, *Photojournalism: Making Pictures for Publication* (Dubuque, Iowa: Kendall/Hunt Publishing Company, 1978), pp. 1–2.

CHAPTER 7

COLOR: A POWERFUL COMMUNICATION TOOL

CONTENTS

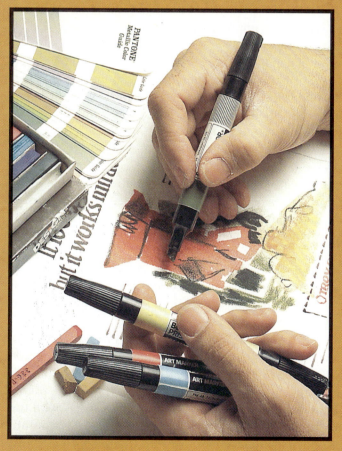

Steve Weinrebe, Stock Boston

► **A COLOR QUIZ**

How much do you know about color? Here's a little quiz with the answers based on research findings. Answers are upside-down at bottom.

1. The most legible combination of ink and paper is:
   a. black on white
   b. blue on white
   c. black on yellow

2. In ads and displays, which color brings the highest returns from females?
   a. red
   b. yellow
   c. green

3. In ads and displays, which color brings the highest returns from males?
   a. brown
   b. blue
   c. red

4. Which colors appear closer to the eye?
   a. warm colors (red, yellow, orange)
   b. cool colors (blue, violet, green)
   c. there's no difference

5. Which color is considered an all-purpose color that has few negatives?
   a. purple
   b. magenta
   c. brown

ANSWERS
1-c, 2-a, 3-b, 4-a, 5-c.

7 The trend in visual communications today is toward bold and colorful graphics. Communicators must use every available tool to make the message effective and make it stand out from its competition. The proper use of color, the judicious use of borders and ornaments, and the proper marriage of ink with paper can all add dimensions to effective printing.

The first step in becoming adept in selecting and using these elements is to develop a sense of how they can help. This graphic sense, or awareness, can be sharpened by studying the work of others. Keep a constant critical eye out as you browse through newspapers, magazines, and even the direct mail communications that fill the mailbox. Try to second-guess the person who designed them. Why was a subhead put here, a border there, an ornament at that position? Why was spot color used there? What did it add to the printed piece to invest in full color rather than spot color or simply printing it in black on white?

When you pass the magazine rack in the supermarket, look at the graphic array. Which magazines seem to be especially attractive? Why? Which magazines seem to communicate at a glance what they are all about? How do they do this?

The head buyer of a major grocery store chain once said he looked at the label on the can before he examined the contents. If the label wouldn't sell, he would reject the product, no matter how fine it might be. The same can be said about printed messages. They must have eye appeal.

Evaluation for eye appeal includes an examination of the printed communication to see if the basic criteria for good selection and use of type have been applied. The communication should be checked for the application of the principles of design. Does it have balance, unity, contrast, proportion, harmony? (These principles are spelled out in Chapter 9.) If the balance is formal, is that appropriate for the type of message?

Then, the piece should be examined to see if these principles have been applied in an unusual or different way to make it stand out from the rest. Are the principles of good typography and graphics used in an unusually arresting way?

Soon you will be able to automatically "score" printed communications as you view them. For instance, an ornament that throws a page out of balance will be spotted in an instant. A boxed item placed in such a way that easy reading of the text is upset will become a source of irritation. You will immediately notice an ornament that clashes with the other elements on the page and destroys unity. And you will be aware of instances when color dominates the page and diminishes effective communication.

A POWERFUL COMMUNICATION TOOL

► The blue of the sky, the red of the sunset, neon lights, paints, wallpaper, color television, advertisements—we live in a colorful world.

Fig. 7-1 ■ Note the effective eye appeal of this book cover. The designer used color and applied principles of design—balance, unity, contrast, proportion, harmony—to attract attention, set the tone, and create interest.

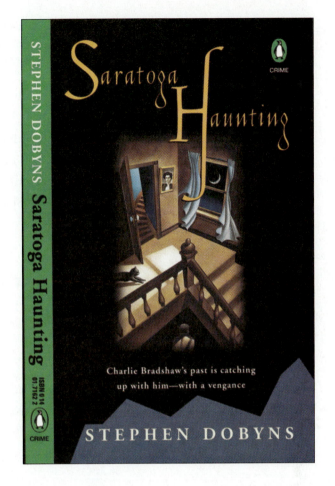

It wasn't always like this. It has only been within the past hundred years or so that we have been able to take advantage of color as a tool in graphic communications. Once a limited number of dyes and pigments were known before the nineteenth century. Now there are thousands of colors of every imaginable hue and intensity. There seems to be no limit on the possibilities of using color. The only restrictions are cost, the ability of the designer, and possibly some limitations imposed by the equipment available.

Even cost is no longer the factor it once was. New methods of preparing color separations and printing plates have cut the cost considerably. Color can now be added inexpensively, with a little creative planning. Printing in a color ink on another color paper can create a piece that breaks out of the dull black on white.

There are several ways in which color can make printed communications more effective. It can help accomplish the first job of any communication—attracting attention. It can create the atmosphere desired. It can help set the mood for a message. Color can provide accent and contrast where they are wanted, and it can help emphasize important points. It can add sparkle to the printed page. It can direct the reader through the message. It can be used in printed materials to help create identity just as it does for schools in flags and athletic uniforms. Think of Campbell's soup! What colors do you visualize?

CREATIVE COMMUNICATION

Here is a plan for creative problem solving. (It is from a booklet produced by the Royal Institute of British Architects, described by Bryan Larson in his book *How Designers Think.*)

The plan includes four steps: assimilation, general study, development, and communication.

The first step is the accumulation and ordering of general information and information specifically related to the problem. This is followed by study of the problem, its nature and possible solutions.

Next, the best solutions are isolated and developed and refined.

Finally, the solutions are discussed with those involved in the project or those who can offer advice and informed evaluation.

However, color is not a cure-all. it will not compensate for poor writing, poor typography, and poor layout. It will not help shoddy printing. The communicator should not try to use it to save an inferior design.

Before taking advantage of this powerful tool, we need to understand several aspects of color. These include:

- How color is reproduced in the printing process.
- The psychological implications of color.
- How colors harmonize or relate to each other.
- How to combine color with type, art, and other elements in a layout for best results.

HOW COLOR IS REPRODUCED

All color comes from sunlight. Reflection and absorption of light produces the effects we know as color. A lemon is yellow because it absorbs all colors except yellow and reflects yellow. In an unlighted room we would not see a yellow lemon. We would not see it at all. Under a dim light, the yellow rays the lemon reflects will be so weak we will see the lemon as gray.

In discussing color with a printer, we need to be familiar with six terms: hue, tone, value, shade, tint, and chroma.

Fig. 7-2 ■ Color work can be done by professional designers on high-speed image workstations. (Courtesy *PrePress Direct.*)

Hue is what makes a color a color. That is, all colors we see are hues. Hue is derived from the ancient Gothic word *hiwi,* which means "to show." Hue is what makes blue blue. *Tone* and *value* are terms used to designate the variations of a hue. They are the lighter tints or darker shades of a color created by adding white or black ink to a hue. Adding black to a color creates a *shade;* adding white makes a *tint.*

Chroma is a term used to indicate the intensity of a color. The chroma of a color is determined by the amount of pigment saturation in the ink that produces the color. Increasing the chroma creates a more intense color.

An artist who wants to create different colors or shades and tints of colors mixes paints on a palette. The printer does the same thing when a spot of color is needed for printing. The inks are mixed on an ink plate and then placed on the press, unless premixed inks are purchased from the manufacturer.

We have been taught that yellow, red, and blue are the three primary colors. All other colors can be created by mixing these primaries. There are, however, additive and subtractive primary colors.

Fig. 7-3 ■ Light rays reflected from a surface create color. A yellow sweater, for example, will absorb all light rays except yellow. It reflects the yellow and appears yellow.

Fig. 7-4 ■ Black is the absence of color. A black object absorbs all light rays and thus appears black. White is the presence of all colors. A white object reflects all light rays and thus appears white.

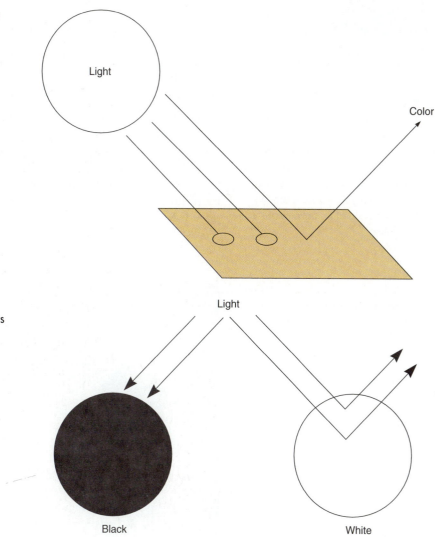

Fig. 7-5 ■ This color triangle shows shades (intermediates between a hue and black), tints (intermediates between a hue and white), and tones (intermediates between a hue and gray). (John Odam, artist, reprinted by permission of Verbum, Inc. from "The Desktop Color Book.")

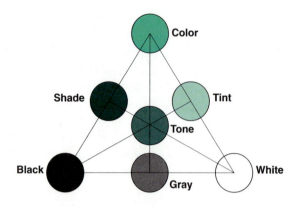

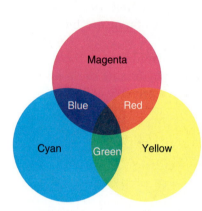

Fig. 7-6 ■ Ink color is called subtractive. The primary ink colors are magenta, cyan, and yellow. Secondary colors are mixed from the primary colors. Magenta and cyan make blue. Green is made from cyan and yellow. Red is made from magenta and yellow. These are the three basic inks needed to make most colors in printing.

The *additive primaries* are blue, green, and red. They are called additive because they produce white light when added together. Additive primaries are the dominant colors of the rainbow. Another good example is a color television image. Color televisions use a red, green, and blue color projection system to create the sensation of color.

The process is different when a printer needs to produce the full range of colors in a full-color illustration. Three colors slightly different from blue, green, and red are used. The printer uses cyan, yellow, and magenta for full-color work. Cyan is a blue green, and magenta is a red violet. These darker colors are called *subtractive primaries*. They are called subtractive because they absorb light. And they are primaries because a full range of colors can be produced by mixing the inks together in various proportions.

In the traditional method of preparing visuals in full color for reproduction, four plates are made through a process called color separation. Each of these plates will print a color of ink in the density required so that when it is combined with an impression from another plate it will create the tone or shade desired. In effect, the printing press

Fig. 7-7 ■ The artist mixes colors on a palette; the printer mixes colors on the printing press.

Fig. 7-8 ■ In printing colors four inks are used: yellow, magenta, cyan, and black. The mixing of the inks is done on paper as it goes through the press.

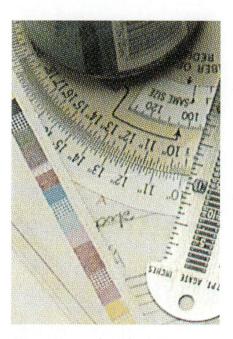

Fig. 7-9 ■ This enlargement illustrates the halftone dot structure of four-color process printing. Looking closely, you will see the individual dots of cyan, magenta, yellow, and black.

becomes the palette. If the people using this process are skilled, the reproduction will be difficult to distinguish from the original.

The printer uses inks called *process inks* in producing printing in full color. Process inks are special transparent inks that are available in magenta, cyan, and yellow. When these ink colors are superimposed, they produce three other colors in the spectrum. Yellow and magenta combined produce red. Yellow and cyan produce green, and magenta and cyan produce blue. Thousands of tints and shades can be reproduced through the combinations of these inks. Black is added to give depth to the dark areas and shadows.

The distinctive sensation we see and identify as a certain color is—to repeat—actually the reflection of light waves that weren't absorbed by the object. For instance, if white light strikes a surface and the surface absorbs green light waves, we see the red and blue light waves that were not absorbed. We see, then, the color magenta, which results from the combination of red and blue.

If the surface absorbs blue light waves, we see the combination of red and green lightwaves, or yellow. And, if the surface absorbs red light, we can see cyan—a combination of the reflected green and blue light.

So, in making plates for full-color reproduction, one plate is made with a green filter and used in printing with magenta ink. A red filter is used for the cyan printer, and a blue filter for the yellow printer. The fourth plate, the black ink printer, is made to add density. Without the black ink impression, the reproduction would appear weak and dark brown rather than black in the shadows.

The process is much more complicated than this brief description, but the point to remember is that it takes four plates and four separate impressions, or runs through the press, to produce a full-color reproduction. It is expensive, but the price is coming down as new equipment for making color separations is developed.

Fig. 7-10 ■ In the traditional plate-making process color plates are made by photographing the full-color art through filters to separate the primary colors. If the original art is continuous tone, such as a color photograph, a screen is used for each exposure as in the creation of halftones from black-and-white photographs. Computers can do the job today.

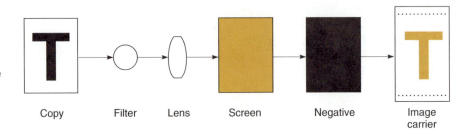

Copy   Filter   Lens   Screen   Negative   Image carrier

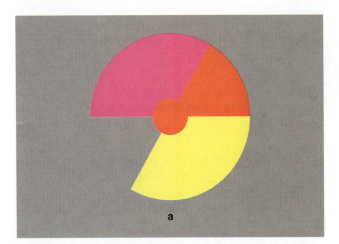

a

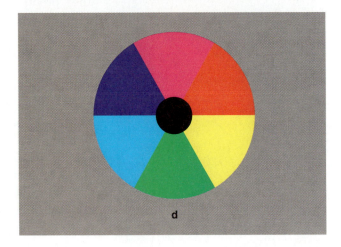

b

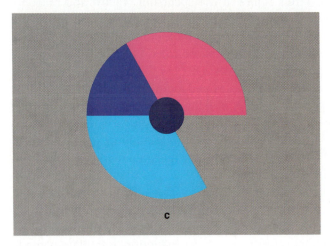

c

d

Fig. 7-11 ■ Superimposing transparent pairs of yellow, magenta, and cyan will produce three other colors in the spectrum. Yellow and magenta produce red (a), yellow and cyan produce green (b), magenta and cyan produce blue (c). The combination of all three colors produces a near-black neutral (d). Thousands of tints and shades result from combinations of these inks in dots of differing sizes.

Fig. 7-12 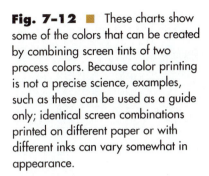 These charts show some of the colors that can be created by combining screen tints of two process colors. Because color printing is not a precise science, examples, such as these can be used as a guide only; identical screen combinations printed on different paper or with different inks can vary somewhat in appearance.

Fig. 7-13 ■ Color artwork is "read" by a scanner, which creates negatives for cyan, magenta, yellow, and black printing plates. (a) Shown here is a scanner from the Hell Chromacom System. (b) Another part of the Chromacom system is the Combiskop. It can make precise color corrections and adjustments to scanned artwork, and it can create a wide range of special effects. (Photographs: Jeffrey Grosscup)

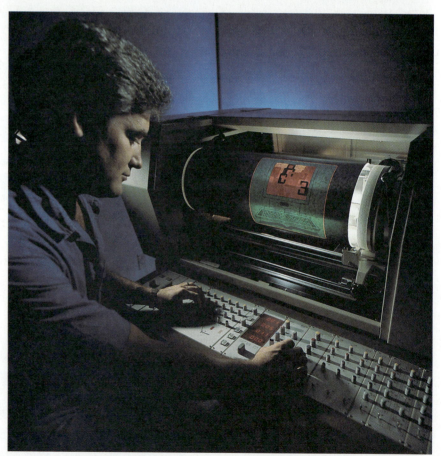

Fig. 7-14 ■ Color bars are included in four-color process proofs. These bars are used to check such things as the density of the color, the amount of ink used, and the quality of color reproduction in screened areas.

YELLOW

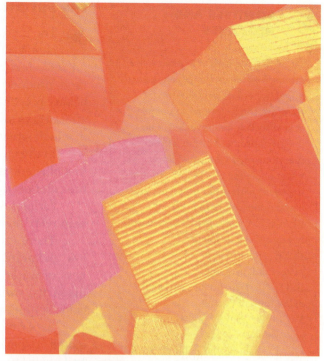

YELLOW AND MAGENTA

YELLOW, MAGENTA, AND CYAN

YELLOW, MAGENTA, CYAN, AND BLACK

Fig. 7-15 ■ The four-color process plates printed in sequence, or progression. Proofs of this sequence are called progressive proofs or "progs."

POSITIVES AND NEGATIVES

There are recognizable pluses and minuses as far as the psychological impact of colors is concerned. Here are the reactions to colors that research has revealed. The positives are listed first. These reactions might be considered when choosing colors and combining them with other elements and companion colors in a layout.

BLACK   Accomplished and worldly/empty and desolate.

BLUE   Secure and peaceful/depressing.

BROWN   Dependable and logical/plain and boring.

YELLOW   Happy and sunny/show-off.

GRAY   Secure and calm/plain and colorless.

GREEN   Calm and natural/jealous.

RED   Power and excitement/aggressive.

PINK   Sweet and soft/femininity.

TAN   Calm and natural/ordinary.

THE PSYCHOLOGICAL IMPLICATIONS OF COLOR

The increase in use of color has led communicators to look to psychologists for help in making the most effective use of this powerful tool. Just as sugar manufacturers have learned, for example, that their product will not sell in a green package, and manufacturers of beauty preparations known that brown jars will remain on the shelf long after others are gone, so communicators must know which colors to use in which situations.

In the case of sugar, tests by marketers have shown that it sells best in a blue container or at least in one where blue is predominant. Blue is the color of "sweetness," whereas green is seen as astringent, like a lime.

Airlines know that proper color schemes in airplane cabins can help relax nervous passengers.

There are warm and cool colors. Fire and sunshine make red, yellow, and orange—warm colors. The shadows of deep forests and the coolness of water make blue, violet, and dark green cool. Night brings on inactivity, while day brings brightness and hope. Thus dark blue is the color of quiet whereas bright yellow is the color of hope and activity.

Experiments have shown that people exposed to pure red are stimulated. Depending on the length of exposure, blood pressure increases and respiration and heartbeat speed up. Red is exciting.

On the other hand, exposure to pure blue has the reverse effect. Blood pressure falls and heartbeat and breathing slow down in a blue environment. Blues are calming.

Advertisements for air conditions use cool colors. Those for furnaces are more effective if warm colors are used.

Unnatural use of color can cause adverse effects. Printing a luscious grilled steak in green not only fails to add to communication in a favorable way but it can also detract by creating a strong sense of repulsion on the part of the reader.

"I have worked with designers who ran halftones of people in blue, green, pink, or some other terribly unnatural color," remarked one designer who reviewed this manuscript. "The results were uniformly terrible."

Blue is the favorite color of the majority of people. It can be used with no fear of adverse psychological effects (unless, as stated, it's used unnaturally). Yellow generates the buoyant happiness of a sunny day. Orange is a happy color, too. And brown is one of the most versatile colors for printing. Men associate it with wood and leather. Many women associate it with leather goods and furs. Like blue, it has no inherent weaknesses and can be used for a wide variety of purposes. Green is also a universally popular color. And purple suggests robes of royalty, the dignity of church vestments, and the pomp and splendor of high ritual.

There are two important points to remember when selecting color for communications. First, warm colors advance and cool colors recede when printed. Reds tend to dominate and can overpower other elements on the page if the designer is not careful. Second, colors in printing should be used as much as possible in their natural associations—green

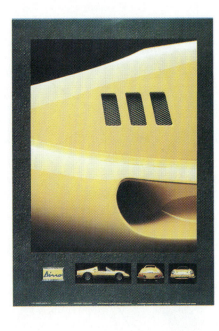

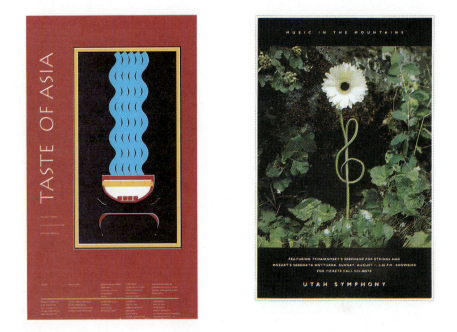

Fig. 7-16 ■ Bright yellow, a happy, active, show-off color is perfect for a Ferrari, and the designer wisely chose to accentuate this color in the poster on the left. Red, a traditional color in Asian art, is a logical choice for the Taste of Asia poster, center. Green leaves and a clever nature motif convey a sense of soothing serenity for a series of orchestra concerts in the mountains. (Left: courtesy Pete Jacaty/Graphtec, Ft. Lauderdale, FL; photographer: Peter Langone. Center: courtesy National Institutes of Health; designer/illustrator Alfred Laoang. Right: courtesy Williams & Rockwood, Salt Lake City, Utah)

forests, blue sky, sunny mornings. (There may be times when the unnatural use of color can create the most effective communication. But remember the risk of repulsion when color is used unnaturally.)

SELECTING COLORS FOR HARMONY

➤ Which colors go well together when printed? Many people can tell instinctively if colors look compatible when printed together, but others need help in choosing color schemes for communications. Luckily, help is available.

In 1899 a Boston teacher, Albert H. Munsell, began research that resulted in a system for distinguishing color. He charted color values on a numerical scale of nine steps ranging from black to white. Munsell's system was adopted by the National Bureau of Standards and slowly added to until it contained 267 different color names.

Out of this came the *color wheel.* Around the wheel are the colors comprising the primary triad of red, yellow, and blue in an equilateral triangle. Halfway between the primaries are the secondary colors. In all, the wheel divides the color spectrum into twelve hues. Five basic color combinations have been devised, which the communicator can use in deciding what colors to use in creating harmonious layouts.

The combinations are:

■ *Monochromatic:* This is the simplest color harmony and is made of different values of the same color. These values may be obtained in printing by screening artwork at different percentages (to show, for example, a tan with a darker brown). Monochromatic harmony works well in printing. Care should be taken not to screen type so that clarity of the type is lost.

Fig. 7-17 ■ Color combinations used for creating harmonious layouts.

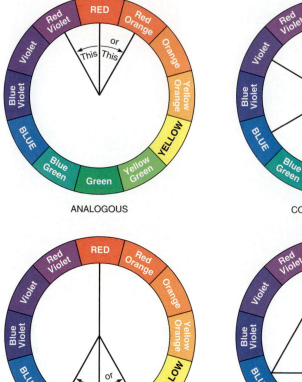

ANALOGOUS

COMPLEMENTARY

SPLIT COMPLEMENTS

TRIAD

Fig. 7-18 ■ A color matching system composed of charts, colored-ink pens, and printing ink, all coordinated, can be used to insure that the printed color matches the color the designer specifies. Pictured here is the PANTONE® Color Selector 1000. Color matching systems are also a part of illustration and page layout software for the electronic designer. (Courtesy Pantone, Inc. All trademarks noted herein are the property of Pantone, Inc.)

■ *Analogous:* These are two colors that are adjacent on the color wheel, such as blue and blue green, or red and red orange.

■ *Complementary:* These are colors that are directly across from each other on the wheel, such as red and green. A complementary selection adds drama because of the contrast of warm and cool colors.

■ *Split complements:* These are colors that are selected by choosing a color on the wheel and finding its complement but using a color adjacent to the complement. A split complementary harmony for red would be blue green or yellow green.

■ *Triad:* This is a combination of three colors, each of which is at the point of a visualized equilateral triangle placed on the wheel. As the triangle is turned to any position on the wheel, its points will designate the three colors of a triad.

Another tool for color selection is a *matching system.* This is composed of samples, or chips, showing the various colors as they will appear in print. It is similar to the collection of swatches found in most paint stores. One widely used such guide is the PANTONE MATCHING SYSTEM®, referred to as PMS. This guide shows the colors as they will appear on coated or uncoated papers.

SOME WAYS TO USE COLOR

➤ There are many ways to take advantage of the powerful communications possibilities of color at very little added cost. The cheapest, of course, is to use colored paper. We are so conditioned to thinking in terms of black ink on white paper that we often overlook this possibility. And we often forget that we could use colored ink on white paper.

Spot color is the process of adding individual colors in printing. One color added to the basic color can do much to make printing stand out at only about a 35 percent increase in the total cost of the job. Each color added means an additional run of the sheet through the press, but it can be well worth it.

Spot color can increase the impact of a printed piece. It can be used to emphasize illustrations or type. More than one spot color can be used in the same layout.

In preparing a layout with spot color, many designers place a tissue overlay on the mechanical (completed layout) to specify where the color will be used, any reverses, the percentage of any screen to be used, and the color itself. Often a small swatch or sample of the color desired is attached. A separate overlay is used for each color.

(Incidentally, ink color *is* affected by the color of the paper. Keep this in mind when printing color inks on colored paper stock.)

Fig. 7-19 ■ Spot color can add impact to a printed communication. This annual report for the Chicago Board of Trade tells the story of that institution's record-breaking year. The reader is paced through a day in the life of a trader, by documenting the significant moments of the trading experience. Here the spot color, red, is used sparingly but dynamically with black. (Courtesy VSA partners, Chicago; Dana Arnett, art director, Curtis Schreiber, designer)

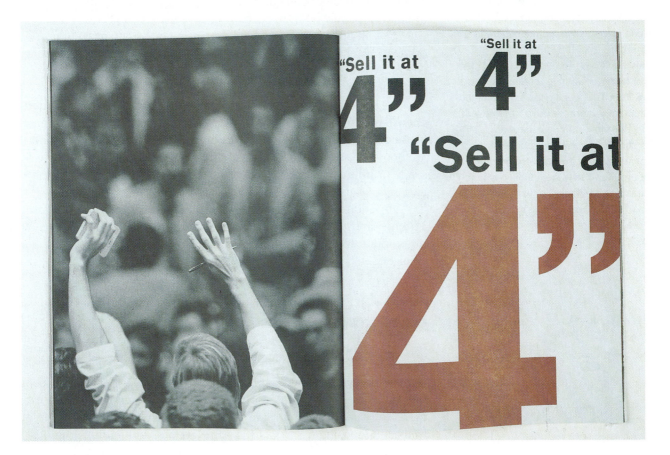

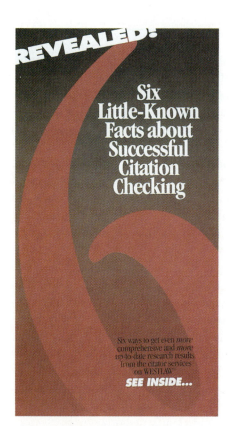

Fig. 7-20 ■ You can often get more color for your printing dollar if you simultaneously print tints of black with the second color, as the designer chose to do in this brochure. The large number six prints 100% red. The background is made up of two over-lapping screens: the black goes from 100% at the top to 10% at the bottom, and it prints over a layer of 100% red. (This effect can be achieved a number of different ways on the desktop, depending upon the software program you use.) Reversing the headline type to white gives the illusion of yet another color. The finished product looks at first glance like more than a simple two-color job.

You can also use simultaneous printing of a solid color and various tints. This can be done on the same press run by screening, or printing type and art made from screened negatives. The density of the resulting tones will depend on the density of the screen. This can be any percentage from solid (100 percent) through half-solid (50 percent) to almost white (10 percent).

Another easy way to obtain effective color is by creating a duotone. A *duotone* is a two-color halftone print made from a screened photograph. Two plates are needed. One is printed in the desired color and the other in black. The result can be a highly dramatic added element to the layout.

The duotone can enable the communicator to add color, warmth, and depth to photographs at a much lower cost than full color—to achieve a unique, artistic interpretation of photographs that is different from the image transmitted with either black-and-white or four-color reproductions.

There is nothing complicated about making a duotone. First you select a continuous-tone photograph. Then two separate printing plates are made from two screened negatives of the photograph. The screened negatives are made by shooting with the screens angled 30 degrees apart, which eliminates the chances of creating an unwanted pattern (called a *moiré* effect) when the plates are printed. By printing the two halftone images in exact register a duotone is created.

A so-called fake duotone is obtained simply by printing a black-and-white halftone on a colored area. This area can be a screen, a solid, or colored paper.

Not all duotones are made by printing one plate in a color and the other in black-and-white. It is possible to print both plates in different colors. A printer can create a three-color or four-color effect by using this technique.

In selecting a color to use with black when printing a duotone, choose one that relates to the subject of the art. Blues and greens, for instance, combine well with black for seaside scenes. Yellows and reds are good for sunsets, and browns or greens can make a realistic landscape of hills and woods. Less often, colors that conflict with the subject may be useful for their shock value.

In addition to duotones, there are tritones and quadrotones. Tritones and quadrotones are three- and four-color halftone reproductions. Like duotones, they can be used to produce subtle or dramatic color effects.[1]

COLOR COMES TO DESKTOP PUBLISHING

➤ The black-and-white world of desktop publishing has become a world of color. Not only are personal computers powerful enough to have the random access memory (RAM) necessary for color separation but they have the necessary higher disk capacity as well. More and more software developers are producing programs to provide color as well as composing text, creating page layouts, and adding graphics.

halftone (black only)

dutone (black and cyan)

tritone (back, magenta and yellow)

quadratone (black, cyan, magenta, and yellow)

Fig. 7-21 ■ Adding color can help create the desired effect. These are examples of the duotone, tritone, and quadratone, compared with a halftone. In the upper left is a duotone created by adding cyan to black, with black having been reduced in highlights and lighter midtones. Lower left is a tritone, which has magenta and yellow added to black. The quadratone, lower right, combines cyan, magenta, and yellow with black.

However, Tim Gill, founder of Quark Inc. and creator of the Quark-Xpress desktop publishing package for Macintosh computers, has a word of caution concerning the use of color in desktop publishing. Gill points out that not only must the technology of desktop color be mastered but also communicators must become skilled at selecting and using color effectively.

"Color provides endless opportunities for bad design, enabling a neophyte to produce a layout predominantly in red and green surrounded by a fuchsia border," he wrote in *Magazine Design & Production*. However, he noted, "as we head squarely toward an era of universal color production . . . the printing industry has already developed the technology to make it possible. Now we must provide the necessary information, training, and education so color desktop technology can be not only used but mastered."[2]

Mike Blum points out that "spot color, Pantone color, and process color screen tints are all attainable without tremendous difficulty" with a desktop publishing system. "If you are considering reproducing color

Fig. 7-22 ■ Complicated color adjustments that formerly were made by the press operator now can be made during the pre-press process on the computer. The process is called trapping, and it takes an experienced graphic designer with sound color knowledge to do it correctly. Trapping means to adjust adjacent color areas to compensate for color registration changes on the press. Usually light colors are spread (enlarged) or choked (reduced) (see explanation below). The designer who can perform this process on the computer can save considerable money.

TRAPPING GUIDE

What is trapping?
- Compensation for press misregistration.
- The key is to overprint or slightly overlap strokes to close an opening.
- The goal is to make the trap unnoticeable to the eye.

When is trapping necessary?
- Whenever PMS colors are touching
- Whenever CMYK and PMS colors are touching
- Whenever there are no common CMYK percentages
- Whenever type is is touching color or photos
- Whenever you are working with gradations and photos

How do I trap?
- Spread (lighter color spreads into darker color)
- Choke (lighter background moves in toward darker color)
- Design out (e.g., overprint, purposely use a white or black outline, drop out background color, etc.)
- Create a bridge color

Trapping Elements

Knockout
Foreground object is cut out, allowing the paper or background color to show through

Overprint
Color objects are printed over the top of one another; can create a third color

Choke
Knockout opening is made smaller (created by overprinting stroke of the background color)

Spread
Object is made slightly larger (created by overprinting stroke of the foreground color)

Fig. 7-23 ■ Here is an explanation of trapping and the various ways trapping can be accomplished. Formerly the job of the press operator, now trapping can be part of the imaging process in computer graphic applications. This is another instance of production moving from the composing and press rooms to the computer.

Black type on white reads 40% more rapidly than type reversed out from black or gray. Poorest legibility is black on red or red on black. Highest legibility is black on yellow.

Black type on white reads 40% more rapidly than type reversed out from black or gray. Poorest legibility is black on red or red on black. Highest legibility is black on yellow.

Black type on white reads 40% more rapidly than type reversed out from black or gray. Poorest legibility is black on red or red on black. Highest legibility is black on yellow.

Black type on white reads 40% more rapidly than type reversed out from black or gray. Poorest legibility is black on red or red on black. Highest legibility is black on yellow.

Black type on white reads 40% more rapidly than type reversed out from black or gray. Poorest legibility is black on red or red on black. Highest legibility is black on yellow.

Black type on white reads 40% more rapidly than type reversed out from black or gray. Poorest legibility is black on red or red on black. Highest legibility is black on yellow.

The type is 9 point Franklin Gothic Book.

—from Adobe *Font & Function*

photographs . . . you need to investigate all of the options carefully before taking the plunge."[3]

The area of desktop color, as with so many areas of electronic publishing, is changing rapidly. It requires skilled visual designers who understand not only the technology but the psychological and visual aspects of using color.

▶ EFFECTIVE DESIGN CHECKLIST

- Use cool colors as the background for black type because they recede and do not detract from the type as much as hot colors.
- When using colors, one color should dominate and the other should be used for accent or contrast.
- Remember that color combinations can add to or detract from the legibility of the type. Black on yellow has high legibility; black on red is extremely difficult to read.
- Select a color that relates to the subject when using duotones unless you wish to create shock value—then use an unnatural color.
- Illustrations reproduced with duotone techniques can reinforce sales, promotional, or information messages.
- A slightly coarser screen works best for producing color halftones to print on coarse paper.
- When using color on newsprint, avoid type with very thin strokes and fine serifs.
- Use red sparingly, but remember that red can give a lift to the printed page. Red is also a good background for white type, if the type is large.
- Blue is an excellent background color. It is good for tints behind black type and it is good for reverses if used full strength. Yellow is too weak to be legible if printed in type masses. Yellow on black has good legibility if used in large types and few words.
- Brown prints well and has good legibility. Its tints are never anemic.
- Generally, body copy should be printed in black or a tint of black when printed on colored paper.
- In advertisements, blue brings the greatest returns from men and red seems to bring the highest returns from women.

▶ GRAPHICS IN ACTION

1. Collect three or four examples of what you consider effective use of color in printed communications. Write an evaluation of each sample, or discuss your choices.

2. Collect three or four examples of what you consider poor or ineffective use of color. Explain what might be done to turn these examples into effective communications.

Generally, delicate types with thin strokes, like ITC Berkeley Old Style (left), are more likely to lose legibility when printed in color than bolder, thicker types like Futura Extra Bold (right).

3. Find examples of what you consider especially creative uses of color. Analyze them and write an explanation of your evaluation of these creative efforts. If you believe they might have been improved, explain what changes you would recommend.

4. Find several pages in magazines or newspapers containing spot color. Try to match the colors with Pantone or another matching system. Analyze the colors and give your opinion about their use and effectiveness.

5. Select two colors to use with the black in the art reproduced below.

Label the various parts with the colors you would use. Keep in mind that you can use percentages of colors. If you have matching color felt pens in a system such as Pantone you might like to try coloring the areas (on a photocopy of the art), or if you are working on a computer with color capability you might scan the art in and complete the project that way. Another way of attacking this project would be to draw a line from each section of the illustration to the margin and label it "60% yellow, 40% magenta," and so on with all the parts you would color. Or, you might want to mount the art on light cardboard, say 8½ by 11, and add an overlay and do your labeling on the overlay. You should add an explanation for your choices of color.

NOTES

[1]*The Desktop Color Book* (San Diego, Calif.: Verbum, Inc., 1992), p. 43.

[2]*Magazine Design & Production,* March 1989, pp. 32–34.

[3]Mike Blum, *Understanding and Evaluating Desktop Publishing Systems* (San Luis Obispo, Calif.: Graphic Services Publications, 1992), p. 27.

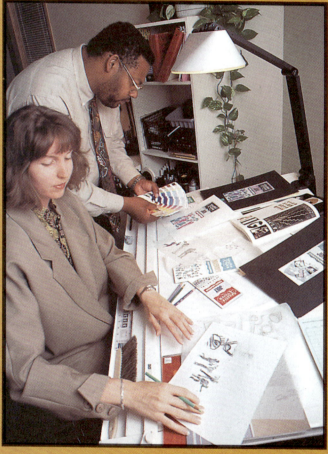
Scott Eklund

CHAPTER
8

PAPER AND INK

CONTENTS

■ **How Paper Is Made**

■ **Characteristics of Paper**

■ **Paper Sizes and Weights**

■ **New Papers for a New Age**

■ **Specifying the Right Paper for the Job**

■ **A Word About Ink**

157

8 No printed communication should be planned without some thought being given to the paper to be used. The proper paper can help the communication do the job. Paper plays an important part in achieving readability and mood as well as durability of the message.

If an "old time" or "antique" theme is planned, consider soft, textured paper. Old style types printed on antique-finish papers will enhance the "feel" of yesteryear. Old style types blend with old style paper. The angular, uneven strokes of the letters harmonize with the roughness and unevenness of soft-finish paper.

A modern look can be achieved better with smooth papers. The detail in a piece of art or the contrast in a photograph will show up much better on a hard-finish paper.

The formal, precise style of many modern and thin typefaces appears at its best on paper that is uniformly smooth and even, with a hard finish. Types with very light letter forms show up best on coated and enameled book papers. But hard-finish papers can accentuate the crude details in the construction of old style letters and make them appear ragged and awkward.

Highly glossed finishes on papers lessen legibility. These papers can even cause eye fatigue and strain. They create a glare that makes reading tiring and difficult. A dull-finish stock is best for long reports and magazines with lots of reading matter.

Anyone concerned with printed communications should know how paper is made, some of its characteristics, and the various types of papers available. Some understanding of paper weights and standard sizes is helpful also.

Fig. 8-1 ■ This catalog for Art Resource, a fine arts rights and permissions representative, uses paper to serve practical and visual needs. The cover stock is a highly textured recycled paper that looks and feels like the kind of canvas that is used for oil paintings. It also stands up well to repeated use. For the inside pages, the designer chose a smooth, coated paper. This type of paper holds the ink on its surface and results in crisp, rich color reproductions. The inside pages are also coated with a clear dull varnish, giving the reproductions added luster. (Courtesy Art Resource)

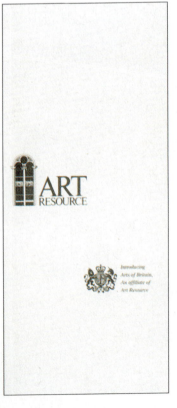

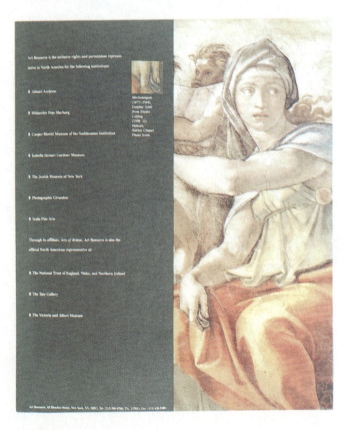

Fig. 8-2 ■ Papermaking in Europe in the seventeenth century. The vatman, coucher, and layman are performing their respective duties. The "pistolet," or heating device, can be seen at the extreme left of the illustration. The wooden hammers of the pulp beater can be seen in the background, upper right. (Culver Pictures)

HOW PAPER IS MADE

➤ Before the early 1700s practically all paper was made by hand. The raw materials—rags—were placed in tubs or vats. They were mixed and beaten into a pulp. The wet pulp was dripped from the tubs by hand and placed in molds made of fine wires stretched across wooden frames.

The milky pulp settled on the frames and drained and became sheets of paper. The damp sheets were then placed in a press, which flattened them and squeezed most of the remaining water out. Finally, the sheets were hung on wires to dry and stiffen.

Although sophisticated machinery has been developed to manufacture paper today, the basic process hasn't changed much. Wood is the most widely used raw material, though some of the high-quality papers are made partially or entirely of cotton and linen fibers. A number of treatments, chemicals, and fillers can be added in the manufacturing process to produce papers with a variety of finishes and other characteristics.

For instance, rosin size is added to create water-repelling qualities so the paper can be used for pen and ink writing, offset printing, or resistance to weather. Fillers, such as clay, are used to improve smoothness, to prevent printing from showing through the sheet (known as the *opacity* of the paper), and to help the ink adhere to the sheet. Dyes and pigments are added to produce papers of various colors.

Paper can be *calendered* (smoothed) by passing it through a series of rollers, and it can be "supercalendered" for an even finer finish. Some papers are produced with a high-gloss, or coated, surface to provide excellent reproduction of photographs and art.

Fig. 8-3 ■ The steps in converting wood into paper are shown in the upper drawing at the right (provided by the Wisconsin Paper Council). The logs enter the pulping machine on the left and leave as a mushy pulp on the right. The process of converting pulp to paper by machine is shown on the lower right. The pulp enters the machine on the left and emerges as a continuous roll of paper on the right.

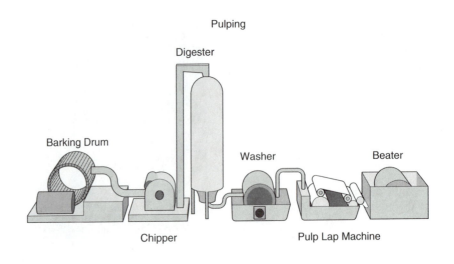

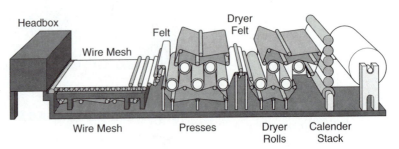

Fig. 8-4 ■ A paper manufacturing machine at the Mead Corporation. "Gingerbelle" contains the machinery illustrated in Fig. 8–3, lower diagram.

Fig. 8-5 ■ Finished paper emerges on the roll in the lower center of this photograph of a huge paper-making machine.

A variety of special finishes is available. Some papers resemble leather, others linen or tweed. Still others are available with all sorts of pebbly and special-effect finishes. These are produced by running the paper through an embosser. Other papers are produced with a watermark or faint design or emblem made by impressing it on the paper with one of the rollers during the process. This roller, called a *dandy roll,* is a wire cylinder for making *wove* (a paper with a uniform, unlined surface and a soft, smooth finish) or *laid* (a paper with a pattern of parallel lines giving it a ribbed appearance) effects.

CHARACTERISTICS OF PAPER

▶ Look closely at a sheet of paper with a magnifying glass and you will discover that paper has two sides. Each side has certain characteristics. The side that was on the wire mesh as the paper traveled through the manufacturing process is called the *wire side.* The other side is the *top,* or *felt,* side. The felt side usually has a smoother finish. The front of a printed piece, especially a letterhead, announcement, or business form, should be printed on the felt side of the sheet.

Paper has a grain. The *grain* is the direction in which the fibers lie in the sheet. Grain affects paper in several ways. For instance, paper folds smoothly in the grain direction. This can be demonstrated by folding a piece of construction paper or cardboard in both directions and noting which direction produces the smoothest fold. For books, brochures, catalogs, and magazines, the grain direction should be parallel with the binding edge of the pages. The pages will turn easier and lay down better.

Fig. 8-6 ■ Supercalendered (or glossy) paper is passed through additional rollers in the finishing process. Here supercalendered paper is coming off the paper-making machine.

Fig. 8-7 ■ Grain is the direction that fibers run in paper, much like in a piece of wood. Grain should be parallel with the binding edge or fold in books, pamphlets, publications, or programs. Pages fold, turn, and lay flat much more easily when printing is with the grain.

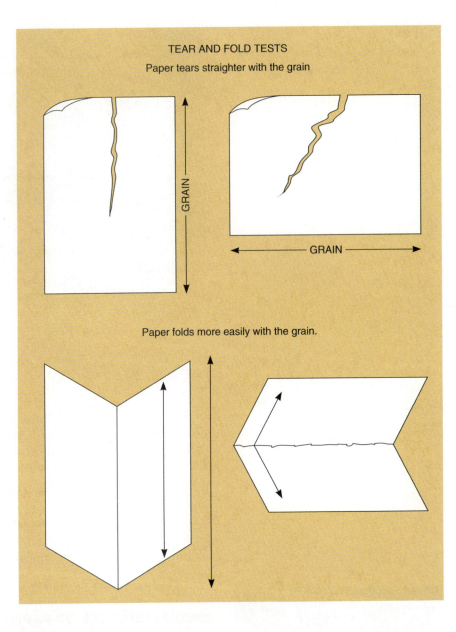

TEAR AND FOLD TESTS

Paper tears straighter with the grain

GRAIN

GRAIN

Paper folds more easily with the grain.

PAPER SIZES AND WEIGHTS

➤ Papers are manufactured in standard sizes and weights. They are identified and selected for printing by these measures. As an example, consider the standard paper used for letterheads known as *bond*. This type of paper is manufactured with a hard surface that will receive printing and writing inks without a blotter effect. The letters won't soak into the paper and become distorted.

Bond papers are made in a basic size of 17 by 22 inches. They will cut into four 8½ by 11 standard letter-size sheets per full sheet. Bond papers come in various weights ranging from 13 to 40 pounds. The most common available weights are 16, 20, 24, and 28. The basic weight is 20 pounds. This means that 500 sheets (a ream) of 17 by 22 bond paper will weigh 20 pounds. You can cut costs—and have a flimsier looking

UNCOATED

Ink pigment and vehicle are absorbed into the paper

COATED

Ink pigment is retained on the surface and the vehicle is absorbed into the coating

Fig. 8-8 ■ Uncoated papers allow the ink to penetrate the paper, while coated papers hold the ink on the surface. Art and photographs are reproduced at their best when coated papers are used.

letterhead—by ordering 16-pound bond paper. Or, you can spend a little more and have a heavier, more impressive looking letterhead by ordering 28-pound bond.

The basic size is different for different kinds of papers. It is thus important to be aware of how papers are classified and sized. The vast number of papers available may make this appear forbidding, but the classification system is really quite simple since nearly all papers can be classified into basic groups. The number of groups varies somewhat but most manufacturers recognize ten. These basic paper groups and the standard sizes for each are listed below. A discussion of the importance of knowing about standard paper sizes is included in Chapter 11, on designing printed communications.

- *Bond* (17 by 22): These are the standard papers for business forms and letterheads. They have a hard surface that works well with pen and ink, typewriter, or word processor. They are available in a large variety of colors, mostly pastels, and most manufacturers provide matching envelopes in standard sizes as well.

- *Coated* (25 by 38): These papers have a smooth, glossy surface. They are used for high-quality printing. The surface can be dull-coated as well as glossy, and there are a variety of other surfaces, such as coated on one side, for labels.

- *Text* (25 by 38): Text papers are available in a variety of colors and finishes. They are used for booklets, brochures, announcements, and many quality printing jobs.

- *Book* (25 by 38): Book papers are not as expensive as text papers. They are used mainly for books, of course, and pamphlets, company magazines, and so on. Book papers are available in a wide range of weights and finishes from antique to smooth.

- *Offset* (25 by 38): These are papers made especially for offset lithographic printing where dampening is a factor. They have sizing added to help the paper go through the offset printing process. They are similar to book papers.

- *Cover* (20 by 26): Cover papers come in an endless variety. Some are of the same texture and color as book papers but of a heavier weight. All sorts of finishes are also available. As the name implies, these are designed for use as covers on pamphlets, magazines, and so on.

- *Index* (22½ by 35 and 25½ by 30½): These papers are made to be stiff and to handle writing ink well. Index cards are examples of this type of paper. Index papers are available in a variety of colors.

- *Newsprint* (24 by 36): This is a cheap paper for printing handbills, circulars, and newspapers.

- *Cardboards* (24 by 36): These are sometimes called *tag board.* They are the heavy stuff used for posters. Lighter weights are used for tickets, cards, and tags. Cardboards come in all sorts of colors and can be colored on one or both sides.

ADD VALUE WITH COLOR

In selecting paper for a communication don't overlook papers in colors. Colored paper and one color of ink can make your piece a two-color job rather than just black ink on white.

The results of a study by the American Paper Institute indicate that use of color can increase results. For instance, a selling message was printed on white card stock, and on a gray cover stock. There were 175,000 pieces of each used. The message on the gray cover stock resulted in 210 more sales than that on the white stock.

In a general way, professional designers suggest that when using colored printing papers, larger, bolder typefaces make the piece easier to read. When colored ink is used with colored paper, reading matter should be kept to a minimum.

NEW PAPERS FOR A NEW AGE

The new technology requires new papers, and now paper mills are producing papers especially for electronic printing methods such as laser and ion deposition. Most have a cotton content of 25 percent to 100 percent. They are available in sizes from 8½ by 11 inches to huge rolls that are designed to run on web-fed presses.

These aren't old papers with new names, but new types of papers created especially for electronic printing. They are designed to cut down the possibilities of trouble as the sheet travels through the press. The cotton content of these papers gives them strength for permanence and brightness for contrast, and just enough stiffness to pass easily through electronic printing machines.

Another feature of the new papers is moisture control, which prevents static buildup that can result from improper moisture levels. Also, the sheets have uniform *porosity*. The amount of air that can pass through the sheet can affect print quality and the ability of the toner to fuse to the paper. Uniform porosity allows an even distribution of air to pass through the sheet.

SPECIFYING THE RIGHT PAPER FOR THE JOB

It is important to list all the information the printer needs to obtain the right paper for the printed communication, along with the other specifications for the job. But before selecting a paper, check to see if it is available. If you select a paper the printer does not have in stock or cannot get quickly from the paper warehouse, you could lose several weeks.

Paper should be specified by listing the basis weight, color, brand name, finish or texture, and grade in that order. The basis weight is the weight in pounds of one ream, or 500 sheets of the paper, cut in its standard size. Just about all papers are listed by weight except some cover

Fig. 8-9 ■ Web-fed presses require paper that will sustain the pressures of high-speed printing as well as help produce a high-quality finished product. Some presses operate at such high speeds their output is measured in the number of feet of paper per minute that goes through the press rather than number of impressions per hour. (Photo by Jeffrey Grosscup)

papers which might be listed by thickness. In listing the color be sure to use the exact term used by the mill. Paper mills, like paint manufacturers, may have their own names for colors and they may have several shades of one color. For instance, a tan paper from one mill comes in English Oak, Chatham Tan, and Monterey Sand. Be sure to check a current swatch book for the color, as mills change colors from time to time.

Next, list the full brand name and the finish or texture. Finally, record the grade. This may seem obvious, but it is important. The grade might be bond, offset, or coated book, for example. If the grade is not listed, you may find yourself making wasted trips or extra telephone calls to the printer or paper supplier.

As an example of paper specification, you might specify the paper for a folder in this manner: 80 pound, soft coral, Gilbert Oxford, antique, text.

Paper is one of the major cost factors in printed communications. It is thus always important to talk with the printer about papers. It is also a good idea to acquire a collection of "swatches" or samples of various kinds of printing papers. These can be obtained from paper wholesalers. A file of paper samples should be a part of every communicator's kit.

Fig. 8-10 ■ It is a good idea to acquire a collection of sample books of various kinds of printing papers, which are available from paper wholesalers and manufacturers.

A WORD ABOUT INK

➤ Although the choice of the proper ink to be used for best results is the job of the printer, communicators should be aware of the role that ink plays in the printing process.

> ## CREATIVE COMMUNICATION

There are two approaches to creative problem solving—prescriptive and descriptive.

Scientists solve problems by the descriptive approach: describing what, how, why. Creative designers use the prescriptive approach: considering what might be, what could be, what should be.

Design involves making subjective judgments—decisions based on awareness of the situation. It brings into play the designer's personal mental abilities as conditioned and stimulated by experiences and knowledge.

There is no infallible, correct solution to a design problem, but the problem and its solution often become clearer as the design process progresses.

Ink has been a part of our civilization for more than 2,000 years. The Chinese used various combinations of ingredients for writing and drawing more than 1,600 years before Gutenberg developed movable type. Early Egyptian literature mentions ink. References to ink are found in both the Old and New Testaments of the Bible. For centuries ink makers produced their product mainly by adding soot, or lampblack, to a varnish made by boiling linseed oil.

In the 1850s the discovery of coal-tar dyes, pigments, and new solvents ushered in the age of modern printing ink. Today ink making is a major industry and science. The National Association of Printing Ink Manufacturers reports that there are approximately 200 ink companies in the United States producing inks in about 400 plants throughout the country. Companies range in size from those with fewer than ten employees to those employing thousands. Industry sales of printing inks are more than $750 million now and are growing at an average rate of about 5 percent a year.

Every printing ink contains two basic parts. These are called the pigment and a vehicle. The pigment is a dry powder that gives the ink its color. Linseed is often used as a vehicle, or liquid that carries the pigment and adheres it to the paper.

The ink manufacturing plant produces two basic types of ink. One is opaque and the other is transparent. The opaque ink will cover a color underneath, either the paper or other ink, completely, so it cannot be used for full-color production. Transparent ink will let a color underneath show through; thus it performs the mixing process on the printed paper to create various colors, tints, and shades, as was discussed in Chapter 7.

Inks are manufactured for compatibility with every type of paper. There are quick-drying inks for high-speed production on rotary presses, inks that harden to resist rubbing, metallic inks that simulate gold and silver, and fluorescent inks that store sunlight and glow in the dark. There are even perfumed inks that provide a subtle aroma for special effects. And there are the inks used with our morning newspaper, which will ruin a white shirt. However, work is progressing toward producing a water-base ink that may solve this problem.

For centuries black was the only color in which ink was available. Through the development of synthetic pigments and a greater knowledge of color technology, a whole rainbow of colors is now available to the ink maker. Color matching to a specific tint, shade, or hue has become an exacting procedure.

We should never overlook the possibilities certain inks can provide for that special effect. Inks, along with all the other supporting elements, combined with type, play a part in the complete printed communication.

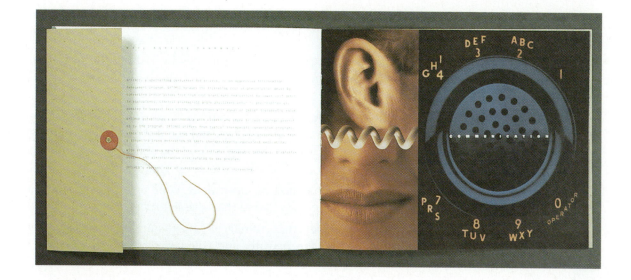

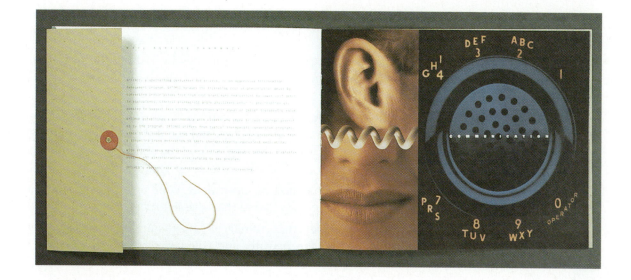

Fig. 8-11 ■ This brochure for a mail service pharmaceutical company uses ink and paper very effectively to reach its audience. The cover stock is a recycled brown paper, and it wraps around to a button and string closure, just like a mailing envelope. Inside, the paper is a glossy stock, which results in rich color reproductions and crisp type. The photo illustrations were created from elements individually photographed in black-and-white and then colored and composited in Photoshop. (Courtesy Kilmer, Kilmer, and James, Inc. Albuquerque, NM and Diagnostek, Inc.)

▶ **EFFECTIVE DESIGN CHECKLIST**

■ When planning printing take into account the standard dimensions of the paper to be used as well as the capacity of the press, to keep waste and cost to a minimum.

■ The finish of the paper can affect the mood of the completed job. Select a paper that prints well and harmonizes with the type and tone of the message.

■ Avoid selecting type designs with delicate lines for printing on rough-finish papers, especially for letterpress and gravure. This is not as critical for offset printing.

■ Remember that colored paper can add another dimension to the printed piece, but select an appropriate color.

■ Consider grain direction when figuring paper stock. If the finished piece is to be folded, the grain should be parallel with the fold.

■ Process or full colors produce most accurately on neutral white paper.

■ Runability, or the efficiency with which the paper can be printed, and print quality are important factors in selecting papers. Discuss them with the printer.

■ If colored ink is to be used on colored paper, check the compatibility of the colors of both ink and paper.

■ Type is most easily read when printed on a soft, white paper.

■ Consider using specialty inks such as metallic or fluorescent inks.

➤ GRAPHICS IN ACTION

1. Start a collection of paper swatches by visiting the nearest paper wholesaler and seeing if samples of the basic types of papers are available.

2. Obtain samples of papers of various weights and textures. Examine them under a magnifying glass and see if you can determine which is the felt and which the wire side of the sheet. Fold them with and against the grain. Note the differences, if any.

3. Research paper making and make your own paper. There are a number of books available that give instructions.

4. Select a paper that would be most suitable for the following. Consider weight, texture, and color. Explain the reasons for your choices.

   a. A brochure announcing an exhibit of famous paintings.

   b. An announcement of an open house at a computer center. The announcement will include high-contrast art.

   c. A magazine devoted to home woodcraft. It will contain much line art.

   d. A newsletter that requires the most economical sheet with the highest opacity.

PUTTING IT TOGETHER

Richard Pasley, Stock Boston

> ## WHAT COULD IT BE?

It could be called a malleable finite cylindraceous cell wrought of parallel axes with azimuthal terminates. It remains one of humanity's best designs because it works all the time; it is cheap, fast, versatile, and, above all else, it is *simple*.

It is a paper clip!

As with paper clips, simplicity is also a great virtue in graphics. Eliminating the unnecessary and concentrating on the simple, the designer can create graphics that will help readers understand information quickly and clearly.

Keeping graphics simple makes them easier to produce and print as well.

9 We took a rather quick trip through the development of human efforts to communicate by means of visuals in Chapter 2. In Chapter 11 we will examine current trends in design. One trend is apparent today: we are in a new age of self-expression in which almost anything goes. But before we try to put all the pieces together in some form, let's take a look at the basic principles that designers have used through the years to produce visual communications that will do just that—communicate.

We have examined the elements that go into making an effective visual communication. Now we can consider the job of actually putting them together in a complete layout. In approaching layout, keep in mind that there are three general categories of materials that people read.

First, there are printed communications that people want to read. These include newspapers, periodicals, and books. Since people are willing to pay good money to obtain these objects, we should strive to make them as pleasant and interesting as possible.

Second, there are printed materials that people must read. These include timetables, government reports, research papers, and income tax forms. Since people must read these materials whether they really want to or not, it is important to make them clear and understandable.

Third, there is material that people must be coaxed to read. This includes propaganda, public relations releases, and advertisements. A greater effort is needed here to lure people into the message and hold them until its end.

In all of these situations, the secret of using typography and art to its best advantage includes an understanding of the principles of design and how they can be employed in printed communications. These basic design principles include the principles of proportion, balance, contrast, harmony, rhythm, and unity. Application of these design principles will help answer the question, How do we put it all together?

We should note that some of the most effective works produced by creative people have been accomplished by deliberately breaking the rules of good design. Before attempting this sort of experimentation, however, we need to understand the rules we are breaking.

THE PRINCIPLE OF PROPORTION

In planning a layout where do we begin? First of all, we must settle on a shape.

Look around you. What are the most pleasing shapes you see? What are the most frequent proportions you encounter? Rectangles, right?

The ancient Greeks recognized the rectangle for all its pleasing qualities, and they built some of civilization's most attractive structures in the shapes of rectangles. In fact, this shape, as illustrated by the Parthenon, became known as the "golden rectangle." Its proportions are about three to five, and it has endured and pleased people down through the ages. Today this rectangle is encountered in doors, windows, table tops, pictures, and even the basic shape of human beings.

Fig. 9-1 ◼ The Japanese designed the rectangular tatami mat centuries ago. It is still cited by graphic designers as an example of pleasing rectangular proportions.

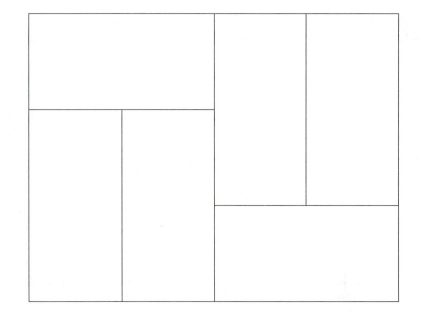

A square shape soon becomes monotonous. The rectangle, though uniform and precise, is not tiring because it offers variety in form.

So, let's settle on a rectangle shape for our layout for a start. Certainly, we can produce effective and interesting layouts by going to squares and breaking out of the rectangular confines. A variation in shape can be the most effective approach for certain jobs when it seems important to be different. But the rectangle will prove most satisfactory for most printed material. Books will fit on shelves properly, brochures will fit standard envelopes, and paper will be used most efficiently. Costs and waste can be kept to a minimum since standard paper sizes are rectangular.

In addition to the dimensions of the page, proportion should be considered when planning other elements in the layout. These include the margins and the relationship of the type and art with each other and the whole.

For instance, margins inside and outside a border should be unequal. Equal white space creates a monotonous pattern. Unequal

Fig. 9-2 ◼ Most books and pamphlets are proportioned to about a 1:1.4 ratio. The height is 1.4 times the width. A square book has a 1:1 ratio. A book with a height of two times its width has a 1:2 ratio. A pleasing inequality in proportions is usually best in graphic design.

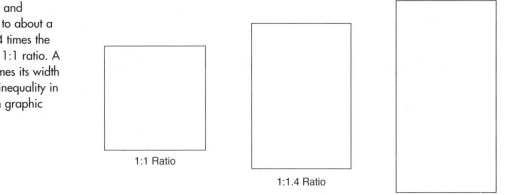

1:1 Ratio

1:1.4 Ratio

1:2 Ratio

Fig. 9-3 ■ Equal margins (*left*) are monotonous. Unequal margins (*right*) are interesting and create better unity.

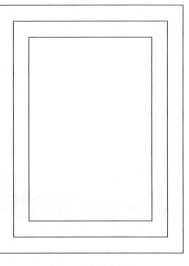

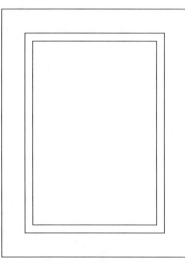

EQUAL MARGINS
Monotonous

UNEQUAL MARGINS
Interesting, better unity

margins break this monotony and present a more interesting layout. Also, the margin outside the border should be larger than that within the border. The border is part of the printed portion of the layout and it should present a feeling of unity with the other printed elements.

In general, we should select shapes of type styles and art that have a proportional relationship to the dimensions of the whole layout. Long, thin types and art go well in long, thin layouts. Short, wide type styles and art carry out the proportions of short, wide layouts. Here again, however, this is a generalization and would not hold true in every layout situation. Each should be considered individually and each should result in a layout that does the job best regardless of what has evolved as the "accepted" practice.

Throughout history the golden rectangle has been the dominant design dimension. It is derived from what mathematicians call the golden section, a formula that was a product of the revival of learning during the Renaissance in fourteenth- and fifteenth-century Europe. The true golden section is a ratio of .616 to 1.0, so that an area 5 inches long would be 3.09 inches wide.

We have settled on standard sizes of 3 by 5, 4 by 6, 5 by 8, and so on for practical purposes such as standard paper sizes and the capabilities of printing presses. Generally the most pleasing page size is considered to be one in which the length is one and a half times the width.

The dimensions of the area of a layout is an important design decision. The first thing the eye notices is the shape of a layout. A layout is said to be well proportioned if its shape is interesting to the eye and its parts are related in shape, but not monotonous in size, and the complete arrangement is attractive and effective.

Once the question of the general proportions of the layout has been resolved, we can consider where to place the elements. We begin by examining the optical center and its relationship to balance.

Fig. 9-4 ■ This rectangle demonstrates the ratio of the golden rectangle, which is .616 to 1.

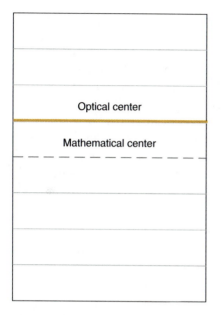

Fig. 9–5 ■ The optical center lies above the mathematical center.

Fig. 9–6 ■ A line on the mathematical center actually looks awkward and below the center. Lines placed on the optical center give a pleasing sense of balance.

The Secret of the Optical Center

The finished layout will be worthless if it does not stop the reader and arouse the reader's interest. We must make critical initial contact. We can do this and arrange the elements in the layout in the most pleasing and effective way possible if we put the "secret of the optical center" into action.

The *optical center* is the spot the eye hits first when it encounters a printed page. If we take any area and look at it, we will find that our eyes land on a point slightly above the mathematical, or exact, center, and slightly to the left. Try it. Open a newspaper and consciously note what you see right off. It will be somewhat above and slightly to the left of the fold. It will take a mighty compelling element to pull your eyes away from this spot.

The optical center is determined by dividing a page so that the upper panel bears the same relationship to the lower panel that the lower panel does to the entire page. That is easier done than said. If an area is divided into eight equal parts, the point located three units from the top and five from the bottom is the approximate optical center.

Luckily we will not have to take a ruler and figure things that closely every time we make a layout. With a little practice in making rough layouts or planning pages, we will get the habit of orienting layouts with the optical center in mind.

We should always take advantage of this natural aid and utilize it as the focal point or the orientation center from which to construct a layout that will make the all-important initial contact. If an element is chosen for this spot that will stop the reader, such as a striking piece of art or a dramatic headline, we are on the way to achieving effective communication.

The optical center, then, is the focal point or fulcrum for placing elements on the layout, and it goes hand in hand with the second principle of layout, the principle of balance.

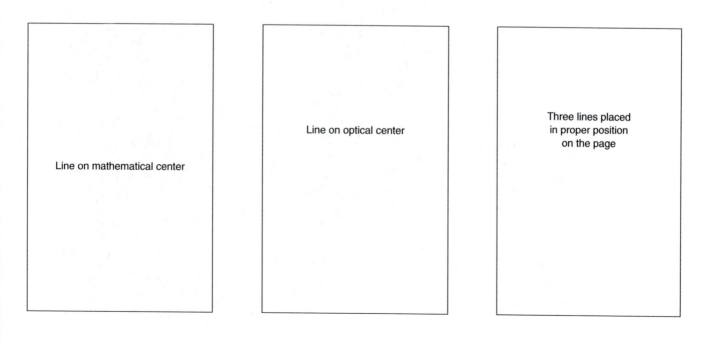

Line on mathematical center

Line on optical center

Three lines placed in proper position on the page

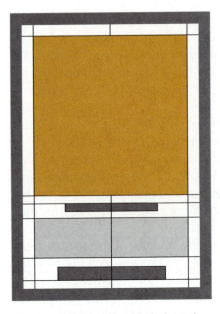

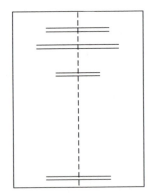

Fig. 9-7 ■ In formally balanced layouts, type lines, illustrations, and other elements are placed left and right of center and above and below center in equal weights for a precise, orderly arrangement.

Fig. 9-8 ■ Symmetrical or formally balanced layouts have elements of equal weight above and below the optical center, as well as to the right and left of an imaginary center line. (Center: courtesy Target Stores; art director: Debra Bistobeau; copywriter: Sarah McNeal. Right: courtesy Pete Jacaty/Graphtec, Ft. Lauderdale, FL)

THE PRINCIPLE OF BALANCE

▶ We need balance in our environment. When things are unbalanced they make us uneasy. Balanced objects look proper and secure.

Balance in printed communications is a must. We must place elements on the page in a way that will make them look secure and natural—not top-heavy, not bottom-heavy. We can do this in two ways. We can balance them formally or informally. (Some typographers call these symmetrical or asymmetrical balance.)

There are times when formal balance is just what is needed. Formal balance places all elements in precise relationship to one another. Formal balance gives us the feeling of formality, exactness, carefulness, and stiffness. Formal balance may be used for luxury car advertisements, wedding announcements, and invitations to white-tie-and-tail events. The *New York Times* and the *Los Angeles Times* occasionally have formally balanced front pages. They help support the image of a no-nonsense, precise publication.

If our communication is formal, dignified, and reserved, a formally balanced layout will help transmit this message. If our target audience has the same qualities, then formal balance may appeal to it.

A formally balanced layout has elements of equal weight above and below the optical center. To the left and to the right everything is the same. If we have a strong display type 6 picas from the top of our layout, we will need a line of the same size 6 picas from the bottom. If we have a piece of art left of center and slightly above, we need a similar element to the right and in the same position. Left and right, up and down, the formally balanced layout has elements of equal size and weight.

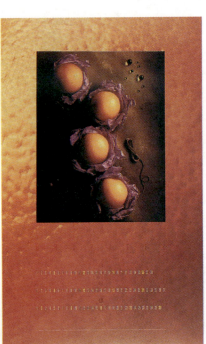

Fig. 9-9 ■ Asymmetrical or informally balanced layouts achieve a stability that is dynamic rather than static. (Center: © 1993 by Carol Orlock. Reprinted by arrangement with Carol Publishing Group. Right: courtesy Business First, Louisville, KY; designer: Stephen Sebree, Moonlight Graphic Works)

Formal balance has its place in layout work, but it is too stiff and uninteresting for many situations. In most layout work, balance is achieved informally. Elements of similar weight, but not necessarily precisely the same, are placed in relationship to one another so that there is weight at the bottom of the layout as well as the top, and to the left and right to balance the whole. Stability is achieved but the balance is dynamic rather than static.

Balance in layout is achieved through the control of size, tone, and position of the elements. It is more a question of developing a sense of balance by constant study and awareness than of following fixed rules devised by someone else.

However, there is a way to go about developing this sense of balance. The starting place, as we mentioned, is the optical center.

If we imagine the optical center as a fulcrum and place elements on the page so that this fulcrum is the orientation point, we will begin to see them fall into balanced positions. It is much like children achieving balance on a teeter-totter (or seesaw, if you prefer). If a child who weighs 80 pounds sits on one end of the teeter-totter and one weighing 40 pounds climbs on the other, what happens if they are the same distance from the fulcrum? The same thing happens with unbalanced layouts—they appear to topple over.

Fig. 9-10 ■ Imagine the optical center as a fulcrum. Place elements on the page so that this fulcrum is the orientation point, and they will tend to fall into balanced positions.

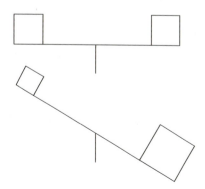

Fig. 9-11 ◼ In these layouts, formal or symmetrical balance is illustrated on the left and informal or asymmetrical on the right. A teeter-totter and fulcrum diagram illustrates the principle of balance.

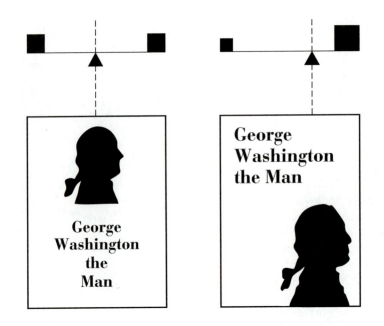

Applying this idea to layout work, if a single line of type is placed on a page it should be at the center of balance, the optical center, for best appearance. The same is true with a single copy block.

If two or more groups of design elements are placed on a page, they should be balanced visually with the optical center serving as a fulcrum.

THE PRINCIPLE OF HARMONY

➤ All the elements in the layout should work together if a communication is going to do its job. They cannot deliver the message to the target audience if they are fighting among themselves. This is as true in visual design as it is among humans.

Fig. 9-12 ◼ Two groups of equal size placed on a page in balance from the optical center (*left*) and one group half the size on the other placed twice the distance from the optical center for proper balance (*right*).

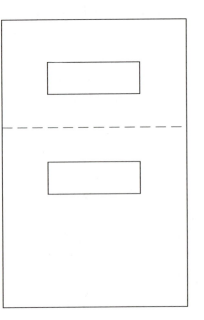
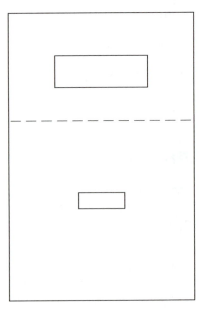

> ### RAISED AND DROPPED CAPS

After planning, if you think you want to mix typefaces, try following this guideline first: Use the bold and other versions of the same typeface for display lines when a single series of the regular face isn't enough.

Before making a decision to mix typefaces, follow this guideline: Use bold and other related versions of the same typeface for display when a single series of the same face isn't enough.

The initial letter is a useful design device. The top example illustrates a raised cap; a drop cap is shown below it. For a more complete discussion of initial letters and their use see Chapters 14, 15, and 18.

In general, layouts achieve harmony in three ways—through harmony of shapes, harmony of types, and harmony of tones. Shape harmony goes hand-in-hand with proportion. The shape of the elements—type and so on—should be the same as the shape of the printed area or the page, and the shape of art and copy should follow this pattern.

Type harmony means that the letter designs of the styles selected should cooperate and blend together and not set up visual discord. Type harmony can be achieved by staying with types of one family and selecting other series of that family for emphasis and contrast.

If different types are used to provide contrast, they should be radically different. Two families of the same race that have characteristics basically similar may not be different enough to provide contrast. They will clash, and destroy harmony. And they can just plain look bad together.

Two families from different races can provide harmony and contrast, but one should clearly dominate. If they are the same—or nearly the same—size, there's a chance that the effect will be jarring and destroy the harmony.

Avoid mixing lowercase and all-cap words. Capitals are formal and dignified and do not harmonize with the irregular shapes of lowercase letters. Stick to one or the other whenever possible.

If boldface type is selected for more than an occasional emphasis, other elements in the layout should be strong as well.

Borders should have shapes in common with the type letter style for type and border harmony. A Black Letter type looks best with a decorative border, and a modern Roman, with its thick and thin letter strokes, goes well with an Oxford rule, which has parallel thick and thin lines.

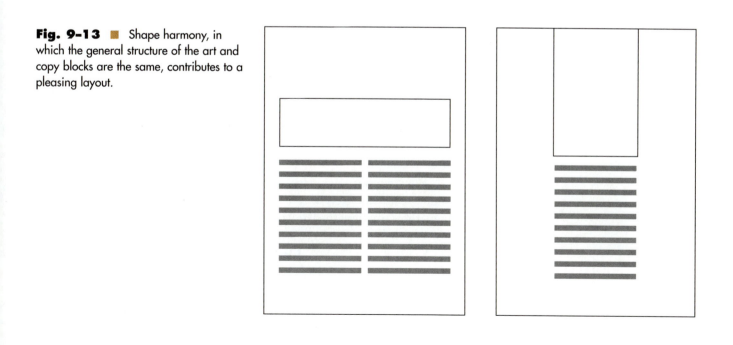

Fig. 9-13 ■ Shape harmony, in which the general structure of the art and copy blocks are the same, contributes to a pleasing layout.

Futura Light

Futura Demibold

Futura Bold

Fig. 9-14 ■ Elements in graphic design should harmonize. Light typefaces should be used with light art and borders, bold types with bold art.

Tone harmony refers to the weights and designs of elements. Bold illustrations and bold types harmonize. Ornamental borders and ornamental types go well together. A straight-line rule will harmonize with a straight-line Sans Serif type.

THE PRINCIPLE OF CONTRAST

➤ What a monotonous world this would be if everything was the same. The changing seasons, the mountains, lakes, and oceans of our earth, the various groups of people who make up the human race, all add interest and contrast to life. Sameness is boring in life, and it can be boring in printed communications as well.

Skilled speakers use voice modulation, pauses, and gestures to make their points and hold the audience's interest. Skilled communicators also use various devices to emphasize important elements in their printed material. In addition, they add variety and interest by applying the principle of contrast.

Contrast gives life, sparkle, and emphasis to a communication. Contrast shows the reader the important elements. And contrast helps readers remember those elements.

Contrast can be achieved by a number of typographic devices. The most obvious of these is the occasional use of italic or boldface types. However, these should be used sparingly, like seasoning in a stew. Too much contrast creates an indigestible typographical mess.

Other ways of achieving contrast include varying the widths of copy blocks, breaking up long copy with subheads, varying shapes of elements, balancing a strong display against a lighter-tone text mass, surprinting (printing type lines on top of halftones or other art), and enlarging one in a group of photos.

A good starting point in achieving contrast in layouts, and a good way to approach handling copy, is to break down the copy into "thought phrases." Thought grouping means taking the copy and positioning it on the page as it might be spoken. Headlines and lines of copy should be written in natural phrases that the reader can take in at a glance.

Suppose we are writing a title for an article and we come up with this wording:

The Miracle of Joe's Discovery

Now, suppose we want to run this head in two lines. How should we divide it? The easy way would be to divide it so both lines would be about the same length. We would end up with something like this:

The Miracle of Joe's Discovery

But that division makes an unnatural pause in the way the reader would decipher the head, since reading is accomplished by grasping the meaning of words in groups of coherent phrases or sentences. So a better way to set the head would be to divide the wording into natural thought groups, something like this:

The Miracle
of Joe's Discovery

This head can be taken in at a glance, and the uneven lines add interest and contrast to the arrangement. (Note: The arrangement of the type lines might be dictated by the "head schedule" used by the publication. We consider this in our discussions of magazine and newspaper layout.)

A little more complex example, but one that better illustrates the principle of contrast, is the way the following simple advertisement is handled. Suppose we have this copy to arrange:

Spend your summer vacation high in the Sierra at Wayside Inn

Let's set this in display type:

Spend Your Summer
Vacation High in
the Sierra at Wayside
Inn

What is wrong? The message is almost incoherent because the lines of type cause awkward and unnatural pauses when the copy is read. Let's use thought grouping to make this easy to read and comprehend. Is this better?

Spend Your
Summer Vacation
High in the Sierra
at Wayside Inn

The next step is to bring the principle of contrast into play. We can add emphasis where it belongs to create a more interesting and memorable message:

Spend your summer vacation
High in the Sierra
at

Wayside Inn

Contrast thus relieves monotony, adds emphasis where it belongs, makes layouts more interesting, and helps effective communication.

Fig. 9-15 ■ Contrast can be achieved and harmony maintained by varying the type sizes and styles but keeping the same family.

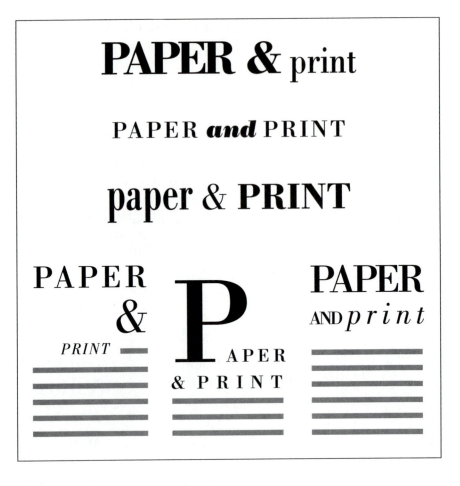

THE PRINCIPLE OF RHYTHM

➤ Layouts that communicate effectively are not static pieces that just lie there on the page. They are alive and they move. In writing, just as in music, life is added by imparting action, variety, and interest to the message. While music communicates with sound, printed communications use art and words to create a beat, or rhythm, by measuring and balancing the movement of vision.

Three ways to get layouts moving include the natural placement of elements, using repetitious typographic devices, and arranging material in logical progression. Let's consider each of these methods.

We can place elements to take advantage of the natural path the eye follows as it travels through a printed page. As mentioned, the eye hits a point slightly above and to the left of the mathematical center of an area. What happens next? The eye travels to the right, then to the lower left, and then across to the lower right in a sort of Z pattern.

If we arrange the elements on the page in a logical order along this Z path, we can take advantage of nature to keep our layout moving.

A beat can be established by repeating typographic devices. Initial letters, boldface lead-ins, numbers or small illustrations, indented paragraphs, italic subheads, all not only provide contrast but if placed in a logical order can help direct the reader through the message and thus give it rhythm and motion.

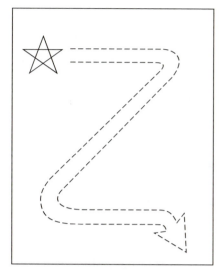

Fig. 9–16 ■ Studies have shown that when a person scans a printed page, the usual eye pattern follows a rough Z through the page. Initial contact is made in the upper left near the optical center, then the eyes move to the right and then diagonally down the page to the lower left and then to the lower right.

THE PRINCIPLE OF UNITY

➤ Unity holds a design together and prevents looseness and disorder. When we see a loose printed communication, our eyes can't find a center of interest and they bounce around with no place to land.

Simplicity is the key here. Unity and simplicity aid communication and eliminate distraction. Keeping it simple is simple. Here are a few ideas:

- Stick to a few type styles, preferably one family if possible.
- Keep the number of shapes and sizes of art and types to a minimum.
- Place art and heads where they won't interfere with the natural flow of reading matter.
- Have one element in an illustration or one illustration in a group of illustrations dominate. Create a center of interest.

Unity can be achieved in ways that are obvious and some that are not so obvious. Obvious ways include enclosing everything in a border, isolating the layout with white space, and using the same basic shape, tone, color, or mood throughout.

Using boxes in a layout can help unify it if they are all similar in thickness, design, and tone. Being consistent in the use of typography is one of the easiest and best ways to ensure unity.

Unity can be achieved by applying what some artists refer to as the *three-point layout method.* So much of life is organized around the unit of three. In the Christian religion there are the Father, Son, and Holy Spirit; in nature there are the earth, sea, and sky; in human needs there are food, shelter, and clothing. In the academic world, the liberal arts are grouped in units of three: natural sciences, social sciences, and humanities. In our governmental structure, we have federal, state, and local governments. And our flag combines red, white, and blue.

When we see three units together we tend to unify them. In layout, headline, art, and copy are the basic three units used to create one

Fig. 9–17 ■ Where should you look? Elements placed in the corners, or scattered, as on the left, create disunity as the eye bounces from one to the other. When elements are grouped together, a center of interest is developed and unity is achieved.

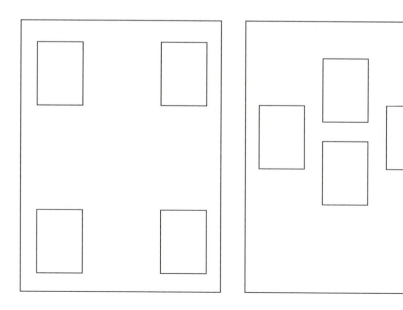

Fig. 9-18 ■ Unity can be achieved by applying the "rule of three." People tend to unify elements when they appear in groups of three.

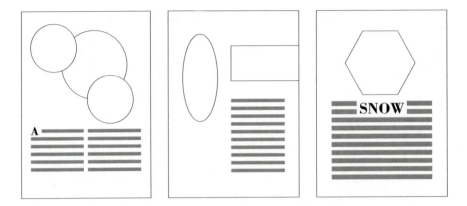

whole. The number of units of art, the number of headlines and subheads, or the number of copy blocks may likely vary within these three basic units. In deciding the number of units for layouts, keep in mind that odd-number units are more interesting than even-numbered ones. Three and five illustrations can make a layout more interesting than two or four.

Which principle of design is most important? This question is somewhat irrelevant. Proportion, balance, contrast, and rhythm must all blend together. However, if all the elements aren't combined in a unified and harmonious composition, attention value is scattered and interest declines. The completed layout must have unity and it must have balance. It must display pleasing proportions, an obvious directional pattern, and type and tone harmony.

Although principles of design can be helpful guides, the positioning of elements and the effective regulation of size, shape, and tone depend more on a sense of correctness and good taste than strict adherence to arbitrary rules. This sense is developed by experience and practice, which increase our awareness of balance, proportion, unity, contrast, rhythm, and harmony.

▶ EFFECTIVE DESIGN CHECKLIST

- Balance can be obtained through control of size, tone, and position of elements.
- Balance can be upset by nonharmonizing typefaces and too many nonessential elements in a layout.
- A unifying force should hold the layout together—white space, borders, and consistency in shape, size, and tone of elements can unify a layout.
- Equal margins are monotonous. There should be more margin outside a rule than inside, but the rule should not crowd the type within.
- Contrast adds interest. It can be achieved by varying widths of copy blocks, enlarging one in a group of pictures, or using italics or boldface, but sparingly.

Fig. 9-19 ■ This advertisement illustrates important principles of design. Note that a strong art element is located at the initial point of contact (upper left), the broken baseball bat acts as a pointer to guide the reader through the advertisement and give it motion. The repetition of oval art shapes add to the motion and guide the eye down to the logo. The tight arrangement of elements reinforces unity as does the use of the baseball bat and baseball. The broken baseball bat humorously reinforces the "assault" message in the headline. (Courtesy Star Tribune. Ad Agency: Fallon McElligott; Bob Brihn, art director; Mike Gibbs, copy writer)

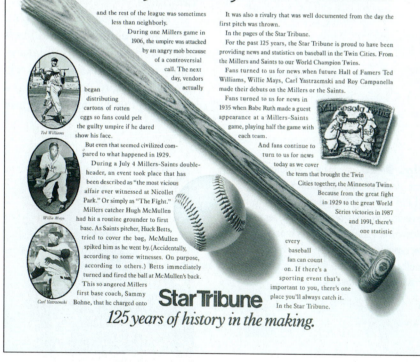

- Orderly repetition of some elements can give motion to a layout.
- Long horizontal or vertical elements will cause the reader to follow their direction.
- The space within a layout should be broken up into pleasing proportions.
- Simplicity is important for attractive layouts. It can be achieved by using very few type styles and reducing the number of shapes and sizes of art.

■ Use design clichés with caution. These include picture cutouts in odd shapes, tilting art or type, setting vertical lines of type, or using mortises, overlaps, or tint blocks.

MAKING THE LAYOUT ON SCREEN OR BOARD

➤ Now it is time to put the principles of design to work. Our tools could be the computer screen or the drawing board. The principles are the same even though the tools are different.

We might approach the construction of a layout by using a simple advertisement to illustrate the points involved. A communication can include a number of parts, in this case a headline, art, copy, and a logo.

The layout is one of three parts of the package the visual communicator might pass on to the producer, compositor, printer, or service bureau if he or she does not create a mechanical. (A mechanical, to repeat, is a layout complete in every way and ready for the printer's plate-making process.) If the mechanical is made elsewhere, the communicator includes the copy for typesetting and the art (photographs or drawings).

Usually, there are three steps in making a layout that is ready for printing: creation of thumbnails, then roughs, then the completed layout. Thumbnails are miniature sketches of ideas for possible arrangement of elements. Roughs are the size of the final layout with just enough detail to guide the person who is putting the parts together to make the mechanical (or comprehensive—called a *comp*).

Fig. 9-20 ■ The computer and imaging systems are taking over the work of the drawing board and T square in creating layouts ready for processing. However, many visual communicators recommend familiarity with the old methods as well as the new. (Richard Pasley, Stock Boston)

Fig. 9-21 ■ This is the dress illustration. (This problem is adapted from *Newspaper Advertising Handbook,* with thanks to the author, Don Watkins, and publisher, Dynamo, Inc. Illustration by Tracy Turner)

Let's go to work and create a rather uncomplicated layout. A good place to start is with advertising layout, as it often includes most of the basic elements—art, copy, head or title, and logo—that designers devise for a printed communication.

Here is the situation. The manager of The Dress Shop has asked a designer to plan a layout for an advertisement to appear in the local newspaper to help introduce the arrival of a new collection of dresses. The manager has the heading, the paragraph of sales copy, the price of the dress, a piece of art showing the merchandise, and the store's logo. The designer has these elements to work with:

If the dress fits, wear it.
Light-hearted summer dresses. With so many prints and styles
to choose from, it'll be easy to find one that fits you like a glove.
$25
(The Dress Shop logo)

The steps the designer uses in planning and making the ad layout are an effective guide for planning all types of printed communications, whether for print media or graphics for television.

Visualization

The first step in developing a layout requires some brainstorming. This is called *visualization.* The communicator's most important job is not done with a drawing pencil, it is done with the brain. The communicator must "see" in the mind's eye how a layout is going to appear. For example, the newspaper publisher wants the paper to look dignified, quiet, and authoritative. How do you perceive such a newspaper's front page in your mind's eye? What sort of headlines, type styles, and nameplate will transmit this image? What do the illustrations look like?

A company wants a brochure for its anniversary picnic. What should be its shape, size, and color? What sort of finished appearance should it have? Brainstorm possibilities and let them bounce around in your head. (Well, it's not quite this simple, as we will see in Chapter 12. Brainstorming in this case must include knowledge of such things as how the brochure will be distributed, but these examples do help illustrate the visualization step.)

Visualization gives direction. It gets us started. It takes an idea or concept and translates it into visual form. Try it and see if this is true. Suppose you have the job of designing an advertisement using this copy:

The surf is up at Waikiki. Take a winter break in the sun and
surf at the Breakers Hotel.

How do you visualize the ad? The possibilities are many: the sun, surf, and sand; palm trees swaying; the hotel and the beach; people surfing. What sort of art would be best, a photo or a drawing? What sort of typeface would say it best? What words would you want to stand out? How would you arouse the reader's interest, make the reader stop and want to know more?

That's visualization

Fig. 9-22 ■ Thumbnail sketches of possible arrangements for The Dress Shop advertisement. (Adapted from *Newspaper Advertising Handbook*)

Fig. 9-23 ■ Headlines on roughs can be indicated in this manner. Guidelines should be drawn to the exact size of the type specified in the comprehensive, but the rough lines only need to simulate the type.

Fig. 9-24 ■ A rough scribble of the approximate size and shape of the art is adequate for rough layouts.

The designer who has to make the layout for The Dress Shop advertisement will not be able to do a lot of creative visualization because the art and copy have already been determined. However, before the layout process begins, our designer friend will visualize several possible arrangements and type styles.

Thumbnails

The next step in producing a layout is to get something down on paper. Generally—once again—three steps are needed to move from the concept to the finished layout. They are the creation of thumbnails, roughs, and comprehensives.

Thumbnail sketches are miniature drawings in which the designer tries out different arrangements of the elements. The goal is to experiment and settle on the most effective placement of the headlines, art, and copy to achieve two goals: (1) make the most attractive arrangement possible by putting into practice the principles of effective design by applying the basics of good typography, type selection, and arrangement; (2) to construct a working blueprint that can be understood and followed by everyone engaged in the production of the communication.

We don't have to be artists to produce thumbnails, or even roughs for that matter. Headlines can be indicated by drawing guidelines to indicate the height of the types to be employed and then filling in between them with up and down strokes.

For easy work and best results, try using a soft pencil for making thumbnails and roughs. The best are either 2H or HB. If softer pencils are used, they are likely to smudge and need to be sharpened more often (pencils numbered 2B to 6B are very soft). Harder pencils are difficult to use, will punch holes in the paper, and the lines are light and difficult to erase. Pencils numbered 3H to 9H are hard. You can obtain 2H or HB pencils at most stationary sections of discount stores or at art supply houses, and they do not cost much.

Art in thumbnails and roughs can be indicated by an outline of the general shape of the illustration, shaded to match its tone.

GESTALT DESIGNING— TRYING TO SEE THE WHOLE PICTURE

Some designers find it helpful at the visualization stage of the game to bring to bear on a design problem Gestalt psychology. This is a theory of perception that features the idea that images are perceived as a pattern, as a whole rather than merely a group of distinct parts.

This theory was developed by a group of German psychologists in the early years of the twentieth century. The word *gestalt* means, in a general translation, configuration. One rather simple example of this complex theory might be the realization that the whole is greater than the sum of its parts.

In making a layout, for example, we should consider the impact and perception of the completed form as it will be interpreted by our target audience. This interpretation is affected by the many demographic and sociologic characteristics of the audience.

An excellent explanation of Gestalt can be found in *The Encyclopedia of Human Behavior* by Robert M. Goldenson (Garden City, New York: Doubleday & Company, 1970), pp. 505–509.

Fig. 9-25 ■ Lines can be sketched for roughs to indicate body matter. The size of the copy block and the width of the lines should be exact, however.

Body copy or copy blocks can be designated by squares, rectangles, or whatever shape the set type takes. Lines should be drawn in these areas to simulate the width of the type and the leading.

A very rough approximation of the size and shape of the elements is adequate when making thumbnails. Roughs need to be more exact.

Quite often we will need to make several thumbnails before we find an arrangement that we believe to be the best. An easy way to get started is to take a sheet of layout paper the size of the finished layout and fold it into quarters or eights. This will give four or eight areas for thumbnails in exact proportion in the finished layout.

As an example, the designer working on the Dress Shop advertisement might make thumbnails in areas 1 by 2 inches, or one-fourth the 4 by 8 size of the finished advertisement. Since this is such a small area in which to work, it is more likely that the designer will use a 2 by 4 or a full-size 4 by 8 area.

With a little practice most communicators can produce credible thumbnails. This is the first step in the creation of advertising layouts, and it is the first step in creating layouts for newspapers, magazines, brochures, and other printed communications.

After experimenting with the various possible arrangements, the layout artist selects the one that appears to be the most effective. A rough layout is then produced with the thumbnail serving as a guide.

Producing Rough Layouts

The rough layout is a drawing the actual size of the finished advertisement. All elements are presented fairly clearly and accurately as far as size, style, spacing, and placement are concerned. It is not quite as finished as the comprehensive, however.

Display type is lettered in and art is sketched in the same size and tone as in the final product; there is enough detail so that the art is a close approximation of its final form. Quite often a copy of the original art will be made and pasted in place on the rough.

Text copy, or reading matter, is still indicated by drawn copy blocks, but these are made precisely as the finished product will look, with lines drawn, or "comped," to indicate the type size and leading to be used. Sometimes "greeking" or simulated type is used for copy blocks in roughs.

There are a number of methods available for producing display lines and headlines for beginning layout work. People planning careers as graphic artists will, of course, want to develop lettering ability. One of the procedures used to develop this skill is useful for communicators who want to have some layout skill but who do not necessarily want to go beyond the rough stage in layout work. The technique is *comping style*.

Both reading matter and display type can be comped for rough layouts. The results will be accurate enough to give the precision of the finished product and realistic enough to show how it will appear.

Reading matter is comped by drawing lines to indicate the type size and the leading or space between lines. This is done in two ways.

An ordinary pencil can be used to draw two thin lines to indicate the tops and bottoms of the x heights of the lines of type.

Or a chisel-point pencil can be used to draw a solid line to represent the lines of type. This kind of pencil can be obtained at most art supply stores. If the point is too wide to represent the size of type desired, it can be shaved down with a single-edge razor blade. A double-edged blade should not be used since it isn't sturdy enough.

Pencils for comping body type should not be too soft. They will not hold the point long, and it will be easy to smear the comped lines. Layout artists recommend HB or 2H pencils.

The procedure for comping solid lines of reading matter includes these steps:

1. Tape the paper to be used on a flat surface (a drawing board is best). Use a T square to be sure the paper is lined up square with the edge of the surface so the T square can be used to draw straight lines.

2. Draw a light outline of the area the type will occupy (the copy block) with the T square and a triangle.

3. Select the type for the finished layout. Indicate the proper leading between lines. Now make small dots vertically in the area to be comped to indicate the base of the x height of the letters to fill the area.

4. Check to see that the pencil point is the same as the x height of the type selected.

5. Use the straight edge of the T square as a guide to draw the lines to represent the lines of type.

If the pairs-of-lines method is used, the same procedure is employed except that dots are placed to represent both the top and bottom of the x height of the letters.

After some practice with full lines, try comping with equal paragraph indentations and lines that are ragged right, ragged left, and centered.

Display type can be comped by tracing. The tools required are a complete alphabet of the size and style of type to be used, a drawing board, a T square, a piece of tracing paper, a ruler, and a hard pencil with a sharp point. The steps include:

1. Draw a light baseline for the type on the tracing paper.

2. Place the tracing paper over the alphabet at the point where the word should begin. Be sure to line the drawn baseline up with the baseline of the alphabet.

3. Trace the first letter in the head or display line in outline form.

4. Proceed to trace the rest of the letters in the line. Take care to space the letters properly and to line each up evenly on the baseline. Time spent in doing the job carefully will pay dividends in the end.

5. Fill in the outlines and erase the guidelines as much as possible.

Fig. 9-26 ■ The two-line method of indicating reading matter on layouts. The two lines indicate the x height of the type chosen.

Fig. 9-27 ■ The solid-line method of indicating reading matter for copy blocks on layouts. The solid line is the same height as the x height of the type selected and the same width as the text block. This can be done with a pencil, or, as in this example, on the computer.

Lorem ipsum dolor sit amet, consectetuer adipiscing elit, sed diam nonummy nibh euismod tincidunt ut laoreet dolore magna aliquam erat volutpat. Ut wisi enim ad min- im veniam, quis nostrud exerci tation ullamcorper suscipit lobortis nisl ut aliquip

Fig. 9-28 ■ Another way to indicate reading matter for copy blocks on electronic layouts is to use "dummy copy." In this case, a Latin text is used to fill in the text block, accurately showing type style and size.

The letters can be filled in with pencil, ink, or felt pen. After a little practice, you will be surprised at the realistic results that can be obtained even with Scripts and Cursives, Black Letter, and ornamental types. If color is needed, the letters can be filled in with colored pencils, felt pens, or ink.

The display lines can be cut out and pasted on the layout. Sometimes the display lines can be traced in outline form and the image transferred to the layout. This is accomplished by rubbing the back of the traced area with a soft pencil. Then the line is placed in position on the layout and the letters traced again. The pencil coating on the back of the tracing paper will act as a carbon to transfer the image to the layout. Again, the letter can be filled in with colored pencils, felt pens, or ink.

There are alphabets of display type that can be transferred to a layout by rubbing. The procedure is the same as when tracing. A baseline is drawn and the letters are lined up for even horizontal and correct vertical spacing. Instead of tracing letters, you transfer them from the master alphabet to the layout by rubbing them with a ballpoint or rounded-point instrument.

Alphabets are also available in printed sheets and in pads of individual letters. The letters can be assembled in display lines and pasted on the layout.

The Comprehensive

The final step in constructing the layout is the comprehensive. Often this is followed by creating a mechanical, which is a pasteup or camera-ready layout completed exactly as it will appear when printed. The comprehensive requires careful work, and many graphics students prepare comprehensives for use in their portfolios. In the comprehensive the illustrations and headlines or titles are shown exactly as they will appear in print. If there is extensive body matter it might be indicated by using "greeking" or simulated type.

When the comprehensive is completed it is mounted on illustration or prepared grid boards and covered with a protective flap, as described in Chapter 10.

In the case of our advertisement, proofs of the type and art are pasted into place to make an exact rendering of the advertisement as it will appear in print. This is called a mechanical. It then can be used for making the printing plate.

But if our comprehensive goes to someone else who will make the camera-ready mechanical, we have one more step to accomplish—the markup.

The Markup

In much communication work, particularly advertisements, brochures, and flyers, the working layout is a rough that includes instructions for the compositor or printer. This is called a *markup.* The markup, illustrations, and type copy are turned over to the printer. As we noted, comprehensives—a further step—also need to be marked up.

All instructions to the printer are written—often in a color to prevent confusion with what is to be set in type—and circled. One method

Fig. 9-29 ■ In the traditional method of making a layout a thumbnail is selected and used as a guide in making a full-size rough. Instructions for completing a comprehensive are added indicating things such as type styles, line widths, and spacing. When work is completed on a computer, the thumbnail (often with instructions added) is used as a guide in actually making the comprehensive.

of markup on a comprehensive is to cover it with a protective flap of tracing paper taped to the top of the illustration board or grid and to write instructions on this flap. Abbreviations are used whenever possible and a sort of code is developed based on basic printing terms.

Instructions on a marked-up rough or comprehensive might include:

■ The family, series, and size of all type faces.

■ The length of all the lines of type, plus the leading between lines.

■ The line setting, such as centered, flush left, or flush right.

■ Any special instructions for the particular job in question.

Below are the most frequently used terms for indicating instructions on roughs:

TIPS FOR ORDERING TYPSETTING

The following suggestions for ordering typeset matter can save money and help ensure that the finished product will be what you want.

■ Specify the typefaces for reading matter and headings and make certain that the printer has these faces and sizes. If this is not certain, the notation "or equivalent" should be included on the purchase order or instructions.

■ Specify the type size in points. If you are not certain exactly what size you want, do not hesitate to ask the compositor to recommend a size.

■ For reading matter, keep the line measure about 39 characters. Remember that one and a half times the length of the lowercase alphabet is considered an ideal measure.

■ Give the line measure (width) in picas, not in inches.

■ Specify any copy that is to run ragged. Otherwise the compositor will justify the lines.

■ Designate the leading desired (the space between the lines).

CAPS	Set in all capital letters
U & lc or clc	Set in capitals and lowercase letters
lc	Set in all lowercase
pt	Abbreviation for point size of type
BF	Set in boldface
8 on 10	(Also written as a fraction, 8/10.) The top number indicates the point size of the type and the lower number the leading between lines (in this case, 8-point type set on a 10-point base, or 8-point type leaded 2 points)
18	Set copy block 18 picas wide
8/10 × 18	Often the type size, leading, and line length are combined like this
] [	Center this line
[	Set flush left
]	Set flush right

The family names of types to be used are often abbreviated: Bod. for Bodoni, Bask. for Baskerville, Cent. for Century, and so on.

Copy blocks are indicated by letters circled on the rough and the same identifying letters are placed at the top of the page of the typed copy: Copy A, Copy B, and so on.

Illustrations can be keyed to the layout with numbers or letters and indicated as Photo 1, Photo 2, or Photo A, Photo B. Different practices may exist in different shops. Always check that the producer of the printing understands the instructions and how they are coded.

The techniques used to lay out effective printed advertisements can be used to advantage by anyone working with the printed word.

► EFFECTIVE DESIGN CHECKLIST

■ Use visualization. A designer's most important tool is still the brain.

■ Integrate the verbal (words) and visual (graphics) elements so they work together to do the job in the most effective way.

■ Feature the most important idea or selling point in the layout.

■ Check every element in a layout—each should be irreplaceable. If an element can be eliminated or replaced, it should be eliminated or replaced.

■ Determine the form and arrangement of the layout by the task it is intended to perform.

■ Graphic elements in a layout should facilitate quick and easy comprehension of the message, offer additional information, or set the mood desired.

Fig. 9-30 ■ The comprehensive layout for The Dress Shop advertisement. This comprehensive was made on a computer using the selected thumbnail as a guide.

■ Remember that if the layout doesn't get the attention of its intended audience, it will not be read.

■ Avoid using Scripts, Black Letter, and decorative types for headlines. If they are used it should be for a special reason, the line should be very brief, and it should not be in all capitals.

MAKING LAYOUTS ON THE COMPUTER

➤ Designers who are working with computers and other electronic publishing equipment recommend that you follow six steps when creating a visual communication. The first two steps are the same as the ones we discussed in planning a layout using traditional tools. The others involve the use of the computer.

The steps are:

1. Create thumbnails in the traditional way.

2. Create a full-size rough in the traditional way.

3. Translate the dimensions, type specifications and art, plus whatever elements you use, such as rules and dingbats, to a page layout on the computer.

4. Print the layout you've created and make any refinements such as editing, changing type sizes, shifting art, or whatever seems to make for a more effective layout.

5. Make a final print.

6. Be sure to save your creation.

Designers who create layouts on the computer have developed a vocabulary of their own. Many of the terms used have the traditional definition, others are new to the world of design and printing. Most likely the terms that have evolved with the advance of electronic design will become more common and there will be more of them. Some of the traditional terms will fade into history.

Here are some of the more common new terms you will be encountering on your trip through the world of desktop publishing:

■ *Anchoring:* placing an imported graphic in a spot on a certain page. In this way it will move with the text if more text is added before or after it.

■ *Default:* automatic setting of the desktop publishing program, if you do not instruct the computer to make changes. Example: the preset space between words in the word processing program.

■ *Downrule:* the vertical line that separates columns.

■ *Drop cap:* a large initial letter cut into a paragraph of type within an article. (It doesn't have to be a cap—see examples elsewhere in this book, especially the chapters on magazine and newsletter design.)

■ *Footer:* information at the bottom of each page such as page number, date of issue, name of publication (traditionally called the folio line).

■ *Header:* same as footer but at the top of the page.

■ *Initial:* a large letter that is raised above the baseline or cut into and extending below the first line of an article.

■ *Landscape orientation:* type or layout printed across the 11-inch direction of an 8½ by 11 inch sheet of paper turned sideways.

■ *Portrait orientation:* type or layout printed on the 8½-inch dimension of an 8½ by 11 inch page.

■ *Raised cap:* a large initial letter that starts at the baseline of the type being used in text matter and extends above the letters. (But see comment with the definition for a dropped cap.)

▶ GRAPHICS IN ACTION

1. Find in advertisements, art, headlines, magazine pages, or other printed material one example of each principle of design. Mount them neatly as exhibits and write captions explaining how the exhibit illustrates the principle. Type the captions and paste them on the exhibit adjacent to the illustrations.

2. Study the design of the front page of a newspaper. List the ways you believe the principles of design have been applied (for example, an italic headline may have been used for contrast). Evaluate the page from a design standpoint and point out any changes you might make if you were redesigning the page.

(*Note:* The two exercises that follow can be done either the traditional way or on a computer.)

3. Define an area 6 by 9 inches on plain white paper (or to be printed on plain white paper) or on layout paper. Next use this space to make a layout that by itself will identify you and your main interest to someone else. Use your name or nickname (try to keep it to about five or six letters). Be creative. Select a type style that might enhance your layout and art or other graphics to tell the story. (*Example:* One student in the author's class was tall and thin and was an end on the football team. He made a tall, slim football player and lettered "Bill" in large condensed type on the jersey. He found the football player in clip art and resized it on his computer.)

4. Define an area 5 by 7 inches on plain white (or to be printed on plain white paper) or on layout paper and arrange the following information in the area. The information will be part of a cover for a booklet. Sketch the words or reproduce them with whatever tools are available to you. Remember to apply the principles of design. Use whatever illustrations or graphic devices you wish. The copy is:

A Self-Guiding Tour of ___ (choose a city: Paris, New York, Moscow, Tokyo, your hometown), Walking Tours Publishing Company, Your Town, Your State

(*Hint:* The first step should involve visualization and thought grouping).

CHAPTER 10

PREPARING FOR PRODUCTION

CONTENTS

© Churchill & Klehr

10 In previous chapters, we have discussed some new trends in the graphic arts. They have brought about many new ways of doing things, and as a result we all are using a variety of methods to prepare for production. Let us review several ways of moving a message from an idea to a target audience:

■ The whole process can be accomplished on the computer.

■ Traditional pasteup methods can also be used. That is, art, type, and rules are brought together on a grid and pasted up.

■ Or, we can employ a combination of methods, using both the computer and pasteup.

In smaller shops one person might perform the whole production process. In larger shops, such as the production departments of large-circulation magazines and newspapers, several designers and technicians might perform essential functions, with the visual communicator coordinating the efforts of each of these people. Regardless of your situation it might be valuable to understand the basic process as it is practiced in all three variations listed above.

First, let's consider what happens when your job is to work with typeset copy and graphics obtained in the traditional way. There are a number of steps to follow in preparing copy for production. Many of them have been discussed so far, but several still remain. For example, here is a statement with a headline:

> Graphic Arts Defined For The Communicator*
> Graphic arts is defined by Webster as "the fine and applied arts of representation, decoration, and writing or printing on flat surfaces together with the techniques and crafts associated with them." For the communicator, graphic arts might be defined as the process of combining all the typographic and artistic materials and devices available in a way that facilitates communication.
>   Graphic arts is not the technique of arranging type, illustrations, borders, and other devices to create an unusual visual experience. Rather, the selection and arrangement of materials should be to achieve the transfer of messages from a source to a receiver.

It is to be printed in a newsletter for communicators. What must be done to transfer the copy to typeset copy ready to be printed?

Some of the preproduction tasks that must be performed include determining the style and size of type for the headline and the amount of space the piece will occupy in the publication. After it is set in type it will have to be proofread for errors.

These steps, along with cropping and sizing art and marking the layout to ensure that the specifications are clearly understood by all who will be working on the job, are part of preparation for production.

---

*While standard English usage calls for lowercasing articles, coordinate conjunctions, and prepositions, regardless of length, unless they are the first words in the heading, many newspapers capitalize the first letters of all words in headlines. We will follow this pattern in this chapter.

Some people working in communications do the entire process themselves. In other situations designers and technicians do much of the work. But all who work in the world of printed communications will find a knowledge of the steps in preparing for production worthwhile.

COPY-FITTING WITHOUT FITS

> Old-timers in the industry could squint at a piece of typewritten copy and tell within a fraction of an inch how much space it would occupy when set in a certain size of type. They called it "casting off" type. We call it *copy-fitting*.

Copy-fitting is a pesky business until you get used to it. However, proficiency can come quickly with a little practice. There are some things to remember from the start. For one thing, copy-fitting is an estimation. There is no exact method of fitting copy. The formulas have to be leavened with judgment.

One problem with copy-fitting is that every letter of every font of type, along with the spaces and punctuation marks, has a slightly different width. If they were all the same, copy-fitting would be simple. But since this is not the case, we have to use some judgment and make allowances in estimating how much space to designate for copy in layouts.

There are five situations in which copy-fitting might be used in planning printed communications. They include:

1. Estimating how much space a headline or title will take when set in a specific size and style of type.

2. Estimating how much space typed copy will occupy when set in a certain size and style of type on a predetermined width.

3. Finding out what size of type to use if the typed copy must fit a predetermined area in a layout.

4. Finding out how much copy to write to fill a certain space when the size and style of type have been selected.

5. Finding out how much space copy that has already been set in type or printed will occupy when reset in another size.

All of these calculations can be made easily with an understanding of only two copy-fitting methods. One is the unit-count system for display type, and the other is the character-count system for reading matter.

Copy-Fitting Display Type

The *unit-count system,* which is used to determine the size of display lines, headlines, and titles for articles, is based on the assignment of units for the letters, numerals, punctuation, and space in a head or title line. The units are assigned on the basis of the letters' relative widths.

Of the twenty-six letters in the lowercase alphabet, eighteen are virtually the same width. These eighteen are assigned a unit value of 1.

All of the other letters and punctuation marks are assigned unit values in relation to these eighteen. For instance, *m* is about one and a half times wider than *x,* so while *x* has a unit value of 1, *m* has a unit value of 1½. The lowercase *i* and *l* are about one-half the widths of *x*, so their value is ½.

Below is a typical unit-count system for display type:

1 unit	All lowercase letters (except *f, l, i, t, m, w,* and number *1*), all spaces, larger punctuation such as ?, ¢ , $, %
½ unit	Lowercase *f, l. i, j, t;* capital letter *I,* spaces between words; most punctuation
1½ units	Lowercase *m, w;* all capital letters except *M, W, I*
2 units	Capital *M* and *W*

In solving a copy-fitting problem for display type, the first step is to determine how many units of the size and style of type will fit into the width selected and then see if the lines of the title or headline fit that limit. We can find this by taking a sample of the type and measuring the units that fit into the width.

For example, the headline noted earlier in this chapter was:

Graphic Arts Defined
For The Communicator

Let's say we want to set it in 16-point Optima Bold type on a line 15 picas wide. Will it fit?

We first have to determine how many units of the type selected will fit into a 15-pica width. We can do this by taking a sample of the type and counting the units in a 15-pica line.

←————— 15 picas —————→

This is 16-point Optima Bold

Here is how the units will count out:

This is 16-point Optima B

1½ 1 ½ 1½ ½1½ 1 1½ ½ 1 1 ½ 1 ½ ½ 1½ 1 ½ ½ 1½ 1 ½ 1½ = 22

Now we know that the maximum number of units of this type that will fit into a 15-pica width is 22. So we check the lines we want to use to make sure each does not exceed 22 units. If we count the units according to our system, we will discover that the top line contains 18½ units and the bottom line counts 20½ units. Both are under the maximum, so the head should fit nicely.

←————— 15 picas —————→

Graphic Arts Defined
For The Communicator

That's all there is to the unit-count system. Communicators who work with type in planning brochures, newspapers, company magazines, and other publications soon discover that if they count everything as 1 unit and then make allowances if there are many wide or narrow letters in a line, they can estimate the proper fit quickly and easily.

Those who work on newspapers or magazines that use the same typefaces in each issue for headings, titles, and headlines can make up sample sheets of frequently used head forms and determine the maximum counts for each line. The maximum (and minimums) can then be noted on these style sheets, or *head schedules,* as they are called. (Head schedules are discussed in detail in Chapter 16 on newspaper design.)

Copy-Fitting Reading Matter

Several methods of copy-fitting are used in planning the reading matter for printed communications. Two of these methods are not very reliable so we look at them just briefly. It is assumed that the copy to be set will be justified. Designer Edmund C. Arnold points out that type set ragged right (unjustified) takes up at least 3 percent more space than justified type. So if copy-fitting estimates are being made on type set unjustified, the estimate should be increased by at least 3 percent and even at that it will not be a tight estimate.

The copy-fitting method often used in publication work is the *word count system.* This involves counting the number of words in the manuscript and then determining how much space that many words will occupy when set in a certain type on a specified width.

One easy method of doing this is to obtain a sample of the type style set in the specified width and calculate the average number of words per line. Then you multiply this average number of words per line by the number of lines of type in a column-inch (1 column wide by 1 inch deep), which gives the average number of words in a column-inch. Finally, you divide this number into the number of words in the typed copy. The result is the number of column-inches the copy will occupy when set in type.

Another method, but one that is seldom used, is the *square-inch method.* The area to be filled with type is determined, and its square-inch capacity is calculated. Then the average number of words in a square inch is multiplied by the number of square inches designated in the layout. This method is used in determining the number of words needed for booklets or other multiple-page productions.

The most accurate method of copy-fitting, however, is the *character-count method.* It is universally accepted and used in communications work. It is based on determining the number of characters in the copy and then the number of typeset characters needed when the copy is set in type.

There are several ways of counting the characters in the copy. One is to find the average number of characters in a line and multiply this number by the number of lines. Some word processors and computers make a character count when you write copy. Others will keep a running word count.

CHECK THE SPELLING CHECKER

The spellchecker is a marvelous thing. Just type your copy and run it through the spell check. Even a poor speller produces spelling bee quality work.

Wait just a minute. Don't put all your trust in the spellchecker. Words that are spelled correctly but still completely gum up a sentence can slip by the spellchecker.

Here are some examples collected from a daily newspaper. Can you spot the wrong words that slipped by because they are spelled correctly?

He said he would to it again if hot caught.

The car can over she curb and mit the fence.

The President kill meat the Senate today

It is mime do to at as I please.

(*Note:* The author wrote this copy using WordPerfect. When the copy was checked with the spell checker, the total number of words in the copy was indicated.)

Next, the number of characters in a line of type in the designated width is determined. Suppose we wish to set our sample copy in 10-point type, with 2 points of space between each line (10/12 or 10 point leaded 2 points) on lines that are 15 picas wide. We must determine how many characters will fit into each line.

(*Note:* In large publications the number of lines to fill a certain area in a column are predetermined and matched with the word processors or computers being used. The reporter or writer is asked to produce a certain number of lines.)

Manufacturers of fonts usually supply this information in the form of a certain number of characters per pica. In addition, you can obtain charts to help in the calculation. Here are some examples of typical types and their characters per pica:

Bookman, 10 point	2.60 characters per pica
Bernhard Modern, 10 point	2.99 characters per pica
Palatino, 10 point	2.70 characters per pica
Futura, 12 point	2.50 characters per pica

For our illustration, let's assume that we have selected Palatino. In 10 point, this type has 2.7 characters per pica. If we decide to set copy in lines 15 picas wide and multiply this width by the number of characters per pica (15 × 2.7), we will find the number of characters per line will be 40.5.

Now, if we divide this number of characters per line into the number of characters in the copy (665), we will discover the number of lines of type (665 ÷ 40.5 = 16.419, or 16.42). We will have 16.42 or 17 lines of set type. Since we have determined that we will have 2 points of space between lines, each line will occupy 12 points (10 plus 2) or 1 pica. The copy when set will occupy an area 15 picas wide by 17 picas deep.

Here is how it worked out when the copy was set in Palatino according to our instructions:

Graphic arts is defined by Webster as "the fine and applied arts of representation, decoration, and writing or printing on flat surfaces together with the techniques and crafts associated with them." For the communicator, graphic arts might be defined as the process of combining all the typographic and artistic materials and devices available in a way that facilitates communication.

Graphic arts is not the technique of arranging type, illustrations, borders, and other devices to create an unusual visual experience. Rather, the selection and arrangement of materials should be to achieve the transfer of messages from a source to a receiver.

In summary, then, to find out how many lines typed copy will make when set in type we proceed as follows:

1. Determine the size and style of type.

2. Determine the width of typeset lines desired.

3. Calculate the number of characters in the typed manuscript.

4. From tables, or working averages, find out how many characters of the specified type will fit in 1 pica and multiply that by the width of the lines in picas.

5. Divide the number of characters in the typed manuscript by the number of characters in one line of type. (*Note:* 6-point type will have twelve lines per inch; 8-point, nine lines; 9-point, eight lines; 10-point, seven lines and a little over; 12-point, six lines, assuming that all these are set solid.)

6. Multiply the number of lines of type by the point size of the type with the space between lines added to find the total depth of the area in points. To convert to picas divide by 12.

HOT TYPE, COLD TYPE, RUBBER TYPE

➤ First there was hot type, type made by casting molten metal. Then there was cold type, type made by making an impression on paper (for example, a typewriter or a computer's laser printer is a cold type generator). Now, there is rubber type. This means that type created on a computer can be made bigger, smaller, fatter, skinnier, bulging, slanting, mashed together, or spread apart.

When it comes to copy-fitting, there is a temptation to use type as if it is made of rubber. If a line is too long, you can squeeze the type together so it will fit. If the line is too short, you can spread things out.

Sometimes this method of copyfitting on the computer is used: If there is more copy than can fit in the space you have allotted for it in your layout, you can either expand the layout or edit the copy, deleting words and sentences until it fits. Or you can change the font or size of type and reflow the copy. This procedure can be repeated until everything fits.

A better solution, sometimes, might be to adjust the size of a title or headline composed on a computer: simply scale it a point or two up or down to fit, so as to improve the page's appearance.

Here are some other common copy-fitting situations you may encounter:

1. What size type should I use to fit the copy into a given area? *Solution:* Scan type specimens and decide on a size that seems to be about right. Calculate the number of lines in this size that you believe will fit into the space. Next, find the number of characters of this type that will fit into a line of the specified width. Multiply your estimated number of lines by the number of characters in each line.

If the total is less than the number of characters in the copy, try a smaller size. If, on the other hand, the total is more than the number of characters in the copy, a larger size will be needed. If one size is too small but the next size is too large, select the smaller size and have it leaded out by adding space between lines as needed.

2. How many words will I have to write to fit into a specified space when I have selected a style and size of type? *Solution:* This crops up most frequently in writing cutlines or short takes of copy for advertisements or brochures, or short takes for boxed type, and so on. First, determine how many characters of the type will fit into the width that has been selected. Next, calculate the number of lines of the type that will be required for the given depth.

Then, set the word processor or typewriter line stops to a length of line that contains the number of characters needed for the typeset lines. Write the required number of lines. These lines will run very nearly line for line with the lines when the copy is set in type.

3. I want to use some copy that has already been set into type. But I want to use it in a different size and width of type. How do I calculate the changeover? *Solution:* First, find the average number of characters in each typeset line of the original. If you know the type style, this can be determined from charts if they are available. If tables are not available, several lines of the original can be counted to determine the average character count per line.

Once the average number of characters per line in the original has been determined, multiply that number by the number of lines in the original to find the total number of characters. Next, calculate the number of characters per line in the new setting. Divide this by the number of characters in the original. The result should give the number of lines in the new setting.

Example: We would like to reprint an item that was originally printed in 6-point Bodoni, 12 picas wide. There are 5 lines in this original. We would like to reprint it in 10-point Bernhard Modern on lines 14 picas wide. How much space must be allowed for this new setting in a layout?

First we must determine that the 6-point Bodoni has an average of 47 characters per 12-pica line. There are 5 lines, so there are 235 characters in the item. Next, we find that there are 2.99 characters of 10-point Bernhard Modern per pica from our charts, or 41.86 characters per 14-pica line. If we divide 41.86 into 235 we will find that the new setting will take 5.6, which is to say, 6 lines.

Copy-fitting may appear forbidding, but with a little practice the communicator can master this vital tool for planning printed communications. And accurate copy-fitting will mean dollars saved when the compositor doesn't have to reset copy that was estimated inaccurately.

PREPARING COPY FOR THE PRESS

Use Standard Editing Marks

If hard copy is produced (copy printed on paper as opposed to computer storage of material), it should be typed on standard 8½ by 11 white paper and typed double-spaced. Copy should never be sent to the printer on little slips of paper or small note sheets. This is inviting problems. All copy should be edited carefully to make sure there are not mistakes.

The standard editing marks generally used in marking copy are shown in Fig. 10–1.

Fig. 10–1 ■ Standard editing marks for correcting copy before it is set into type. These marks differ from proofreading marks.

Correction Desired	Symbol
1. Change form:	
3 to three	③
three to 3	three
St. to Street	St.
Street to St.	Street
2. Change capital to small letter	
3. Change small letter to capital	d
4. Put space between words	the time
5. Remove the space	news paper
6. To delete a letter and close up	judgement
7. To delete several letters or words	shall always be
8. To delete several letters and close up	supererintendent
9. Delete one letter and substitute another	Receive
10. Insert words or several letters	of time
11. Transpose letters or words, if adjacent	receive
12. To insert punctuation (insert mark in proper place)	

comma	⌄	parentheses	{ or }
period	x or ⊙	opening quote	
question	?	closing quote	
semicolon	;	dash	1/m or 1/n
colon	or ⊙	apostrophe	
exclamation	!	hyphen	=

13. To start a new paragraph	¶ or ⌐ It has been
14. To center material	⌐ Announcing ⌐
15. Indent material one side	Categories
	a. the first
	b. the second
16. Indent material both sides	one two three four
	five six seven
17. Set in bold face type	The art of
18. Set in italics	The art of

Catching the Errors

After the compositor sets the type, or if it is set with computer equipment, the communicator will be supplied with *proofs* (also called *galleys*). These are usually made on a copying machine or laser printer if the type was set "cold type." In the unlikely event that the type was set with a "hot type" machine, galley proofs will be provided. (The term is a holdover from the days when virtually all type was set from metal and placed in a tray, or galley, from which sheets were pulled for proofing.)

Most proofs, however, are supplied on reproduction paper. This is a high-quality white paper. Such proofs should be marked with a non-reproducing blue liquid or fine felt pen, unless other arrangements have been made with the production department.

There are standard proof marks to be used in marking proofs. They are similar to editing marks, but some are slightly different.

Measure Twice, Cut Once

The old carpenter rule that says measure twice, cut once can apply to visual communications. The interpretation for us is that you cannot be too vigilant in seeking out and correcting errors before they appear in the final product. An error in print is with you forever.

The time spent checking, reading, and checking again before the image is printed is time well spent, and it can save money as well. Here are some ideas concerning proofreading:

- Adopt a stylebook for your output, even for a small newsletter. Use it as a guide and follow your style faithfully.

- Proofreading has two parts: one to seek typographical errors, and another to check the proof with the original to see that it conforms in every way.

- Two people can make the job easier and more efficient. One is a "reader" who reads the original, while the other person checks the proof.

- Quite often in a public relations firm, advertising agency, or publishing house where more than one person reads proof each proofreader uses a different color pencil.

- Read proofs with a pen or colored pencil, never a lead pencil. Furthermore, never make erasures on proofs.

- In book work, corrections are indicated by making a mark on the spot where the mistake occurs and the correction beside the line in the nearest margin (see Fig. 10–3).

- In newspaper, newsletter, and other publication work the error is indicated by a line drawn from the error to the margin, with the correction mark made in the margin.

- Graphics need special care in proofing. Charts and graphs should be checked for mathematical accuracy as well as for typographical errors.

- The person or persons who read proof should initial the copy when they have finished.

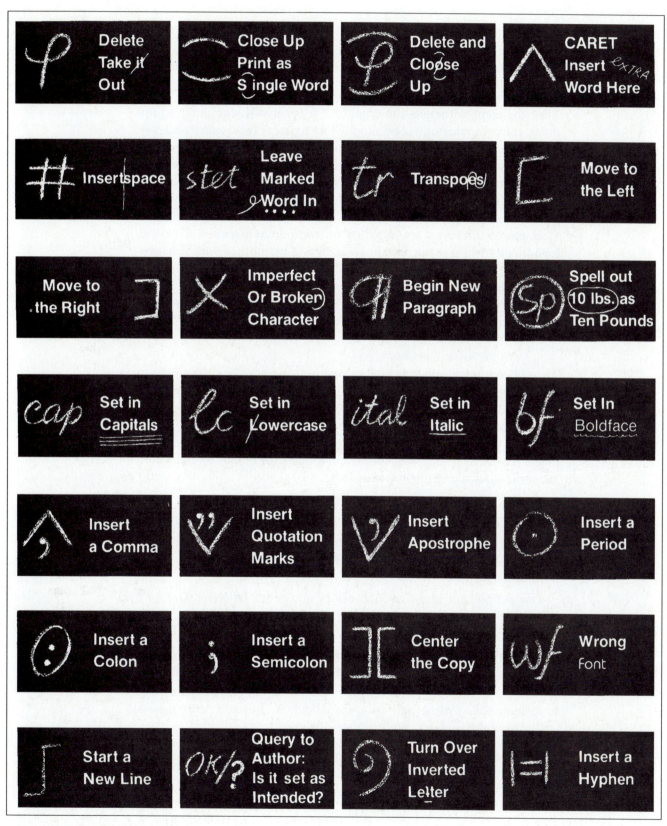

Fig. 10-2 ■ Standard proofreading marks. Note some differences between editing marks and proofreading marks.

Catching the Errors

After the compositor sets the type, or if it is set with computer equip-ment, the comunicator will be supplied with *proofs* (also called *galleys*). These are usually made on a copying machine or laser printer if the type was set "cold type." In the unlikely event that the type was set with a "hot type machine, galley proofs will be provided. (The term is a holdover from the days when virtually all type was set from metal and placed in tray, or galley, from which sheets were pulled for proofing.) Most proofs, however, are supplied on reproduction paper. This is a high-quality white paper. Such proofs should be marked with a nonre-producing blue liquid or fine felt pen, unless other arrangements have been made with the production department.

There are standard proof marks to be used in making proofs. They are similar to editing marks, but some are slightly different.

Measure Twice, Cut Once

The old carpenter rule that says measure twice, cut once can apply to visual communications. The interpretation for us that you cannot be too vigilant in seeking out and correcting errors before they appear in the final product. An erort in print is with you forever.

The time spent checking, reading, and checking again before the image is printed is time well spent, and it can save money as well. Here are some ideas concerning proofreading:

- Adopt a stylebook for your output, even for a small newsletter. Use it as a guide and follow your style faithfully.

- proofreading has two parts: one to seek typographical errors, and another to check the proof with the original to see that it conforms in every way.

- Two people can make the job easier and more efficient. One is a "reader" who reads the original, while the other person checks the proof.

- Quite often in a public relations firm advertising agency or publish-ing house where more than one person reads proof each proofread-er uses a different color pencil

- Read proofs with a pen or colored pencil, never a lead pencil. Furthermore, never make erasures on proofs.

Fig. 10-3 ■ A typeset galley that has been proofread and marked for correction.

WORKING WITH THE PRODUCTION DEPARTMENT

➤ The people who do the actual production work for the designer or editor can provide valuable suggestions, often gleaned from long experience, which can make the communication more effective.

Whenever we work with production department personnel or commercial printers, we should agree on certain conditions and specifications for our communication. Here are the principal accepted "trade customs" of printers in the United States:

1. *Quotation:* A price quotation not accepted within sixty days is subject to review. All prices given by a printer are based on material costs at the time of the quotation.

2. *Orders:* Regularly placed orders, verbal or written, cannot be cancelled except on terms that will compensate the printer against loss incurred as a result.

3. *Experimental work:* Experimental or preliminary work performed at the customer's request will be charged at current rates and may not be used until the printer has been reimbursed in full for the amount of the charges billed.

4. *Creative work:* Creative work, such as sketches, copy, dummies, and all preparatory work developed and furnished by the printer, shall remain the printer's exclusive property and no use of the such work shall be made, nor any ideas obtained from it, except upon compensation to be determined by the printer. This compensation would be in addition to the original agreed upon price.

5. *Condition of copy:* If copy delivered to the printer is different from that which was originally described by the customer and on which a quote was made, the original quotation may not apply and the printer has a right to give a new quote.

6. *Materials:* Working mechanical art, type, negatives, positives, flats, plates, and other items when supplied by the printer remain the printer's exclusive property unless otherwise agreed in writing.

7. *Alterations:* Work done on changes from the original copy will be quoted at current rates and an accounting will be given to the customer.

8. *Prepress proofs:* The customer should insist on proofs before a job is printed, and the printer should insist that the customer mark the proof with an "O.K." or "O.K. with corrections" and signed. The printer cannot be held responsible for errors in proofs if proofs were marked O.K. Changes should not be made verbally.

9. *Overruns and underruns:* Overruns or underruns not to exceed 10 percent on quantities ordered, or the percentage agreed upon, shall constitute acceptable delivery. (Note: If you need exactly 10,000 copies be sure the printer knows this. Under this custom he could deliver as few as 9,000 copies on a 10,000 order and still be technically correct as far as filling the order is concerned. But he should bill you for 9,000 copies.)

Whether we set type in house or order it set by a compositor, it is important to write out all instructions and be sure the instructions are perfectly clear. Typesetting costs will be reduced and better quality will result.

It is an old axiom in the printing trade that the compositor follows copy, mistakes and all, "even if it flies out the window."

Before ordering typesetting:

- Read the copy and correct errors in spelling, punctuation, capitalization, and grammar.
- Check for paragraph and list item numbering, if any, as well as indentation, page numbering, and general format.
- Copy should be double spaced, on one side of a sheet, and paginated in sequence.
- Long tables and other matter that is to be set in a special way should be typed on separate pages.

10. *Terms:* Payment shall be whatever is set forth in the quotation or invoice unless you have made previous arrangement with the printer. Claims for defects, damages, or shortages must be made by the customer in writing within fifteen days of delivery.

Both the printer and the customer should understand all conditions concerning the printing and delivery of orders. Most commercial printers will supply their customers with a copy of these accepted trade practices. It is very important that these practices are understood and that the copy and instructions you give to the printer are perfectly clear to all involved. This can't be emphasized enough.

When contacting a printer for the first time it is a good idea to look over samples of work produced in the shop to see the type and quality of printing it has done for its customers.

In addition to understanding the customs of the trade, it will save time and money as well as help you get a satisfactory job if you make sure you have answered the following questions and communicate the information to the production department or printer.

1. When is the job needed? The more lead time the printer has, the more care can be taken in production.

2. What sort of paper is best suited for the job? How durable should it be? If the cheapest paper available is specified, how will this affect the quality of the job?

3. What about color—for the paper and/or the printing?

4. Are the photos or illustrations of satisfactory quality to reproduce well? If there are shortcomings, the printer should point them out so the communicator will know what to expect when the finished job is seen.

5. Are the specifications and instructions on the layout, copy, overlay (mask), and illustrations clearly understood by both the communicator and the printer?

The more details we can give the printer about the job, the better the chance that our expectations will be fulfilled. Printers are skilled craftspeople—or they should be—and they can provide many helpful suggestions if they know just what we want done.

Instructions for compositors and printers must be clear, concise, and legible. There are some universally accepted abbreviations for marking copy. However, there can be variations from place to place, and it is important that both the communicator and the printer agree on those being used. Instructions generally are of three types: (1) for cropping and sizing art, (2) for marking layouts, and (3) for marking reading matter. Art instructions are considered in Chapter 6.

Instructions for layouts and reading matter should include:

- Type size in points. However, for very large display type, inches and centimeters are used in some shops.
- The type family by name, such as Caslon, Stymie, Times Roman.

- The family series, which could be condensed, light, medium, bold, extra bold, light italic, and so on.

- The posture of the letters, whether all capitals, all lowercase, capitals and lowercase, small capitals, swash letters, or other special characters.

- The width of the lines in picas.

- The leading between lines.

- The justification—whether the lines are to be set flush left, centered, flush right, or justified. Usually, the justification is obvious by the comp lines on the layout.

In addition, it might be necessary to indicate if parts of the copy are to be set indented, in italics, boldface, or in some other special way.

This list may seem formidable, but it can be mastered quickly. There are a number of shortcuts for marking copy and they can be understood with a little practice. For instance,

8/10 Caslon Bd. Itl clc × 15

or

8/10 Caslon Bd. itl U&lc × 15

(either U&lc or clc mean capital and lower case)

means "Set this in 8-point Caslon bold italic capitals and lowercase letters with 2 points of leading in a line 15 picas wide."

The designation 8/10 comes to us from the days of linotype composition when the term "8 on 10" meant to cast 8-point type on a 10-point slug. This was the equivalent of putting 2 points of leading between the lines.

When a brochure, advertisement, or general printing layout is made, most of the instructions are written on the layout sheet outside the actual layout. Any instructions written within the layout should be circled to indicate that they are not to be set in type. All instructions should be clear and accurate. After all, the specifications are like those an architect would put on a blueprint. The builder is expected to follow them precisely. The printer is expected to follow the layout's specifications precisely.

A DESKTOP DESIGNER'S TOOL KIT

In addition to the hardware and software of a desktop publishing system, other tools can prove helpful. Certain reference books may prove to be time and error savers if kept within reach of your computer. Especially helpful are a word divider that just lists words with their proper divisions but with no definitions for speedy reference, a spelling dictionary, a stylebook, and an almanac.

A number of rulers are available; several include a number of functions. Especially helpful would be a collection of rulers. Multi-function rulers can be found that include several of these features on one ruler.

SELECTING A SERVICE BUREAU

Some visual communicators have encountered this problem: They have taken a document to a local service bureau for high-quality output. The service bureau calls and reports it can't print their file.

Check your sevice bureau first. Here are some questions to ask:

- Are your systems compatible for the projects you want to do?
- What are the features of their hardware and software?
- What sort of help can they give you for the type of work you want to produce?

It can be helpful to do all this before you complete your project. This is especially true when you are up against a deadline.

The rulers should provide you with:

- Inches, fractions and decimals of inches, picas, points, and metric divisions, if possible. (As international trade barriers go down, we may see a revival of the metric system in this country.)
- Screen percentage table. It is especially helpful if the ruler shows screening in type or illustration, not just in screened blocks.
- Line spacing scales, solid rule scales from about 4 to 72 points, and type sizes from 4 to 72 points.
- Conversion tables including picas to inches and points to inches.

Other rulers or charts can be obtained to show keyboard command shortcuts.

In previous chapters several tools of the trade have been mentioned that will prove helpful for either desktop or traditional design. Let's take a look at the tools needed for the traditional method of creating layouts for platemaking. This could also prove helpful for those working with the computer. As an art director with twenty years in the production of award-winning design work wrote in *Electronic Publishing,*

> To become truly "publishing friendly," (computer) hardware and software throughout the publishing industry will have to become more standardized. And, schools will have to provide desktop publishing students with enough training so that they are better prepared to step right into positions requiring the use of desktop publishing systems.
>
> In the meantime, keep those X-acto blades and rubber cement jars handy.[1]

X-ACTO BLADES AND RUBBER CEMENT

Some basic tools and materials are needed to complete design projects if you are using the so-called traditional methods or your computer has "crashed" and you need to meet a deadline.

- *Paper:* Two kinds of paper will prove useful for drawing thumbnails, roughs, and comprehensives. One is *transparent tracing* and the other is *layout paper.* Layout paper is white and not as transparent as tracing paper but it still can be used for tracing. Both can be obtained in pad form in sizes from 8½ by 11 to 19 by 24. Paper weights of 16 or 24 pound work well for layouts.
- *Rulers:* Two types of rulers will come in handy. One is a 12- or 18-inch etched steel and the other is a *pica rule* or *graphic arts rule* with both inch and pica scales.
- *T square and triangle:* A good 24-inch T square and an 8- or 12-inch triangle are musts. A T square with a plastic edge should never be used for cutting. Obtain a T square with a steel arm for cutting. A plastic triangle should also not be used for cutting. It could become nicked and useless for drawing straight lines. (It is a good idea to have a steel T square, triangle, and straightedge for making cuts with a knife or razor blade.)

- *Pencils and pens:* The most useful pencils for layout work are 2H or HB. Felt pens come in handy too.
- *Erasers:* Magic Rub pencil and art gum work well.
- *Masking tape and rubber cement:* Both will come in handy for tacking down art on grid or layout paper and for many other uses. Rubber cement thinner is needed to thin our rubber cement when it thickens in the jar. It also can be used to loosen something that has been pasted down with rubber cement.
- *Scissors and art knives:* A good pair of scissors and an X-acto knife or single-edge razor knife will take care of the cutting needs for starting in layout work.

Only a few additional items are needed to add pasteup capability to the tools required for layout. These include:

- *Nonreproducing blue pencils and pens*
- *A waxer:* An inexpensive hand-held model works fine.
- *A burnisher:* Burnishers are either in roller or stick form. If much pasteup work is done, the roller is most satisfactory.
- *White correction fluid or graphic white paint:* These fill in shadow areas or cover blemishes in the pasteup.
- *Preruled grids* or plain white bristol, about 4 ply.

STEPS IN BASIC PASTEUP

➤ Once the layout has been completed and all the images to be used are assembled, the next step is to paste them into position as shown in the layout. Then this pasted-together form is photographed for

Fig. 10-4 ■ Traditional tools of the trade. This graphic designer is working with some of the traditional tools of the trade. A wide selection of pencils and pens is always helpful. Rubber snakes are, of course, optional. (© Churchill & Klerh)

Fig. 10-5 ■ Scaling Art in Four Easy Steps.

Scaling Art

Steps in scaling art using the diagonal line method:

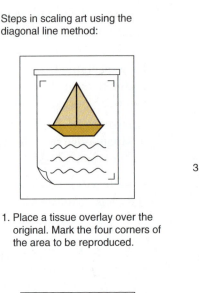

1. Place a tissue overlay over the original. Mark the four corners of the area to be reproduced.

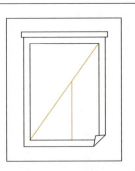

3. Mark the desired width on the bottom line of the original area. Example: If you want to reduce the original to 5 inches from 8 inches, measure across the width from left to right to 5 inches. Then draw a perpendicular line from this new width to extend through the diagonal.

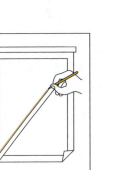

2. Connect the corner marks on the overlay to make an outline of the original image area, and then draw a diagonal from one corner to and beyond the opposite corner.

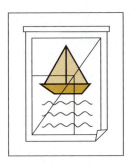

4. Mark the final size of the width and new depth (where the vertical and diagonal lines intersect) on the overlay and retape it over the original. Show the cropping and final size as well.

plate making. The process is called *pasteup*. It can be accomplished by following ten steps:

1. Prepare the grid or base sheet.

2. Double check all elements for errors and compare them with the layout to make certain they are all available.

3. Apply wax to the backs of the type and art forms.

4. Trim the excess paper from the type and art forms.

5. Position the elements on the grid or base sheet.

6. Check all elements to be sure they are square.

7. Burnish the form to affix the elements to the grid.

8. If halftone negatives are to be stripped in by the printer, affix a window (usually red plastic) the exact size of the halftone.

9. Add borders and rules, usually in tape form.

Fig. 10-6 ■ The pasteup process. Guidelines are drawn with a nonreproducing blue pen or pencil. Then the elements are affixed in position, usually by using a waxer to coat their backs so they will stick to the grid. The body type in the illustration is an example of greeking (simulated type that makes no sense). (Adapted from Graphic Products Corporation, Rolling Meadows, Illinois 60008)

Fig. 10-7 ■ (a) In pasteup the elements are placed into position on grids with preprinted guidelines in nonreproducing blue. (b) The completed pasteup is photographed and a printing plate is produced. The grid lines will not show in the final printed product.

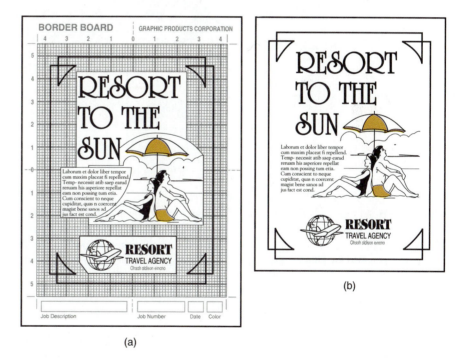

10. Make a copy on a copying machine and proof the copy. Then add an overlay to protect the pasteup.

In step 1 a piece of illustration board or a preruled grid (in nonreproducing blue, which will not show up in printing) is fastened to a drawing board or flat, perfectly smooth surface. It is critical that everything be square and true. The grid should be lined up on the surface with a T square and then held in place with small pieces of tape in the corners.

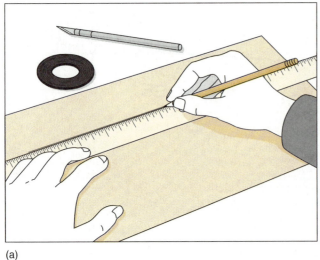

(a)

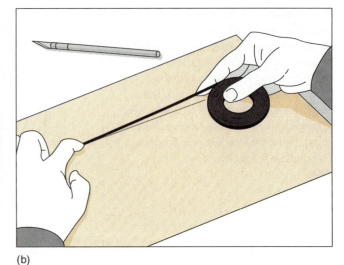

(b)

(c)

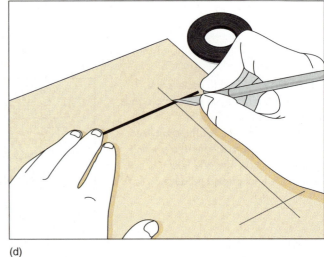

(d)

Fig. 10-8 ■ To apply border tape: (a) Draw a faint pencil line, nonreproducing blue guidelines, or use a guideline on the pasteup grid for aligning the border tape on the layout. (b) Press the end of the tape into position and unroll enough tape to go just beyond the length required. (c) Carefully lower the tape into position along the guideline and gently smooth it into place. (d) Trim the tape to the desired length and firmly burnish it into place.

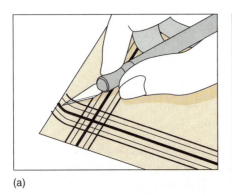

(a)

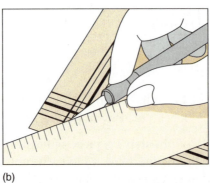

(b)

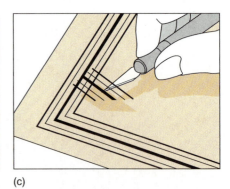

(c)

Fig. 10-9 ■ To create attractive mitred corners on a pasteup: (a) Place the border tape in position but overlap the ends of the tape beyond the corner of the box. (b) Lay a straight edge on the overlapped area and cut carefully on the diagonal. (c) Remove the excess material and press the border into position.

Fig. 10-10 ■ Borders can be customized and their widths narrowed if desired. (a) First cut the border to the desired width. Next, slide an art knife under the border and remove the excess. (b) Finish the border by adding rules to create different effects and press it into position.

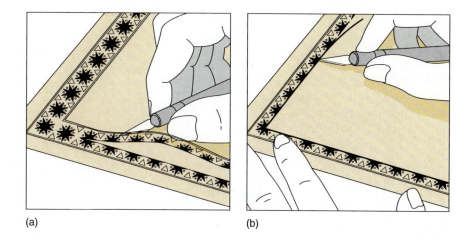

(a)   (b)

Next, the nonreproducing blue lines on the grid are used to position the heads, art, body copy, and other elements. Nonreproducing blue pencils or pens can be used to mark the spots where the elements are to be placed. If art is to be bled (printed to the edge of the page) it should extend about ¼ inch beyond the outside dimensions of the page margins for trimming after printing.

Rubber cement or melted wax is applied to the backs of the assembled images. They should be trimmed as closely as possible to the print area but care should be taken not to cut into any images. It may prove more satisfactory to wax after trimming, depending on the size of the elements.

The various elements with adhesive applied are placed in position on the grid. Great care is taken to make sure everything is straight and square. A T square is used to line elements horizontally, and a right-angle triangle with one edge placed on the edge of the arm of the T square is used to line them up vertically.

When adjacent columns of reading matter are lined up or when lines are added to a column of reading matter, a Haber rule is a handy tool. A *Haber rule* is a plastic rule marked with type sizes and various leadings so that, for instance, two lines of 8-point type leaded 2 points can be lined up evenly. The point of an art knife is handy for moving small elements on the grid for alignment.

If a halftone negative is to be stripped in later, the exact area is drawn on the grid with a nonreproducing blue pen and the area is coded (such as "photo A"). The photograph is similarly identified and sized to fit the area exactly.

Once all the elements are in place, the entire pasteup is burnished to ensure that everything is firmly in place. There are several types of burnishers, but the rubber or ceramic roller is the most frequently used. A sheet of clean white paper is placed on the images for burnishing to help keep the pasteup clean and prevent smearing during the burnishing process.

If the pasteup is to be produced in more than one color, the additional color areas are placed on an *acetate overlay sheet.* The entire pasteup is often protected with a cover sheet, or *frisket,* taped as a flap over the completed grid.

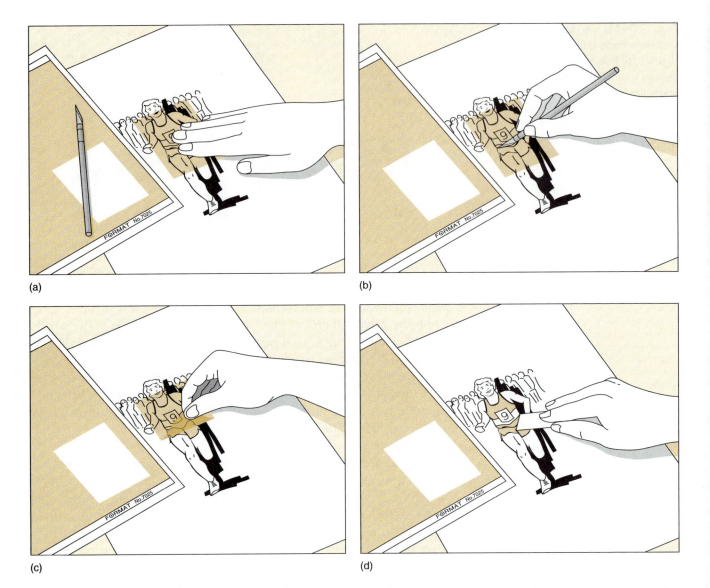

(a)

(b)

(c)

(d)

Fig. 10-11 ■ To apply shading film to art: (a) Cut and remove enough shading film from a backing sheet to cover an area slightly larger than the drawing. Smooth out any air bubbles. (b) Cut lightly around the outline of the area to be shaded on the artwork. (c) Remove all excess shading film. (d) Burnish the film until it appears as if it were actually printed on the artwork.

▶ **EFFECTIVE PASTEUP CHECKLIST**

■ Border tapes used with care can add a pleasing element to your pasteup (see Fig. 10–8).

■ Mitre border corners for neater, more professional-looking pasteups (see Fig. 10–9).

■ Use creativity and customize borders (see Fig. 10–10).

■ Shade art for a more realistic effect. Use shading films for shading or for color overlays (see Fig. 10-11).

■ Masking film can be used to create *overlays* for color printing.

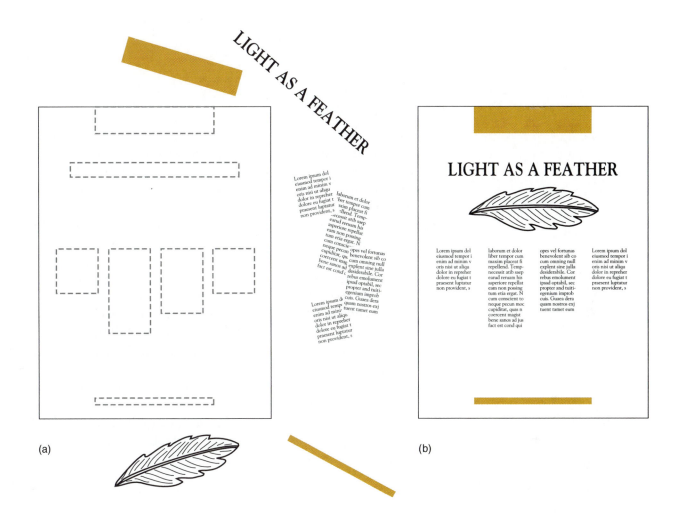

Fig. 10-12 ■ (a) The individual pieces of art and copy and their positions on the grid or pasteup board (often a lightweight white bristol cardboard). (b) The completed pasteup. A protective flap of lightweight paper or tracing paper can be taped to the back and folded over the face of the pasteup.

Follow these steps:

1. Cut a piece of masking film (red or amber is used most frequently) large enough to cover the area to be printed in color and tape it firmly at the top of the layout.

2. Cut around the outline of the area to be printed in color.

3. Peel off the taped large piece of masking film. The outline form remaining can be affixed to a clear polyester overlay ready for the camera.

4. Care must be taken to place the red masking film cutout over the original layout to obtain a perfect register.

▶ **GRAPHICS IN ACTION**

1. Take the front page of a daily newspaper. Measure the width of the columns in picas. Determine the maximum unit counts of the headline types used on the page for various column widths. Then rewrite this headline for a newsletter so it has proper thought grouping for a column width of 18 picas:

```
Auxiliary gift shops, and
gift cards
provide yet another way to
care for patient needs
```

2. Use the copy that defined graphic arts at the start of this chapter. Assume you want to set it in 10-point Palatino (2.70 characters per pica) leaded 2 points, in a column 12 picas wide. How deep would the space be when the copy is set in this space in this size and style of type?

3. Assume you want to print the copy used to demonstrate copy-fitting in this chapter (Graphic Arts Defined For the Communicator) as an envelope stuffer for your business. Your business is: Your Name and Address Graphic Designers. You want 5,000 flyers, 6 by 9. Go through the steps for making an image that can be used by a printer. Use either a computer or the traditional methods. Make a list of all the information you would want to discuss with the printer.

4. Take your project created in No. 3 to a printer and obtain an estimate of the cost of printing this job. Discuss with the printer the trade customs and other information you would need to determine in having your project printed.

5. Practice using the tools you have for creating visuals. Use either your computer or the traditional methods. Try making shadow boxes and other special effects.

NOTES

[1]"A computer and DTP software don't necessarily add up to savings," *Electronic Publishing,* January 28, 1994, p. 15.

CHAPTER 11

DESIGNING PRINTED COMMUNICATIONS

© Churchill & Klehr

Fig. 11-1 ■ The purpose of design is to communicate. Whether "new age," traditional, or something in between, printed communications should exhibit the attributes of good design principles—*and* be legible and readable. (Courtesy U&lc)

11 "Chaos can be fun," said Stephen Doyle, whose design firm determined the appearance of *Spy,* a satirical New York magazine that some considered startling and others called outrageous.[1]

Some observers of the world of visual communication believe the 90s will be remembered as the age of chaos. The clean-lined designs of the Modern era of the 1950s and 1960s have evolved into a "new age" of self-expression in which anything goes. Some say the cutting edge of design today is characterized by careless mixing of type sizes and styles, using type horizontally and upside down, throwing in art in all sorts of colors and all shapes and sizes, piling letters on top of each other, and just having fun with the tools of design.

Not everyone agrees with this "new age" approach to design. The graphic design magazine *U&lc* calls this new design trend "pluralism." Many communicators wonder if the essential function of graphic design is getting lost in the melee.

As we consider visual communication in the next chapters as it applies to everything from envelopes to magazines, keep in mind that the purpose of design is to communicate. The best design does just that. It might be "new age" or more traditional or a mixture of both, depending on the purpose and the audience to whom it is aimed.

Every time an image is impressed on a piece of paper, the ultimate effect is communication. No matter whether the production is an elaborate magazine, a metropolitan newspaper, or a letterhead, the same care should be taken to ensure that it is doing all it can to perform this function to the fullest.

Every printed communication should exhibit the attributes of good design principles—and be legible and readable. It is now time to put to work the principles of layout and design, the use of type and illustrations, and the role of paper and ink as well as the various methods of production in creating printed communications.

In this chapter we consider some of the various types of printed communications all of us working in the profession will encounter at some time during our careers. Then, in succeeding chapters we examine the design of advertising, magazines, newspapers, and newsletters. By developing a basic understanding of the graphics of communication we can go from there to the area of industry in which we might wish to specialize.

First we consider brochures since they are so closely related to newspapers, magazines, and newsletters. Then we examine stationery, programs, and books and pamphlets.

DESIGNING THE BROCHURE

➤ They are called brochures, folders, flyers. Regardless, the basic approach to their design is the same. A folder can be thought of as a finished brochure that is folded, and a flyer as a single-sheet handbill. We will refer to them as brochures to prevent confusion.

Note: Spy magazine didn't last. The publisher folded it in February, 1994, after 78 issues were published.

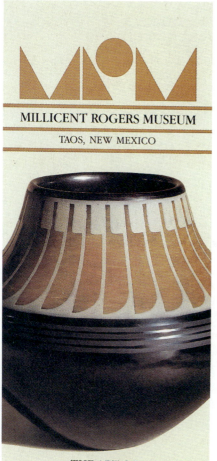

MILLICENT ROGERS MUSEUM

TAOS, NEW MEXICO

THE ART OF
NORTHERN NEW MEXICO

Fig. 11–2 ■ A rather simple design, but look how many good decisions were made to create an effective brochure cover page. Note the bold, attention-getting art, the museum logo made with triangles and a circle to create MRM, the use of colors that say "Northern New Mexico." (Courtesy Millicent Rogers Museum, Taos, New Mexico)

Let's say we are to design a brochure that will be part of an organization's communications mix. The brochure will serve as an informational piece, or an introduction to prospective members. Where should we begin? How do we move from inception to the completed project?

Planning

While adjustments must be made to fit the particular situation at hand, there are some steps that can serve as a guide in handling any brochure or folder design execution from start to finish. *Planning* is the first step. The more details that can be worked out in the early stages of the project, the more effective and cost-efficient the end product will be. Planning should include (1) forming a statement of purpose, (2) determining the audience and its characteristics, (3) making a checklist of the essential information to be included, (4) listing the benefits to the audience of the information, and (5) making a timetable for execution and distribution.

The planning could be organized around the "three Fs" of communication—function, form, and format. Consider the brochure's *function*. What is its purpose? What are some possibilities? Usually these purposes will fall into one of three or four alternatives. It might announce a workshop or program of some sort. It might be used mainly to provide information. (In this case, we need to determine if the brochure is an end in itself or a supplement to other communications such as an advertising campaign or a lecture series.)

Perhaps the brochure is to serve several functions. It might be a mail-out announcement and at the same time a bulletin board notice. It might be part of a series of brochures that the audience will be encouraged to keep in a binder for future use or reference.

The distribution method and the life expectancy of the brochure should play a part in design planning. Will the brochure be mailed, distributed in an information rack, or handed out at a meeting? Will it be used just to announce an event, or will it have more permanent use?

It will also, of course, be necessary to consider budget factors. How much money can be spent on the production? Money can be a limiting factor on the size, number of illustrations, use of color, quality of paper, and so on.

As this preliminary visualization of the situation progresses, a form may begin to evolve since form follows function. What should the physical size be? What shape should the brochure have? There are a number of possibilities. It could be simply a flat sheet; it could be folded in any number of arrangements.

Now might be a good time to start considering a rough dummy. Try this. Settle on a size and take a blank piece of paper and see what can be done with it. For example, suppose we decide our brochure will be printed on an 8½ by 11 standard typewriter-size sheet of paper. We have determined that the brochure will have a multi-informational purpose and that it should be easy to mail, place on information racks, and pass out at meetings.

What can we do with this piece of paper to make the most effective brochure?

Fig. 11–3 ■ A number of good design decisions are illustrated by this brochure. Note the achievement of unity through design and color and how the color and an icon are used to emphasize important points. A key design decision was to place the order form in an outside column. When the form is detached, the brochure and its message remain intact. (Courtesy American Psychological Association)

There are a number of alternatives. The first is to make the brochure a flat sheet, printed on both sides. This could be punched to be kept in a ring binder. Or it could be designed as a combination flyer and bulletin board notice. One side would be designed as a poster and the other could contain general information, or be left blank, or have an address box for mailing.

Other possibilities might include folding the sheet of paper in certain ways. But before we can explore those possibilities, we should become acquainted with paper finishing and folding operations.

Folding

If we are going to produce a brochure or pamphlet that requires folding, that operation should be a part of the planning. Michael Blum, a printing instructor, wrote in *In-Plant Printer* that "approximately 35 to 40 percent of the labor cost of the average printing job is in finishing."[2]

Modern equipment is capable of producing many different types of folds. But all folds are basically either parallel or right angle. *Parallel folds* are used for letters where two folds are required to fit the letter into the envelope. This same fold, when the sheet is held horizontally, becomes a six-page standard—also called *regular*—fold.

An *accordion fold* is another parallel fold. It, too, is popular for brochures and envelope stuffers. The most basic parallel fold is a simple fold to make a four-page brochure. The two-fold accordion made from an 8½ by 11 sheet is popular for brochures as it creates a handy size that mails easily in a number 9 or 10 commercial envelope. It also has good design possibilities. Accordion folds can be made with additional folds to create eight, ten, or more pages.

A popular fold for invitations and greeting cards is the *French fold*. This is an example of a right-angle fold, which is made with two or more folds at right angles to each other. The French fold is also used to create an eight-page publication that can be saddle stitched if desired and trimmed off at the head, or top, of the folded sheet.

Folding machines can handle signatures of many pages to create booklets and publications of twelve, sixteen, twenty, twenty-four, or

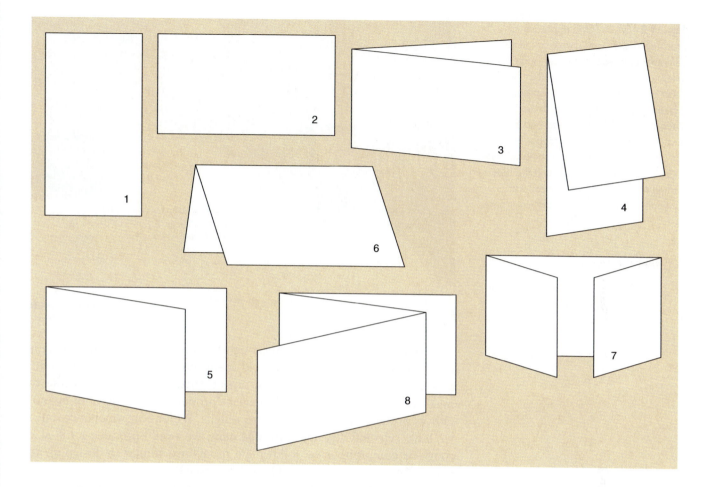

Fig. 11-4 ■ The possibilities presented by various types of folds should be considered in brochure planning. Here are some alternatives: 1, vertical parallel fold; 2, horizontal; 3, book fold; 4, short fold vertical; 5, short fold horizontal; 6, tent fold; 7, gate fold; 8, z or concertina fold.

more pages. Some machines are equipped with pasting attachments to produce paste-bind booklets (booklets with the pages pasted rather than stapled).

There are many other options for folding depending on the equipment available. These options should be considered when brochures and other printed communications are planned. Thus it can be quite worthwhile to discuss all possible options with the printer or binder operator. Sometimes the capability to make certain folds can spark ideas for a new and unique way to design the brochure.

Now take the blank sheet of paper and experiment with the fold possibilities for your particular brochure. How many alternatives can you devise considering all the factors that went into the planning so far? Keep in mind that you would want to preserve the basic dimensions of the format you have in mind for your brochure in selecting folding alternatives.

Planning the Format

Once a size is determined, the format can be planned. This should include (1) the size and form of the margins, (2) the placement of heads and copy blocks, (3) the use of borders, illustrations, and other typographic devices, (4) the selection of type styles—and the overall determinations of how the principles of design will be applied.

Fig. 11-5 ■ One approach to brochure design is to create an attention-getting headline for the cover page and follow up with contents related to the headline. Here the two-page spread explains the headline. The subhead elaborates on the main head and the art and copy complete the message. Note the use of the yellow moon, the same art style on both cover and spread, and the blue barline to create unity, balance, and continuity. (Courtesy State Farm Insurance)

Now we can begin making rough layouts on paper. A good idea is to take several sheets of paper, fold them into the final brochure form, and sketch roughs of possible arrangements. Some designers like to make thumbnails in smaller but exact proportions to the final layout. Others prefer to work with full-size roughs. Whichever we choose, once we have selected a general arrangement, we would produce a full-size rough or comprehensive, following a procedure similar to designing an advertisement. Then we would mark the rough and submit it plus typed copy and illustrations to a printer. Or we might have the type set and then do the pasteups for comprehensives or completed mechanicals. These would be photographed and the negatives used to make plates for printing.

Two Ways to Design Effective Brochures

Although the design for the brochure may evolve out of the preliminary planning, if we find it difficult getting started, there are other ways to approach the overall design. One might be called the "headline method," and the other the "attention to action" approach.

In the *headline method* we devise a brochure outline around the headlines to be used. First is the feature head, or the title for the brochure. This head stresses the most compelling reason for the target audience to read the brochure. It should set the theme for the brochure by answering the question, Why should I bother to read this brochure?

This feature head can become the title line for the brochure, and it can be amplified by *main support heads*. These can number two or three to six or more, and they become the heads for the copy blocks in the brochure. Often each copy block and head cover one topic or point to be made.

If the copy block under the main support head is long and involved, it can be broken down by "reinforce heads" or subheads, each

Fig. 11-6 ■ This award-winning brochure that doubles as a bulletin board poster was designed by Amy Harten Graphics, Champaign, Illinois, for the University of Illinois at Champaign-Urbana.

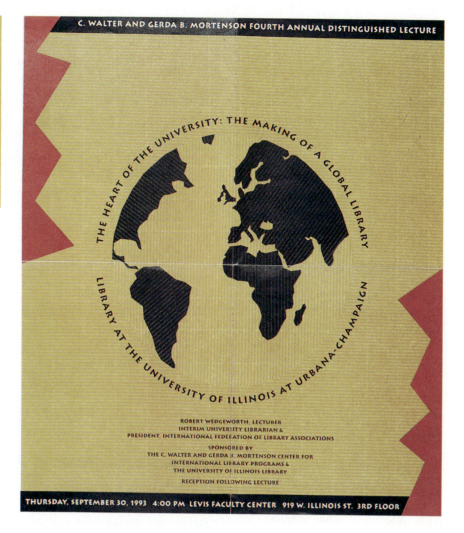

with a brief copy block. This approach can be used as an outline for writing the brochure copy as well.

The *A-I-D-C-A (attention, interest, desire, conviction, action) formula* some advertising copywriters use, as explained in Chapter 12, can be a handy guide in planning brochures. The parts of the formula that are relevant to the situation can be used to check the copy and to plan the layout. This method also helps to organize the material in an orderly and forceful manner.

➤ EFFECTIVE DESIGN CHECKLIST FOR BROCHURES

- Work with the pages as the units readers will see. For example, if the brochure is four pages, the two inside pages should be designed together. If the brochure has two parallel folds, to make six pages, the three inside pages should be considered as a unit.

- In designing facing pages, cross the gutter with the same care as if designing magazine spreads.

▶ **A MINI COURSE IN DIVISION**

Quite often when designing brochures we want to create a format of three pages on each side of a sheet of paper. This requires dividing the sides into thirds when making a grid or template for the layouts.

Here's a quick way to divide an area into thirds.

Just multiply its width in inches by 2 and the result will be the width of one-third of the page in picas.

Say you have an 8½ by 11 sheet of paper and you are planning accordion or parallel folds to create a six-page folder with each page 8½ inches by one-third of the width. Multiply 11 by 2 and the result in picas will be 22. Each one-third segment of the sheet will be 22 picas wide by 8½ inches deep.

Some other examples:

- An 8½ inch width times 2 equals 17 picas wide for each third.

- A sheet 14 inches wide will have three 28-pica segments.

- A sheet 9 inches wide will have three 18-pica segments.

- Apply all the basic design principles—balance, proportion, unity, contrast, harmony, rhythm—when laying out a brochure.

- Define the margins for the pages first and work within them when making layouts. Use ample margins and avoid a jammed-up look.

- Stress simplicity and careful organization in layouts.

- If the rough layout is to be examined and approved by another person before production and the roughs are on thin paper, cut the spreads apart. Paste them on heavier backing for a more impressive presentation. A protective flap or cover taped at the top will help, too.

- Check to see if all possible readers' questions are answered.

- If a mail-in coupon or registration form is included in the design, place it where it can be detached easily and where it will not destroy pertinent information such as a program listing when it is removed.

- Use big, bold display when the brochure is to double as a bulletin board announcement.

- Have the purpose and content dictate the design: The announcement of an event calls for stronger display than an informational brochure does.

- Don't try to achieve too much in one brochure. Designers often need to limit the quantity of information to be included in a single brochure.

CHOOSING THE RIGHT PAPER

▶ Choosing the right paper for a brochure or any other printed communication requires making two basic decisions. One is *selecting the proper finish and weight*. The other is *planning the size* of the printed piece to obtain the most paper for the least amount of money.

Once the format of a job has been determined, the next step is to select the best paper. This should be done after deciding the mood of the message, the type styles, and the kinds of art being used. All will play a part in determining which papers will work best.

In addition to antique finishes, machine finishes, bonds, and coated papers, there are papers of bold colors, pastel colors, iridescent colors. Nearly every color imaginable is available to call attention, set a mood, or add distinction. There are even "duplex" papers with a different color on each side.

The printing process and mailing costs will play a part in the paper choice. Offset and bond papers are closely related and are finished to take the water involved in offset printing and writing with ink. Screen printing can be accomplished on almost any kind of paper or other material.

In selecting papers, their reflectance or brightness and opacity should be considered. The more light the paper reflects, the brighter it will appear. This is its *reflective* quality. A glossy paper will appear bright, will show the contrasts in art to their maximum, and will bring out the tones. These papers will print colors vividly. However, glossy papers can be tiring to the eye if used for large amounts of reading matter.

Fig. 11-7 ■ In preparing a mechanical for a brochure, the "lay," or arrangement of pages on the grid, should be such as to ensure proper order for printing. Usually, several pages are printed on one sheet which is folded and trimmed after printing. This is the arrangement of pages on a mechanical for a typical eight-page brochure.

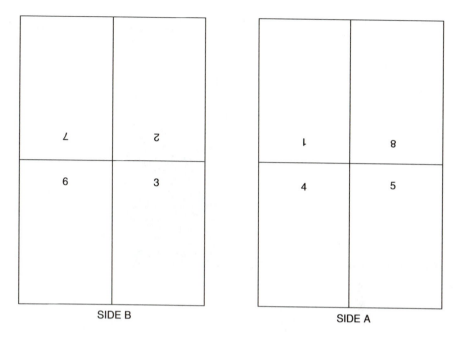

SIDE B   SIDE A

The *opacity* is the ability of a paper to help prevent printing on one side from showing through to the other side. Opacity is an important quality to consider when selecting brochure paper that will be printed on both sides.

Since the paper has such an important effect on both the design and the quality of the printing, it is helpful to obtain samples of possible papers to use, preferably with printing on them, from the printer or paper company before starting a design project.

Another aspect in selecting paper is its size in relation to the size of the printed piece. As was noted in Chapter 8, unless papers are manufactured in rolls, they are produced in standard-size sheets.

This creates no problem where letterheads are concerned. Since the standard letterhead is 8½ by 11 or 5½ by 8½ inches, and the standard bond paper sheet is 17 by 22, four 8½ by 11 sheets or eight 5½ by 8½ sheets can be cut from each full sheet with no waste.

But it is worthwhile to understand how the printer prices and cuts paper stock. Sometimes a slight adjustment in the format of a project can create significant savings in paper costs.

Here is how it works. Say we are planning a brochure. It will be a simple, four-page folder with each page measuring 8 by 10 inches. The folder will be created by using a parallel fold on a 10 by 16 sheet. We have decided that the folder will look best if printed on machine-finish book paper. The standard size is 25 by 38. We require 5,000 brochures.

The printer will calculate the number of 25 by 38 sheets needed and cut them to make 5,000 of the 10 by 16 sheets. This is the formula that will be used:

$$\frac{\text{Paper width}}{\text{Brochure width}} \times \frac{\text{Paper length}}{\text{Brochure length}} = \begin{array}{c} \text{Number of 10 by 16s} \\ \text{that can be cut} \\ \text{from a 25 by 38 sheet} \end{array}$$

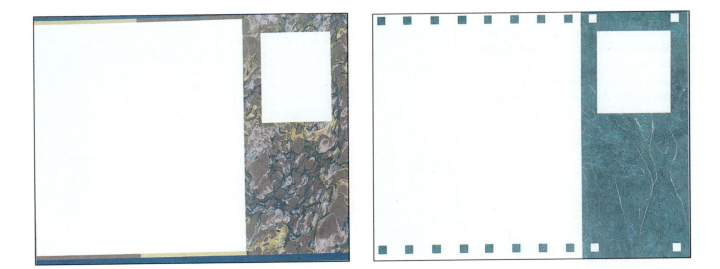

Fig. 11-8 ■ Paper is available in many colors, designs, and textures. This pre-printed paper can add much to the effectiveness of a brochure, memo, or flyer at a minimal cost. It can be used in a laser or ink-jet printer. Software is also available that makes designing printed materials "a snap." (Courtesy PaperDirect)

Fig. 11-9 ■ Careful planning that considers paper sizes can be cost efficient. On the left, six cuts, possibly eight if paper grain is not a factor, produce 7 by 10 inch sheets from a 25 by 38 sheet. By reducing the size just 1 inch for both width and depth to 6 by 9 inches, sixteen cuts can be obtained. The paper cost would be decreased by about 50 percent.

That is, the printer will divide the widths and depths to get the most cuts out of a sheet. This may be affected by the grain of the sheets if the brochure is to be folded, especially if printed on heavy stock. However, in this case, we get

$$\frac{25}{10} \times \frac{38}{16} = 2 \times 2 = 4 \text{ 10 by 16 sheets from each 25 by 38 sheet}$$

If the 4 is then divided into 5,000, we find that 1,250 full-size sheets will be needed for the job. We will be billed for that number plus about 5 percent for spoilage in printing and processing.

However, if the brochure is designed for a 6 by 9 page rather than 8 by 10, it can be printed on a 9 by 12 sheet cut out of the 25 by 38 size.

$$\frac{25}{12} \times \frac{38}{9} = 2 \times 4 = 8 \text{ 9 by 12 sheets from each 25 by 38 sheet}$$

Now the job will require only 625 sheets, cutting the paper cost in half even though the brochure page size is only reduced by 1 inch in one direction and 2 inches in the other.

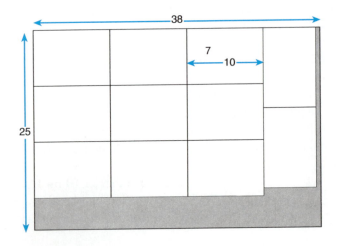

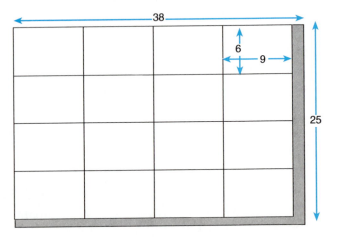

LOGO DESIGN

In designing an effective logo, you have to stretch your imagianation and be creative. These are international symbols. Can you match them with their meanings?

A Lost Child   D Florist

B Keep Frozen   E Go This Way

C Snack Bar

1

2

3

(Answers: 1-C, 2-B, 3-D)

The economies of choosing sizes for the final printed products that correspond to standard paper sizes cannot be overemphasized. A designer can always choose a unique size, but that designer must be prepared to pay for higher levels of waste. Also remember that sizes that can be cut efficiently from bond papers will not cut efficiently from book papers because of the different standard sizes. One designer has pointed out that beginners often design a communication on standard office (8½ by 11) paper and then specify book papers for production. This causes confusion and increased costs.

In planning printing needs, quite often paper can be saved by printing more than one job on the same sheet of paper. Money-saving procedures such as this can be worked out if the communicator and the printer have developed good rapport.

DESIGNING EFFECTIVE STATIONERY

Letterheads, statements, invoices, envelopes, business cards, and other printed materials needed to help us function in our work environment may not appear to offer much challenge. However, even something as deceivingly simple as a business card should receive thoughtful consideration. The principles of good design apply here just as they do for all printed communications.

The design of these items should be coordinated so they all work together to create the desired impression. Often it is effective to use the same layout but perhaps in a smaller size for statements and invoices, envelopes and cards, as is used for the letterhead. And even though a different design may be chosen for each, depending on its use, it is worthwhile to use the same logotype or typeface for the name of the organization on all printed pieces. This will help build recognition and memorability.

Creating A Logo

Designers keep two basic considerations in mind when creating a logo. The first is the characteristics that will make it suitable for printed communications. The second is its adaptability to all the identity requirements of the organization.

An effective logo should identify the organization when it stands alone. It should be simple enough to reproduce well on office copiers and more sophisticated printing equipment. It should reduce or enlarge without losing its design subtleties. It should reflect the tone of the organization, and it should not become outdated as times and styles change.

The logo should be executed with consideration of the possible expansion of the organization or company into new areas or activities. And the design should be suitable for use on vehicles, work clothes, uniforms, and so on.

One of the country's most prestigious design firms is Chermayeff & Geismar Associates, which has created corporate identity programs for such firms as Xerox and Chase Manhattan Bank. It also devised the official American Revolution Bicentennial symbol.

Fig. 11-10 ■ "Where to position the logo and the type, which typeface works best visually and best represents the client, and what size and shape the letterhead should take are some of the things that make every letterhead job an exciting challenge," according to "A Letterhead Production Guide" by the Gilbert Paper Company. Here are some possibilities for locating the logo.

Fig. 11-11 ■ The design can be incorporated into a total identity and marketing program for a business or organization.

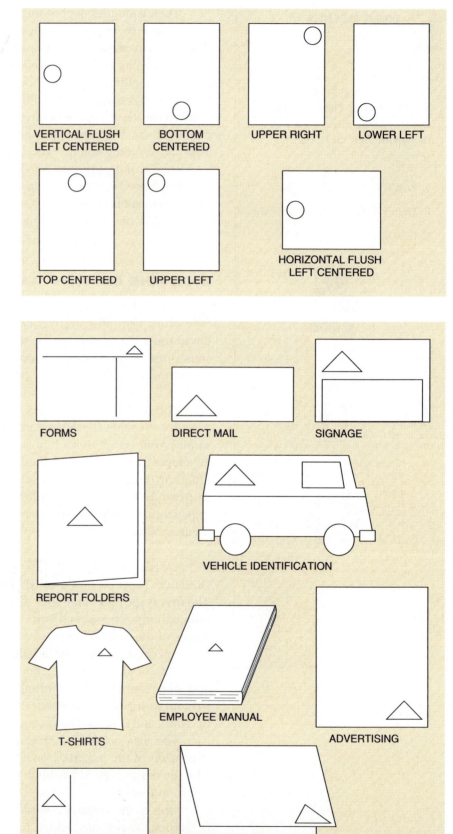

The firm follows the same philosophy for each project regardless of its size. This philosophy is stated in its promotional brochure: "Design is the solution of problems, incorporating ideas in relation to the given problem, rather than the arbitrary application of fashionable styles."[3]

How Chermayeff & Geismar handles a project might provide helpful insights for the neophyte designer. Their work on the Carousel Center is a good example.

Carousel Center is a large shopping center in Syracuse, New York. It was developed by Pyramid Companies as a flagship shopping and convention complex. The Center was created to be a major destination for movie goers, shoppers, and conventioneers.

A late eighteenth century restored carousel was used to set the theme for the festive atmosphere of the Center. A six-story atrium and convention facility creates an observatory for vistas over the New York state lake region.

The design process for Carousel Center drew on many talents—an architect, an interior designer, lighting consultants, engineers, and graphic consultants. Chermayeff & Geismar was hired to create a logo, marketing graphics, and environmental artwork.

Fig. 11-12 ■ (a) In its original, schematic design work for the Carousel Center, Chermayeff & Geismar's design team first made a palette of pastel colors to coordinate with the tiles used on the shopping center floor. (b) The completed logo was combined with a Futura Light typeface. (c) For the initial presentation to the client, the logo was applied to shopping bags, T-shirts, and other promotional materials. (d) The logo as it would appear on trucks. Note how the number on the parking lot standard is coordinated with the logo palette. (e) The logo as it would appear on large information signs at the Carousel Center, (f) A proposed interpretation of traditional carousel designs used in the Center.

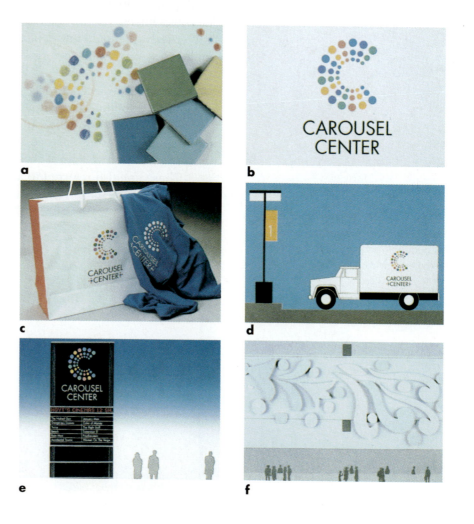

The first step was research. The design team investigated carousel motifs but decided the logo should reinforce the modern spirit of the Center's architecture, and the festive atmosphere of the shopping arcades.

For the logo, a color palette of pastel colors was selected to coordinate with decorative tile patterns used on flooring throughout the Center. This was incorporated with an abstract "C" rendered on a Macintosh computer coupled with a Futura Light typeface.

The logo and graphic identity device were applied to shopping bags, T-shirts, stationery, etched glass mockups, and promotional materials for the initial presentation to the client. After the completion of their preliminary work, Chermayeff & Geismar's design underwent numerous changes.

The Letterhead

Often the letterhead is the initial contact the receiver of a message has with the sender. Not only that, but many times the letter is the only contact made between an organization and its prospective clients. The letterhead, then, carries the weight of creating an impression as well as transmitting a message.

The letterhead should make a statement about its originator. The type styles selected and their arrangement help set the stage for the message. Effective letterhead design generally should be neat, dignified, and orderly. It should have character but not be obtrusive. It should be unique but restrained in terms of type sizes, tonal values, and use of space.

Letterhead designers suggest that the most effective results are obtained by skillfully accentuating the name of the firm, product, or logotype in relation to the other less important type elements while maintaining harmony, balance, and tone. In seeking this goal, designers usually consider two approaches: traditional or modern.

These are also referred to as formal and informal letterheads.

Fig. 11–13 ■ Traditional layout in letterheads with symmetrical balance. (Courtesy Woodbury and Company, Inc., Worcester, Mass.)

Fig. 11-14 ■ Creativity is more important than complicated design. Note the logo here. It is unique and memorable although rather simple to create. The logo has been blended with essential copy for the letterhead, envelope, and business card. Note, too, how white space and color were applied in the individual parts of this stationery trio. The placement of color did not interfere with the function of each, but did help in unifying the package and making it unique. (Courtesy the Marlin Company and Foodwear, Springfield, MO)

In the *traditional design,* type groups are usually arranged in either a square or inverted pyramid. If a trademark or symbol is used, it is centered. Sometimes rules are included but if they are, the formal symmetry is maintained. One feature of the inverted pyramid arrangement is that it forms a downward directional motion toward the message.

The *modern approach* is to create a basically asymmetrical arrangement while maintaining the principles of good design. The type can be arranged on an imaginary vertical line or it can be counterbalanced. If larger type is used for the company name on the left of the page, a smaller two or three-line address may be placed on the right for balance.

Rules are sometimes used to add motion to the letterhead. Decorations can give a letterhead individuality, but they should be selected and used with discretion. Color should also be considered. Remember, though, that the typographic embellishments should not draw attention away from the type.

Papers are available in a variety of finishes—linen, woven, pebble—to add individuality and distinction to a letterhead. If a paper with a textured finish is selected, it's a good idea to examine the inking and reproduction abilities of the paper.

Margins are important in letterhead design regardless of the arrangement selected. Side margins of type lines should approximate fairly closely the usual line width of the typed message. Sometimes elements such as the name and position of the person sending the messages are placed on the right of the page, to balance the typed name and address of the recipient of the letter.

Some organizations insist that long lists of officers be included on a letterhead. This can cause design problems, but they can be solved. If

Fig. 11-15 ■ This dramatic letterhead was designed by Clifford Stoltz for Planet Interactive, a multimedia developer. Its appeal is aimed at educational, corporate, and museum target audiences. "Our intent was to visually represent the idea of interactive media with all of its layers and movement," he noted. The images were created in Adobe Photoshop and the layout was completed in Aldus Freehand. (Courtesy Stoltz Design, Boston, MA)

only a few names are involved, they can be listed across the bottom of the sheet. The other obvious alternatives are to list the names down the left or right margins. These lists should be kept as unobtrusive as possible. Sometimes printing them in a lighter color will help. Of course, placement of all elements should always be made with consideration of the format of the letter to be typed on the sheet.

A typographically effective letterhead printed on a carefully selected stock that reflects the character of the organization can create a favorable impression and help project the desired image.

Special Processes

There are several processes that can be used in producing letterheads and other printed communications, which can add effectiveness and distinction. They include engraving, embossing, hot stamping, thermography, and die cutting.

Engraving   Engraving is an excellent method for projecting a high-quality, prestigious image. The sharp lines and crispness of an engraved announcement or letterhead project elegance, strength, and dignity. It reproduces fine lines and small type well. And it brings out the subtleties of shadings and patterns in a design.

A chromium-coated copper or steel plate with an etched-in design plus a smooth counterplate are used on a special engraving press. The plate is covered with ink, then wiped dry. The ink remains in the etched portions. Paper is fed into the press, and the impression transfers the ink to the paper.

Keep in mind that most engraving plates are limited to 4 by 8 inches. Also, paper selection is critical because of the stress exerted by the press. Paper lighter than 20 pounds should never be used.

Embossing   This technique is enjoying great popularity. It uses heat and pressing paper between dies to produce a raised effect. It provides a distinctive element to a printed communication, and introduces a third dimension for added memorability. Often new life can be added to an old logo by using embossing.

Embossing can be done in three styles: *blind, deboss,* and *foil-embossed.* Blind embossing uses the process without ink or foil. Debossing is embossing in reverse. The image is pressed down in the paper rather than raised. Foil embossing uses a thin material faced with very thin metal or pigment.

Usually the embossed effect works best alone. The visual impact is impaired when printing or color are added to the embossed image. When using embossing remember that the paper is formed, or molded, and this will use more of the paper than the layout might indicate. So type and other elements should not be too close to the embossed area.

Hot Stamping   Hot stamping uses the same heat-pressure process as embossing, but it goes one step further by transferring an opaque foil material to the surface of the paper. A variety of foils and designs are available, but the most common hot-stamping techniques use gold or silver foils.

Hot stamping is used for greeting cards, ribbons, paper napkins, and so on. With the introduction of new hot-stamping presses it is also becoming a popular technique for business cards and letterheads.

In hot stamping, a very thin ribbon of foil is fed into a press and releases its pigment onto the paper when pressed between a die and a hard, flat surface as heat is applied.

Hot stamping is expensive. It can cost as much as 10 to 15 percent more than engraving or embossing. Also, the process can discolor certain colors of paper stock, especially browns, yellows, and oranges.

Thermography   Thermography produces a raised printed surface by dusting the wet ink printed on the surface with a resinous material. This material is fused to the ink with an application of heat. The image is permanent and chip-proof and crack-proof. It is considered by some to be similar in appearance to engraving, but it can be added anywhere on a sheet of paper and is not limited by a plate size, as is the case with engraving. It can also be used with any color ink.

Die Cutting   Die cutting is rather like cookie cutting, except paper instead of dough is used. It can be an effective and dramatic attention-getting device. The cuts can be straight, circular, square, rectangular, or a variety of special shapes. Lasers are now being used to cut dies.

Delicate or lacy patterns, which tear easily, should be avoided. Also, since it is difficult to maintain a tight register in the die press, elements should not be designed close to the cuts.

Die cutting is not expensive compared with some of the other special-effect processes, but care is needed in selecting paper with sufficient strength to take sharp, clear-cut lines.

Fig. 11-16 ■ This brochure was a first-place winner in a national contest. It was made more effective with the use of die cutting. Designed by Richard Maul, it was produced by the Engineering Publications Office, University of Illinois at Urbana-Champaign.

Fig. 11-17 ■ Raised printing can add a dimension to business cards, stationery, and announcements. Such printing can be produced by thermography. Here the process is illustrated from *Sign of the Windmill,* publication of the Van Son Holland Ink Corp.

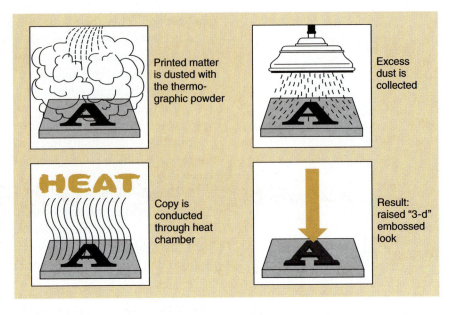

Printed matter is dusted with the thermographic powder

Excess dust is collected

Copy is conducted through heat chamber

Result: raised "3-d" embossed look

► EFFECTIVE DESIGN CHECKLIST FOR LETTERHEADS

■ Letterhead design should never interfere with the purpose of the letterhead, which is to convey a message.

■ The *monarch size* (7¼ by 10½) can add dignity for professionals such as doctors, designers, architects, and executives.

■ When color stock is used the color should fit the character of the

Fig. 11-18 ■ Here is an example of creative die cutting. This distinctive letterhead was designed for in-house use by Chikamura Design of San Francisco. Note the design and placement of copy. It blends with the image created by die cutting and leaves ample space for the message area. The design of the "T" and "F" for telephone and fax creates unity because of treatment similar to the logo design. The business cards work both in two- and three-dimensions. Inside each 3-D card resides a smooth touchstone pebble and an accordion-fold insert listing the firm's clients. (Courtesy Chikamura Design)

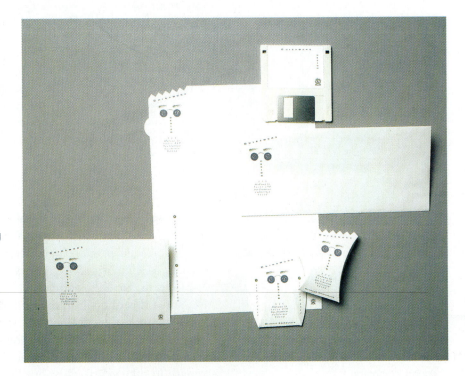

organization or the service it renders. It should not interfere with the typed letter.

■ Half-sheets (5½ by 8½) can save money, and they can be folded twice to fit a 6¾ envelope.

■ The logo should be original, stimulating, imaginative, and straight-forward. It should be adaptable as well.

■ The weight, color, and texture of the letterhead paper should be compatible with its envelope.

■ Always keep in mind that a letterhead is a platform for words.

THE ENVELOPE—A TALE OF DIVERSITY

➤ The part played by the envelope in printed communications begins with the vast size and diversity of materials available. Here is another tool that if used properly can make communications effective. The communicator should be able to sort out the different styles of envelopes and select the best one for the job.

But there are so many to choose from! The Old Colony Envelope Company, which produces the most extensive line of envelopes in the United States, offers more than 1,700 different styles and sizes. Other converters (which is what the envelope people call themselves because they take flat sheets of paper and cut and fold and glue them to create envelopes) also offer envelopes in hundreds of sizes and styles for thousands of uses.

Fortunately, though, they have settled on some basic sizes and grades that are easy to sort out and that will take care of most of the designer's and commulciator's needs. Selecting and using just the right envelope need not be difficult. There are four main points to consider: (1) sizes and styles, (2) paper weight and texture, (3) graphic design, and (4) Postal Service regulations.

The sizes of envelopes are given in inches with the shortest dimension first. A 6 by 9 envelope is 6 inches wide and 9 inches deep. Designations also include the location of the opening and the styles of the flap and seam. There are several devices for closing the envelope, and each should be considered.

For example, most standard stationery envelopes are "open side" with the seal flap and opening on the long dimension. "Open end" envelopes have the seal flap and opening on the short dimension. Flap styles are called pointed, square, wallet, and mail-point. Seam styles are determined by the construction and location of the parts of the paper folded and glued to form the finished envelope. These styles include a diagonal seam that is used most commonly in business correspondence, a pointed flap used for announcements, and side seams used for mailing programs and booklets. A center seam is used in making envelopes that must be rugged to withstand heavy duty.

Envelopes can also be classified by the way they close. There are gummed flaps, flaps with metal clasps for added security, and "button-and-string" tied-down flaps, which were designed for envelopes to be

ENVELOPES
STANDARD STYLES AND SIZES

The envelope manufacturers and the graphic arts industry have settled on a variety of standard sizes and styles. Although a number of others are available, these are the most common:

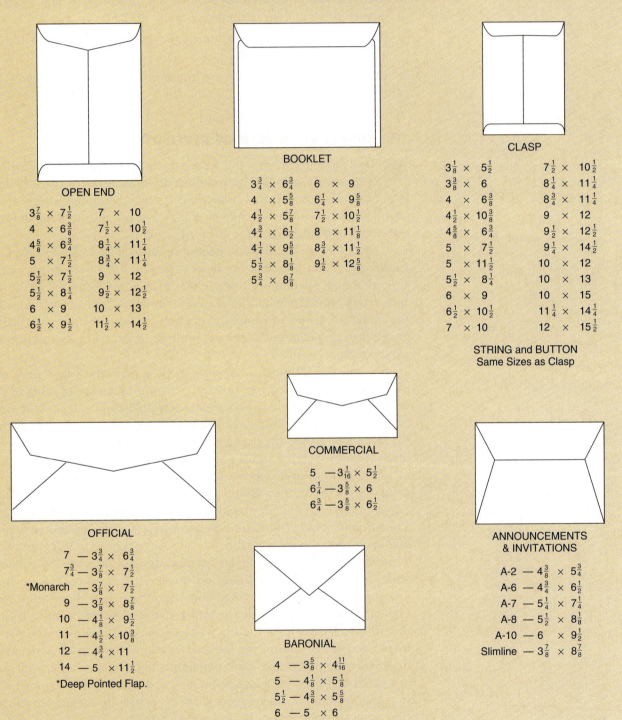

BOOKLET

$3\frac{3}{4}$	$\times$	$6\frac{3}{4}$	6	$\times$ 9
4	$\times$	$5\frac{5}{8}$	$6\frac{1}{4}$	$\times$ $9\frac{5}{8}$
$4\frac{1}{2}$	$\times$	$5\frac{7}{8}$	$7\frac{1}{2}$	$\times$ $10\frac{1}{2}$
$4\frac{3}{4}$	$\times$	$6\frac{1}{2}$	8	$\times$ $11\frac{1}{8}$
$4\frac{1}{4}$	$\times$	$9\frac{5}{8}$	$8\frac{3}{4}$	$\times$ $11\frac{1}{2}$
$5\frac{1}{2}$	$\times$	$8\frac{1}{8}$	$9\frac{1}{2}$	$\times$ $12\frac{5}{8}$
$5\frac{3}{4}$	$\times$	$8\frac{7}{8}$		

CLASP

$3\frac{1}{8}$	$\times$	$5\frac{1}{2}$	$7\frac{1}{2}$	$\times$	$10\frac{1}{2}$
$3\frac{3}{8}$	$\times$	6	$8\frac{1}{4}$	$\times$	$11\frac{1}{4}$
4	$\times$	$6\frac{3}{8}$	$8\frac{3}{4}$	$\times$	$11\frac{1}{4}$
$4\frac{1}{2}$	$\times$	$10\frac{3}{8}$	9	$\times$	12
$4\frac{5}{8}$	$\times$	$6\frac{3}{4}$	$9\frac{1}{2}$	$\times$	$12\frac{1}{2}$
5	$\times$	$7\frac{1}{2}$	$9\frac{1}{4}$	$\times$	$14\frac{1}{2}$
5	$\times$	$11\frac{1}{2}$	10	$\times$	12
$5\frac{1}{2}$	$\times$	$8\frac{1}{4}$	10	$\times$	13
6	$\times$	9	10	$\times$	15
$6\frac{1}{2}$	$\times$	$10\frac{1}{2}$	$11\frac{1}{4}$	$\times$	$14\frac{1}{4}$
7	$\times$	10	12	$\times$	$15\frac{1}{2}$

STRING and BUTTON
Same Sizes as Clasp

OPEN END

$3\frac{7}{8}$	$\times$	$7\frac{1}{2}$	7	$\times$ 10
4	$\times$	$6\frac{3}{8}$	$7\frac{1}{2}$	$\times$ $10\frac{1}{2}$
$4\frac{5}{8}$	$\times$	$6\frac{3}{4}$	$8\frac{1}{4}$	$\times$ $11\frac{1}{4}$
5	$\times$	$7\frac{1}{2}$	$8\frac{3}{4}$	$\times$ $11\frac{1}{4}$
$5\frac{1}{2}$	$\times$	$7\frac{1}{2}$	9	$\times$ 12
$5\frac{1}{2}$	$\times$	$8\frac{1}{4}$	$9\frac{1}{2}$	$\times$ $12\frac{1}{2}$
6	$\times$	9	10	$\times$ 13
$6\frac{1}{2}$	$\times$	$9\frac{1}{2}$	$11\frac{1}{2}$	$\times$ $14\frac{1}{2}$

COMMERCIAL

5	—	$3\frac{1}{16} \times 5\frac{1}{2}$
$6\frac{1}{4}$	—	$3\frac{5}{8} \times 6$
$6\frac{3}{4}$	—	$3\frac{5}{8} \times 6\frac{1}{2}$

OFFICIAL

7	—	$3\frac{3}{4} \times 6\frac{3}{4}$
$7\frac{3}{4}$	—	$3\frac{7}{8} \times 7\frac{1}{2}$
*Monarch	—	$3\frac{7}{8} \times 7\frac{1}{2}$
9	—	$3\frac{7}{8} \times 8\frac{7}{8}$
10	—	$4\frac{1}{8} \times 9\frac{1}{2}$
11	—	$4\frac{1}{2} \times 10\frac{3}{8}$
12	—	$4\frac{3}{4} \times 11$
14	—	$5 \times 11\frac{1}{2}$

*Deep Pointed Flap.

BARONIAL

4	—	$3\frac{5}{8} \times 4\frac{11}{16}$
5	—	$4\frac{1}{8} \times 5\frac{1}{8}$
$5\frac{1}{2}$	—	$4\frac{3}{8} \times 5\frac{5}{8}$
6	—	5×6

**ANNOUNCEMENTS
& INVITATIONS**

A-2	—	$4\frac{3}{8} \times 5\frac{3}{4}$
A-6	—	$4\frac{3}{4} \times 6\frac{1}{2}$
A-7	—	$5\frac{1}{4} \times 7\frac{1}{4}$
A-8	—	$5\frac{1}{2} \times 8\frac{1}{8}$
A-10	—	$6 \times 9\frac{1}{2}$
Slimline	—	$3\frac{7}{8} \times 8\frac{7}{8}$

Fig. 11-19 ■ Standard envelope styles and sizes.

used over and over again. Some converters have other patented closures such as self-sealing adhesives.

We can design the printed material and then seek the proper envelope. However, time and money can be saved and a much more effective communications package produced if we consult a listing of styles and sizes of envelopes first. See Fig. 11–19 for such a listing.

When selecting an envelope, we need to consider the size and bulk of the material to be inserted and how it is to be stuffed. An envelope for inserting by hand should be from one-eighth to one-fourth of an inch wider and one-fourth to three-eighths of an inch longer than the material it contains. If a machine at the printing plant or at a mailing firm will be used, the inserter should be consulted. The whole package must be compatible with the mechanical system.

Once the size and style have been selected, thought should be given to the envelope paper stock. There are impressive envelopes, envelopes that attract attention, and envelopes that harmonize in texture and color with the messages they contain.

All envelopes, however, need to conform to Postal Service regulations. The Postal Service classifies envelopes as nonmailable, mailable with no surcharge, and mailable with possible surcharge. Since the regulations are subject to change, they should be checked before printing is designed to be sent through the mails.

Graphics for Envelopes

The envelope can introduce the contents. It can help create the stage setting for the message. Often this communications bonus is overlooked and little attention is paid to envelope graphics. Good envelope graphics produced with some thought can aid in getting the container opened. Direct-mail advertisers know this, and they do all they can to design envelopes that will get the prospect to look inside.

Envelope graphics should be determined by the nature of the message and the sender. The types selected and their arrangements should harmonize with those used on the message.

There are three principal categories of envelope graphics: those designed for direct-mail advertising, those to accompany letterheads, and those for pamphlets or publications. Direct-mail envelopes are designed to use every device possible and proper to attract attention and get the prospect to open and read the contents, just as art or headlines are used to lure a reader to read a newspaper or magazine advertisement. The envelope is an integral part of the whole sales plan.

The graphics of envelopes that accompany letterheads should extend the basic letterhead design. The same types, logos, and symbols used on the letterhead but in suitable smaller sizes can help create the tone and recognition impact of the message.

The graphics of envelopes used for publications or pamphlets should reflect the contents and project the same type and tone harmony.

In other words, whatever the purpose of the envelope, there should be a strong visual relationship between it and the contents. This includes the graphics as well as the color and texture of the paper.

Fig. 11-20 ■ Envelope graphics are important. The envelope is often the initial contact with a target audience. It can attract attention, lure the recipient to open it and peruse the contents, it can set the tone of the message, and it can make a statement concerning the sender.

These envelopes were designed in Quark Xpress and printed on an Apple 360/600 DPI laser printer. Each envelope is hand die-cut, so no two are alike. Julio Lima says of his design: "In the modern world things seem to be losing a personal touch. I try to let my customers know they are special to me, and therefore I take the time to correspond with them in a personal way." (Courtesy It! design, Orlando, FL)

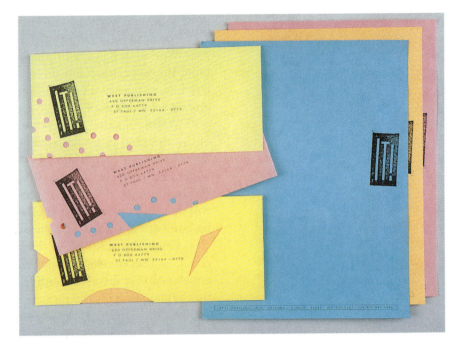

Sometimes business reply cards or envelopes accompany a mailing. Here again, certain Postal Service regulations govern the graphics, sizes, and information that can be included. The designer should become familiar with these regulations.

THE BUSINESS OF CARDS

➤ Business cards are like letterheads—they can be formal or informal depending on the person or organization they identify. Most *formal cards* are carefully arranged to preserve balance and dignity. The copy should identify, explain, and locate. That is, it should emphasize the name of the person or firm, tell the nature of the business or service, and give the address and telephone number. In the formally balanced card all elements are balanced along a visual vertical line down the center of the card with attention paid to the optical center.

Informal cards still retain the attributes of good design and typography, but are less rigid in arrangement. The designer has greater freedom in selecting type styles and arranging them on the card. Scripts, Romans, Sans Serifs, or Square Serifs can be used along with rules and small symbols or logos as long as they reflect the nature of the organization or service. Of course, all the essential information should be included in legible typefaces.

There are several standard sizes for cards. The generally accepted business card is identified as a number 88. It is 2 by 3½ inches. Resist the temptation to be different by using a different size. Odd-sized cards are often thrown away, and they will not fit the standard desktop file systems for business cards that serve as an excellent reference source for busy people.

PHONE NUMBER

NAME OF BUSINESS
DESCRIPTION OR SLOGAN

JANE D. SMITH   1200 PINE STREET
                                 CITY AND STATE

Fig. 11-21 ■ Traditional layout for a formal business card.

Fig. 11-22 ■ Modern design for business cards, emphasizes symbolism and bold display for recognition and memorability.

In preparing business card layouts, don't place the type lines too close to the edge of the card. A margin of 12 to 18 points should be allowed on smaller cards and at least 18 points on larger cards. If a card is a number 88, 3½ inches wide, the type should be designed in an area 18 picas wide.

PROGRAMS

➤ Programs for plays, concerts, and other events do not necessarily follow a standard size or style. Quite often, too, the limitations imposed by budget restraints may create an interesting design challenge. Of course, the same basic criteria for good layout and typography used in all graphics work still apply.

The simplest plan for a program is a single sheet. The dimensions should follow the principle of good proportion while cutting most economically from the paper size chosen.

There are several common formats for programs, depending on number of pages and content. Most four-page programs with printing on two pages are designed with a title page on page 1 and the program itself on page 3. If three pages are printed, the program copy occupies the second and third pages. If a menu and a program are included, the usual format is the title page, the menu on page 2, and the program on page 3.

The typography should be consistent on all pages. A single family, with italic or oblique if contrast is needed, is usually best to lend harmony and a pleasing appearance. If other type styles are used, they should be used sparingly, for heads or for contrast, as long as they harmonize in design and tone.

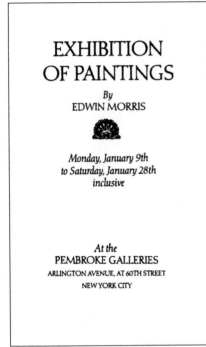

EXHIBITION
OF PAINTINGS
By
EDWIN MORRIS

*Monday, January 9th
to Saturday, January 28th
inclusive*

At the
PEMBROKE GALLERIES
ARLINGTON AVENUE, AT 60TH STREET
NEW YORK CITY

Fig. 11-23 ■ Title page for a program, illustrating proper word grouping, proper type choice for the subject, and good balance and unity. (From *U&lc,* publication of the International Typeface Corporation)

Lines of dots or dashes are used to separate items on many programs. These devices are known as *leaders.* They are also used for setting what is called tabular material such as financial statements. Hyphens or periods can be used in place of leaders, with a standard separation between each period or hyphen. Most designers find that 1 or 2 ems is about right.

BOOKS AND PAMPHLETS

➤ Communicators often become involved in writing and designing books and pamphlets. It is thus helpful to know a few principles and practices concerning the format and design of these publications. They are treated very briefly here as, once again, the basic tenets of good design and typography apply.

Let us begin by considering the standard arrangement used in the book industry and see how it can be helpful to us. This standard arrangement is followed for an average book and followed or modified depending on the size and nature of the book or pamphlet.

The order of arrangement of the contents of a typical book includes, from front to back, the following pages and sections:

Cover
Half-title
Title page
Copyright information
Dedication
Preface
Acknowledgments
Contents
List of illustrations
Introduction
Text
Appendix
Glossary
Bibliography
Index

All of the segments except the copyright information, which often includes the printer's imprint, generally begin on right-hand pages. The copyright information and printer's imprint usually appear on the back of the title page. This order of contents can be used as a guide for orderly arrangement. Of course, items can be eliminated. For instance, on booklets the cover can also serve as the title page. Even many full-sized books do not contain all of the sections.

The half-title is a page containing only the title of the book usually placed at the optical center. The title page gives greater prominence to the title and usually includes the author's name. The publisher's name and address and the date are often included on the title page. These are arranged and designed to harmonize with the content and to have proper balance on the page.

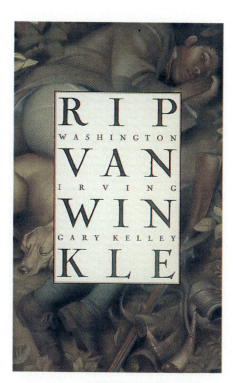

Fig. 11-24 ■ This elegant children's book was designed by Louise Fili. Take a look at the cover page (left). Fili has used a mortice within full-page art of the sleeping Rip. The proportions of the mortice are the same as the page. The text and illustration on the two-page spread are framed within similarly proportioned boxes. Note the generous leading of the text and the dynamic initial cap that invites the reader into the story. The first three lines were carefully planned to complete the opening sentence in all caps. Note also the treatment of running heads and folios. (Courtesy Louise Fili, Ltd. Illustrations by Gary Kelley)

A colophon can be included, usually at the end of the book. It describes the technical aspects such as typefaces, paper, and printing techniques. For example, this book contains a colophon; turn to the page following the index.

Harmony is an important design consideration, and the types used should work together throughout the book. The preface and acknowledgments are usually set in the same style and size of type as the text matter. Other material is often set in a smaller type size.

Some typographical features of book design that apply to booklet planning include folios, running heads, and margins. *Folios* are the page numbers of a book. The standard practice is to use Roman numbers (xii or XII) to number pages of the sections preceding the text, called the *preliminaries,* or front matter, and Arabic numbers for the text and ending sections, called the *back pages.*

The numbering of the preliminary pages begins with the half-title. It is important that the numbers are placed consistently throughout the book.

Running heads are the lines at the top of pages that identify the book or chapter and often contain the page number. These heads usually consist of the title of the book on the left-hand page and the title of the chapter on the right. Running heads on preliminary pages ordinarily identify the contents of these pages.

Running heads offer the opportunity of adding a little variety and contrast to the page. But they still should harmonize with the title page and the body matter. Here are some examples of running heads:

Graphic Communications Today

Chapter 1: Why Visual Communication?

Part IV: The Visual Arts

Fig. 11-25 ■ Margins are important elements in book design. Progressive margins (top) and progressive margins with hanging shoulder notes (bottom) are shown.

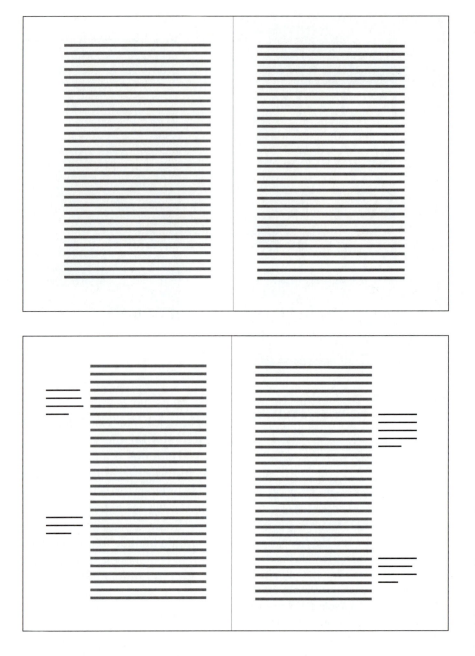

Margins play an important role in book design. They frame the type much like a mat frames a work of art. They help the eye focus on the type area and create a pleasing appearance to the page.

Book designers recommend that there be more margin at the bottom of the page than the top. This will help prevent the appearance of the type falling out of the page. The inner margin should be smaller than the outer margins. This will help make two facing pages appear as a single, unified whole. Careful attention to margins will not only enhance the appearance of a book but will help legibility as well.

Much care is taken in setting type and arranging elements for books. If some of the practices of page layout that are standard in book production were followed closely by others in the printed communications field, much of what we read would be improved.

▶ EFFECTIVE DESIGN CHECKLIST FOR BOOKS AND PAMPHLETS

■ Eliminate widows. *Widows* are the final words of a paragraph carried over from one column to the top of the next, or from one page to the next. They often contain only a word or two. This practice breaks the unity of a paragraph and creates an uneven contour to the column or page.

■ Do not end a column or page with the first line of a paragraph.

■ Do not divide a word from one column or page to the next.

■ Avoid more than three consecutive lines ending with hyphenated words.

■ Prevent "rivers of white" from flowing down columns. *Rivers of white* are obvious gaps between words that run down the columns. They are the result of poor and uneven spacing in the lines of type. To avoid rivers of white use a smaller type face on the same measure; use the same typeface but in a longer measure; set the copy ragged right; use the same measurement but a more condensed typeface.

A PRACTICAL PROJECT IN DESIGN AND PRODUCTION

▶ A Sacramento, California, graphic designer, who interviewed and hired many young designers right out of school and found them lacking in understanding the production end of the business, decided to do something about it. He created a course in which students engage in hands-on designing and the actual production of what they design.

The designer, Michael Kennedy, who owns Michael Kennedy Associates in Sacramento, has taught the course at California State University, Chico.

Fig. 11-26 ■ Two problems encountered in preparing reading (or text) matter for attractive design and pleasant reading. In the top example, the righthand column contains a widow, the last line of a paragraph carried to the top of the adjoining column. The lower example contains rivers of white, vertical gaps in successive lines caused by excessive spacing between words. Both situations should be eliminated.

Eliminate widows. *Widows* are the final words of a paragraph carried over from one column to the top of the next, or from one page to the next. They often contain only a word or two. This practice breaks the unity of a paragraph and creates an uneven contour to the column or page.

Book designers recommend that there be more margin at the bottom of the page than the top. The inner margin should be smaller than the outer margins. This will help make two facing pages appear as a single, unified whole.

Careful attention to word spacing will not only enhance the appearance of a book but will help legibility as well. Much care is taken in setting type and arranging elements for books. If some of the practices of page layout that are standard in book production were followed closely by others in the printed communications field, much of what we read would be improved.

CREATIVE COMMUNICATION

"Eureka, I've found it!"

What a happy moment when the editor or designer "sees the light" and solves the problem.

But psychologists tell us that after we have collected information about the problem, clearly defined it, and started on a solution, it can be helpful to forget it. Well, not forget it entirely. Just withdraw attention from it for a while.

Often we can then return to the problem with a fresh attitude and a new approach that can lead to a better solution than if we continued working without interruption.

Psychologists call this the "Eureka syndrome"—the "sudden" emergence of an idea or solution to a problem.

The course begins with students examining a variety of projects produced by working designers, from the creation of thumbnails to finished printing. The main task of the course is to develop a design project that is printed in process color.

The assignment is the same for each student—designing a business card. All the cards are combined on a grid to create a poster. The poster is printed in full color, and some of the posters are trimmed so that each student receives 100 of his or her own business cards. The students are involved in all the steps of the production process. They use a variety of materials from colored pencils to torn paper.

The class meets once a week, and it follows this general schedule:

- *Week 1:* The procedure is first to work on the full-color art, then on the typeset copy. This week rough ideas are worked out in pencil sketches. Students contemplate how best to use the color materials that are available.

- *Week 2:* Students now narrow down their ideas to one or two and create a full-size sketch. They write an explanation of how the final art will be reproduced.

- *Week 3:* The final art for the color portion of the card is prepared. The art for each card is trimmed to exactly twice the size of the poster to fit the grid format.

- *Week 4:* The artwork for each card is mounted on the grid. It is photographed, and an 8 by 10 color transparency is made of the entire layout. Color separations are made by a laser scanner. The cards, which have been gang-produced, are now 2 by 3½ inches with about ¹⁄₁₆ inch all around for trim. They are separated and the students add typeset material to their individual cards on an overlay. They can have the type printed in black or reversed to white. The final step is to specify the instructions to the printer on a tissue overlay.

- *Week 5:* The artwork is sent to the printer. The printer produces two proofs, one in full color and the other a blueline. The students check the proofs for color, registration, and accuracy; then the proofs are returned to the printer to prepare for printing.

- *Week 6:* The class spends the day at the printing plant and follows all the steps in the production process. When the posters roll off the press each student receives 25 posters plus 100 business cards cut from the full sheets.

The cost is covered by a small course fee and sizable donations from companies involved in the project. The major contributor has been the printer Georges + Shapiro Lithograph of Sacramento.

"This is a rare opportunity for students to understand the relationship between design and the printing process," says Joel Shapiro, one of the owners of the printing firm.[4]

The project benefits the university as well. Posters are mailed to high schools and junior colleges in the area to acquaint students with the university and its design program.

Fig. 11-27 ■ Poster produced by the design students. Designer Michael Kennedy has used this project in his classes since 1987. The students not only learn all aspects of visual communication from design to production, but end up with a valuable tool they can use. Jobs have resulted from their work in the class.

 GRAPHICS IN ACTION

1. Select the type to use to design a coordinated 8½ by 11 letterhead, number 10 commercial envelope, and number 88 business card for your own use. If you are associated with an existing business or service, use their name. If not, devise a fictional name for a firm in your major field of interest. The type and its arrangement should reflect the characteristics of the business or service. Design the letterhead, envelope, and business card.

2. Outline the procedures you would follow to create an informational brochure for an organization with which you are associated. This brochure would be printed on an 8½ by 11 sheet that would be mailed to prospective members. Its objective is to convince prospects that they should consider joining the organization.

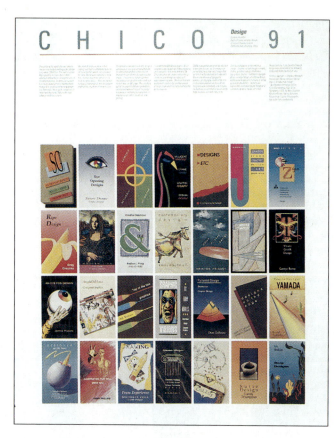

Fig. 11-28 ■ This is another of the posters produced by the design students. The individual business cards were cut from the printed posters.

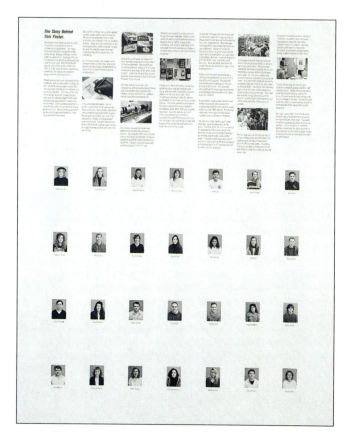

Fig. 11-29 ■ Each student's photo is printed on the back of his or her business card. These have proved valuable for the students when they start to make contacts in their search for jobs. Prospective employers have been impressed.

3. Prepare a rough dummy for the brochure planned above.

4. Design one letterhead in the traditional format and one in modern design for a company, either existing or fictional. Use the same copy for each. Use an ornament or devise a symbol. Consider using a rule for the modern format. Analyze the two designs and decide which would be most appropriate for the company.

5. Plan and design the cover (book jacket) for your autobiography. Select types and ornaments or borders that you believe would best fit the subject and enhance the cover. The use of ornaments or borders is your decision. The cover size is 6 by 9 inches.

NOTES

[1]"Design Today," *Chicago Tribune*, October 13, 1993, Sec. 5, p. 4.

[2]*In-Plant Printer*, April 1982, p. 48.

[3]"Design By Number," *HOW*, January/February 1988, p. 71.

[4]"Hands-On Education," *HOW*, November/December 1988, p. 66.

ADVERTISING DESIGN

© Churchill & Klehr

12 After examining all the parts of a complete graphic communication, the time arrives for putting these parts together. One approach to the design of magazines, brochures, newspapers, and all other forms of printing the communicator might be responsible for, is to study advertising design.

There are several good reasons to approach the application of graphic design from an advertising base. Some of the best talent in the communication field works in the world of advertising. Advertising is a pacesetter in the use of art, type styles, and the arrangement of elements on the printed page.

In addition, advertising makes a good starting place because all the steps, from conceptualization to the finished comprehensive or mechanical layout, can be followed quite easily. All the principles of design can be seen in action in one comparatively small area. A well-designed advertisement will contain, often on one page or less, balance, proportion, unity, contrast, and rhythm. These principles are put to work to create a communication that does a specific job.

There is another benefit. Quite often communicators who specialize in editorial functions or public relations, for instance, have to coordinate their efforts with those of advertising personnel. A common task might be a special supplement for a newspaper, a special section for a magazine, or an advertising campaign that requires support from public relations professionals. As with most areas of endeavor, when mutual understanding exists among the various professionals engaged in an effort, the work goes more smoothly and the result can be more effective.

The study of advertisements can help stimulate creative ideas for brochure and magazine page layouts. Sometimes the arrangements of elements in an advertisement can be adapted to editorial content. For example, does the placement of the elements in the advertisement produced here in Fig. 12–1 trigger ideas for placement of elements on a magazine page? A possibility is shown in Fig. 12–2.

Of course, the creation of a layout is only one small part of the advertising process, just as it is only one part of any communication effort. It cannot be completely isolated from the other steps in effective communication. But even this brief look at advertising design should help us understand something about the process of advertising communication. In addition, since most advertising is communication that forcefully attempts to motivate people, examining the techniques used by advertising professionals can help those in other areas of the profession.

DESIGN AND ADVERTISING COMMUNICATION

Advertising communication differs from most other communication in two ways. Here the communicator pays to have the message circulated. As a result, the communicator has more control over the message than, say, the public relations professional who distributes a press release. The source pays, so the source can specify when and where the advertisement will appear. The source decides the size and content of the message as well.

America's best export is America.

InterNorth and several other large American corporations have been engaged in a unique business-to-business relationship for five years in nations of the Caribbean Basin. Called Caribbean-Central American Action, it is the initiative of an international partnership to encourage development of strong, market-oriented economies.

The freedom and stability of the Western Hemisphere will depend largely upon the economic models its nations choose to adopt. The cooperative role of U.S. businesses can do much to ensure that those

models provide productive freedom and a better way of life for the people of the region.

Balance-of-trade figures tell only part of the story of America's success in international business. The rest of the story is the incalculable benefit in sharing the best of America with other nations.

Americans don't export just goods and services. We also send abroad the compelling evidence of how well our system works, and the inspiring model of what free people can achieve for themselves in a free system.

That's why our InterNorth International company and other international companies take pride in sharing the best of America with the rest of the world. Our most valuable export is our nation's 200-year-old success story.

InterNorth is a diversified, energy-based corporation involved in natural gas, liquid fuels, petrochemicals, and exploration and production of gas and oil.

INTERNORTH
We work for America.

International Headquarters, Omaha, Nebraska 68102
© 1983, InterNorth, Inc.

Fig. 12-1 ■ This advertisement could be used as a guide in making a layout for a magazine page (see Fig. 12–2).

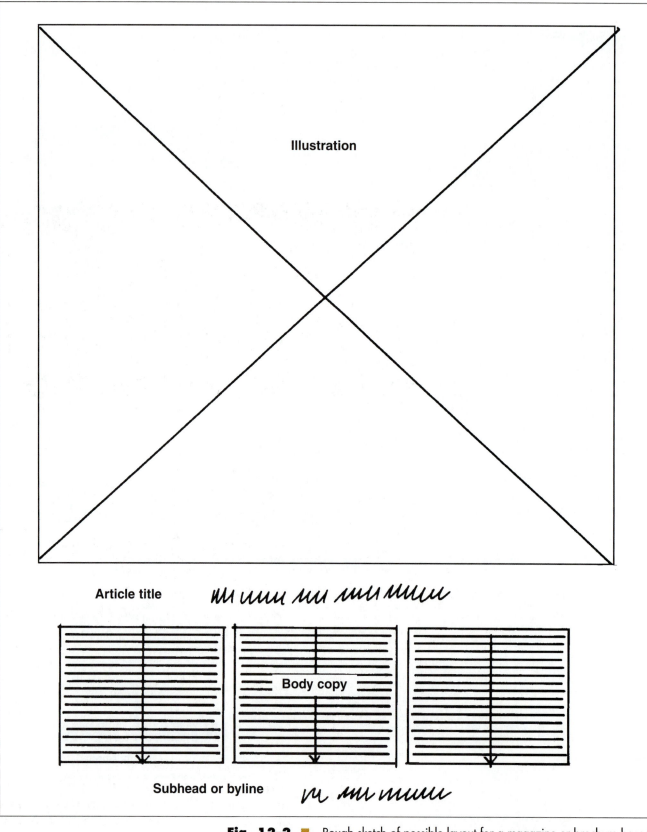

Illustration

Article title

Body copy

Subhead or byline

Fig. 12-2 ■ Rough sketch of possible layout for a magazine or brochure based on the Internorth advertisement. Advertisements can be good idea sources for communicators.

Although the source has final say in the message, the actual advertising layout can be created by designers who work for an advertising agency, those who work for the medium that delivers the message, such as the newspaper, radio station, magazine, or television station, or the staff of the advertising department of the source—a business or organization, for instance. Quite often the strategy and its execution is accomplished by a team with representatives from an advertising agency and the client in consultation with representatives of the advertising deparment of the particular medium.

Advertising communication is aimed basically at getting people to do something or accept something, often against their will or initial inclination. Therefore advertising communication must use all the attributes of the communication process to attain maximum effectiveness. This includes typography and graphics.

Advertising communication is *persuasive communication.* So is most public relations communication and much newspaper and magazine editorial content. This makes them sort of cousins under the skin. Better newspapers, brochures, and other printed materials can be designed by studying the techniques of the advertising designer. Since typography and layout cannot be separated from the message they present, the most effective design cannot be created without understanding how that design is linked to the message.

A quick trip through the advertising copywriting process will help us understand the importance of linking the layout with the message.

The Strategy Platform

The first step taken by most advertising copywriters is to form a "strategy platform" as a guide for the actual writing. Usually more than one person is involved in devising the strategy platform. The account executive, copywriters, and layout people work together as a team. (In a one-person shop, of course, it will be a one-person project.)

The strategy platform is based on extensive research of the source and its product, the media to be used, and the target audience. It is a written statement that answers questions such as the following:

1. Who is the target audience?

2. What is the most important idea in this whole project?

3. What are the most important selling features?

4. What other important features of the product or idea should be considered?

5. What action do we want from the target audience?

The job of the copywriter and the layout artist is to integrate the verbal and visual elements they believe will be most effective. The goal is to get the desired "action" out of the target audience in the most effective and least expensive way.

Quite often copywriters and layout artists work together to accomplish this. Sometimes one person, if that person knows typography and graphics as well as the techniques of effective copywriting, does the whole job.

ARTWORK HELPS

Illustrations increase readership of advertisements. McGraw-Hill's Laboratory of Advertising Performance reports a study of 3,406 business-to-business ads showed that ads with artwork performed better than ads without it.

Some findings:

■ Ads with artwork made contact with the target audience 32 percent better.

■ Ads with artwork aroused interest 26 percent better than ads without.

■ The ads with artwork had 22 percent more people say they preferred the product than the ads without artwork.

Arranging Information: A Useful Formula

There is an old tried-and-true formula that advertising copywriters often use to arrange the information they believe most effective to create a selling message. This formula plots the message from start to finish, from attention to action, in a series of five steps. This has been dubbed the A-I-D-C-A approach.

The A-I-D-C-A approach is effective in planning all sorts of communications. But few communicators outside the field of advertising are aware of it.

Let's see how the formula is applied to the communications process. Before any communication can take place, we must make an initial contact with the target audience. The audience will not listen if we do not get them to look up from what they are doing or stop them from turning the page.

This process of *getting attention* is the A of the formula. Whether an advertisement or a layout for a magazine article is being planned, the communicator must first capture the attention of the audience. Typography can do it. Effective words presented in the right type style can do it. Effective art can do it too. The designer must blend the words of the copywriter with the skills of the typographer.

The A for attention is followed by I, which stands for *interest.* Something written in the copy and arranged in the layout must stimulate the reader's interest quickly.

Well, we have attention, and we have aroused interest. What happens next? The target must be given a strong shot of *desire.* This means desire to acquire the product, to know more about it, or to endorse the idea or whatever the objective of the message might be. In writing a narrative, for instance, we must build up the reader's interest to make that reader want to continue through to the end. The D is for desire.

Depending on the purpose of the communication, the C may or may not be pertinent. If an advertising layout is trying to sell the reader a product, now is the time for *conviction.* However, if this is a brochure explaining an activity, C may not be needed. It all depends on the type of communication. But C in an advertising message, or in an editorial, is the clincher, when the message has sold the prospect. Here is where the communicator closes the pitch and has the prospect ready to put money, or support, on the line.

Finally, it's back to A, but this time the word is *action.* Action is the means for accomplishing the communication's purpose in the first place. If a communication does not provide the target audience with a way to take action or let them know action has been or will take place, very little will happen. In advertising, action can be generated by a number of devices—limited time offers, send in that coupon, get in on this special deal, price good until the end of the week, and so on.

The A-I-D-C-A formula provides a plan to keep things moving, to establish the rhythm and motion needed for a dynamic layout. The communicator can use this formula to help in placing elements on a page for a dynamic, alive layout such as the one illustrated in Fig. 12–3.

Fig. 12-3 ■ This advertisement illustrates several design principles and techniques including application of the A-I-D-C-A *(attention-interest-desire-conviction-action)* formula. The background art and headline give it motion and direction. The broken line of the head underscores its humor and mirrors the design of the center lamp. The art and copy are well-balanced without being too static or formal. The layout perfectly reflects the ad's central message: "We've got the expected and the unexpected." (Courtesy Target Stores; Ad Agency: Martin/Williams)

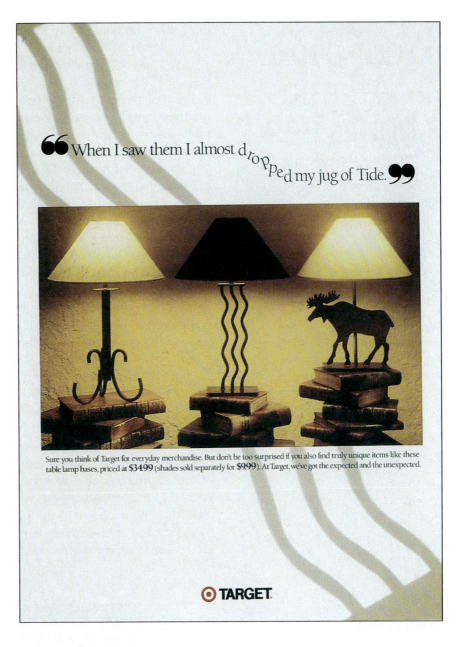

Graphic Elements

Whether the advertisement designer uses the A-I-D-C-A formula or has another approach to the task, the graphic elements of an advertisement facilitate quick and easy comprehension of the printed word. They can supply additional information that the written word cannot convey well, and they can help set the desired mood.

Let us take a quick look at how these elements can be put together into an effective advertisement. Most of these techniques are applicable to all types of printed communications—they aren't just the private domain of the advertising world.

Art can be used in advertising for many different purposes. The most obvious and most frequent use is to simply show what a product

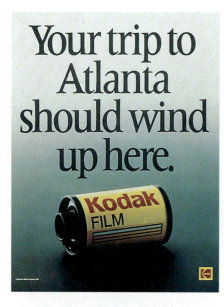

Fig. 12-4 ■ Often retentive advertising is an important part of an advertising plan for an established product. Here the product, Kodak film, is shown with a clever headline in a simple but effective layout. Notice how reading the headline leads you right down to the product. (Tausche Martin Lonsdorf)

looks like. Product art is most effective, however, when readers are already aware of their need for the type of product being pictured.

Art can be very effective by showing a product being used. Art of this sort can stir to consciousness a need or desire for the product that the reader had not felt before. It can also reinforce a headline designed to attract a particular target market or make the wording that does this unnecessary in the headline, leaving room in the reader's mind for something else that might make the complete ad message more effective. Art showing a product being used should include people with whom the intended readers can or want to identify.

Art can also demonstrate the happy results of owning or using the product or service or patronizing a particular establishment. This may be shown either realistically or symbolically. Usually this type of illustration is associated with emotional, imaginative copy. This kind of art is especially helpful if the advertiser wants to reach persons who have not felt a need for the product. It attracts the interest of hard-to-motivate prospects by making them want to experience the same joy and satisfaction as the pictured users. It arouses their interest in the product or service, hopefully enough so they will read the rest of the ad to find out more.

Such art can take a positive or negative approach, or two pictures can be used, one negative and the other positive. For instance, they can show the predicament and the solution or some other sort of before-and-after situation. Advertisers have found this format to be very effective.

Closely related to "happy results" illustrations are those that imply psychological relationships between the product and its users. This type of art emphasizes the background and environment of the product's users or portrays people with whom readers would want to be associated. This art must be reinforced by imaginative, emotional copy.

Art used in advertising copy can show real products and real people in actual situations; it can also be abstract and symbolic. Symbolic

Fig. 12-5 ■ An approach that can be effective in advertising design is to pose a problem and provide a solution. This advertisement for Healthtex shows old blue jeans with the knees worn out and the solution—Healthtex! Note the integration of the headline with the art. (The Martin Agency)

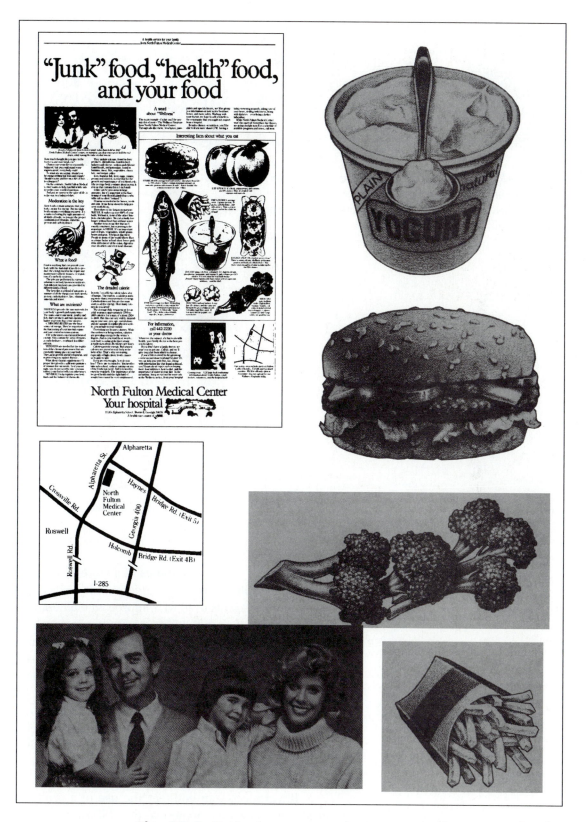

Fig. 12-6 ■ Here is a newspaper advertisement created by using a number of art sources: computer-generated clip art, a line art diagram, and a continuous-tone photograph converted to line art by the halftone process. (Courtesy American Newspaper Publishers Association)

Fig. 12-7 ■ In creating an advertisement the designer will test the layout possibilities by making a number of thumbnail sketches. Then a full-size rough is created prior to completing a more detailed "comp" or a "ready" for plate-making mechanical. (Courtesy American Newspaper Publishers Association)

art can reflect various attributes of a store or product—stylishness, reliability, durability, convenience, femininity, masculinity, gaiety, seriousness. Symbolic art is used to reinforce an element of the product's image. This type of art is difficult to create but it can have great impact and memorability. It is a real challenge to the communicator's creativity to come up with ideas for symbolic art that are not trite or too obvious.

Quite often art can be used much more effectively than words to demonstrate features of a product and how it is made and works. Cutaway techniques or greatly magnified illustrations of product details that may never be seen by the user in normal circumstances can be effective in certain situations and for certain products. This kind of art goes well with factual copy and is a graphic way of presenting tangible evidence that a product can perform as promised.

Illustrations can connect the use of a product with a national or local current event. A picture of a blizzard can remind people of the need for all sorts of bad weather gear, especially if a blizzard is raging outside at the time the advertisement appears.

Fig. 12-8 ■ What more graphic illustration could Wrangler have used than this to show its product in use? The headline, art and color tell the tale—earthtones and a rugged product. The action—a cowboy hits the dirt—pulls the target audience into the advertisement. There's humor here (except for the cowboy) as pratfalls are a sure way to get laughs. Humor is a sure-fire tool to increase reader interest. The art is so forceful little copy is needed to put the pitch across. (The Martin Agency)

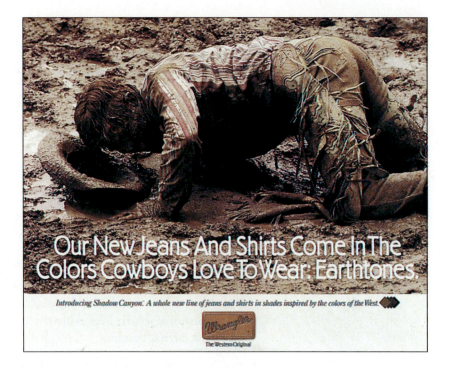

Headlines for Advertisements

The headline is the most important single typographic element in an advertisement. Its primary function is A—attention. In addition to attracting attention, an effective headline states or implies a benefit. It should contain a verb if possible, and active verbs far outperform passive verbs. The good headline identifies the target audience and gets the reader involved.

The headline for an advertisement might be developed from the copy, as it is for a news story or magazine article. It can also tie in with the illustration.

Some ad copywriters say if the headline doesn't get the reader's attention, the rest of the ad will never be read. If it attracts the wrong kind of readers, those who don't want, don't need, or can't afford the product, the ad won't do its job.

How long should a headline be? Basically a headline should say enough to attract the attention of the target audience and make them want to read the rest of the ad. But keep it short. There have been successful Volkswagen ad heads with just two words:

Think Small

Nobody's Perfect

However, use as many words as necessary to do the job. One of the most famous heads in all advertising history had eighteen words:

At Sixty Miles an Hour the Loudest Noise

In This New Rolls Royce Comes from the

Electric Clock

The communicator has many choices when deciding on the type of headline for an advertisement. There is the "news" headline:

Wammo Now Has Flamastan

The news headline should be set in a type style that makes it look like a newspaper headline.

The selective headline emphasizes appeal to the target audience and helps sift out the target from the mob. A headline for Haggar slacks zoomed in on the target like this:

The Slacks for the Untamed Young Man

Benefit headlines stress advantages. The most effective benefit headlines do not boast, they stress benefits to the target audience:

You'll Have No Maintenance Costs for Five Years

Promise headlines, those that offer a reward for use of the product or adoption of the idea, should be followed by proof in the copy that the promise will be kept. Clearly related to the promise head is the "how to" or advice headline:

How To Get More Interest on Your Savings

Here, again, proof should be offered in the copy.

The command headline gets readers involved because they are urged to act. Tactfully and subtly written, it can be very effective, but if the command is too strong the prospect might take offense at your arrogance. "Do Yourself a Favor, Buy from Us" is a much more effective approach than "Buy from Us, We're the Best."

Label headlines in advertisements are weak, just as weak as label heads on news stories or articles. A label head simply states a title or obvious fact. "Arrow Shirts" would be an advertising label head; "Lions Club Meets" would be a label head on a news story.

There are many other types of advertising headlines. Some pose a question ("Do You Suffer from Headaches?"); others attempt to arouse curiosity ("How Many Beans in This Jar?"), and still others challenge ("Go for It!"). These heads are effective if done well, but they usually violate the basic rule that a headline should reveal what an ad is about. They can arouse curiosity enough to make the reader read on, but if the copy does not satisfy that curiosity, the head may make an enemy for the sponsor of the ad.

Fig. 12-9 ■ This headline identifies the target audience and holds out a promise to lure the target audience into the advertisement. Also note the correct use of negative leading between the lines. The ascenders and descenders do not touch.

To improve your accounts receivable, shift your point of view.

CREATIVE COMMUNICATION

The creative communicator can be frustrated by accumulating either too little or too much information.

Effective creative solutions require adequate information. Superficial research results in superficial design.

On the other hand, too much information that is not relevant to the goal of the layout can muddy the waters and cause confusion.

The creative communicator should make an effort to gather enough information to understand the design problem thoroughly. However, irrelevant information should be eliminated.

Creativity is aided by concentration on information pertinent to the solution of the problem.

Copy in Advertisements

Copy is the printed words in an advertisement. It is made up of the headline and the body information. These, together with the illustrations and *logo* (the name of the firm in a distinctive design) plus any other typographic devices, make up the components of an advertising layout.

The person who makes the layout should understand something about what makes an effective piece of body copy. The key word is *words*.

Copy is composed of words, and the best copy is composed of the best words that can be found. Words that stop you in your tracks, words that sell you, words that get you going, words that reflect the consumer's point of view rather than the seller's. "You" words help draw the audience into the message. "Selling" words help the copy get action.

> Those who write advertising copy . . . should, I believe, constantly bear in mind that, if advertising copy is to be at all effective in contributing to the eventual sale, it should not venture beyond its limited province of informing favorably; of inciting curiosity; of building belief; of creating understanding; of developing the urge to investigate and see for oneself.[1]

The copywriter must understand the product thoroughly, know what it can do, how it does it, and its assets and shortcomings when compared with similar products. The writer must also have a clear idea of the target audience. The key to successful communication here, as it is in all other areas, is to be able to create common understanding and believability. An understanding of the target audience's characteristics and behavior is vital.

THE ADVERTISING CAMPAIGN

All the skills of the designer working with personnel in the advertising agency or its client are brought into play when an advertising campaign is created and executed. A look at a successful campaign can provide insights valuable to anyone involved in graphic communications.

An advertising campaign in its most fundamental form is a series of advertisements that repeat one basic message. The first step in developing a campaign is intensive research to determine the "position" of the product, service, or idea to be promoted, that is, where the advertiser desires to place his or her client or product in the minds of the target audience. For instance, Avis, the car rental firm, developed a campaign around its position by advertising "we're number two." The campaign emphasized that because of this position Avis tried harder than its competition.

A plan of action is developed that includes the objectives of the campaign, major selling points, goals, and a budget to carry out the plan. Although millions of dollars have been spent on campaigns by large corporations, campaigns do not necessarily require a large expenditure of money. Many successful campaigns have been short term and relatively inexpensive.

Such a campaign was the "Electric Drought" campaign created for the Sierra Pacific Power Company by Doyle-McKenna and Associates, Inc., both of Reno, Nevada, a city in a semidesert region of the mountain West. The goal of the campaign was to tell target audiences the situation faced as a result of drought conditions and to secure their understanding of measures to be taken.

Here was the problem. A nationwide drought greatly reduced the availability of low-cost hydroelectric power. Sierra Pacific normally purchases this power from sources in the Pacific Northwest. Because of the shortage of power the utility had to pay more for electricity. This resulted in its seeking a substantial rate increase from consumers.

The state public utility commission permits fuel and power purchase costs to be passed on to customers once a year. But the commission must approve the amount of increase. Sierra Pacific found it necessary to seek a 10 percent rate increase in this situation.

Research indicated that six out of ten Sierra Pacific customers had no idea of the effects of the drought on the power supply. Much of this research was obtained through focus groups, in which a cross section of the population met with advertising agency and utility personnel who elicited their opinions and perceptions.

The agency and the client, after studying the findings, set the following objectives for the campaign:

1. Build awareness quickly with employees, the media, and the public that a nationwide drought was causing unusual conditions that would increase power costs and electric rates.

2. Create strong recall for this message in the brief five-week period before the rate increase was sought.

3. Establish an effective base of believability that the drought was the "villain" and Sierra Pacific and its customers were both victims.

4. Show steps the utility was taking to help mitigate the increased costs and hold down rates as much as possible.

The strategy devised and the action taken included:

1. Informing Sierra Pacific employees of the drought impact on rates and preparing them to answer customer inquiries.

2. Conducting news conferences which included an aerial tour of drought-stricken reservoirs.

3. Placing advertisements on television and in newspapers. Large space advertisements were used to demonstrate how the company relied on other areas for hydroelectric energy. The advertisements also emphasized that the drought was creating unusual problems.

The campaign targeted the total market area of the utility, but placed extra emphasis on reaching and developing understanding among the influential persons in the community.

No campaign, whether an advertising, public relations, or editorial effort, is completed until it is evaluated to determine if the goals have been reached. In this case, at the end of just five weeks, research

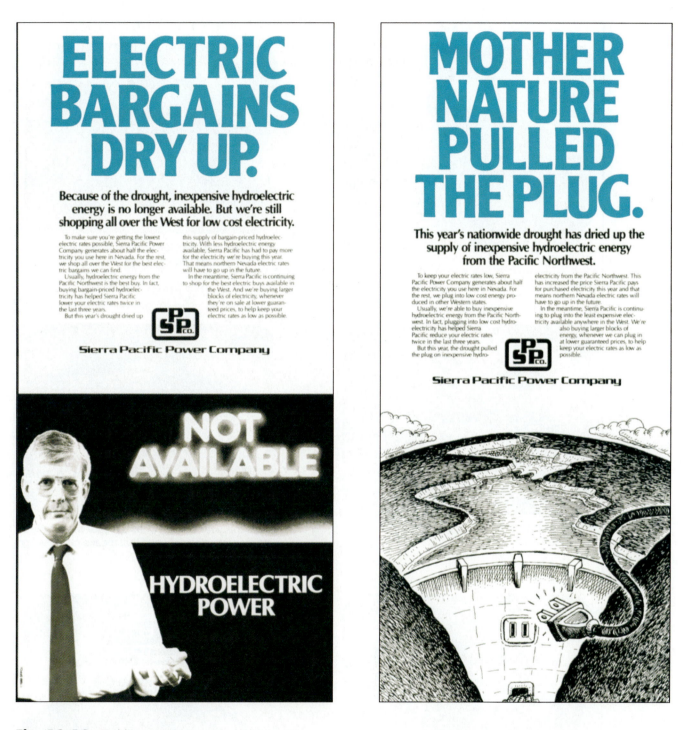

Fig. 12-10 ■ Newspaper advertisements created for the Sierra Pacific campaign explaining the drought situation. (Couresy Sierra Pacific Power Co., Stan Berdrow, vice president, communications and public affairs; Bob Alessandrelli, manager, creative and production services; Doyle-McKenna & Associates, Inc.)

showed 77 percent of the public could recall the drought messages. This, agency and utility officials felt, was an unusually high awareness score.

All told, 57 percent of the public believed the drought was the cause for a rate increase. Five weeks previously 60 percent had no idea that the drought would cause electric bills to go up. Instead of the utility being blamed for the rate increase, a majority of the public was convinced the drought was the real culprit.

1. About half the electricity you use is produced here in Nevada...

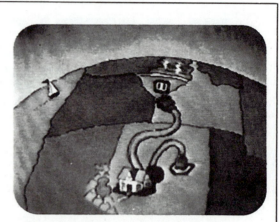

2. But, to keep rates low, Sierra Pacific Power Company plugs into other low cost sources...

3. Like surplus hydroelectric power from the Pacific Northwest.

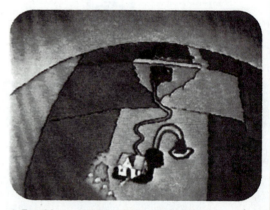

4. But this year's drought has cut back this supply of inexpensive electricity and that means rates may go up.

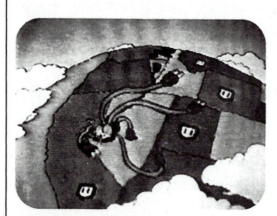

5. So, Sierra Pacific is searching all over the West for other electric bargains...

6. ...to keep your rates as low as possible.

Fig. 12-11 ■ Television storyboards for the Sierra Pacific campaign. This was a 30-second spot.

A Multimedia Advertising Campaign

The visual communicator working in the fields of advertising and public relations quite often will find the most effective approach is a multimedia production. The designer is challenged to create graphics to be used on a variety of surfaces. And, the visual communicator should look beyond a single medium in planning strategy.

For example, a successful multimedia campaign was carried out by Suburban Propane & Petroleum of Whippany, New Jersey. The company set a goal of increasing sales in new installations, water heaters, and ranges by 5 percent compared to the previous year.

A three-month promotion was built on a theme that was modeled after the Olympic games. It was called "Gallons for Gold." The campaign was conducted at 820 district offices located throughout the United States and at the headquarters office. The locations were dubbed "countries." Targeted were 8,000 employees—drivers, customer service personnel, secretaries, managers, corporate staff, and support personnel.

Promotional products were distributed at the "opening ceremonies" and then at "special events" during the medal competition by managers in printed T-shirts and caps. A sales competition was held each week utilizing a different event. One week it was a ski jump to "leap to new levels," and another it was a marathon to "run with the winners." The promotion's mascot was Fillmore the Lion (to fill more tanks with propane). Fillmore was imprinted on a variety of items used in the campaign. See Fig. 12–12.

Gold, silver, and bronze awards were given at "closing ceremonies." All sales goals were exceeded. In the case of ranges, the sales were 200 percent of the goals and new installations were 43.8 percent above the company goal.

Fig. 12-12 ■ Items the visual communicators at Suburban Propane & Petrolane created for its campaign to increase sales and service. The very successful campaign demonstrates the value of employing a communications mix. (Courtesy Promotional Products Association International)

CREATIVITY AND STRATEGY

▶ In developing a campaign or a single advertisement, two words can be especially helpful for the designer—*creativity* and *strategy.* Creativity in advertising design means, in part, finding a new and unique way to present an idea graphically. Strategy means developing a plan to present this message in a way that will achieve the desired goals.

Creativity and strategy are not just helpful to the designer of advertisements. They can be applied to the creation of any communication.

Identify, Illustrate, Simplify

Those who design billboards have a lesson to teach the visual communicator. They say an effective billboard has three elements: a large illustration, a short message, and a clear identification of the source or sponsor. Billboards, the oldest form of advertising, offer us a challenge and a good way to try our hands at effective communication for several reasons.

1. A billboard must deliver its message quickly and to the point. Advertising professionals say the billboard must make contact and deliver its message in about 8 seconds.

2. The billboard has intense competition. In a commercially zoned area billboards can stand shoulder to shoulder as they vie for attention.

3. There is considerable resistance to billboards because opponents point out that they can pollute our visual environment.

Billboards and signs come in all sizes and shapes, but in our abbreviated look at this medium we will confine our concern to the regulation outdoor poster sizes:

■ The poster panel, which measures 12 feet high by 24 feet long. The copy area is 10 feet 5 inches high by 22 feet 8 inches long.

■ The bulletin, which is 14 feet high by 48 feet long.

Advertisers consider several advantages of billboards as an advertising medium. They include:

1. The billboard provides excellent reach at a reasonable price. Research has indicated that a well-placed board can reach 86.7 percent of the adults in an area.

2. Often billboards can be located at a place where the product or service can be obtained.

3. The billboard reaches most automobile riders between the age of 18 and 49—the group most advertisers want to reach.

4. Billboards provide repetition of the message—repetition is one of the requirements for making an impression on the target audience.

5. Illuminated billboards do a selling job 24 hours a day.

Designing a billboard layout can be a worthwhile activity for the visual communicator. Selecting a simple theme and presenting it in a

Fig. 12-13 ■ Repetition and unity are musts for a successful series of advertisements. Here are two of four newspaper ads which received a national second place for the Newspaper Association of America and the American Academy of Advertising's annual student competition. Nicole Marquis used a hard-hitting "testimonial" headline, which is actually the first sentence of her longer copy block. The photographs were carefully printed as vignettes to help the ads carry a more "informal" feel "without destroying the otherwise orderly designs," Marquis said. "In a sense, the upper copy block is really a very long continuation of the header." A reverse block carries the "traditional" copy block. The photos were scanned on Nikon Coolscan and imported to PageMaker 4.2, where the layouts were created. Client: National Committee for the Prevention of Child Abuse. Creative director and copywriter: Nicole Marquis; photographer: Dylan Coulter. Both are advertising students at the University of Oregon's School of Journalism and Communication. (Courtesy Dr. William E. Ryan, instructor.)

concise, attention-getting manner that will appeal to a target audience can be an interesting challenge.

There are several approaches to consider in designing a billboard. You can make a claim, offer news, remind the target to do something, make a comparison. Some tools to employ might be humor, symbolism, and creativity.

Here are some points to consider in making a layout for a billboard:

■ Three elements—art, headline, logo—are plenty.

■ The number of words should be limited to no more than ten—less is better.

Fig. 12-14 ■ A billboard may appear to be a simple visual design challenge. But, it must attract attention and tell the story with art and words that can be absorbed and remembered by someone in approximately 8 seconds. (Courtesy Target Stores)

■ Large illustrations get attention.

■ Use bold colors and type styles.

■ Tie in art with headline.

■ Unity of elements is important.

■ Plan to make only one point.

■ Emphasize the sponsor.

We will end this chapter on advertising design with some exercises in making miniature billboard layouts, included in the Graphics in Action section.

Fig. 12-15 ■ This ad is a composite: The coffee cup, pencil and "Top Ten List" card were shot as knockout photos and scanned atop an earlier photograph taken of wood-grained contact paper using a Nikon Coolscan. Designer Dustin Welch felt the contact paper gave a stronger sense of the wood grain needed to simulate the David Letterman desktop. Two computer files were combined to give the type (Courier) a staggered and more real "typed" look. The ad was assembled in PageMaker 4.2; the headline, copy and taglines were also created in PageMaker. To give it a "funky" look, it was decided to print the piece in black and white and color it with markers by hand. This print ad was part of a campaign which received a national first place from Citibank's annual student advertising competition. Client: Citibank. Creative director and copywriter: Chris Ribiero; art director and photography: Dustin Welch; production and photography: Mark Rose. All of the team members are advertising students at the University of Oregon's School of Journalism and Communication. (Courtesy Dr. William E. Ryan, instructor.)

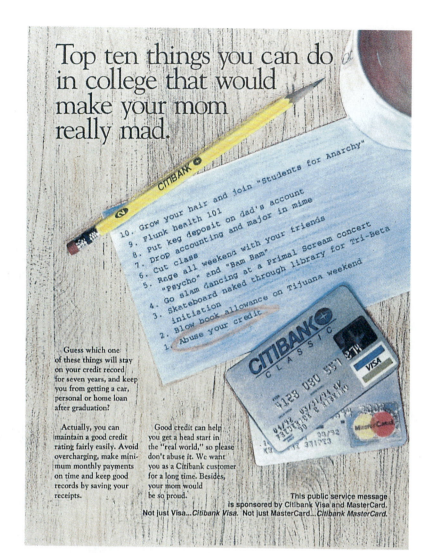

➤ EFFECTIVE DESIGN CHECKLIST

■ Generally, the most effective layout will lead the reader through the advertisement by the design and placement of the elements.

■ In advertising layout, art can be used to stir to consciousness a need or desire that was not felt before.

■ In an advertisement, art that contains people should show people with whom the intended readers can identify.

■ Even though the Z pattern takes advantage of the way the eye often scans a page, if all ads followed this route none would stand out.

■ The design, as well as the copy, should emphasize benefits.

■ White space can be used to unify a layout if it is kept to the outside of the space in which the elements are placed.

■ One item usually should stand out in an advertisement layout, or one item should be emphasized. But the amount of emphasis is a creative decision and most likely will vary with each situation.

▶ **GRAPHICS IN ACTION**

1. Select two or more of the headlines used as examples on page 260. Visualize how you would design art to illustrate the messages of the headlines. Make rough sketches of the art.

2. Use the idea in No. 1, but find art in magazines, clip art books, or art programs on your computer to use as illustrations.

3. Prepare a layout for a billboard for your favorite charity or non-profit organization. You want to evoke an emotional response in the audience. The billboard will be 12 feet high and 24 feet long. Make your layout 4 inches by 8 inches. Add a margin to reduce the actual layout area to the proportions as explained in this chapter.

4. Find an advertisement in a newspaper or other publication that you believe is poorly executed. Redesign it and explain what you did and why.

5. The advertisement shown on this page contains many design and typographical flaws. Redesign it and produce a 5 by 7 inch image ready for publication. Use any art and typestyles, borders, or other graphic devices you desire. (This project could be executed in color or black and white.)

NOTE

[1]Walter Weir, *On the Writing of Advertising* (New York: McGraw-Hill, 1960), p. 7.

DESIGNING FOR PUBLIC RELATIONS

CONTENTS

© Churchill & Klehr

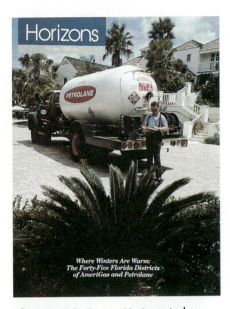

Figure 13-1 ■ *Horizons* is the publication for the employees of the companies that make up UGI Corporation. It is bright and it features employees in action. Note that the light of this cover attracts the eye, there is good unity and contrast, the name of the company is obvious but not dominating, and the employee is doing something. The white logo has excellent visibility, as does the teaser in white on the dark palm-tree background. This cover illustrates the fact that design does not have to be complicated to be effective. Jocelyn Canfield Kelemen is writer-designer as well as editor of *Horizons.*

13 WHAT IS PR?

One of the most misunderstood terms in the world of communication is *public relations.* All sorts of activities from passing out door-prize tickets to greeting patrons as they enter an establishment have been called public relations.

While these pursuits do involve relations with the public, they are far removed from a planned program as it is created and implemented by the professional public relations practitioner. An understanding of the public relations process can pay off for the visual communicator.

Public relations activities require a huge amount of visual materials. They include annual reports and publications, newsletters, brochures, tabloid-format newspapers—virtually everything from envelopes and reply postcards to hard-bound books. The world's largest commercial printing firm, R. R. Donnelley and Sons, produces its *The Lakeside Classics* series of hard-bound books for stockholders each year and has done so since 1903.

A look at a planned public relations effort can offer us some insight into the graphics the designer may be asked to create, and it may open doors to opportunities. For instance, the huge Ruder-Finn, Inc., New York City based public relations firm has established Ruder-Finn Design, its in-house graphics facility.[1]

Ruder-Finn Design produces complete communication services for its clients. These include such visuals as corporate identity items, brochures, training manuals, how-to booklets, posters, annual reports, point-of-sale display units, and three-dimensional exhibits.

The professional public relations practitioner defines the process something like this:

> Public relations is the planned effort to influence public opinion through satisfactory (preferably *exemplary*) performance and two-way communication.

The application of this definition involves advising management, evaluating public attitudes, analyzing the organization's policies and procedures as they affect the interests of the publics (groups of people with particular interests in the organization) and the community. Activities include implementing programs and actions designed to earn public understanding and acceptance.

To accomplish the goal, public relations people lobby, do publicity activities, work on advertising efforts, and work with the media, as well as advise management on policies and procedures.

One approach to handling a public relations program used by those in the field is to follow a four-step plan. In sequence, it includes these procedures:

■ Research to define problems and gather all the information needed to work on them.

■ Planning to set short- and long-term goals, a timetable for reaching them, anticipation of what can go wrong or might need adjustment

Fig. 13-2 ■ This cover for the *Regional Review* of the Federal Bank of Boston illustrates the excellent design work produced for public relations communication programs. Can you analyze this cover and determine why it would be suitable for the client as well as effective in reaching the publics for which it is intended? (Courtesy Federal Reserve Bank of Boston, Ronn Campisi art director. Illustration by Jean Tuttle.)

Federal Reserve Bank of Boston

REGIONAL REVIEW

FALL 1993 VOLUME 3 NUMBER 4

Also: After the Credit Crunch · Economic Forecasting

the BYTES of INVENTION

Our traditional system of protecting intellectual property searches for ways to absorb exotic new digital creations

as the program proceeds and what to do about it, plus what will be needed to accomplish the goals.

■ Action and communication—to do something and let publics know what is being done.

■ Evaluation to see if the goals have been reached and to see what worked well and what could have been done better. In addition, evaluation is not just after-the-fact. It involves monitoring and assessing that begins with the research phase and continues throughout the program. That way, the practitioner has a better grasp of what's going on.

As you can see, the various visual communication tools we have examined and will examine in future chapters can play a part in the world of public relations. Rather than repeat what has been said and rehearse what will be said about these tools, let's look at one of the most important activities of a public relations facility—producing the annual report. The author was associated with the public relations department of a major corporation, where he noted that it took one full-time person four months of his work year to plan and produce the annual report.

THE ANNUAL REPORT

➤ The first step in producing the annual report is, of course, planning. One approach is to plan a theme for the report. This could stress one aspect of the company each year. Themes could include such things as the company's personality, its reputation, its strengths and

Fig. 13-3 ■ Skill in newspaper design often is applied in the world of public relations. The designer of the *Grand Canyon Railway Territorial Times* needed newspaper layout knowledge. Before layout work started, the project required intense research into "old West" style typography as well as the history and characteristics of the Grand Canyon area. (Courtesy Grand Canyon Railway and Grand Canyon Trust)

weaknesses, and what its publics want to know about it. Other themes might include:

- The steps being taken to increase earnings in the future.
- What is happening outside the organization that will affect its ability to accomplish its goals.
- How the company has improved its image in the community and what it is doing to be a good citizen.
- The greatest accomplishment during the year.

Before we go further, it should be understood that the best plans for impressive visual communications can be constricted by the budget. The designer should understand this aspect of the project before spending a lot of time on design goals that outstrip the available money.

A timetable should be created as one of the first steps in producing the annual report. This could include scheduling for photographs, art, stories, financial report, printing, and distribution.

Fig. 13-4 ■ In the past, annual reports were dull financial reviews aimed at the serious investor public. Research has shown that investors come from all demographic groups and that the reports are becoming important communication tools. BellSouth has created this striking report that incorporates visual graphics with readable text to tell its story and rally support from all present and potential stockholders. (Courtesy of BellSouth Corporation)

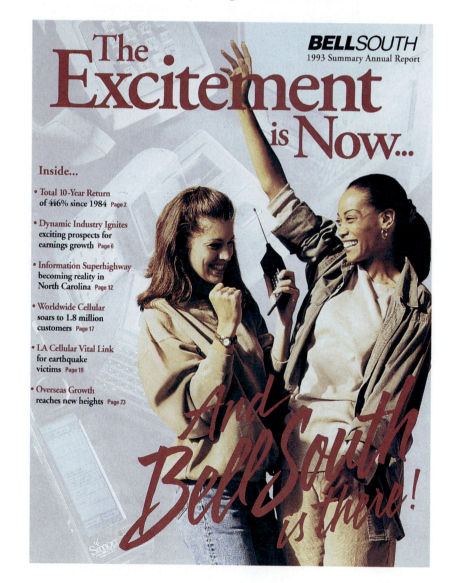

(*Note:* The Securities and Exchange Commission mandates that the annual report must be distributed within 90 days after year-end figures have been compiled.)

As part of the planning, the communicator should research the company's shareholders. A demographic picture of shareholders should play an important role in determining the direction the design and contents will take. For instance, the annual report can be a valuable communication tool if the target audience will make use of it. It can be more than just boring statistics and financial statements. A New York Stock Exchange study revealed that the average shareholder owns shares in about three and a half companies. So there is the aspect of competition with the annual reports of other companies to consider.

It will be helpful to study the annual reports of competitors as well as other similar organizations.

The parts of the annual report include:

- *The cover:* It should be meaningful and not just nice decorative art. A tasteful design that reflects the company image works well.

- *The table of contents:* If the report is long—say, twenty pages or more—it should have a table of contents.

- *Letter to shareholders:* A fixture in annual reports; it should be from the president and/or chief executive officer and should discuss the concerns of the shareholders as revealed through research. It should be readable—most likely written by the public relations department.

- *Financial highlights of the year:* Expanding the chief executive's letter.

- *Main text:* Two approaches to this element might be considered. One would be a straightforward review of the year, department by department; another is a theme approach.

- *Core financial statements:* Prepared by the firm's accountants.

As mentioned, there are a number of possibilities for themes. In addition to those mentioned, company history might be considered on its anniversary years; a cross-section of customers might work; and an annual report featuring outstanding employees could produce some good internal public relations as well as make an interesting report.

The author of this text was involved in producing an annual report the theme of which traced the product from its raw material stage until it reached the consumer. The report brought many favorable comments from stockholders.

When it comes to designing the annual report here are a few things to keep in mind:

- The Securities and Exchange Commission requires that body type should be at least 10 point so all shareholders can read it with ease.

- Keep reverses to a minimum, and use good basic design techniques. The annual report is no place to be cute with design.

- Most likely you will be required to include photographs of executives and others. If so, don't always use mug shots; try to show people in the report doing something.

Fig. 13-5 ■ This two-page spread is from the BellSouth annual report. These exciting, attention-grabbing layouts are a far cry from the stilted, formal financial pages of annual reports produced in the past. (Courtesy of BellSouth Corporation)

Fig. 13-6 ■ The annual report is a good communication tool that can be utilized to rally support from the important stockholder public. BellSouth included this reply-card pitch in its report to build up a mailing list of stockholders who might contact Congress when issues of importance to them and the company are considered by lawmakers.

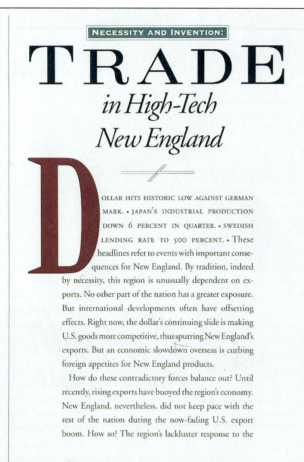

NECESSITY AND INVENTION:

TRADE

*in High-Tech
New England*

DOLLAR HITS HISTORIC LOW AGAINST GERMAN MARK. • JAPAN'S INDUSTRIAL PRODUCTION DOWN 6 PERCENT IN QUARTER. • SWEDISH LENDING RATE TO 500 PERCENT. • These headlines refer to events with important consequences for New England. By tradition, indeed by necessity, this region is unusually dependent on exports. No other part of the nation has a greater exposure. But international developments often have offsetting effects. Right now, the dollar's continuing slide is making U.S. goods more competitive, thus spurring New England's exports. But an economic slowdown overseas is curbing foreign appetites for New England products.

How do these contradictory forces balance out? Until recently, rising exports have buoyed the region's economy. New England, nevertheless, did not keep pace with the rest of the nation during the now-fading U.S. export boom. How so? The region's lackluster response to the

By Jane Sneddon Little

The author thanks Michael Jud and Garrett Solomon for valuable research assistance

6 REGIONAL REVIEW • WINTER 1993   ILLUSTRATION BY TIM LEWIS

If necessity is the mother of invention, in New England she's the grandmother of trade.

Fig. 13-7 ■ A two-page spread utilizing the A-T-S-I (art-title-subhead/byline-initial letter) approach, as explained in Chapter 15, for a public relations publication noted for its outstanding design. Notice how the art grabs the reader and reinforces the theme of the article. Note that the large initial letter (in red) does not overpower the text because of the body type size, the leading, and the use of white space on the page. Note, too, that title lines and by-line are all centered for unity and consistency. This is from the *Regional Review* of the Federal Reserve Bank of Boston, Ronn Campisi, art director. The illustration is by Tim Lewis.

A PR DESIGN SUCCESS STORY

➤ Design requirements for a public relations effort do not always include printing on paper only. The designer should keep in mind all the materials and devices available. Here is an example of a successful public relations plan that was built primarily around just two items: a T-shirt and a mug. But, both display creative design with a goal in mind.

The Bridgeport Hospital in Bridgeport, Connecticut, set a goal of improving employee morale and creating a better image in the community. Morale was low, and the community image was poor after two bad situations involving two physicians. The hospital did not have any sort of program of relations with the media.

A theme was developed: "Bridgeport Hospital: A View of the World," to depict the hospital as a leader in the region and beyond. A humorous, four-color design was created and printed on posters placed around the hospital and used on T-shirts and mugs.

Fig. 13-8 ■ This two-page spread is from *The Process of Discovery*, a publication that reviews the year's activities of the National Center for Supercomputing Applications. Note the placement of elements. The subtle use of the enlarged, tone-downed art taken from the small art on page 23 and used to frame page 22 is an example of the principle of unity applied in a creative and appropriate manner. (Reprinted with permission of National Center for Supercomputing Applications at the University of Illinois, Urbana-Champaign. Photography by Thompson-McClellan, Champaign.)

The T-shirts were given away personally by the president and the chief operating officer of the hospital during a 2-hour period for each of the hospital's three shifts.

All 2,500 employees were made aware in advance of the T-shirt distribution, so all who were interested knew they would be available. Shirts were also sent to the media. Ceramic mugs with the theme's graphic on them were presented to key individuals at meetings both in and outside of the hospital.

Of the 2,500 employees, 2,300 picked up a shirt over the three shifts, with several employees asking to purchase additional shirts. Favorable feature stories appeared in the media. The T-shirts are now being sold in the hospital gift shop, and the mugs are being used as gifts to key hospital visitors and new employees.[2]

Fig. 13-9 ■ The creative visual communicator looks beyond the obvious in devising media for a campaign. In this project, the T-shirts became communications tools, as did the printed poster. (Courtesy Promotional Products Association International.)

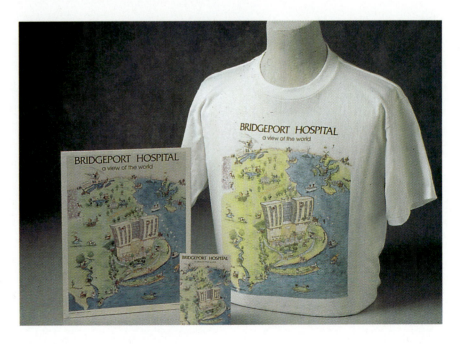

▶ **GRAPHICS IN ACTION**

1. Assume your client is a hotel near the campus of the university you attend or one with which you are familiar. The hotel would like for you to come up with a plan to increase the patronage of parents who come to town to visit their sons or daughters. Brainstorm this idea and outline your program.

2. Create a graphic to implement the plan you devised in No. 1. (This project could be limited to one design or expanded to creating the visuals for a complete program, depending on the emphasis you want to place on this aspect of visual communication.)

3. You have your own graphic design studio. You recently bought a major PostScript font library for your computer. You want to inform your clients of your expanded capabilities. Plan an information program to make your clients aware of this addition.

4. Carry No. 3 forward by creating an example of a visual (brochure, newsletter, etc.) to be used in executing the plan.

5. Scan the daily newspaper to see if you can find a story concerning a public relations problem. It might be some problem caused by a civic body (such as an action by the city council), or it could be unfavorable publicity reflecting on a local business or a person in the news, for example. Brainstorm ideas for a response and the graphics that could accompany the response.

NOTES

[1]"Stop Worrying and Love the Mac," *Graphic Arts Monthly,* October 1992, pp. 92–93.
[2]With special thanks to Richard G. Ebel of Promotional Products Association International.

CHAPTER
1 4

DESIGNING THE MAGAZINE

CONTENTS

© Cindy Charles, PhotoEdit

This chapter and the one that follows are for those in visual communications who find that their jobs will involve producing or helping to produce a magazine, and for those who aspire to careers in the exciting field of magazine publishing.

14 BIG AND SMALL MAGAZINES ARE BASICALLY THE SAME

➤ "I need help!" The voice on the other end of the line was a familiar one to the journalism instructor. Deborah had been one of his advisees when she was a student. She had opted for the radio/television sequence of courses. She had no interest whatsoever in the print media and avoided the graphics courses, while taking the bare minimum of writing and editing courses.

After she spent two years in an entry-level position at a television station, opportunity came knocking at Deborah's door in the form of a job offer as information officer for the local real estate board. The increase in salary was substantial and the future opportunities appeared bright.

The board members explained Deborah's duties.

"Of course you will continue publication of our monthly magazine," one member remarked.

Deborah didn't get the job.

Most people visualize one of the popular publications when magazines are mentioned. *Reader's Digest* or *TV Guide,* with their more than 15 million copies an issue; *Time, Newsweek, Sports Illustrated, Good Housekeeping, Better Homes and Gardens, Glamour, Seventeen,* and *Rolling Stone; National Geographic,* with its stunning photography, or *Scientific American,* with its precise, detailed text and charts. These are formidable publications. Planning and producing a magazine on such a scale would seem to require technical knowledge that is beyond the abilities of many communicators.

But the same principles of selecting type and illustrations and placing them on a page in the most effective way possible apply to small eight-page association publications as they do to these giants. And the small association monthly can be just as attractive in its way and do just as effective a job of communicating with its target audience. It does take planning and the application of basic principles of good design. We begin by discussing general planning and then move on to the specifics of magazine design.

First of all, the design and production of a magazine can be fun. Of all the areas of printed communications, none is more interesting and challenging. Also, the satisfaction of accomplishment when you hold the printed copy of your magazine is rarely exceeded in any other communications activity.

Where do you begin? Although our concerns are layout and design, we cannot separate this from editorial planning.

In the ideal situation, the staff will include a design specialist—the *art director.* This person has the primary responsibility for the creative aspects of producing the magazine.

Fig. 14-1 ■ A good example to illustrate the need for the complete visual graphic communicator to become skilled in the design of multiple media is the magapaper. This magapaper, which includes the design of a magazine for its front and back covers, becomes a tabloid newspaper when it is unfolded. (Courtesy Farm Bureau News)

The art director should be versed in all the visual aspects of a printed communication, especially type selection and arrangement for effective readability, legibility, and suitability. He or she should be experienced in the production end of the business as well.

There are many examples of outstanding design in magazines, but there are also examples of designs that are beautiful as works of art, yet hamper the effectiveness of communication. These can include using decorative rules and borders that create barriers rather than unity or advancing hot colors that dominate the visual area.

Too often the tip-off that a publication is in trouble is its use of "screaming" graphics—which figuratively shout for help as the publication goes down for the third time. Too often a publication will suddenly take graphics seriously for the first time when it hits turbulent waters. Examples in recent years include the old *Saturday Evening Post,* a giant in its day, in the months before its demise in 1969, and the *Chicago Daily News* in the final weeks of its life in 1978.

GOOD DESIGN AIDS CONTENT

➤ As in all printed communications, good magazine design must aid and illuminate the content. The combination of good design and poor content can fail, whereas what appears to be poor design and good content can sometimes survive and even prosper. Obviously, however, we should aim for good design *and* good content.

This partnership concept—good content and good design—extends to the editor and art director. The editor should attempt to keep design within the limits of its function while encouraging the art director to provide creative advice that results in the bright and unique. Both should strive to produce a publication that will attract and hold readers.

The editor who has a good art director as a partner is fortunate indeed. However, in many of the more than 10,000 periodicals of various sizes and shapes that appear each month in America, the editor and art director are one and the same. This is especially true with small house publications for business and industry and organizations like the local Girl Scout council, real estate board, and so on. Many of the entry jobs in communications involve producing these small magazines.

Let us assume, then, that we are going to design a magazine from the ground up, or that we are going to give an existing magazine an overhaul to make it more effective. The first step is planning. Time spent on planning and writing the plans down on paper will pay for itself over and over again.

LONG-RANGE DECISIONS

➤ In designing or redesigning a magazine there are several long-range decisions that should be made immediately. These include:

■ *The function, or purpose, of the magazine:* We should determine exactly why it is being published, what we hope to accomplish by sending it out into the world.

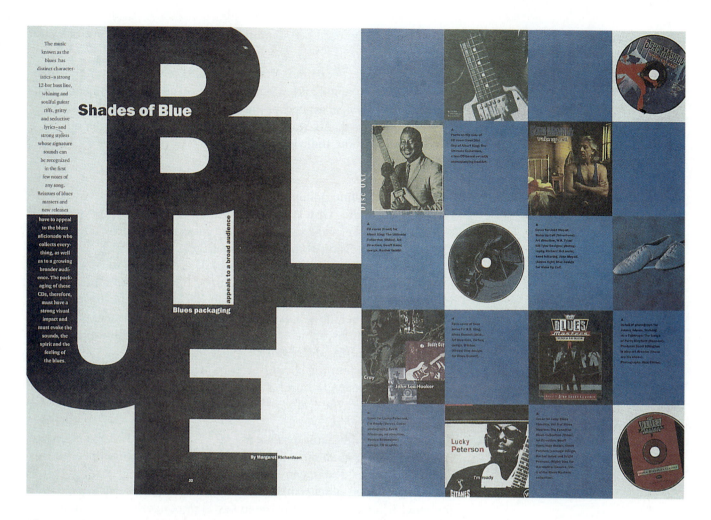

Fig. 14-2 ■ Big and bold. That is the trend in much graphic communication today. This two-page spread is from *U&lc* the publication of the International Typeface Corporation. This layout has a number of interesting features. Consider the use of reverses in the arrangement of the copy. The placement of the ten pieces of art is such that they do not fight. This spread is an example of a layout that will not only attract attention, but will hold the reader for some time as there is much to study and contemplate.

■ *The personality of the magazine:* Printed communications, like people, project images. What sort of image do we want our magazine to project? Is it dignified and reserved or is it informal and aggressive?

■ *The audience we wish to attract:* What sort of person do we want to read our magazine? What are our readers or potential readers like, where are they located, what are their interests?

■ *The formula for our magazine:* This means the kinds of information, articles, and features we will include in each issue and how this material will be presented.

■ *Will our magazine contain advertising?* If so, how will our editorial formula affect the potential for advertising? Will our target editorial audience be a target market for certain goods and services? If so, the advertising people take over here and determine the markets, appeals, and potential advertisers who will be interested in what we have to offer.

■ *When and how often our magazine will appear:* If the publication is a weekly, timeliness is usually an important factor in the formula, and the design format should reflect this timeliness.

■ *Design and typographic decisions:* These will include the basic format—the page size, margins, number of columns per page, and the typefaces to be used for standing heads, article titles, captions, and body matter.

■ *Editorial style decisions:* Standard practice for spelling, grammar, punctuation, capitalization, and so on, as well as decisions concerning all the physical aspects of the magazine can be included in a *stylebook* or manual. All staff members should use this stylebook as a guide while doing their jobs.

Title and Cover Policies

The title or headline policy has to be determined. Two philosophies are usually found here. One is to adopt one or two families of type for all titles and the other is to select specific types for each article.

Another decision concerns the magazine cover policy. For example, what will be the logo (or nameplate) design, what sort of art will be used on the cover, how will the various typographic elements be used from issue to issue? Other typographic decisions to be made in the planning stage include the arrangement of heads, subheads, masthead, regular feature titles, table of contents, column widths and placement, and/or placement of advertising.

All of this planning should be done with the basic tenent of effective magazine design in mind. *The physical appearance of the publication should reflect the editorial content and appeal to the audience for which it is intended.*

Much of a magazine producer's success is related to the ability to isolate the target audience and build a product that will appeal to this audience. Proper design can help us achieve this goal.

For instance, a magazine devoted to religious concerns should look the part. It must by its appearance say "I'm concerned with religion," just as a magazine must say "Let's go hunting and fishing" in its look if it is to appeal to the hunting and fishing enthusiast. A magazine aimed at businesswomen should wear a different typographic "suit" than one appealing to structural engineers. These stylistic differences need to be considered in the initial planning stages.

Visualization in Magazine Design

The next step for the editor or designer is *visualization*—the construction of mental pictures—of the magazine's eventual appearance.

One word of caution. Although our magazine's appearance may say "hunting and fishing," it is important that a new and unique way be found to say it. And it is important that we say it without resorting to screaming graphics. Our publication should stand out from others that are trying to say the same thing. Thus our planning needs to include a study of the competition and how it is saying what we want to say.

In planning the initial design, then, we must always keep the potential reader in mind. A scientific magazine, for instance, appeals to a precise, orderly mind. It should use precise, orderly types—medium Sans Serifs; clean, sharp modern Romans, such as the Bodonis; straightforward solid line rules and thick-and-thin straight-line combinations of the Oxford rules. It should have accurate and clear-cut placement of

Fig. 14-3 ■ This cover from *Field & Stream* accomplishes the four functions of a cover: It identifies the magazine in a way that sets it apart from others, it attracts the attention of the intended target audience, it sets the tone or mood of the contents, and it lures the reader inside. (Reprinted with permission of *Field & Stream,* a publication of Times Mirror Magazines, Inc.)

elements. Color should be used for emphasis where it is needed, but color should never come on so strong that it shouts.

Scientific American is considered one of the best-designed magazines, and it applies these typographic principles with great success even though it might appear rather forbidding to the reader who is not especially interested in the world of science.

Whatever basic design approach is chosen, it should not be changed in the future without a great deal of study and replanning. The basic design plan should remain constant, as it can help achieve identity and continuity from one issue to the next. It should help the reader recognize the magazine instantly, just as *Time's* distinctive red color, all-cap nameplate in Roman type, and cover art have for years.

As the general planning progresses, we should also keep in mind the admonition of one magazine designer, "If you're dull, you're dead."

SCIENTIFIC AMERICAN

Can the Growing Human Population Feed Itself?

As human numbers surge toward 10 billion, some experts are alarmed, others optimistic. Who is right?

by John Bongaarts

Demographers now project that the world's population will double during the next half century, from 5.3 billion people in 1990 to more than 10 billion by 2050. How will the environment and humanity respond to this unprecedented growth? Expert opinion divides into two camps. Environmentalists and ecologists, whose views have widely been disseminated by the electronic and print media, regard the situation as a catastrophe in the making. They argue that in order to feed the growing population farmers must intensify agricultural practices that already cause grave ecological damage. Our natural resources and the environment, now burdened by past population growth, will simply collapse under the weight of this future demand.

The optimists, on the other hand, comprising many economists as well as some agricultural scientists, assert that the earth can readily produce more than enough food for the expected population in 2050. They contend that technological innovation and the continued investment of human capital will deliver high standards of living to much of the globe, even if the population grows much larger than the projected 10 billion. Which point of view will hold sway? What shape might the future of our species and the environment actually take?

Many environmentalists fear that world food supply has reached a precarious state: "Human numbers are on a collision course with massive famines.... If humanity fails to act, nature will end the population explosion for us—in very unpleasant ways—well before 10 billion is reached," write Paul R. Ehrlich and Anne H. Ehrlich of Stanford University in their 1990 book *The Population Explosion*. In the long run, the Ehrlichs and like-minded experts consider substantial growth in food production to be absolutely impossible. "We are feeding ourselves at the expense of our children. By definition farmers can overplow and overpump only in the short run. For many farmers the short run is drawing to a close," states Lester R. Brown, president of the Worldwatch Institute, in a 1988 paper.

Over the past three decades, these authors point out, enormous efforts and resources have been pooled to amplify agricultural output. Indeed, the total quantity of harvested crops increased dramatically during this time. In the developing world, food production rose by an average of 117 percent in the quarter of a century between 1965 and 1990. Asia performed far better than other regions, which saw increases below average.

Because population has expanded rapidly as well, per capita food production has generally shown only modest change; in Africa it actually declined. As a consequence, the number of undernourished people is still rising in most parts of the developing world, although that number did fall from 844 million to 786 million during the 1980s. But this decline reflects improved nutritional conditions in Asia alone. During the same period, the number of people having energy-deficient diets in Latin America, the Near East and Africa climbed.

Many social factors can bring about conditions of hunger, but the pessimists emphasize that population pressure on fragile ecosystems plays a significant role. One specific concern is that we seem to be running short on land suitable for cultivation. If so, current efforts to bolster per capita food production by clearing more fertile land will find fewer options. Between 1850 and 1950 the amount of arable land grew quickly to accommodate both larger populations and greater demand for better diets. This expansion then slowed and by the late 1980s ceased altogether. In the developed world, as well as in some developing countries (especially China), the amount of land under cultivation started to decline during the

JOHN BONGAARTS has been vice president and director of the Research Division of the Population Council in New York City since 1989. He is currently a member of the Johns Hopkins Society of Scholars and the Royal Dutch Academy of Sciences. He won the Mindel Sheps Award in 1986 from the Population Association of America and the Research Career Development Award in 1980–85 from the National Institutes of Health.

RICE PADDIES (these are in Indonesia) provide the principal food for more than half the world's population. In many parts of Asia the terrain prevents farmers from using mechanized farm equipment; to grow and harvest a single acre of rice can demand more than 1,000 man-hours. Still, Asian countries now produce more than 90 percent of all rice grown.

1980s. This drop is largely because spreading urban centers have engulfed fertile land or, once the land is depleted, farmers have abandoned it. Farmers have also fled from irrigated land that has become unproductive because of salt accumulation.

Moreover, environmentalists insist that soil erosion is destroying much of the land that is left. The extent of the damage is the subject of controversy. A recent global assessment, sponsored by the United Nations Environment Program and reported by the World Resources Institute and others, offers some perspective. The study concludes that 17 percent of the land supporting plant life worldwide has lost value over the past 45 years. The estimate includes erosion caused by water and wind, as well as chemical and physical deterioration, and ranks the degree of soil degradation from light to severe. This degradation is least prevalent in North

Fig. 14-4 ■ The precise, careful graphics and type arrangements of *Scientific American* might not appeal to everyone, but they are just right for a publication aimed at people interested in the sciences. Even though the layout appears uncomplex, note how many design decisions had to be made. (Copyright 1994 by Scientific American, Inc. All rights reserved. Photograph by Steve Vidler, Leo de Wys, Inc.)

The Four Fs of Magazine Design

One way to approach the physical design of a magazine, is to consider the "four Fs" of magazine design—function, formula, format, and frames.

Function The *function* part of this approach is obvious, but it will be helpful to jot down the things the magazine should accomplish. Will it be an internal magazine, meant for members of an organization or employees of a company? Or will its appeal be external, aimed toward people outside the organization? Or will it have a combined goal of dual appeal, internal and external? Will it be aimed at recruiting new members or new support? Will it be a "how to" publication, or will it be a publication that relies on layouts with lots of photos? All these functions will affect the physical form of the publication.

Formula The *formula* is the unique and relatively stable combination of elements—articles, departments, and so on—that make up each issue. The elements that should be considered in devising the formula for a magazine include the sort of articles to be included, such as fiction, uplifting essays, interpretative pieces, or whatever.

Fig. 14–5 ▪ *National Geographic, an American tradition, has always used a standard cover format. The design has gained product recognition through the years with its yellow frame. Note the excellent legibility of the reverse type and the use of a Script for Sicily. Balance, unity, proportion, and harmony are all incorporated in this cover design. (Photo by William Albert Allard © 1995 National Geographic Society)*

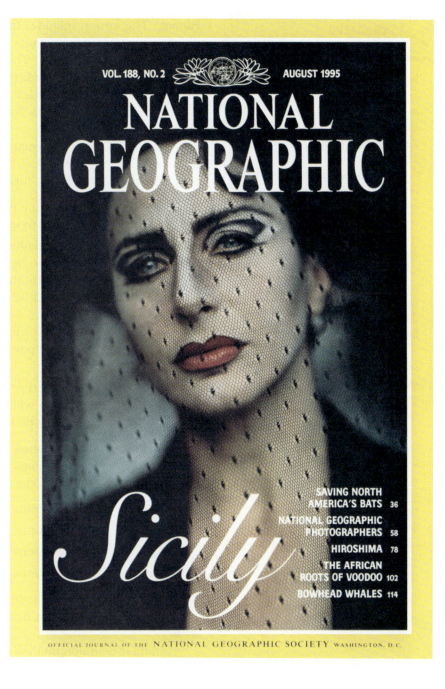

The formula also includes the sort of illustrations, drawings, and/or photographs to use. It includes the departments that will be a regular part of each issue as well as editorial or special interest columns, poetry, cartoons and jokes, fillers, and other miscellaneous material. Efforts should be made to produce content that has balance and consistency—and variety to prevent dullness.

Once we have defined the function of the magazine and developed the formula to achieve this function, we need to consider our special typographic concerns—the format and frames of the publication.

> ### CREATIVE COMMUNICATION

Is experience the best teacher?

The idea battleground in design is free-thinking, free-flowing, open-ended, no-rules creativity versus knowledge, discipline, experience. The struggle goes on.

Some psychologists have found that experience can restrict creativity. Some experienced editors or designers might not view a problem with a fresh outlook. They might classify it with past problems and select solutions from past experience. Only if the problem type cannot be recognized is it studied in depth. Otherwise, old solutions are fitted to new problems.

What is the answer? Creative problem solvers suggest the answer might be brainstorming—using group interaction to stimulate individual thought. Participants are encouraged to generate as many ideas as possible without evaluating them. After a period of time, the ideas are grouped, duplicates and obviously impractical suggestions eliminated, and the others rank ordered.

Format   The *format* includes the basic size and shape of the magazine plus the typographic constants or physical features that stay the same from one issue to the next. These constants include the cover design, masthead, break of the book (space allocation), placement of regular features, folio line techniques, and techniques for handling *jumps,* or the continuation of articles from one part of the publication to the other.

Magazines select a format, or basic design pattern, incorporate it in their stylebook, and stick to it. There are a number of things we must consider when deciding the format of our publication. These include:

1. The press capacity of the printer who produces the magazine plus the most efficient way to use paper with a minimum of waste.

2. Ease of handling and mailing. How will the publication be delivered to the reader? If it is to be mailed in an envelope, that could be a factor in determining its size. How will the publication be handled by the reader? If it will be the type of publication that is kept and filed, it might be wise to select a size that will fit standard file cabinets or binders. If it is the sort of publication that will be carried around in a pocket or purse, that is another factor to consider in determining size.

3. The content. Large picture layouts require elbow room to be effective. If the publication will use many picutres or diagrams, a large page size will probably be best.

There are, however, some common format dimensions that have evolved. One set of dimensions determined by designers sorts out magazines by size according to the sizes of the type areas. For example,

Pocket:	2 columns wide by 85 lines deep
Standard:	2 columns wide by 119 lines deep
Flat:	3 columns wide by 140 lines deep
Large:	4 columns wide by 170 lines deep

(*Note:* The lines used to measure depth are agate lines, based on agate type, which is 5½ points in height. There are fourteen agate lines in 1 inch.)

Another common method of classifying magazines is by page size:

Miniature	4½ by 6 inches
Pocket	6 by 9 inches
Basic	8½ by 11 inches
Picture	10½ by 13 inches
Sunday supplement	11 by 13 inches

There are variations to these standard sizes, however, and not all magazines will fall into these categories.

The most common magazine page size these days is the basic 8½ by 11 inches, or slight variations thereof. The size represents the most efficient use of paper, is easy to address and mail, and fits nicely in binders and file cabinets. From the graphics point of view, the basic page is large enough to permit good use of art and to give considerable latitude for interesting layouts.

Frames Magazine *frames* are the outer page margins, the white space between columns of types and pages, and the use of white space to "frame" the various elements such as headings, titles, subheads, by-lines, and art.

A basic decision must be made regarding page margins. There are two possibilities. One is to use *progressive margins.* In this type of margination, as explained in Chapter 5, margins are designed to increase in size as they progress around the page. The gutter margin, or inside margin, is the smallest. On the right-hand pages the margins increase clockwise, and on the left-hand pages they increase counterclockwise. Progressive margins may be chosen if the designer wants to give a visual impression of high quality, or "class."

Fig. 14-6 ■ White space is an important design element. This page demands attention even though it consists only of the title, subhead, by-line, and a small initial letter. The title is unified with the text but it is printed in light blue, a cool color, and it does not hamper easy reading. Note the little icon in the lower right to indicate continuation to the following page. (Courtesy *National Wildlife*)

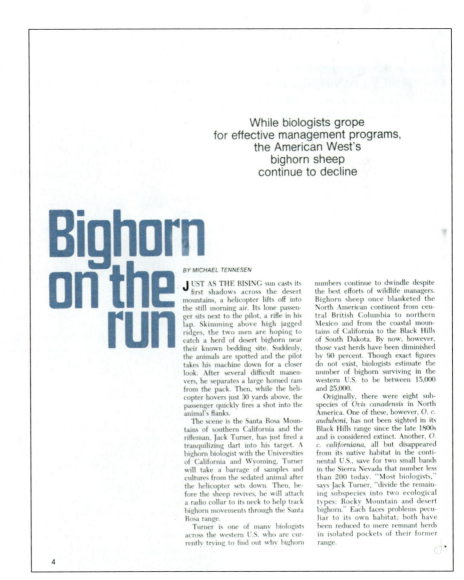

While biologists grope
for effective management programs,
the American West's
bighorn sheep
continue to decline

Bighorn on the run

BY MICHAEL TENNESEN

JUST AS THE RISING sun casts its first shadows across the desert mountains, a helicopter lifts off into the still morning air. Its lone passenger sits next to the pilot, a rifle in his lap. Skimming above high jagged ridges, the two men are hoping to catch a herd of desert bighorn near their known bedding site. Suddenly, the animals are spotted and the pilot takes his machine down for a closer look. After several difficult maneuvers, he separates a large horned ram from the pack. Then, while the helicopter hovers just 30 yards above, the passenger quickly fires a shot into the animal's flanks.

The scene is the Santa Rosa Mountains of southern California and the rifleman, Jack Turner, has just fired a tranquilizing dart into his target. A bighorn biologist with the Universities of California and Wyoming, Turner will take a barrage of samples and cultures from the sedated animal after the helicopter sets down. Then, before the sheep revives, he will attach a radio collar to its neck to help track bighorn movements through the Santa Rosa range.

Turner is one of many biologists across the western U.S. who are currently trying to find out why bighorn numbers continue to dwindle despite the best efforts of wildlife managers. Bighorn sheep once blanketed the North American continent from central British Columbia to northern Mexico and from the coastal mountains of California to the Black Hills of South Dakota. By now, however, those vast herds have been diminished by 90 percent. Though exact figures do not exist, biologists estimate the number of bighorn surviving in the western U.S. to be between 15,000 and 25,000.

Originally, there were eight subspecies of *Ovis canadensis* in North America. One of these, however, *O. c. auduboni*, has not been sighted in its Black Hills range since the late 1800s and is considered extinct. Another, *O. c. californiana*, all but disappeared from its native habitat in the continental U.S., save for two small bands in the Sierra Nevada that number less than 200 today. "Most biologists," says Jack Turner, "divide the remaining subspecies into two ecological types: Rocky Mountain and desert bighorn." Each faces problems peculiar to its own habitat; both have been reduced to mere remnant herds in isolated pockets of their former range.

4

Regular margins, or those with identical dimensions, are most common. They should take up about half of the total area of the page. Quite often the *folio lines* (page number, name of magazine, date to appear on each page) are placed in the margins of magazine pages. This is another typographic decision to make.

Another white space or frame decision concerns the space between columns. A minimum of 1 pica of white space should be allotted here. Less will make the page look too crowded. A pica and a half is not too much. On a basic 8½ by 11 inch page or larger, 2 picas of white space between columns on a two-column format is about right. Too much white space between columns will destroy unity and make the page appear fragmented.

There is a tendency for those new at the game to crowd elements and jam them together. Don't be afraid to use plenty of white space; make a minimum of 1 pica between art and body copy, between head and subhead, and between all other elements.

Fig. 14-7 ■ Added impact can be obtained by bleeding art. Bleeds are illustrations that are extended in one or more directions to the very edge of the page. In this page the art was bled to the middle of the gutter on the left and beyond the edge of the page on the right. This single page has great impact as a result of close cropping and the bleed technique. (Page designed by Jocelyn Canfield Kelemen for *Horizons* magazine of the UGI Corporation)

Electric Utility Offers Hands-On Training Center

The Electric Utility Division's **Dundee Training Center** was just a good idea for several years until it was built during 1991 and 1992. The site is set up to develop construction standards and provide underground and overhead "hands-on" training to electrical operations employees.

The training center is designed to simulate a realistic electric distribution system, though none of the transformers nor any of the equipment at the site is electrically energized.

At the site, there are several utility poles, including an "upside down" pole with the transformer framed at ground level, making it easier and safer to instruct a group. One section of the site is devoted to underground electrical lines and equipment, including pad-mounted residential transformers, which step power down from high primary voltage to lower residential voltage.

The site is used on a monthly basis. ■

Counterclockwise from above, left: Engineers from the standards department use the training center to test construction materials. Pictured here are (from left) Bill Hritzak, who runs most of the training sessions, Walter Grodzki and Rich Secor, who are installing termination ends on cables in a residential transformer box.

At left: Ken Reese and Norm Williams work on the same project.

Above: In addition to on-the-ground training, some of the trainees go up in bucket trucks to get a first-hand look at equipment. Pictured here are Bill Hritzak and Tommy Cope.

Once concrete decisions are made concerning the function and formula of a magazine and the basic format, including handling of the frames, we can turn to the specific elements that will be combined to make our typographic package. But before we do, there are two areas that we should address: basic terminology and redesigning an existing publication.

BASIC MAGAZINE TERMINOLOGY

➤ Following are some basic terms that anyone engaged in magazine editing, design, or production should understand:

- *Bleed:* The extension of an illustration beyond the type area to the edge of a page.
- *Break of the book:* The allocation of space for articles, features, and all material printed in the magazine.
- *Contents page:* The page that lists all the articles and features and their locations.
- *Cover:* Includes not only the front page but the other three pages making up the outside wrap of the magazine as well.
- *Folio:* The page number, date, and name of the periodical on each page or spread.
- *Gutter:* The margin of the page at the point of binding, or the inside page margin.
- *Logo:* The magazine's nameplate, appearing on the cover, masthead, and so on.
- *Masthead:* The area, often boxed or given special typographic treatment, where the logo, staff listings, date of publication, and other information regarding the publication is listed.
- *Perfect binding:* A binding method that uses a flexible adhesive to hold the backs of folded signatures together while they are ground to size and more adhesive is applied. The cover is put in place while the adhesive is still wet.
- *Saddle stitch* (also called *saddle wire*): The kind of binding in which staples are driven through the middle fold of the pages.
- *Self-cover:* A magazine cover printed on the same paper stock as the rest of the magazine.
- *Sidestitch* (also called *sidewire*): A method of binding in which staples are driven through stacked printed sections (signatures) of the magazine.
- *Signature:* A large sheet of paper printed on both sides and folded to make up a section of a publication. For instance, four pages might be printed on each side of a sheet and then the sheet folded and cut to make an eight-page signature.

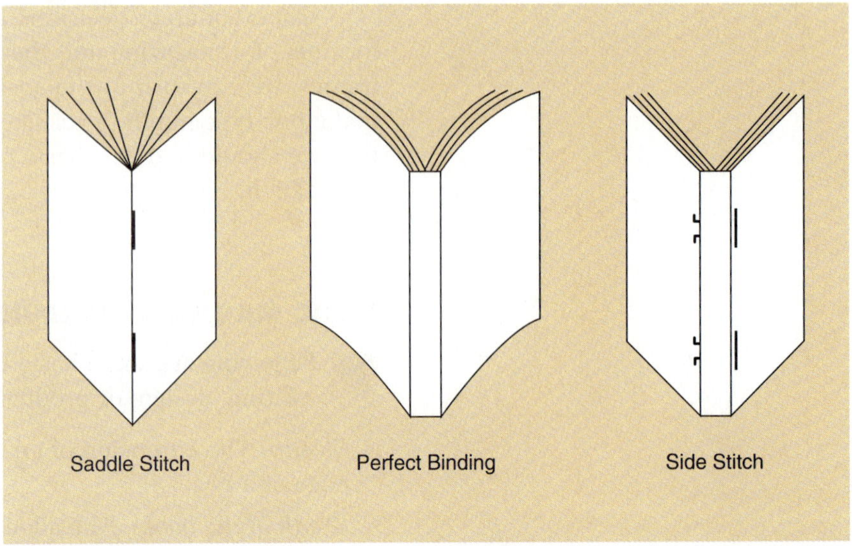

Fig. 14-8 ■ Binding styles for magazines.

Saddle Stitch   Perfect Binding   Side Stitch

Fig. 14-9 ■ Magazines are printed in signatures. Signatures are groups of pages printed on one sheet. Here is a test page of a 12-page signature (6 pages on each side) ready to be checked for correct color and arrangement before the press run is started. Note the color bars at the bottom of the sheet. (Courtesy Heidelberg Harris)

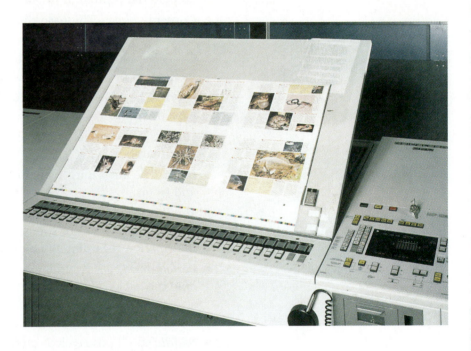

REDESIGNING A MAGAZINE

➤ The general approach to designing a new publication can be used to redesign an existing magazine as well. But there are a few additional points we need to consider before creating a new look for an existing publication.

The first step in redesigning should be a complete study of the present format. Every item from the smallest typographic device to the logo should be examined. The primary examination should center on the audience and its needs. This might require contact with the audience through research and surveys to find answers to questions such as:

1. Does the present format do a good job of bringing the editorial content and the audience together?

2. Does the present design give the audience what it wants?

3. Will a different format serve the audience better?

4. Does the audience prefer different kinds of illustrations (photos instead of diagrams, for example)?

Changes must take into account factors that may not be obvious. Talking with the printer and compositor is important. It might be impossible to produce the changes sought with the equipment available. Much time and effort could be wasted planning changes it would be impossible for the equipment to duplicate.

If the publication is produced in house, on equipment we possess, the equipment manufacturer can be a valuable source of graphic and redesign ideas and equipment capabilities.

We should solicit ideas from as many sources as possible but not abdicate the job of decision-making. A publication designed by a committee usually turns out to be a hodgepodge collection of graphic ideas that is seldom effective.

We must also avoid the tendency to design by "shotgun." This is the temptation to try to outdo graphic design on each succeeding issue by packing each issue with more attention-getting graphics than the one before. Shotgun design is seen more and more, often to the detriment of the publications on which it is practiced.

If the publication carries advertising, our study should include the types of advertising, the most common sizes, and their present arrangements on the pages. For example, a proliferation of small ads will present problems in page layout that could be avoided if the magazine runs fewer but larger ads.

While it might not be possible to control the size and design of the advertisements, which usually come to the publication from a variety of sources, it is possible to control the arrangement of the ads on the pages.

Steps in Redesign

Once a thorough study of the present design has been made, the redesigning process can begin. Below is a useful step-by-step outline for overhauling a publication.

1. *Start at the back.* Magazines are designed from the back to the front. Why this backward approach? First of all, a new design usually means a new logo or new cover design. This indicates that there is something new inside—and there had better be! A new label for the same old can of beans does not fool anyone very long. Another reason for starting with the back is that's where most of the design trouble usually can be found. Those little mail-order ads, fillers, and jumped conclusions of articles get dumped in the back. So, clean it up first and then go on to the features. Plan a basic uninterrupted reading pattern, but start with the back.

2. *Group, consolidate, organize.* Analyze the small items and rearrange them. This will often lead to an organizational format that will improve the appearance of the whole publication. How can that be? Well, the secret of a well-designed publication is *departmentalization.* Grouping related items together creates an orderly plan that makes sense to the reader. It helps sort out the contents of the publication.

   If small ads are carried, consider them first. What is their typographical tone? Are they crammed with lots of copy? Do they try to scream at the reader with large, bold type, heavy borders, lots of reverses? Separate them into groups and arrange the groups by sizes. If they are scattered helter-skelter throughout the magazine, group them together in some way—perhaps by subject category. Arrange them on a layout sheet in an orderly pattern (see Figure 14–10). Ads are more effective if grouped by subject matter—schools, camps, travel, trading post—rather than being scattered randomly throughout a publication.

3. *Analyze departments and their heads.* Too many departments—household hints, sports shorts, and so on—can clutter a publication in two ways. It is difficult to design effective layouts if many short departments must be accommodated. Also, the constant repetition of many similar department heads can lead to a choppy format. Check to see if departments can be combined or eliminated if there are too many in the publication.

   When redesigning department or section heads, keep in mind the criteria for good heads: The head should blend well with the copy, help say what the department is all about, and be uncluttered with illustrations and ornaments. If illustrations are used, they should be simple. Avoid art that could become dated in heads—art that is in fashion now but probably will be out soon. The head should be clean, brief, and to the point. It should be easy to adapt it to one-, two-, or three-column widths.

4. *Consider the constants.* There are other constants to review in addition to department heads. (Constants are the typographic devices that do not change from issue to issue.) These include the table of contents, masthead, editorial section, letters section, fillers, next issue's previews, and special advertising sections.

   The entire sequence of constants must be handled individually and then collectively to present a harmonious whole. In designing the constants as well as all other parts of the total format, all the principles of design and type selection we have discussed should be put into practice.

5. *Finally, the cover.* Most communicators are tempted to redesign the cover right off, but we leave it to last for a very good reason. A thorough study of all the factors that must be considered in designing a magazine will provide a bonus. Designing an effective cover now should be easy. Even though the cover is considered last it probably is the most important element in the entire format. It is the display window—what people see first. It can cause the reader

Fig. 14-10 ■ An effective way to reduce advertisement clutter in magazine design is to group the small ads under an appropriate heading or headings. This aids the advertiser, too, as it helps flag the target audience. (Courtesy *Nevada* magazine)

to pick up a periodical or pass it by. The ideas about cover design in Chapter 15 are useful in redesigning as well as in creating a new publication.

➤ **EFFECTIVE DESIGN CHECKLIST**

■ Provide for ample margins and white space. If the margins and white space between the columns are inadequate, the entire magazine will have a cramped, jammed-up appearance.

■ Define editorial and advertising content clearly. If the reader cannot tell easily where one begins and the other ends, the whole publication will appear disorganized and confused.

Fig. 14-11 ■ This layout of the opening page of an article for *Flux* magazine was produced by students at the University of Oregon School of Journalism and Communication. This was the strongest photograph of the "shoot," and both the editor and art director wanted it run BIG. A horizontal layout would have placed the man's face on the crease, so designers chose to create a vertical layout of this story to set it off and to emphasize the vertical lines of the man and the dog in the photograph. The title box and type were run in two colors. Client: *Flux* magazine. Art director: Jamie Kaineg; art associate, Sean McLaughlin; photographer: Michael Shindler. (Courtesy Dr. William E. Ryan, instructor)

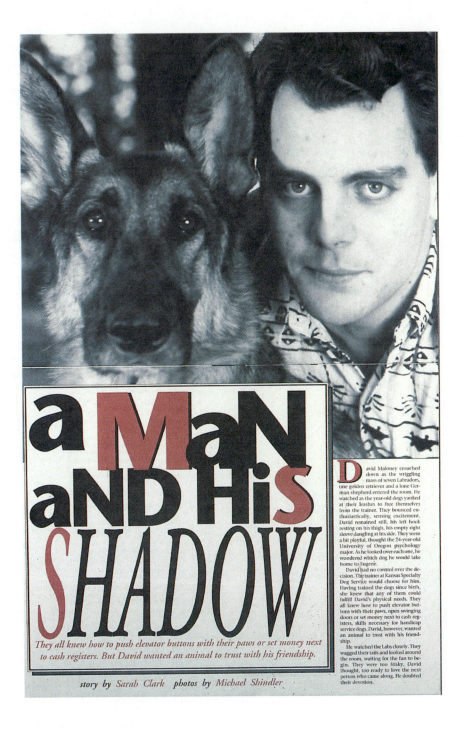

- Make sure type styles relate to content. The typefaces and illustration designs must harmonize with the editorial content. Some designers call this "type and content marriage." Good type marriages are a sign of professionalism.

- Pictures should be selected and cropped for content first. Do the pictures help eye movement through the page? If art causes eye movement out of the page or through the page in an uncontrolled way, the page patterns are those of a beginner, and we want to be pros.

Fig. 14-12 ■ The computer has taken over as the tool of choice in the world of magazine design. Here a designer creates a magazine page using the VariColor Macintosh layout work station. Stations like this are designed to handle complex pages with lots of graphics. (Courtesy PrePRESS Direct!)

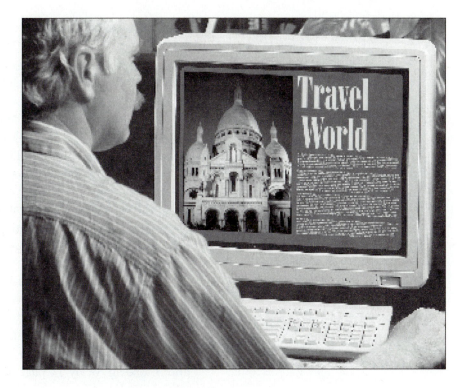

■ Special departments should relate to the basic editorial theme of the magazine. Unrelated departments, especially if there is a proliferation of them, tend to break down the basic editorial impact of the magazine.

■ Check the last pages as well as the first. The back of the book should not be a dumping ground. The final pages should be well organized if the entire package is to be as attractive as possible.

■ The table of contents should be neat, clean, and functional. If the table of contents and the masthead are cluttered, crowded, or disorganized, redesign them.

■ Everything should blend together. Check to see that the stories and articles are laid out to present a unified magazine package. If they seem to be individually designed with no thought given to what else is contained in the issue, they need work.

■ Check the body type—the basic reading matter type. It should be a clean, readable design—preferably a Roman face that is big on the body. Check the leading and see if the type size is near the optimum for the width of the columns.

■ Consider the design from the reader's standpoint. Some magazines are designers' dream productions but nightmares for readers. Don't let layouts become ego trips. Make them functional. See that each element in each layout is there for a purpose. That purpose should be to attract the reader, hold interest, and make reading a pleasant experience.

➤ **GRAPHICS IN ACTION**

1. Select a magazine that appeals to a special interest audience and analyze its design and typography. Try to determine how the design, selection of type styles, and arrangement of design elements were made to appeal to the target audience. If there are shortcomings in the design, explain the changes you would recommend.

2. Develop a formula for a small magazine. Have its target audience be a group or organization, special-interest or hobby, to which you belong or to which you have a special affinity. Make a written plan to present to possible financial backers of the proposed magazine.

3. Develop a format for the small magazine to carry out the philosophy of the formula developed in No. 2. (Both Nos. 2 and 3 can be combined with Graphics in Action Nos. 4 and 5 in Chapter 15 for a major project. It might be well, then, to restrict the size of the magazine to, say, eight or twelve pages, depending on the amount of time that can be devoted to this project.)

4. Design a basic cover layout for a magazine for an organization of which you are a member or for the magazine proposed in Nos. 2 and 3. Use an 8½ by 11 page with a type area 44 by 57 picas.

5. The page included here has many design faults. It should be completely redesigned to be effective. This could include using art that is apropos to the content and will attract and lure the reader into the article. Design a 3-column, 8½ by 11 page to replace this page, using the same length text. This project could be done on your computer or with traditional tools. Start by brainstorming and making thumbnails.

By Judi Prats
Kent State University

VOLUNTEER PR SERVICES

Make more of

your education by

getting involved in

volunteer PR. It can

broaden learning

experiences,

widen contacts for

future references

and increase

your knowledge in

practictioning

S o you're planning on graduating and landing that big deal job writing news releases with your initialed Parker Bros. pen, seated at your very own Formica-topped desk in your very own plastic-plant-decorated office.

It's the real thing. Your big break.

But that big break doesn't come in an all inclusive 9-5 package deal, neatly adorned with one hour lunches, 15 minute caffeine breaks and the option to leave the office a half hour early in order to avoid the Dodge'em cars on the freeway.

No, the job doesn't stop when the "Happy Days" reruns come on.

There are things to be taken away from the office besides a new leather-smelling briefcase or your first "real" byline.

You've got to be a part of community involvement. This means doing VOLUNTEER WORK — a dreaded task that you thought would finally leave you alone after diploma presentation

This volunteer work, although possibly more extensive (yet not as colorful) as selling carnations in the Student Center, may take on the task of petitioning to get a hospital levy passed or handing out flyers to support a candidate.

This community involvement is more than an exercise in seeing how many clubs or groups recognize your name — it's an achievement of personal goal attainment. This goal is to make yourself a total person, handling with finesse the complementary roles of Joe Businessman and Joe Citizen.

You have to be conscious that your big break doesn't stop when the title Account Executive is tacked to your name.

It continues throughout your career, in making yourself a success inside the office and out.

And, just like we learn how to write news releases and snap photographs and run the lithography press (with a little assistance) we must also be educated in the seemingly unrewarded activities like peddling pumpkins and signing up blood donors.

PRSSA is the bridge to those "unrewarded" efforts that tend to be associated with asking for too much money and begging for too much time. These volunteer activities are indeed rewarded.

Donate time to become active in your community

They are looked at admirably when placed on a resume, but more importantly, they are thought of warmly when the doer looks back and realizes how he has helped to achieve the desired goal, whether it be a convention to Chicago or the renovation of a theatre.

The activities of PRSSA don't stop with working on accounts or escorting Bloodmobile victims to the food table, there is the social side of public relations that dare not be ignored.

PR practitioners have acquired a reputation for knowing how to have a good time. This is a talent that must also be fostered in our college days.

So, the next time you hear one of the PRSSA officers sprouting off about getting involved with the accounts, selling whatever, or attending a wine and cheese party — just remember, that it's all a part of the degree.

INSIDE AND OUTSIDE THE MAGAZINE

© Scott Eklund

15 In the previous chapter, we laid the groundwork for successfully designing or redesigning a magazine. Now we are ready to put our plan into action. The designer faces the task of creating prototype page layouts that will be examined and evaluated by everyone involved in the project.

DESIGNING THE MAGAZINE

➤ How does the designer proceed? What are the first steps in the actual creative process?

We are living in a visual age, a world of visual excitement. It takes the combined talent of the artist, the knowledge of the psychologist, and the skills of the designer and printer to produce pages that will encourage the reader to anticipate each issue and reach for one particular magazine among all the others seeking attention.

The Break of the Book

The first decision to be made in crossing the bridge from the planning stage to the layout stage is what is known as *the break of the book.* This is the terminology editors and art directors use to designate what is going to be placed where.

There are several basic philosophies concerning how to break the book. One is called the *traditional plan.* Under this arrangement, the constants—the regular columns and features, the masthead, the table of contents, and any editorial page material plus the advertisements—are grouped in the first few and the last few pages. The middle pages are reserved for the current issue's main articles and stories. The strongest article in the issue is used as the lead article for this middle section. Several major magazines that use this method of breaking the book include *Reader's Digest, Smithsonian,* and *National Geographic.*

Another approach is called the *front to back system.* In this arrangement, features and articles are spread throughout the magazine. A great many company and association publications follow this approach with perhaps only a contents page at the front of the book.

Of course, the editor and designer can strive to be different and create an entirely new plan.

Laying Out the Pages

Once basic decisions are made, it is time to go ahead and place the graphic elements on paper. This is done with a layout or *grid sheet* for each page. These grid sheets can be obtained for most standard magazine page sizes and column widths from graphic supply concerns or they can be made and reproduced on a duplicator or office copier.

Grids are available in quarter scale, usually four to an 8½ by 11 inch sheet, for making thumbnails. Some editors start their layout work by folding sheets of blank paper into proportionate small sizes, as in making thumbnails for advertisements, but slitting them so they are actually blank miniatures of the full size. It is possible, too, to make a miniature ruler with a strip of cardboard and label it with an inch scale

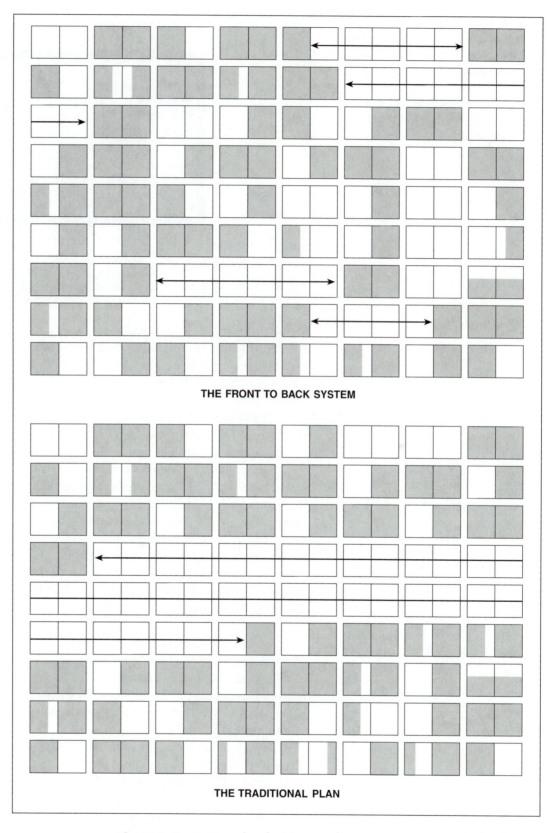

THE FRONT TO BACK SYSTEM

THE TRADITIONAL PLAN

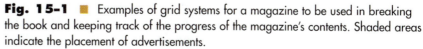

Fig. 15-1 ■ Examples of grid systems for a magazine to be used in breaking the book and keeping track of the progress of the magazine's contents. Shaded areas indicate the placement of advertisements.

Fig. 15-2 ■ Whether magazine page layouts are created on a drawing board or computer screen the principles of good design are the same. Here is a rough of a magazine page layout displayed on a SuperMatch 21 monitor by Macintosh. (Courtesy DTP Direct, Edina, Minnesota)

to the proportion of the full-size sheet. For instance, on the miniature ruler for making thumbnails, one-fourth of an inch might equal 1 inch on a full-scale ruler. Another approach is to cut a cardboard grid that has pica squares ruled on it in nonreproducing blue and have 1 pica equal 1 inch.

The designer uses these tools to rough in all the material the full-size layout will contain and then uses the resulting thumbnail as a guide in keeping things straight when full-size layouts are made.

An easy way to keep account of progress in laying out a magazine is to put the full-size layouts for each page in numerical sequence up on the office wall. Using a small piece of masking tape, the pages can be taken down, worked on, and replaced.

This method of planning an issue has two advantages. The status of the whole issue can be seen at a glance and facing pages can be seen side by side. It should be kept in mind that the magazine reader sees two facing pages at a time, and good planning should include making sure that these pages are compatible.

Screens Will Replace Drawing Boards

The use of pencil, pens, and paper and layout and grid sheets is rapidly diminishing. *Time* now uses a device in its layout department that replaced layout sheets, art knives, and waxers. The new device is called the Vista, and when it went into use it was believed to be the only one of its kind in the world.

The machine has two adjoining video screens. The story, headline, art, and other graphic elements that the designer wants to place on a page are displayed on one screen. The other screen is a monitor that shows what the completed page will look like in color. The designer can move the elements around, alter their sizes, and arrange them on the screen just as most art directors now arrange them on paper. As a *Time* staffer noted, the machine "gives you the freedom to revise and adapt quickly. It can turn the work of hours into as little as twenty minutes."

Whether a magazine is laid out with a ruler and pencil or felt pen, or whether it is composed on state-of-the-art equipment, the basic principles of good design in general and magazine design in particular still apply.

PLANNING THE COVER

▶ All pages of printed communication are important, but if one page must be singled out as the most important of all in magazine design, it has to be the front cover. The cover creates the all-important first impression. It not only identifies the publication but also says something about its personality.

A good front cover should accomplish four things:

■ It should identify the magazine in a way that sets it apart from the others.

■ It should attract attention, especially from the target audience.

■ It should lure the reader inside the magazine.

■ It should set the tone or mood of the magazine.

In addition, when the magazine is sold in supermarkets or on newsstands, the cover plays an important role in the selling process.

Every cover should automatically carry certain information. In addition to the logo, the date of issue, volume, and number should appear—especially if the magazine is the type that will be filed and indexed for future reference. The price, if the magazine is sold, should be included. This seems self-evident, but it is surprising how many small magazines fail to include this pertinent information on their covers.

Self-Cover or Separate Cover?

One of the first decisions that has to be made is whether the magazine will be self-covered or have a separate cover. A *self-cover* is a cover printed on the same paper stock as the body of the magazine. Many magazines invest in a more expensive and more substantial paper stock for the cover.

However, the self-cover has its advantages. It is, of course, less expensive. In addition, for the small publication on a limited budget, the self-cover can provide color on inside pages at virtually no extra cost. This is possible because most magazines are printed in *signatures,* or sections of pages in units of four, with the number of units in a signature decided by the press capacity. Thus, when color is purchased for the cover, it can also be used on the other pages of the signature containing the cover. This could be four, eight, sixteen, or even thirty-two pages, depending on the size of the magazine and of each signature in its manufacture.

Another cover decision concerns advertising. A very limited number of publications sell the front cover page at a premium as a source of income. These include a few business and professional publications. One is *Editor & Publisher.* However, most editors find front-cover advertising objectionable. The question about cover advertising might be whether the interest-arousing and selling asset of a strong cover should be sacrificed for the additional money obtained by selling the front cover.

Many editors have found that a cover that sets the theme for an issue, identifies what the issue is all about, or ties in with a strong lead article works best. Others report that covers with closely cropped human interest pictures are good attention-getters.

Covers That Sell Contents

A trend today is toward greater use of the cover to sell the contents. More and more *blurbs* are being used on covers. These teasers are designed to lure readers into picking up the magazine for the contents.

In designing blurbs it is important to realize that the cover is the magazine's store window. It is the poster or billboard that will advertise

Fig. 15-3 ■ Simple design can be the best. This neat layout for the cover of a quarterly financial report is just right in its trim, uncomplicated arrangement. Note how the white of the page frames the cover and how the typefaces used are lined up with the art. The art is more than a pretty picture; it shows UGI workers making tests of the water. (Courtesy UGI Corporation, Jocelyn Canfield Kelemen, writer-designer)

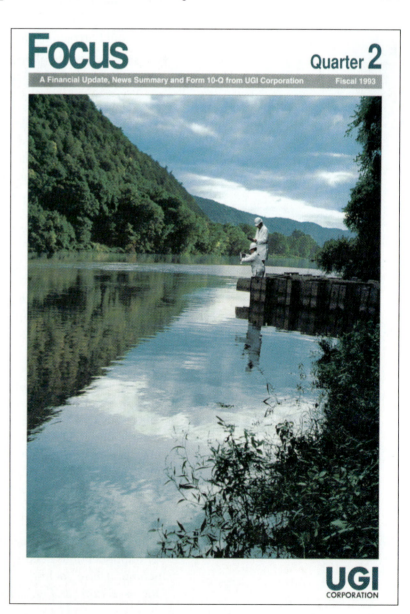

Fig. 15-4 ◼ This dramatic cover (below) and cover story (right) demonstrate the skills of the visual communicator in creating and designing. The designer did not attempt to clutter the cover or the story with a lot of type and distracting layout techniques. However, the use of a hot color and white in the lettering on the cover made it legible without being distracting. The designer let the illustration tell the story with great effect. (Courtesy *JD Journal,* corporate magazine of Deere & Company)

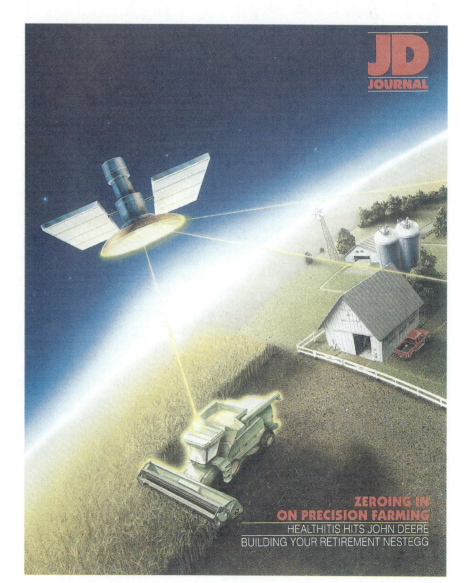

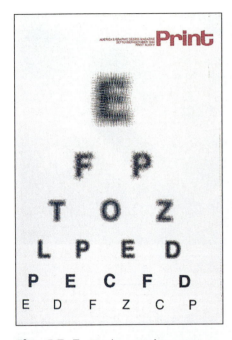

Fig. 15-5 ■ A magazine cover does not have to be complicated to be effective. Dylan Coulter created this cleaver *Print* eye exam chart using PageMaker 5.0. The typeface is Helvetica; it was carefully manipulated to affect this "graduated and distorted look" in Photoshop. The *Print* nameplate was scanned on a flatbed color scanner and cleaned up in Photoshop. Coulter distorted the largest point sizes most and decreased the fuzzy effect with each successive smaller sized line up to the last line, which is smallest but razor sharp. Client: *Print* magazine. Art direction and design: Dylan Coulter, University of Oregon School of Journalism and Communication. (Courtesy Dr. William E. Ryan, instructor)

and, hopefully, sell what the publication has to offer. Blurbs should be written and designed much like the copy on posters and billboards—short and to the point. The message should be one that can be taken in at a glance. Advertisers say a billboard message should be read in five seconds. Blurbs on magazine covers should be equally short, never more than three lines of type for each blurb.

Blurbs should also relate closely to the article titles. In one magazine recently, the blurb on the cover announced "Solar Pioneers." The title of the article referred to was "To Catch the Sun." Readers might have trouble relating the two. Make sure the blurbs can be identified with the articles or features quickly and without confusion.

Traditionally, the blurb was placed along the left side of the cover. This was because of the way many magazines were stacked on newsstands so that they overlapped and only a portion of the left side of each cover was visible to the passerby. However, it isn't necessary that this pattern be followed for most magazines today.

Consistency Is Important

The inside cover pages and the back cover can cause some design problems. The key to designing these pages is consistency. Select a graphic pattern for these pages and stick to it. If the magazine runs advertising on the inside front cover and on both back-cover pages, the problem is easily solved. Usually the cover pages sell well because of their high impact. The back cover is seen almost as much as the front cover, and the inside cover pages receive high viewing as well.

But if advertising is not a part of the covers, the designer needs to adopt a cover design philosophy. *Context,* the magazine of the DuPont Corporation, uses the back cover as a contents page. It includes color photos and short blurbs for each major article along with the masthead and the post office mailing permit tag plus an area for the address sticker.

The address sticker can be a problem. It is unfortunate that many magazines have fine front-cover illustrations and designs only to have them marred with an address sticker and, in many cases, the comptuerized code for the checkout counter. Cover planning should include consideration of this problem. Some magazine designers solve it by using a mailing wrapper or envelope. If, however, costs or other factors rule this out, it might be worthwhile to incorporate the address area into the design, as *Context* does.

It is possible to include some regular features on the inside covers; for instance, the inside front is an excellent spot for the contents page for a small magazine. The better-designed magazines avoid running large amounts of reading matter on the inside covers and solve some outside-back-cover problems by extending the front-cover illustrations to cover the back as well.

The *Reader's Digest* solves the problem nicely by using the front cover as a blurb and contents page and filling the back outside cover with a full-page illustration.

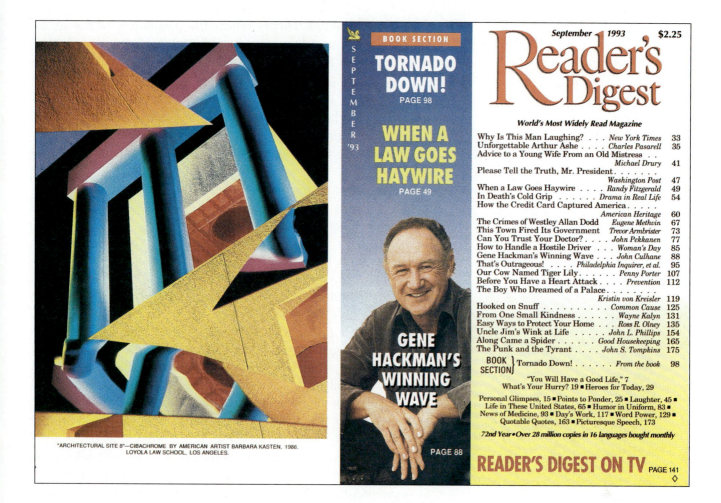

"ARCHITECTURAL SITE 8"—CIBACHROME BY AMERICAN ARTIST BARBARA KASTEN, 1986.
LOYOLA LAW SCHOOL, LOS ANGELES.

Fig. 15-6 ■ The *Reader's Digest* uses the front cover as both a table of contents and a display area for teasers. Art is used on the outside back cover. Both techniques can be used for company or organization publications.

Cover Design Preparation

A good preparation for designing the cover of a magazine is to browse through an assortment of magazines and see how well the designers have used the attributes of good typography to help accomplish the job of the cover. Ask yourself the following questions to guide your evaluations.

1. *Does the cover identify the magazine and reflect its personality?* The logo should be large enough to be recognized immediately and the style should be compatible with the magazine's personality. (An artist can be commissioned to make a distinctive logo for the publication at a reasonable cost.)

A strong, aggressive type such as a Sans Serif, Square Serif, or Roman in boldface would be good for a bold, aggressive magazine. A medium or light old style Roman is a good choice for a dignified publication. Scripts or light or medium Romans with swash first letters project an image of gracefulness. Square Serifs or strong modern Romans are good for scientific or technical publications, but they should not be too bold. There are enough type styles available to project almost any image desired.

Cover illustrations should reflect the personality of the magazine, too. Most magazines use a combination of type and illustrations to project their identity in the cover design.

2. *Does the cover attract the target audience and get its attention?* The type styles and illustrations used should relate to the audience and reflect its characteristics and interests. If a magazine is appealing to an aggressive target audience, using a lot of elements on the cover will project the image of a magazine that is full of vitality and action.

3. *Does the cover lure the reader inside?* The basic cover design consists of a strong logo at the top and an illustration relating to the tone of the magazine or the theme or, possibly, the lead article. Designers have found, however, that type is the most effective means of luring the reader inside. If blurbs are used, check to see if they appeal to the target audience. Check, too, to see if there is an element of timeliness. Blurbs should stress the benefits the reader will receive by turning to the articles being touted.

4. *Does the cover create identity from issue to issue?* Once a type style for the logo is adopted it should continue from issue to issue. The placement of the logo plus the date of issue and so on should also be basically the same from issue to issue. The general approach to handling blurbs should be consistent. There should be enough consistency in the cover design to create continuity and identity from one issue to the next.

5. *Does the cover contain the essential information?* Check to see that the date, price, and volume and issue numbers are present. It is surprising how often the lack of these essentials isn't noticed until after page proofs are made.

ESSENTIALS OF PAGE DESIGN

➤ There are two points to keep constantly in mind during the designing of a magazine. One is that the reader sees two pages at a time. The other is that all the basic principles of design—balance, proportion, unity, contrast, rhythm, harmony—should come into play.

The A-T-S-I Approach

With this in mind, we can plan the actual design of the pages in the magazine. A good way to get things started is the art-title-subhead and/or byline, initial-letter approach, or the *A-T-S-I formula.* It is a simple and safe way to make layouts attractive and functional. Once this basic concept of magazine page arrangement is mastered, the designer can experiment with more daring use of white space and placement of elements.

In building a page using the A-T-S-I approach, a large attention-getting photograph or other art is used to attract the reader. This is followed by a well-conceived title line. The subhead or byline, or both, are designed to move the reader toward the start of the article. Then the ini-

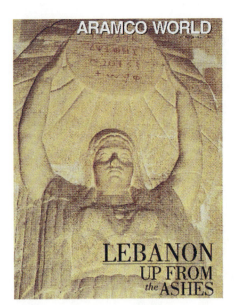

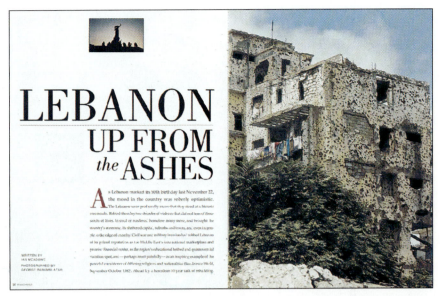

Fig. 15-7 ■ One approach to cover design is to select a lead article and feature it on the cover. In this instance the superbly designed *Aramco World* used the same typestyle and arrangement for the cover as for the article. Note the flush right lineup of the title and application of the A-T-S-I formula plus the utilization of white space as a design tool. (*Aramco World;* design by The HILL Group)

tial letter signals the beginning of the article and serves as a bridge to the reading matter from the other elements in the design.

The Axis Approach

Another method of arranging the elements on a magazine page in an orderly manner is called the *axis approach.* Here the title, subhead, and byline, if used, follow one of the basic rules of good magazine design—*line up the elements.* But here they are lined up on an axis. The axis usually is one of the between-columns alleys.

In placing elements on a magazine page there are a number of points to keep in mind:

1. *First and most important, square up the elements.* This means to line things up and keep things even. Square up the elements where the eye tends to square them. For example, the top of a small illustration above another should line up with the top edge of a large illustration nearby. Type should be lined up along the margins of the type area, or if the lines are indented they should be lined up on the designated indentation. Cutlines for art that is bled to the outer edge of the page should be lined up with the type form and should not be placed in the white area, or margins, of the page.

2. *Distribute the elements throughout the layout.* Elements should not be bunched up all in one place. If the art, title, blurbs, and byline are placed at the start of the story, the page can be thrown out of balance. In addition, it will leave the page with columns of dull, gray type. Place the elements around the page to create better balance and to make the page more interesting.

3. *Keep the elements from fighting each other.* Illustrations that are next to each other but are unrelated will fight, especially if one is not large enough to dominate. Articles in side-by-side single columns will fight each other for the reader's attention. Elements

Fig. 15-8 ■ Humdrum contents pages are giving way to upbeat design that reflects and adds unity to the design of the entire magazine. These contents pages demonstrate the trend and illustrate the work of the designer to attract readers and help define what they will find inside the magazine. (Reprinted with permission of *Technique* © Mar./Apr. 1994. For subscription call 1-800-272-7377)

should be placed so they will harmonize and create a unified whole rather than causing dissonance and disunity.

4. *Be consistent in making layouts.* Those just starting in magazine graphic work sometimes attempt to gain variety and interest by changing the types and styles of subheads and initial letters within one article. They end up with the layout counterpart to the Victorian house cluttered with gingerbread. Consistent use of a carefully chosen style on such items will help layouts achieve simplicity, harmony, and attractiveness.

One school of typographical thought contends that all heads should be in the same type family to preserve consistency and harmony. Many magazines follow this philosophy and use the same types and basic arrangements of elements for all articles throughout every issue.

Other designers say that type should be used to establish an individual mood for each article. Begin by studying the tone and feel of an article, as that will help in selecting and arranging graphic elements to ensure attractiveness and compatibility of graphics and content.

5. *Avoid monotony.* Although the layout should be consistent, an effort should be made to make layouts fresh and unusual. Ask these design questions constantly: Would this article work better with a wider column? Could I use a larger type size for this head? Would

Fig. 15-9 ■ Look at the design devices used to make this page interesting and lively, yet rather structured in the placement of elements. The A-T-S-I technique is applied, but subtly. Freeform art is combined with rather rigid modern Roman and sans serif types. The initial letter and PULL in the title are Bodoni and help unify the elements. The art is bled to the left and the same art form is used as background for the examples. Note the placement of the page number and by-line as well as the solid triangles and icon used to emphasize the points in "Guidelines." (Reprinted with permission of *Technique* © Mar./Apr. 1994. For subscription call 1-800-272-7377)

a rule placed here be effective? How would this look with an over-sized initial letter? Is this page too gray, and do I need to use a pulled quote in single or double column width or some other device to give it punch?

6. *Don't overdo bleeds.* Bleeds are a powerful tool for the magazine designer and there is a temptation to overdo them. Don't. And don't bleed art in a helter-skelter manner. Too many bleeds or too great a variety of bleeds creates a haphazard look that destroys simplicity and beauty in a layout.

7. *Avoid placing large pictures on top of small ones.* When small pictures appear immediately under large ones, the smaller ones look crushed. Normal placement of a group of pictures should build them up like toy blocks so they don't seem to topple over.

8. *Keep flashy arrows and fancy artistic devices to a minimum or, better yet, avoid them altogether.* These devices now look old-fashioned. Today the rule is for clean and simple designs that look neat and

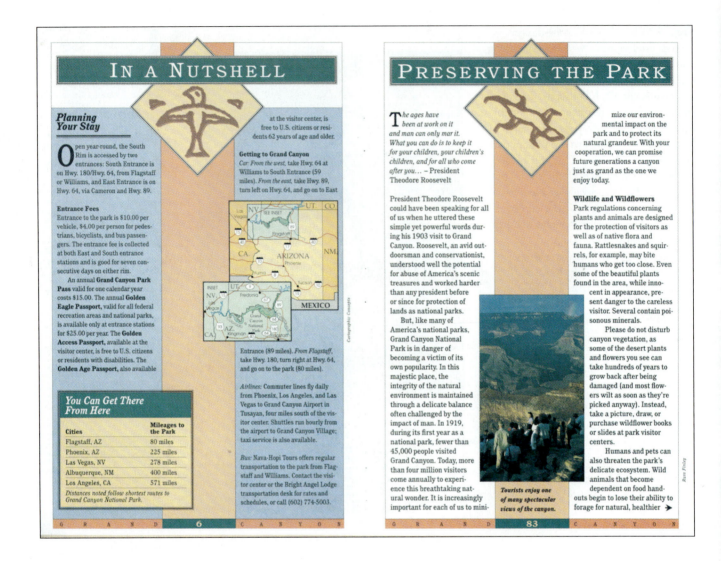

Fig. 15–10 ■ Here are two pages from the *Grand Canyon Magazine*. Look at the design decisions that were made for a 5½ by 8½ page. The use of headers and footers of consistent design, icons, and colors, as well as type faces on pages 6 and 83 demonstrate unity and consistency. The choices also help create the image of the Grand Canyon and its National Park. (Courtesy American Park Network's *Grand Canyon Magazine*)

modern. Studies have shown that readers do not like pictures with rules around them (but in some cases rules can help frame a picture and define the area it occupies), type printed over art (surprinting), oval-shaped art, and similar effects.

9. *Keep the pages dynamic.* Today the rule is simple, uncluttered, dynamic designs. In printed communication the message must be alive to be effective.

Traditionally, printed pages have had a strong vertical thrust. Pages that consist basically of reading matter usually are designed with the vertical column dictating where the copy is placed. As a result, most magazine pages consist of two or three columns of vertical, gray reading matter separated by a thin strip of white space.

This vertical flow is monotonous and if pages are to look alive this flow should be broken up by initial letters, subheads, illustrations, and/or white space.

Fig. 15-11 ■ This is a well-organized page in which the title can be read at a glance. Notice how the various elements are lined up and that a consistent ragged right type setting is carried through in the title, subhead, and caption lines. (Courtesy *Smithsonian*)

By Robert Wernick

The Greatest Show on Earth didn't compare to home

John Ringling ran the world's most famous circus, and when he built a house and museum, he made them into a three-ring extravaganza

A bronze version of Michelangelo's *David* commands ordered parterres and colonnades of the sculpture garden courtyard, 350 feet long, of The John and Mable Ringling Museum of Art.

John Ringling, the Circus King—some six-foot-four in his silk stockings, 270 pounds, an estimated $200 million in capital assets—was a formidable figure to encounter at any time; seldom more so than on the day in the early 1920s when he summoned an architect to his office and announced that Mable wanted them to build a house.

It was to be a house worthy of a man who was the youngest, and last survivor, of the five Ringling brothers who had built one of the greatest circuses of their time, which they called, with pardonable pride, the "Greatest Show on Earth." The house would be called Ca' d'Zan, Venetian dialect for the "house of John." It would rise from the shores of Florida's Sarasota Bay, beginning with a grand marble staircase with a large boat dock where Mable could board her gondola, and rise to a tower that would dominate the palm-flecked coast. It would have 30 lofty and luxurious rooms—banquet room, ballroom, game room—and its various facades were to contain features of two of the build-

Photographs by Marvin E. Newman

63

Making Pages Interesting

Here are a few points to keep in mind when arranging elements on magazine pages to change direction and make the pages more interesting:

■ *A vertical plus a vertical can equal monotony:* A page of all single-column copy and single-column illustrations will tend to reinforce the vertical thrust and continue the monotony. Change the direction somewhat to make the page more interesting. This means adding a horizontal thrust. White space can be used to do this. Titles can be spread over several columns. A strong horizontal picture can be used. All will help create a visual change of direction.

> **CREATIVE COMMUNICATION**
>
> Know when to stop.
>
> The creative process can be endless. On the other hand, a puzzle has an answer. A mathematical problem is either right or wrong and that is the end of it.
>
> But the creative design process can go on and on. There is no one final, absolutely correct answer. In creative design one of the skills worth developing is knowing when to stop.
>
> Knowing when to stop involves knowing the capabilities of the equipment and the materials available, the characteristics of the target audience, and the attributes and limitations of the medium used to transmit the completed layout in its final visual form. It is also simply recognizing when you have produced a good design that no longer needs "perfecting."

- *A change of form can make a page interesting:* Generally we think in terms of squares and rectangles. A change of form from the single vertical or horizontal unit can help create interest. For example, an L-shaped arrangement of illustrations provides a change of direction and adds variety to the page.

- *There is movement in the content of art:* Quite often the center of interest in an illustration can help create a change of pace. The direction the subjects are looking or the direction a moving object is going can create motion on a page. But we must be sure the direction is leading where we want the reader to go. Such illustrations must be placed in a position that ensures the direction is *into* the article, or the page, rather than away from it.

- *White space is a good directional tool:* Breaking out of the standard margination, with more white space at the top or side of the page, with uneven column endings, can help break up vertical thrust. Color used in charts and graphs or in multicolumn heads can draw attention away from the vertical movement of the columns.

Although we have emphasized some rather fixed typographic rules for making magazine designs, the challenge always is to strive for the fresh and unusual. But the fresh and unusual should still be in balance and help to create a harmony among the elements as well as presenting a unified whole.

Allen Hurlburt, magazine art director, explains adherence to the basic principles of good design combined with creativity in describing his philosophy on balance:

> The balance in modern layout is more like that of a tightrope walker and her parasol than that of a seesaw or measuring scales. A tightrope walker in continuous and perfect balance is not much more interesting than someone walking on a concrete sidewalk.
>
> It is only through threatened imbalance, tension, and movement that the performance achieves interest and excitement. For the modern magazine designer and the tightrope walker, balance is a matter of feeling rather than formula.[1]

USEFUL DESIGN ELEMENTS

A number of design elements lend themselves especially to magazine design. These elements can also be used for brochures and similar printed communications.

Initial Letters

Initial letters are in. We seem to go through periods when they are popular and other times when they aren't. One of the advantages of modern computer typesetting is the ease with which devices such as initial letters can be used. In the days of hot type composition, it was expensive to use initial letters. Slugs had to be sawed and fitted.

Initial letters can be effective typographic devices. They can aid the reader in bridging the gap between art, title, and article. They can

Fig. 15-12 ■ Initial letters are receiving increased attention. Initial letters add variety to a page and break up the gray reading matter, but they must be planned with thought.

FOR A MOMENT there I was afraid my first trip to Cuba was going to be my last. I was staying at Havana's Hotel Nacion-al, an elaborate 1930s structure with close to 500 rooms, many of which over-look the sea, and a fraying roman-ticism from the days when it played host to the Duke of Windsor, Erol FLynn and

AT LAST. After what seems like years of wait-ing you are here.What a dilemma. Should you suc-cumb to the alllure of Aspen

YOU'RE GETTING THE house ready for a holiday party, and you need a centerpiece quickly. But you have no flowers and no time to run to the florist or nursery. What do you do? If you live in a mild-winter area, grab the clippers and step out-side: there's probably a wealth of greenery to choose from.

Our feet—with 26 bones, 33 joints, and 19 muscles each—are a wonder of nature. We not only ask them to walk 115,000 miles in a lifetime and torture them with ill-fitting shoes, but we pressure them with two to three times our weight when we jog.

It was my first attempt at hitch-hiking in 20 years, and we were getting nowhere fast. My partner and I had haunted the same remote strip of highway in the nmountains of central Kyyushu for an hour now.

Natural gas is composed chiefly of methane, a molecule made of one carbon atom and four hydrogen atoms. The chemical simplicity of gas and the absence of

WHEN IT IS RAINING and millions of bi-cylclists have pulled on slickers of yellow and blue and red, and the city is awash in soft, wet color when the streets are mirrors calling down shimmering images of the bordering plane trees—that, I think, is the best time of all to first see Shanghai.

The sounds came from directly behind him. *Purr . . . click . . . swish. . .* Carlton Conlan Connager instinctively stepped to the side of the corridor, and the Patient Transport Vehicle hummed its way past him.

Fig. 15-13 ■ *The Champion Magazine uses the same typeface for the title as is used for the reading matter to carry the reader into the article. The declining type size makes a natural reading flow. The title is printed in red, as is the reverse line (Fungus boosts growth), a hot, advancing color which catches the reader's eye and gives added emphasis to these important design elements. (Courtesy Champion International Corporation)*

Fig. 15-14 ■ *(Oppostie page) Cut-in heads can break up the gray of the printed page and add life and brightness. The variety of possibilities is endless but the rules of good typography should be applied in selecting types, spacing, and line length, and in placing rules.*

have a unifying influence. They can open space on the page, breaking the monotony of columns of type. They also can help provide balance if placed properly.

In addition, initial letters can be used in the same type style as the title of the article to give unity and consistency throughout. (A different type style tends to destroy harmony. In some cases, though, magazines have used different type initials effectively by selecting the same typeface for the initials as is used in the magazine logo. But care must be taken to ensure type harmony among head and subhead, initial letter, and body type.)

Care is also needed in placing initial letters. An initial letter should never be placed at the top of a column except at the beginning of an article. It should be placed far enough from the top of a column so it will not confuse the reader. Nor should it be placed too close to the bottom of a column.

The distances between initial letters should be varied throughout an article. They should be placed in unequal spots in the copy and they should never line up horizontally in two adjacent columns.

Adopt a standard method of handling initial letters. There are a number of possibilities. Two common types are rising initial letters and dropped initial letters. Rising initial letters extend above the first line of the body copy. The baseline of rising initials should line up with the baseline of the first line of the body copy. A dropped initial is cut into the body copy with the top of the letter lined up with the top of the letters in the first line of copy.

Many possibilities exist for handling initial letters beyond the standard rising or dropped initial. We can contour body copy around the initial. We can set the first two or three words in the copy after the initial letter lowercase, all caps, or small caps. But whatever style we choose, it should be used consistently throughout the article or magazine.

If the first sentence of an article is a quote, we have to figure out a way to handle the quote mark with the initial letter. There are several alternatives. We can use quote marks from the body type, or from the same type as the initial letter, or leave them out. The latter alternative, however, can cause confusion for the reader.

Always be aware when using initial letters that, as with many typographic devices, poorly planned ones look a lot worse than none at all.

Titles

The trend is toward short titles. The reader should be able to read the title as a unit and not have to read each word alone. The space between words in titles should never be wider than the lowercase *x* of the type being used. And a title should never be extended to fill an area if it means putting so much space between words that the unity of the line is destroyed.

Letterspacing, the placing of more space than normal between each letter in a word, should be used very carefully if at all. If words in a title are letterspaced, the space between the letters should be minuscule. And the space between any lines in a title should be tight. Too much space between lines can destroy unity.

Exploring the North

40

Hunting for fossils or mushrooms, caring for the animals, and downing hearty home-cooked meals are a few of the pleasures of a Nova Scotia farm.

Many early settlers of the county rumbled down into the region via the "Great Pacific Wagon Road."

aliquam erat volutpat. Ut wisi enim ad minim veniam, quis nos- trud exerci tation ul-lamcorper suscipitiu lobo rtis nisl brut aliquip ex allo como do conse quat. Duda la autem vel eum iriure dolor in hendrerit id vulput inate velit esse mole stie euta conse quat, vel illum dolore leneu feugiat nulla facilisis at vero eros odio net accumsan et iusto elan odio dignissim bodi qui blandit praesent luptatum zzril

Peterson recently completed a multimillion-dollar deal for construction of a hotel and golf course in Shanghai.

aliquam erat volutpat. Ut wisi enim ad minim veniam, quis nostrud exerci tation ullamcorper suscipit lobortis nisl ut aliquip ex ea commodo consequat. Duis autem vel eum iriure dolor in hendrerit in vulputate velit esse molestie conse quat, v e l illum dolo re eu feug iatnu salla facil is isat vero er os et ac cum san et iusto odio dignissim qui blandit

Lorem ipsum dolor sit amet, consectetuer adipiscing elit, sed diam nonummy nibh euismod tincidunt ut laoreet dolore magna Ut wisi enim ad minim

"Out here I just sit back and let it go."
–Alcide Verret

aliquam erat volutpat. Ut wisi enim ad minim veniam, quis nostrud exerci tation ullamcorper suscipit lobortis nisl ut aliquip. Lorem ipsum dolor

"I need to be able to turn around at the end of the day and see the results of my labor—to see a hillside that I yarded."
—AL REINHART, 32, LUMBERJACK

TO BE STUCK IN THE SAHARA WITH A DEAD CAR IS NEVER A PLEASANT PROSPECT

aliquam erat volutpat. Ut wisi enim ad minim veniam, quis nostrud exerci tation ullamcorper suscipit lobortis nisl ut aliquip ex ea commodo consequat. Duis autem vel eum iriure dolor in

OVER THE CLIFFS FOR EGGS

hendrerit in vulputate velit esse molestie consequat, vel illum dolore eu feugiat

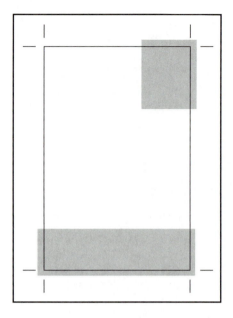

Fig. 15–15 ■ Bleeding art to the extremities of the page can give it greater impact and added weight as a design element. In planning bleeds the layout should indicate the bleed extending about ⅛-inch beyond the margin for trimming after the page is printed.

Script or Cursive types should never be letterspaced. They were meant to be joined or to give the illusion of being joined—the whole point of these types is their resemblance to handwriting. Never use Scripts, Cursives, or Black Letter types in all-capital letters in titles. They are extremely difficult to read.

Avoid using an inappropriate type style for a title. An agricultural magazine ran an article about a new combine, a large piece of machinery, in Coronet Script. (The flowing lines of the script did not help create the image of a rugged machine.) The incongruous use of type can destroy the harmony of elements, design, and editorial content that makes a completed layout so effective.

Also be careful with stylized titles, in which an artist has added flourishes or sketches to the letters. Sometimes this can be effective because it is unusual; other times it is just plain amateurish, and it can destroy the proper horizontal direction of the line as well.

Bleeds

Bleeding art, that is, extending it beyond the normal type area into the margin to the edge of the page, can add variety to the page and impact to the art. It can help create a change of direction to break up monotony, and it can create the impression that the illustration goes on and on.

Bleeds are good design devices, but they should be used with thought. If bleeding will give greater impact to the layout, use it. If the photo content is such that an image of a vast expanse can be enhanced by bleeding, do it. If a change of direction or a breakout from the monotonous can be accomplished by bleeding art, bleed it. But give it some thought first. Also, be sure to check with the production staff or the printer about any possible mechanical limitations for handling bleeds.

Captions

Editors and art directors agree that, in theory at least, a good piece of art should not need a caption. It should tell the story all by itself. Well, that would be great if the art could talk. But often art needs assistance—a caption—in telling the story. A good caption should be as brief as possible and it should add information, not simply restate what is obvious in the art.

How should captions be handled?

One rule of thumb in magazine design is always include a caption unless there is a compelling reason to leave it out. Have you ever been frustrated by a lovely scene used in a magazine to set a mood or present a pleasing visual experience and then searched through every page to try to find out where the scene was located? Never frustrate your readers.

There are two basic approaches to placing captions. One is to place them adjacent to the art they describe. The other is to cluster captions to refer to several pictures in a spread or an article. In either approach, the designer should make it easy for the reader to match caption and art.

Avoid all-capital-letter captions. Settle on a caption width that is never wider than the width of the art. A caption that is narrower than the art lets air into the page, while captions wider than the art look awkward. Select a type style that harmonizes with the body type. Often an italic of the body type works well. Avoid caption widths that violate the optimum line length formula (one and a half times the lowercase alphabet). If captions are wider than the formula, divide them into two or more columns under the illustration and leave a least a pica of white space between the columns.

Crossing the Gutter

When a layout extends through the *gutter*—the margin between two facing pages—onto the adjacent page, be very careful in crossing that gutter. In fact, avoid crossing the gutter except in the center fold of a saddle-wire-bound publication. On a two-page spread, crossing the gutter may be needed for unity and maximum impact. But care should be taken in running a photo across the gutter because the fold may detract from its effectiveness. If a photo that contains people is used, the center of interest may be destroyed or someone's face creased.

Also be very careful in crossing the gutter with type. In fact, this should be avoided if there is a chance problems will arise. A head can be placed across the gutter if it is planned carefully so that the crease comes between the words. Care must be taken, too, to see that the pages line up in printing and the head is in a straight line from one page to the other.

Placing Advertisements

There are a number of layout patterns for placing advertisements on the page. One plan is especially suitable for magazine design. This is to fill full columns with advertisements and leave full columns open for editorial matter.

Some magazines, especially the shelter publications (as the "homemaker" magazines are called), use an "island" makeup plan for inside pages. Advertisements are isolated, usually in the center of the page, and surrounded with reading matter.

In planning the graphics for your magazine, remember that in today's world people are constantly being exposed to improved graphics and new graphic techniques. A publication must be concise, complete, and attractive. The trend is toward simpler layouts with bigger and fewer pictures, shorter but bolder heads and titles, larger and bolder initial letters. More tightly edited stories, concisely written, can provide the space needed for better display.

▶ EFFECTIVE DESIGN CHECKLIST

■ Square up elements. Square items with the margins. Keep even (that is, line up) the top edges of illustrations that are similarly placed. Square up elements where the eye tends to square them. For example, the top of a small illustration above another should line up with the top edge of a nearby large illustration.

Fig. 15-16 ■ The "magazine" plan for placement of advertisements. Full columns of advertisements leave full columns for editorial matter. This is an arrangement for single-column advertisements. (Courtesy *Minnesota Monthly*)

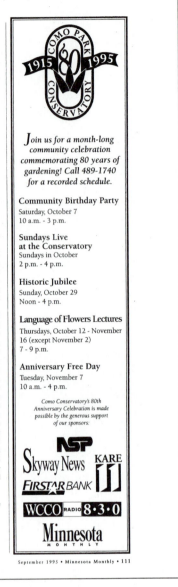

- Distribute elements throughout the layout. Bunching illustrations, title, subhead, and byline at the start of the story creates imbalance and can leave columns of gray type.

- Keep elements from fighting each other. An illustration or a head placed alongside another can fight it. Keep peace in the family by isolating unrelated heads and illustrations.

- Be consistent in making layouts. Select a pattern for handling heads, captions, and all other graphic elements and stick to it for continuity, identity, and consistency.

- Seek the fresh and unusual. Seek new ways of doing things, study the work of others, and don't be afraid to experiment. But keep the new and unusual within the bounds of sound principles of design.

- Use good judgment with bleeds. There are so many ways to bleed photos that there is hardly a wrong way. However, remember that varying bleeds too much will bring a haphazard look to pages. "Minibleeds," or small photos that are bled, usually are not effective. Some designers say the full-page bleed is the only acceptable one.

■ Don't place initial letters at the tops of columns, except at the start of the article. Adopt a consistent typographic plan for handling initial letters. Also, avoid placing subheads at the top of columns as this can confuse the reader.

■ Don't place cutlines in the margins. If you design a bleed for a page do not place the cutline so it extends into the margin. Stop the cutline at the margin.

■ Don't place big pictures on top of little pictures. The little pictures will look crushed. The same principle applies to advertisements. In placing ads on the page it is better to put the bigger ads at the bottom of the columns and build them up like building blocks.

■ Don't use arrows, pointing fingers, and other fancy ornamentation unless there is a good reason, such as creating an atmosphere or mood. Dynamic designs are usually neat, clean, and open.

➤ GRAPHICS IN ACTION

1. Find a one-page magazine layout that includes the title, byline, a subhead, art, and initial letter, etc., and design a two-page spread based on this page. Increase the size of the body type area by one-third and add additional art as you see fit. Prepare a grid for the layout on paper or light white posterboard at least 11 by 17 inches. Each page will have three 14-pica columns with 1½ picas of space between 10-inch-deep columns (you may have or can purchase prepared grids to fit these dimensions). If you complete this project on your computer, create the spread one page at a time, unless you are lucky enough to have a large two-page monitor, and mount your pages on the posterboard for display and evaluation.

2. Find an article in a newspaper or news magazine and design a cover for a "standard" (3 columns by 119 lines) size magazine based on this article.

3. Find an article in a pocket-size magazine such as *Reader's Digest, TV Guide,* or *Prevention* and redesign it for a flat or basic-size page.

4. Use the formula you developed for a small magazine in Chapter 14 Graphics in Action No. 2 to develop a plan for breaking the book for the publication.

5. Make a complete dummy (a rough simulation of a completed magazine; it contains the layouts for all the pages in the order in which they will appear in print) for the small magazine you developed in Chapter 14 Graphics in Action. The dummy should carry out the magazine's formula and format philosophy in its design.

NOTE

[1]Allen Hurlburt, *Publication Design* (New York: Van Nostrand Reinhold, 1976), pp. 28, 31.

THE NEWSPAPER AND THE DESIGNER

© Bob Daemmrich, Stock Boston

16 This is the age of graphics in newsrooms across the country. More and more advertisements are appearing in the help-wanted columns of newspaper trade publications seeking young people with visual communication skills and an understanding of the newspaper profession. Here are some phrases from advertisements that appeared in *Editor and Publisher* magazine.[1]

> . . . *needed immediately for news design, page layout, and graphics . . . work full time on news design, page layout . . . strong page design skills required . . . knowledge of page layout techniques . . . seek copy editor who can design attractive pages . . . design pages, write headlines . . . strong editing and layout skills . . . experience in editing, graphics, layout, management . . . photo and page-layout skills essential . . . work full time on news design, page layout, and graphics . . .*

But, before we go on, we should recognize that a knowledge of newspaper design isn't just for journalists or graphic designers aiming at careers in the industry. A knowledge of newspapers and newspaper design can be valuable for:

■ Advertising professionals who must deal with the print media. They also can be involved in helping produce newspaper advertising supplements or newspaper-format advertising publications.

■ Public relations people who can talk the language of the newspaper industry with media professionals. They can be involved in producing public relations publications with a newspaper format. Take a look at the "newspapers" in Chapter 13. They are public relations tools.

Design has come to the fore as an important—even vital—part of producing the more than 1,700 daily and 8,000 weekly newspapers in the Untied States and Canada. In 1979 a group of newspaper designers organized the Society of Newspaper Design with 22 North American members. Today its membership has grown to more than 2,200 with members in 42 countries as well as Canada and the United States.

One approach to the understanding of any creative skill is to examine what has gone before and consider how that history affects practice today. Will Durant wrote in the preface of *The Story of Civilization* that the study of history will help people "see things whole, to pursue perspective, unity and understanding."[2]

A study of the past is especially helpful in newspaper design. Many of the practices, page arrangements, design forms, and even terms used today were developed during the evolution of the physical form of newspapers. Many of the design changes being initiated today are efforts to break out of this tradition to make newspapers more attractive and more readable for today's audience. Moreover, a study of the past may help us avoid repeating its mistakes.

Fig. 16-1 ■ The modern newspaper. The *Washington Times* is a consistent winner in the annual competitions of the Society of Newspaper Design. Its design is considered one of the very best in the United States.

In this chapter we trace the development of newspaper design and see where it seems to be going in the computer age. In addition, we examine designing and redesigning newspapers in the light of present trends.

Fig. 16-2 ■ John Peter Zenger's *New-York Weekly Journal* in typical Colonial era "bookish" newspaper format.

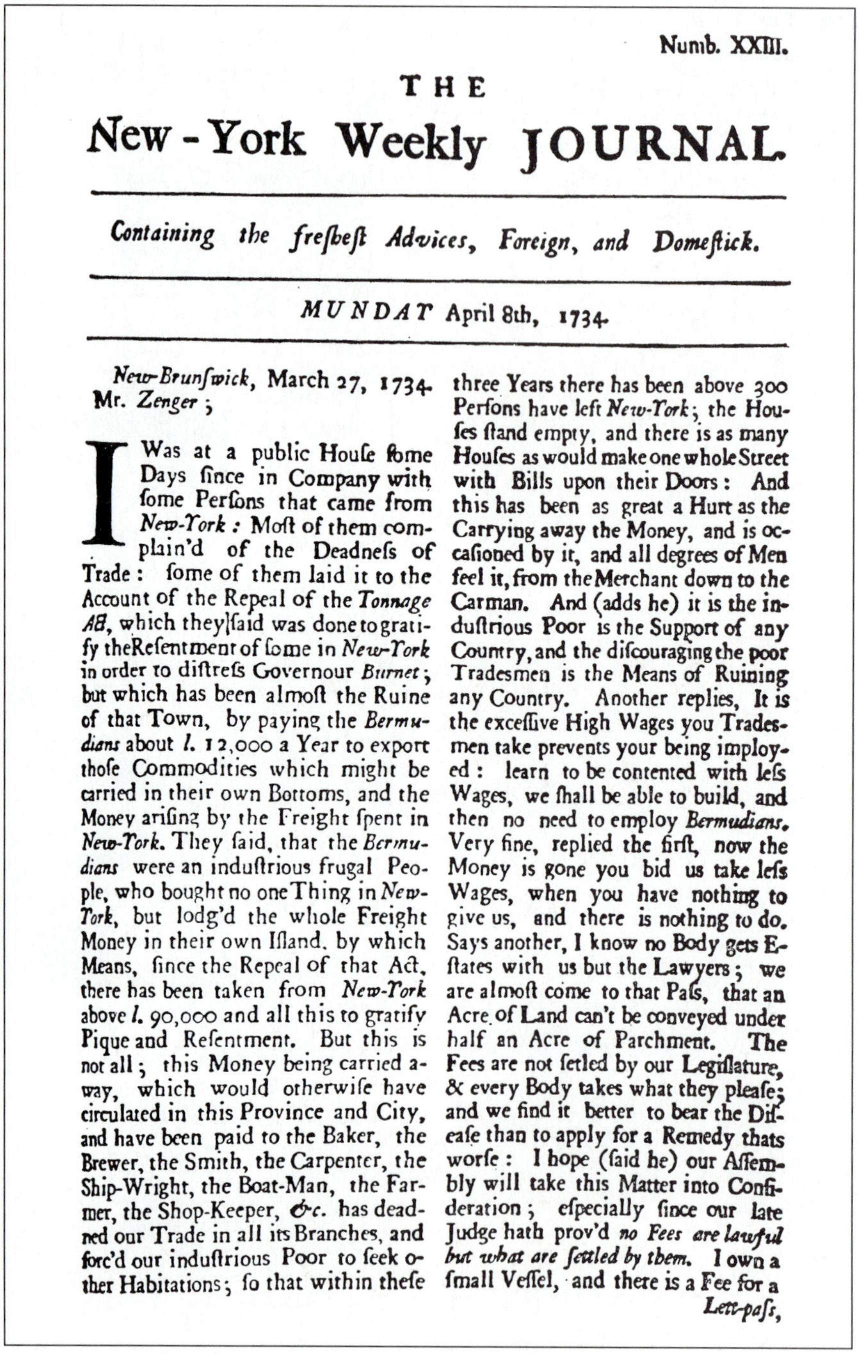

Fig. 16-2 ■ John Peter Zenger's *New-York Weekly Journal* in typical Colonial era "bookish" newspaper format.

THE COLONIAL ERA NEWSPAPER FORMAT

➤ The first newspaper designer in America was a renegade Englishman who fled his country one jump ahead of the sheriff. Only one issue of his newspaper was printed, and it was promptly suppressed.

Benjamin Harris arrived in Boston sometime in 1690. The single issue of his newspaper, *Public Occurrences, Both Foreign and Domestic,* appeared on September 25, 1690. Fourteen years passed before another newspaper was produced in what is now the United States. The *Boston News-Letter* was issued by John Campbell, the postmaster. It continued publication for 72 years.

Both newspapers were produced in a format similar to that of the early newspapers in England. They were the first of what might be called the Colonial era of American newspaper design. They were small and made little or no effort to display the news. However, they did have some distinctive typographic characteristics that some designers today would endorse.

Public Occurrences was four pages about 7½ by 11⅜ inches in size. It was set in type about the size of 12 point in columns about 17 picas wide. There were two columns to a page, and the columns were separated by white space rather than column rules. Two three-line initial letters appeared on page 1. They were the only typographic efforts to add variety to the body matter.

The *Boston News-Letter* followed a similar pattern.

The Colonial era newspapers were produced by printers rather than journalists or publishers. Many of these printers were book and general commercial printers first and newspaper producers second. They used the same typefaces for their newspaper printing and their book work. As a result, these newspapers resembled early-day books in page format. They were set in large types on wide columns, and the columns were usually separated by white space. A few printers used vertical rules between columns.

Many of the design changes in recent years have included a return to some of the characteristics of the Colonial newspaper. These include the larger body type, wider columns, and white space rather than rules to separate the columns.

During the more than 200 years that elapsed between the Colonial format and the format of today, newspapers went through some wrenching changes in appearance. The designer of newspapers—whether the newspaper is a metropolitan daily, a company employee paper, or a university or school weekly—will find it worthwhile to trace these changes and see how newspapers evolved.

TRADITIONAL NEWSPAPER FORMAT

The traditional format dominated newspaper design for nearly a hundred years. But as newspapers proliferated, competition began to affect the business. There was a increasing effort to be first with the news, to obtain the largest circulation, to get the most advertising, to make the most money.

The large margins of the Colonial newspapers were reduced to get more news and advertisements on the pages. Body matter was set in smaller type so more material could be fitted on the page. In the 1800s, eye-fatiguing 6-point type for reading matter was common.

Column widths were reduced until the 13-pica column became standard. Instead of ample white space, vertical rules were placed between columns so they could be crowded more closely together.

Fig. 16-3 ■ The traditional format emerged in the middle 1880s and dominated newspaper design in the United States for a century. This is Joseph Pulitzer's famous *World,* which was published in New York City.

Increasing interest in the news, especially during the Mexican War (1846–1848), led to greater display of titles on news stories. There had been an occasional head on stories before the 1840s. Most, however, were of one to four lines, and all were restricted to a single column.

The Mexican War seems to have been the event that triggered the expansion of headlines. Additional lines were added with short dashes between each unit. These units became known as *decks.* The short dashes were and are called *jim dashes.* During the Civil War it was not uncommon for a newspaper to print a headline with up to twelve decks employing as many as six different type styles.

There was good reason for restricting headlines to single columns rather than using multicolumn heads, which we would do if a big news story broke today. Some of the larger newspapers were printed on the Hoe type-revolving cylinder press. The type was held in place on the big rotating cylinders with the help of wedge-shaped column rules anchored in the curved bed of the cylinder. Most column rules were made of brass, and printers were reluctant to cut them.

There were the design aesthetics of the era as well. Printers believed that to "break the column rule"—to spread a layout over two or more columns—disfigured, a page. The *New York Herald* ran two-column headlines in 1887, but it left the rule between the columns in place and divided the headline on either side of the rule. The rule ran right through the headline!

When decks of more than one line were composed, the practice was to center each line. This led to the headline pattern called the *inverted pyramid,* in which each succeeding line is smaller than its predecessor and all are centered to give the appearance of an upside-down pyramid.

The single-line head or one-line deck became known as a *crossline* or *bar line.* If the line filled the column width, it was called a *full line.* These terms are still used today.

Other traditional headline patterns were developed. A head in which the first line is a full line and each succeeding line is indented, usually an em, and justified became known as a *hanging indent.* The *Wall Street Journal* uses a hanging indent in its head schedule.

A head in which the top line was set flush left, the middle line centered, and the third line flush right with all lines as nearly equal in length as possible was called a *step head.* Step heads could be two, three, or even more lines deep but all had a step-down pattern.

During the "yellow journalism" era, which started in the 1890s, more and more multicolumn headlines appeared. Headlines became larger and bolder. The single-line *banner head* that stretched across the width of the page made its appearance.

All these typographic innovations became part of the traditional pattern of newspaper design.

Fig. 16-4 ■ Typical traditional headline forms. This style was popular from the middle 1880s through the early 1900s and is still found in some newspapers. The top all-cap lines are bar lines followed by two-, three-, and four-line inverted pyramids except for the third deck in "Launching A Vessel," which is a hanging indent. The decks are separated by jim dashes, and the heads are separated by Oxford cutoff rules.

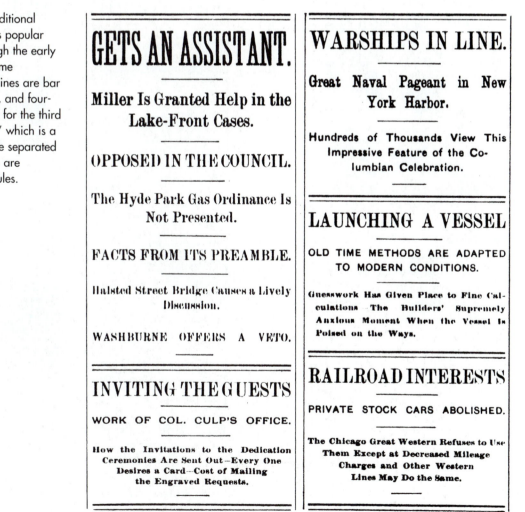

GETS AN ASSISTANT.

Miller Is Granted Help in the Lake-Front Cases.

OPPOSED IN THE COUNCIL.

The Hyde Park Gas Ordinance Is Not Presented.

FACTS FROM ITS PREAMBLE.

Halsted Street Bridge Causes a Lively Discussion.

WASHBURNE OFFERS A VETO.

INVITING THE GUESTS

WORK OF COL. CULP'S OFFICE.

How the Invitations to the Dedication Ceremonies Are Sent Out—Every One Desires a Card—Cost of Mailing the Engraved Requests.

WARSHIPS IN LINE.

Great Naval Pageant in New York Harbor.

Hundreds of Thousands View This Impressive Feature of the Columbian Celebration.

LAUNCHING A VESSEL

OLD TIME METHODS ARE ADAPTED TO MODERN CONDITIONS.

Guesswork Has Given Place to Fine Calculations The Builders' Supremely Anxious Moment When the Vessel Is Poised on the Ways.

RAILROAD INTERESTS

PRIVATE STOCK CARS ABOLISHED.

The Chicago Great Western Refuses to Use Them Except at Decreased Mileage Charges and Other Western Lines May Do the Same.

The Tabloid Format Arrives

In the 1920s two cousins, Joseph Medill Patterson and Robert McCormick, who were members of the family that owned the *Chicago Tribune,* started a half-sheet newspaper. The *tabloid* was born. Tabloid newspapers—newspapers with small pages usually half the size of the broadsheet—had been tried before but none had been successful in this country.

But the time was right for a small newspaper, tightly written, full of pictures and snappy headlines, and aimed at the big-city subway rider, to be a success. And a success it was. Soon tabloids were springing up in most major American cities.

As a result of its flashy design, the tabloid was tagged a "sensational" journal. However, the tabloid page size has many assets as a design form and deserves a solid place in the communications spectrum.

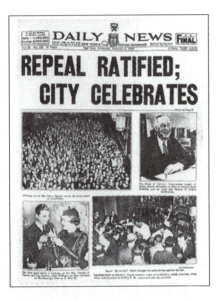

Fig. 16-5 ■ The *Daily News,* New York, was the first successful tabloid newspaper, and it continues today as one of our circulation leaders. The front page uses the poster format, which billboards stories found inside the newspaper.

Fig. 16-6 ■ The tabloid format is gaining popularity as the size of choice for company and organization newspapers. *The Michigan Farm News* has been recognized for its excellent design. The space at the lower left is for the address label. Dennis Rudat is editor and business manager.

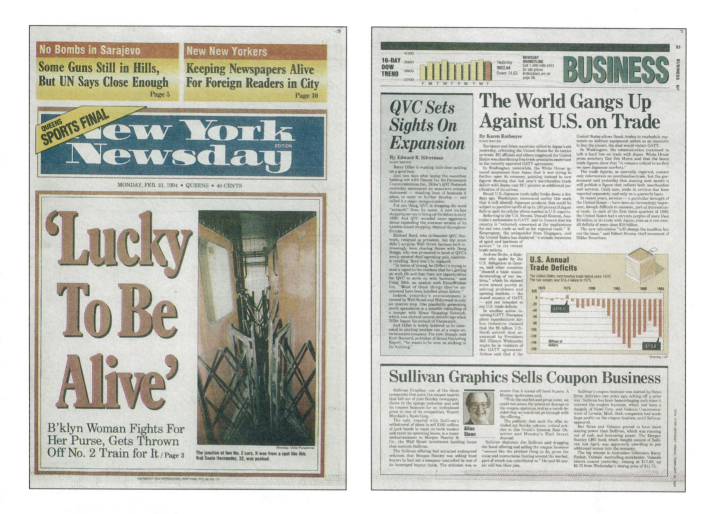

Fig. 16-7 ■ *Newsday*, the superbly designed New York and Long Island tabloid, uses the poster format with a definite magazine-type layout to emphasize stories found inside. *Newsday's* inside pages also have a strong magazine design. *Newsday* pages are good sources of ideas for students and editors or designers of "magapapers." (Copyright 1994, Newsday, Inc.)

Characteristics of the Traditional Format

Narrow columns, along with rigid and precise headline patterns, became trademarks of the traditional newspaper format. Some newspapers continue to use this format. Some designers are adopting traditional characteristics today where they are appropriate to the overall design philosophy. The traditional format is characterized by:

■ Column rules separating narrow columns. The rules are cast on a 4-point base for many newspapers, further cramming the type together.

■ Headlines with a number of decks, all separated by jim dashes.

■ Nameplates often embellished with "ears," or type material on either side at the top of the page. These contain weather, edition logo, promotional material, slogans, and so on.

■ Cutoff rules separating unrelated units such as stories, photos, and cutlines.

■ Rules above and below the folio lines, the full-width lines under the nameplate giving the volume and issue number, date, city of publication, and similar information.

■ Banner heads, sometimes used every day regardless of the importance of the news. These banners are followed by readouts, or decks.

Fig. 16-8 ■ The *Litchfield County Times* maintains the traditional format for its front page. It uses the optimum line width, however, creating a six-column page. This newspaper has won awards in the Society of Newspaper Design competitions.

- Boxes, bullets, ornaments, and embellishments used liberally.
- Many headlines set in all-capital letters, particularly the top decks in the head.
- Types from several families often used in the head schedule.

In addition, the design plans of the front and inside pages of the traditional newspaper usually follow definite preconceived patterns. (These patterns are discussed in Chapter 17.)

As with all design, though, it is difficult to categorically classify the patterns of all newspapers within clear-cut time and design periods.

Some publications changed slowly and some never changed at all. But the traditional approach to newspaper design began to come under serious challenge in the late 1930s and early 1940s with the emergence of what might be called the "functional" design philosophy.

FUNCTIONAL NEWSPAPER DESIGN

➤ The *functional design* philosophy is based on the concept that if an element does not perform a function it should be eliminated, and if another element does the job better it should be used.

John E. Allen led the revolt against the traditional, highly formalized style of newspaper design. His editorship of the *Linotype News,* regarded as the nation's typographic laboratory, and his authorship of three books on newspaper design gave authority to his recommendations. His campaign started in 1929 with what he called "streamlined" headlines. These were heads set flush left and ragged right.[2]

In arguing for the new flush left and for abandoning the complex head designs, Allen made these points:

1. The traditional headline form is difficult to write and often it is necessary to use inaccurate or inappropriate words because of the rigid unit count.

2. All-cap lines are hard to read compared with lines set in lowercase.

3. Flush left heads allow more white space into the page and give heads more breathing room.

4. Traditional head forms are difficult and take more time to set in type.

These points made sense to many designers, and the new style was adopted by more and more newspapers. It was based on the idea that the purpose of typography and graphic design is to make the contents understandable and inviting to read.

Designers examined each element of the newspaper page and evaluated its worth in terms of effective communication. They proceeded from the thesis that if a functional newspaper were to be designed, the first step was to define its function—this is a good starting point for any design project, incidentally.

The functions of most newspapers can be summarized as *informing, interpreting, persuading,* and *entertaining.* The design and layout of any newspaper should help it achieve four specific goals:

1. Increase readability and attract the reader.

2. Sort the contents so the reader knows at a glance which information is the most important and what each part of the newspaper contains.

3. Create an attractive and interesting package of pages.

4. Create recognition so the paper can be readily identified.

Fig. 16-9 ■ The *Christian Science Monitor* was an early convert to functional modern design. Heads were set in capital and lowercase, white space was used in place of column and cutoff rules, multicolumn heads helped break up the traditional vertical thrust, and elements that did not perform a function were modified or eliminated.

A number of innovations in design were adopted in the late 1930s and early 1940s to help accomplish these goals. After the adoption of the flush left headline form with fewer, if any, decks, other efforts were made to let light into the pages and brighten them. White space was used wherever possible. Nameplates were simplified. Often, ears were dropped or cleaned up and typographic embellishments in the nameplate area were eliminated in favor of white space.

The top, and in some instances the bottom, rule on the folio line was eliminated. Vertical column rules were dropped in favor of white space between columns and this white space was increased. A pica of white space between columns was considered minimum for effective separation.

Cutoff rules and jim dashes were scrapped in favor of white space, although some newspapers continued to use cutoff rules if they were thought more effective in designating story and art unit limits.

The new design movement favored fewer banner heads but more variety in layout. The optical attraction of the upper left corner of the page was utilized by placing important stories or photos there rather than subordinating them to the traditional lead story in the upper right corner.

Shorter nameplates were another design innovation. Designers frequently used skyline heads and stories, placed above the nameplate and extending across the width of the page. The traditional nameplate, which extended across the top of the page, was reset in varying widths so it could be "floated" or shifted around on the page and set in two, three, or more column widths for variety and change of pace.

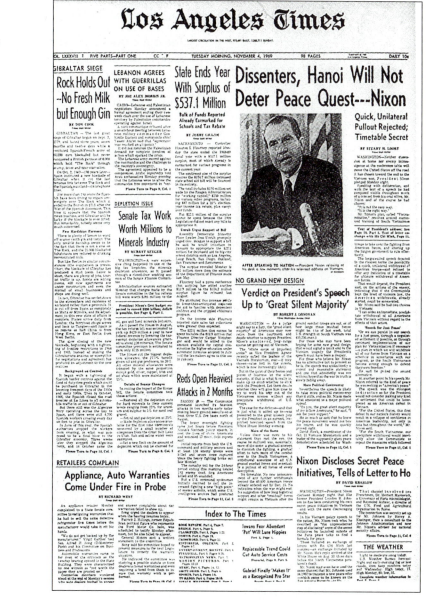

Fig. 16-10 ■ The *Los Angeles Times* was one of the first metropolitan newspapers to adopt the optimum format, replacing the traditional eight-column page with a six-column page, which allows wider columns to make reading easier.

Other functional innovations included good display of a page 1 index and highlighting of inside features to attract the readers to the inside of the newspaper. More photos were used and in larger sizes to give them increased impact. Photos were cropped closely and enlarged. More attention was paid to the bottom half of the page—the area below the fold—to get a better balance and to present a livelier look from top to bottom.

Jumped stories were eliminated as much as possible since readership studies revealed that a story loses about 80 percent of its audience when it is continued to another page.

A horizontal thrust was introduced with the use of more multicolumn heads and photos. This helped break up the dullness of column after column of vertical makeup. Captions were shortened and rules, boxes, and ornaments simplified.

Not all newspapers adopted all of the functional design devices. But more and more newspapers did appear in a format that reflected what had become accepted as a basic tenet of good newspaper design:

The appearance of the newspaper should reflect its editorial philosophy and appeal to its particular audience.

The *New York Times,* traditional yet in its basic design, continues to win awards for its adherence to that philosophy.

THE OPTIMUM FORMAT ARRIVES

In 1937 the *Los Angeles Times* restyled its format to functional design, and that year it won the coveted Ayer award for outstanding newspaper design. Twenty-eight years later, the *Courier-Journal,* Louisville, Kentucky, and its companion newspaper, the *Louisville Times,* became the first metropolitan newspapers to usher in the *optimum design era.* The *Courier-Journal* cut its columns per page from eight to six and widened them from 11 picas to 15.

In the 1960s some newspapers began to appear with a "downstyle" head dress. The *downstyle head* is composed in all lowercase letters except for the first word and proper nouns. It further simplifies newspaper design and eases reading.

In 1965 daily newspaper circulation in the United States was 60,358,000. By 1970 the population stood at 203,302,031 and newspaper circulation was 62,108,000. Ten years later the population had grown by more than 23,000,000 while newspaper circulation remained virtually unchanged. During the decade circulation of all the general circulation newspapers in the country only increased by 115,040.

Editors and publishers recognized that something was wrong. The country had more and more people but not more and more newspapers. They looked at their products and decided steps should be taken to make newspaper reading more attractive.

Following the lead of the *Courier-Journal* and others, many newspapers made two basic changes. The size of the body type was increased from the standard 8 point to 9 and even 9½. Columns were widened to

Fig. 16-11 ■ The *Hartford Courant* as it appeared in 1984, a carefully designed example of the optimum format. (Copyright 1984, Hartford Courant)

approximate the optimum line length for reading ease and speed. This meant changing from the cramped 10½- or 11-pica columns to more comfortable 14- or 15-pica columns.

By the middle 1970s the majority of newspapers had switched to the six-column format for at least their front and section pages. Some newspapers went to five-column pages and virtually all increased the white space between columns.

Fig. 16-12 ■ Today the *Courant* is a member of the redesign era with skyline teasers, color, and a trend that is emerging—the restoring of the period at the end of the nameplate, a practice abandoned by most newspapers years ago. (Copyright 1995, *Hartford Courant*)

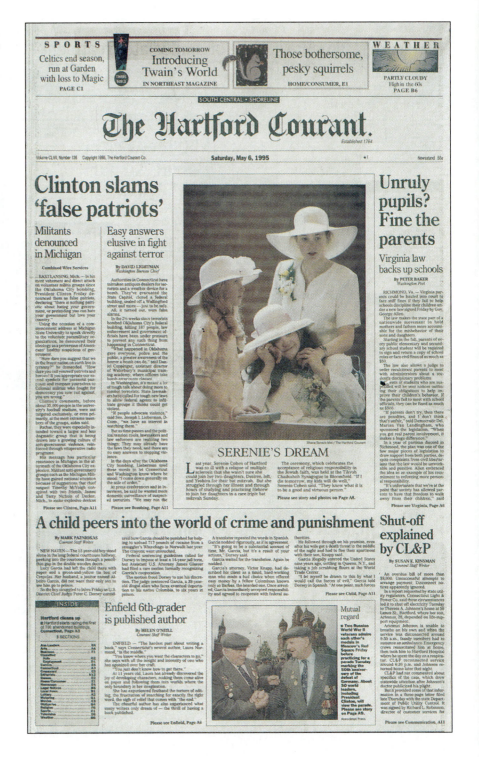

A leader in urging more readable newspapers was Edmund C. Arnold, who succeeded Allen as editor of the *Linotype News* and who has been recognized as one of America's authorities on newspaper design.

"There are many advantages to the op format," Arnold wrote in *Modern Newspaper Design.* He pointed out that "a line length at optimum is an asset because it enhances communication. The reader likes

Fig. 16-13 ■ Metropolitan papers are placing more emphasis on serving outlying areas. The *Hartford Courant* has five "Town News Extra" sections that are distributed in the Sunday edtion to their various regions. Note the map that indicates the area covered by this example. This section contains local news and information that reminds one of the contents of the typical community weekly newspaper. (Copyright 1994, *Hartford Courant*)

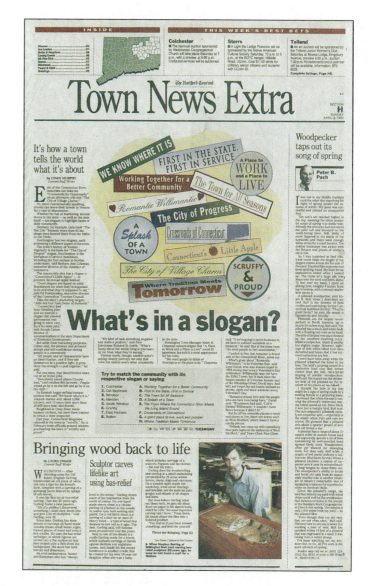

the longer measure, too, even if he doesn't understand the technicalities involved."[3]

However, even though the optimum format made newspaper reading easier and more pleasant, circulation continued static. Many newspapers have again narrowed their columns back to 12 picas and reduced the body type back to 8 point. For them, the intent of the optimum format has been lost.

THE REDESIGNING ERA

➤ Newspaper design today is in a state of flux. The optimum format is with us in spirit if not in actuality. At the same time editors and designers are probing ways to make newspapers more visually exciting. They are struggling to keep up with the rapid changes in life-styles and reader interests. The new technology is also dictating many aspects of form and format.

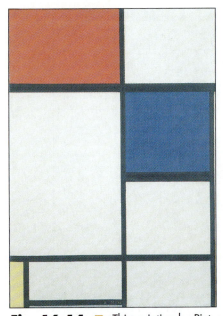

Fig. 16–14 ■ This painting by Piet Mondrian is an example of his style, which inspired the modular makeup of many of today's newspapers. (Private collection. Photo courtesy Sidney Janis Gallery, New York)

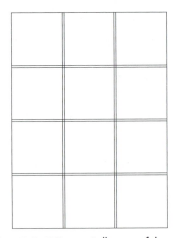

Fig. 16–15 ■ Followers of the International Typographic Style advocate the use of a grid in graphic design. A grid consists of precisely drawn straight lines in rectangles and squares on paper or cardboard printed in nonreproducing ink. It is used for placing elements on a layout. In desktop publishing and computer pagination the grid is created on the monitor. This is a three-column grid.

There is, however, a growing recognition of the importance of blending design with content to develop the most effective communications package. Dr. Mario R. Garcia, a leading designer, wrote in *Contemporary Newspaper Design,* "Improvement in content and emphasis on clear writing and editing, combined with effective graphic innovation should be present" before circulation declines can be reversed.[4]

At the same time, the new technology is opening doors of opportunity for newspaper editors and designers. The mechanical constraints of the past have been eased, allowing the designer to apply what has been called the *total design concept.* This means that instead of being restricted by a page divided into columns, the designer now has an area that can be treated as a blank rectangle (the dimensions of the page) on which to create the most effective layout possible.

The design question has become not how to fill columns but how to create an effective page within its overall dimensions. Some designers have retained the basic vertical approach which has withstood the test of time for so many years. The answer for many others has been found in the *modular* format. This approach to design evolved from the creations of a Dutch painter, Piet Mondrian, and a school of design that is known as the Swiss approach, or the International Typographic Style.

Mondrian did most of his work in the early part of this century. By 1917 he was concentrating his efforts on the use of the primary colors—red, yellow, and blue—combined with black and white, and limiting his art forms to straight lines, squares, and rectangles.

These compositions, employing vertical and horizontal lines at 90 degree angles forming crosses, rectangles, and squares, were typical of Mondrian's art. Mondrian, who lived until 1944, has been an important influence on contemporary art and architecture, as well as on the modular approach to layout of newspapers, magazines, and other printed communications.

As graphic historian Philip B. Meggs notes, "Mondrian used pure line, shape, and color to create a universe of harmoniously ordered, pure relationships. To unify social and human values, technology, and visual form became a goal for those who strived for a new architecture and graphic design."[5]

The International Typographic Style, which we discussed in Chapter 2, was adopted by newspaper designers. Characteristics of this design philosophy that popped up in newspaper design included:

■ Use of a precisely drawn grid.

■ Use of Sans Serif types with Helvetica being a favorite.

■ More type set ragged right.

■ Combining the work of the reporter, visual communicator, and editor to present information in as clear a manner as possible.

The use of the grid, advocated by this movement, has become a standard practice especially in laying out pages for publications. In the modular approach to newspaper design the page is made up of a series of rectangles, with perhaps a square now and then. Each spatial unit, or module, contains a complete story. It is as if each story with its head

Fig. 16-16 ■ Here is a rough of a possible arrangement of illustrations and copy on the three-column grid. The modular approach to newspaper design grew out of the work of Piet Mondrian and the philosophy of the International Typographic Style.

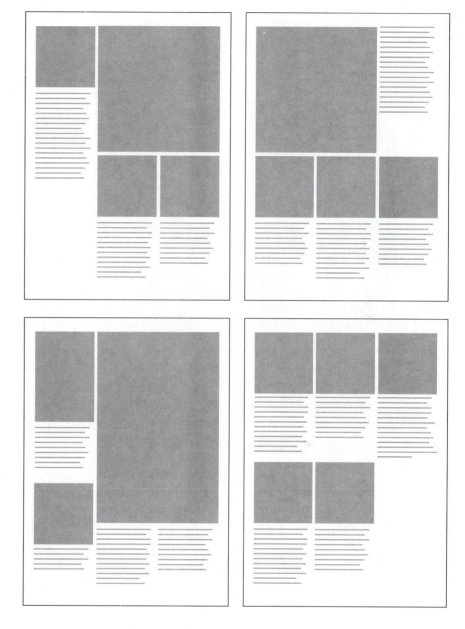

and art, if used, is prepackaged in a rectangle or, more rarely, a square so these packages can be arranged in as pleasing a way as possible on the page.

Designers who have adopted the modular plan—and it works well for large-format magazines and newsletters as well as newspapers—have these suggestions for planning a modular page:

■ Make numerous thumbnail sketches of newspaper pages made up of various combinations of rectangles. Do not use squares as they are monotonous and uninteresting. Keep in mind the basic design principle of proportion. Select the sketch that is most pleasing and use it as the basic design grid for that particular page.

Fig. 16-17 ■ This front page of the *Maine Sunday Telegram* illustrates modular design. The page contains eight distinct rectangles with the news placed within the skyline and nameplate at the top and teasers at the bottom for anchors. There are only five news stories. The page is a good example of the use of principles of design including unity, balance, and contrast.

■ One module should dominate the page and presumably contain the lead story. This module should be placed above the fold, usually in the upper left or upper right —the high-interest sections of the page.

■ Each module should be self-contained, with a rule to define it. However, the rule should not be too heavy, no more than 4 points wide. Some designers specify color for the rules if available. Fairly generous white space, usually 18 to 24 points, can be used instead of rules.

■ Modules contain a head and often art. Modules can be art and cutline only, but they should be considered as packages of information. The elements included should transmit the information as clearly and completely as possible.

■ The trend is toward the use of more line art in newspaper design. Photographs, when used, should be cropped closely to give impact to the center of interest.

Fig. 16-18 ■ Careful attention to inside and section pages is important. Too often all the emphasis is placed on the front page. This section page illustrates an "info package" ("Pineland decays . . .") in which the skills of the reporter, photographer, graphic designer, and editor are combined to tell the story as effectively as possible.

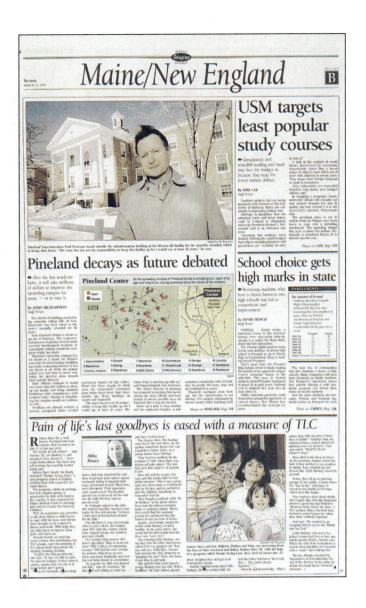

■ Plenty of white space should be used within the rules—around the heads and other elements.

Not all designers are modular format advocates. The corporate art director of The New York Times Company, Lou Silverstein, comments on this design plan in Chapter 17.

It should be pointed out that within the overall dimensions of the page, the designer working with "desktop" equipment has great freedom. Tools that permit the wraparound of type and the easy manipulation of type and art enable the designer to take a "free flow" approach, if that is desired, to creating interesting layouts.

Whenever a newspaper is being redesigned or a new publication is being planned, it is important to precede the actual design work by a publication analysis.

Fig. 16-19 ■ When the *Oregonian* was redesigned these goals were set: Increase newsstand sales, convert Sunday-only readers to daily readers, reduce median age of readers from 51 to 39, reduce the number of people who don't read because of lack of time, gain more public awareness of content and editorial character of the paper. On the left is a front page of the redesigned paper. On the right is a food section page showing the emphasis put on creative use of graphics, which is continued throughout the paper. (Courtesy *Oregonian*, Portland, Oregon)

HOW TO ANALYZE A PUBLICATION

▶ The designer of a newspaper should plan an analysis of the product on a regular basis. If possible, each issue should be evaluated with the editor. This evaluation could start with a few moments spent in browsing through the entire copy.

The overview of the issue should reveal a general impression of whether the typography maintains the character of the publication. For instance, does the whole issue help identify the publication as a conservative newspaper for a conservative community? Does it help say this newspaper is produced by an organization devoted to academic interests or to the manufacture of heavy equipment? The appearance of the newspaper should reinforce its purpose.

The examination should reveal if the arrangement of elements aids communication. Are there barriers? Are the rules, ornaments, or subheads placed so the flow of copy is interrupted to the point that the reader is confused? Does the layout increase readability? Would readers be attracted to this story or that? Or would they be inclined to pass a story by because the layout appears dull? If you were a reader would you want to spend time with this newspaper?

The entire package should do a good job of "sorting" the contents so the reader can find topical matter easily and without confusion.

Once an overall impression has been formed, each of the typographic elements should be examined and evaluated:

1. *Body type:* Is it legible and readable? Roman types have the highest readability. But the Roman used in newspaper design should have rather soft serifs and not too sharp a differentiation in the widths of the letter strokes. The size of the body type should be checked to see if it is large enough for easy reading. Types that are big on the body (large *x* height) are usually preferred. Line length and leading should be examined to ensure their effectiveness.

2. *Headlines:* Is the type selected for the headlines attractive? Does it reflect the tone of the newspaper? Of the feature stories? Even though a bold type is chosen, it should be clear and legible. The same is true for light typefaces. A headline type should have a fairly good unit count. If more than one family is used in a head arrangement, the types should harmonize but one should dominate. Spacing between words and lines should be examined as well as all the factors of legibility, such as the size of the head for the width of the line.

3. *Typographic color:* Have ornaments, bull's eyes, arrows, and so on been avoided? If typographic devices are used, they should enhance legibility rather than detract from it.

4. *Newspaper constants:* Do the standing heads, department and column heads, and the masthead harmonize with the overall effect of the layout? The constants should be alive and not static. Headings such as "The President's Column," "Washington Week," or similar label heads should be redesigned if they do not have an element that can be changed, preferably with each issue, to illuminate the contents and add life.

5. *Pictures and cutlines:* Are the pictures cropped for proper emphasis? Art should communicate a message and not just ornament the layouts. Cutlines should be in a consistent style throughout the newspaper. They should be set in a type style that harmonizes with the other types but still provides some contrast. Cutlines should be set in the proper width, never more than about 18 picas wide. Cutlines under wide art should be broken into columns that approximate the optimum line length. Indented cutlines with ample space between lines brighten a page.

6. *Front page layout:* Can the application of the basic principles of design be seen? Is unity, balance, contrast, and harmony evident in the selection and placement of the elements? Is the optical center used to achieve balance? The front-page design should emphasize the most important story, but usually more than one strong element is needed to make a lively page. However, the page should not be overloaded to the point where it appears to be a conglomeration.

Ear

Nameplate

Folio line

Downstyle
flush left head

Summary sub-head

Byline

Dateline

Cutoff rule

Box

Photo credit line

Cut line

Jump line

Fig. 16–20 ■ This page from the *St. Petersburg Times* illustrates a number of newspaper design terms.

Are there strong elements in the "hot spots"—the four corners of the page? Unless there is a planned vertical thrust to the page, a strong horizontal treatment is desirable. There should be ample but well-planned white space.

7. *Inside page layout:* Is a consistent pattern evident for the placement of advertisements? Advertisements should not be placed

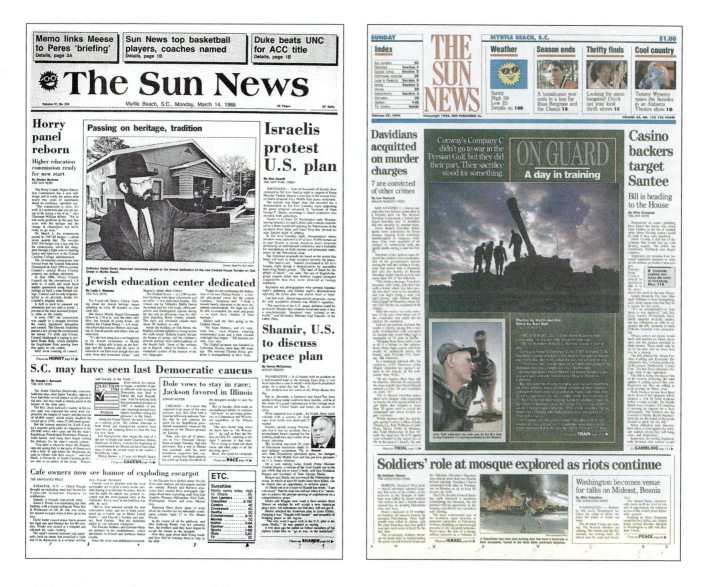

Fig. 16–21 ■ The *Sun News,* which serves a resort area, recently underwent a dramatic change in appearance. The plan was to give the paper a contemporary, distinctive look that would stand out on a newsstand where it had to compete with ten other newspapers. On the left is the newspaper before the redesign. After the redesign (right) the *Sun News* carried fewer front page stories to make room for larger art. The nameplate was given a vertical treatment for a distinctive look. This allowed for more room for top-of-the-page teasers. Century Bold was selected for the headlines with Franklin Gothic for accent. Bylines are in Franklin Gothic and Century Old Style. (Courtesy *Sun News,* Myrtle Beach, S.C.)

haphazardly on a page, and the pattern adopted should be used consistently throughout the newspaper. Advertisements should be placed so they do not destroy reasonable editorial matter display; that is, they should be kept as low as possible on the page. Is there an editorial stopper—a story or art or a combination—on each inside page?

8. *Section pages and departments:* Are these given the same care as page 1? These pages should reflect the purposes and characteristics of the sections in their typographic design. For instance, the sports pages should have headline type that helps to say "This is the sports section," and the family living section should have a typographic dress that helps identify it. The principles of good layout should be evident in these pages as well as in all the others.

Once each part of the newspaper's anatomy has been analyzed and areas of improvement noted, the suggested improvements should be examined to see how they fit in helping to create a unified, attractive publication.

Fig. 16–22 ■ What will the newspaper of the future be like? Here is Don DeMaio's answer. This prototype page was designed for an American Press Institute workshop on the newspaper in the year 2001. DeMaio, graphics director of the Associated Press, believes the newspaper's front page will include a personalized databank for the individual subscriber. One difference in the future, he predicts, "will be the quality of people designing pages. I think that skilled design journalists, working with new technology, will be primarily responsible for the complete news product." (Courtesy American Press Institute)

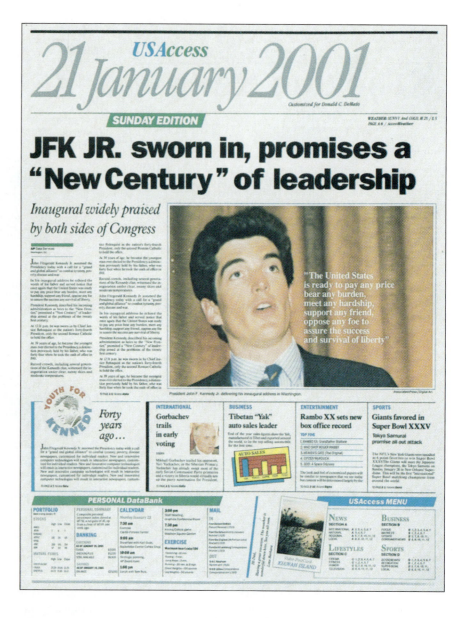

► EFFECTIVE DESIGN CHECKLIST

■ Eliminate barriers. Check to see, for instance, if copy broken by subheads, art, or other typographic devices is easy to follow over, around, or under the devices.

■ Break up long copy for easy reading. Use extra space between paragraphs, pull out pertinent points and box them, use subheads, or indent and illuminate enumerated points with bull's eyes or other typographic color devices. But don't overdo it.

■ Set copy on proper measure for easy reading. Check to see that copy is never set more than two columns wide. Never set it two columns wide if the columns are more than 12 picas. Body matter shouldn't be set more than about 15 picas wide.

- Avoid using overlines with photos. (Overlines are small heads above photos.) Studies show they have no value. If a head is part of the cutline format, it should be immediately adjacent to the cutline.

- Stick to one or two families of type for the head schedule. Plan a basic head schedule with one family of type and use its variations for contrast. If another family is used, use it sparingly and for contrast and accent, rather than basic heads.

- Be cautious with reverses. Be sure reversed type has high legibility. Reverses can be difficult to print well, and they can disfigure a page.

- Crop carefully and enlarge generously. Crop to emphasize the point of interest and eliminate anything that gets in the way of story-telling quality of the photo. Enlarge to give impact and reader interest and do it generously.

- Never run two unrelated photos next to each other. They will tug at the reader for attention, decreasing the impact of each.

- Have a strong element in each quadrant of the front page. The "hot spots" attract interest, and the strong elements will hold the readers and ensure an orderly and balanced layout.

- Watch the folds. In making layouts, be aware of the folds and try to keep photos away from them. Be sure the fold doesn't destroy or maim the subject matter in the photo.

▶ GRAPHICS IN ACTION

1. Select a daily newspaper and study its typography and design. See how many examples you can find that illustrate applications of the principles of design. (*Examples:* A Black Letter used for the nameplate might contrast well with the style of type selected for the headline schedule. Elements placed below the fold help create balance on the page.)

2. Put together a prototype of an entire front page of a newspaper. Materials for such a prototype can be obtained by copying headlines, reading matter, and newspaper constants on a copying machine. Or, if you are working with a computer, they can be scanned to the page. (Use the suggestions in "How to Analyze a Publication" in this chapter as a guide.)

3. Make a design plan for an "ideal" newspaper. Select the page size, types for headlines and features, departments, and all the design elements that you believe should be incorporated in such a publication.

4. Design a small newspaper for an organization to which you belong or design an employee newspaper for a firm with which you are acquainted. If such a newspaper exists now, analyze the typographic and design elements and make recommendations for any changes that would improve the newspaper's format.

5. This project is extensive, so you might want to do it as a team or class effort. Select a nearby community or neighborhood that doesn't have a newspaper (or that seems ready for a competitive newspaper). Plan and conduct the research that you believe should be done. Make a basic design plan for your proposed newspaper that reflects the character of the community and the newspaper you would produce for it.

NOTES

[1]From advertisements in *Editor & Publisher,* March 19, 1994.

[2]John E. Allen, *Newspaper Designing* (New York: Harper, 1947).

[3]Edmond C. Arnold, *Modern Newspaper Design* (New York: Harper, 1969), p. 266.

[4]Mario R. Garcia, *Contemporary Newspaper Design, A Structural Approach* (Englewood Cliffs, N.J.: Prentice-Hall, 1981), p. 23.

[5]Philip B. Meggs, *A History of Graphic Design* (New York: Van Nostrand Reinhold, 1983), p. 23.

CHAPTER 17

DESIGNING AND REDESIGNING NEWSPAPERS

© Mark Richards, Photo Edit

17 Publications all across the country—big ones, little ones, metropolitan dailies, community weeklies, and company and campus newspapers—have discovered visual communications. Constant examination and reexamination of the publication's appearance takes place as editors and designers seek ways to make their product more appealing and attractive.

Many newspapers have created a new position on their staffs for a person who specializes in visual communication—the graphic journalist. The graphic journalist is one who combines the skills of the designer and photographer with those of the reporter and editor to devise methods of presenting information in the most effective way possible.

The techniques of the graphic journalist could prove valuable to the communicator in public relations or advertising as well as to those working on newspapers and magazines.

The graphic journalist combines words, type, art, borders, photographs, drawings, and typographic devices to form a unit of information. He or she also works with the editorial staff in designing and laying out newspaper sections and pages. The graphic journalist must understand design principles and graphic and typographic techniques. In addition, the person must have the editor's understanding of news and information and the opportunities for its visual presentation.

The editors of a publication, working with the graphic journalist, strive to apply the following formula: If the rewards received from reading an article were divided by the effort made to accomplish the task, the result would equal the possibilities of the piece being read.

$$\frac{\text{Rewards received}}{\text{Effort to read}} = \text{Chance of being read}$$

Communicators should keep this formula in mind. People will refuse to read material that is full of barriers, choosing instead the many forms of communication that require little effort to absorb.

Another major reason for the growing attention to graphics is the intrusion into the editorial room of the electronic age. Pagination devices are becoming standard tools for putting together newspaper pages, and many journalists are involved in arranging information units to form a page layout on a video screen. These journalists will make graphic as well as editorial decisions.

DEVELOPING A DESIGN PHILOSOPHY

➤ One of the first steps in sharpening your skills as a graphic journalist, or a communicator who will be involved in the design of printed communications, is to start developing a *design philosophy*. A design philosophy might be defined as your beliefs and attitudes toward all the aspects of graphic design. It would include such things as your preferences for particular type styles for certain situations, how you would project an image through the use of typography and graphics, and how you would apply such subjective values as taste and judgment to your work.

Fig. 17-1 ■ The one newspaper that is credited with starting the graphics explosion in the world of journalism is *USA Today*. When it appeared in 1982 with its emphasis on color and graphics, it became a model for many newspaper redesign plans. (Copyright 1995, *USA Today*. Reprinted with permission)

As Bill Ostendorf, who has helped design more than thirty publications, puts it, "Design is not the implementation of a series of 'correct' or 'right' techniques. Design, like editing, involves taste, judgment, discipline, training, and experience. And it requires some kind of design philosophy."[1]

Design philosophy helps the communicator to bring meaning and direction to the many decisions that have to be made.

How do you develop a design philosophy?

"Unfortunately, no one can really hand you an article or list that provides such a philosophy. You have to develop and nurture your own," Ostendorf notes.[2]

A philosophy of design cannot be acquired by simply reading books or attending classes, but they can help. It requires a career-long effort to learn everything possible about communications—not just design aspects, but also such things as market research, advertising, public relations, statistics, computers and new technological developments, reporting and editing.

The first step in developing a design philosophy is to make a decision to keep working on it. This should include reading lots of books and professional magazines, attending workshops, and studying the design work of others.

THE APPROACH TO REDESIGN

Let us assume that you have just been appointed editor of a small newspaper. This is your first job and you want to do all you can to make the newspaper as effective as possible. It does not matter if this is a large or small community newspaper or a university or organizational publication, the procedure is the same.

Of course, you examine the content of the newspaper to see if it is supplying what the audience wants and needs. In addition, you consider the method of publication and distribution. Your major concern, however, is with the typographic dress the newspaper is wearing. The decision is made to do a complete overhaul of the design. But how will you start and carry out a redesign project?

One course of action is to follow the procedures professional designers recommend. These procedures offer a guide for designing a new newspaper as well as redesigning an existing publication.

A newspaper to be successful must have three qualities: (1) It must contain the information people want and need. (2) It must attract the audience. (3) It must be interesting.

Design can help make a newspaper attract the desired audience and be attractive. It can also make the newspaper interesting.

But before specific design principles are put to work to create the physical appearance desired, a few general guidelines for designing effective newspapers should be reviewed:

■ Typography and graphics can tell the reader what type of publication is being produced. They can say, "This is a hard-hitting, crusading publication." They can say, "This is a dignified publication devoted to accuracy and thoroughness." And they can say, "This newspaper is taking a light, breezy approach to all the activities it is attempting to cover."

Fig. 17–2 ■ This dramatic section opener page demonstrates powerful use of graphics to grab the reader. Too often design efforts are concentrated on the newspaper's front page. Careful planning and creative use of art, color, and type can attract and keep readers involved in the entire package. (Courtesy *the Washington Times*)

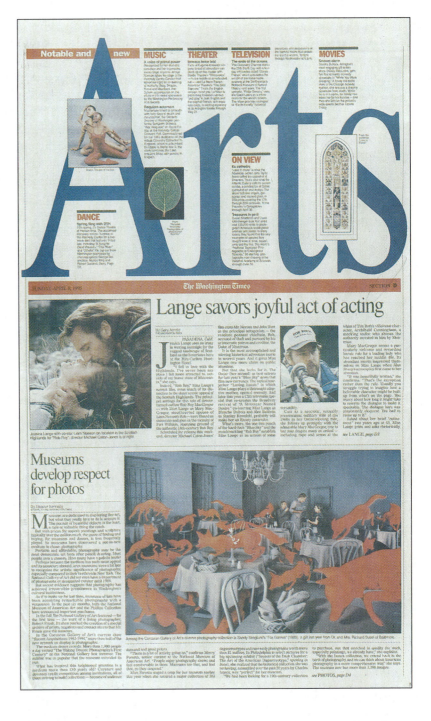

- Typography and graphics can provide instantaneous identification for a publication. Readers should recognize immediately that this is a certain newspaper, not the *Daily Times* from the neighboring town or the *Employees Gazette* from the plant down the road.

- Typography and graphics can help readers spot the various departments or classifications of material the publication contains. They can help the reader sort out the contents and indicate which material the editors believe is important and which they consider of minor interest.

Before the principles of good design are put to work, a thorough study of the situation should be made. Everyone in the organization should become involved. The editorial, advertising, production, circulation, and marketing departments should participate. An analysis of the market and reader demographics should be part of the research.

When the *Oregon Statesman,* a 45,000-circulation daily in Salem, was redesigned, the designer spent a week carefully reading copies of the newspaper to become familiar with its form and content. Then decisions were made based on a realistic look at the resources. This included the limitations of staff and equipment. Also, consideration was given to how changes could be made within the framework of the ongoing work schedule, and what could be done considering the size of the "news hole" (the area that could be devoted to everything but advertisements) and the entire newspaper.

The Redesign Plan

Once a study of the present format and resources is completed, a plan of procedure and a timetable can be organized. Many designers follow a step-by-step outline that looks something like this:

1. Research and set the goals.
2. Survey the readers for their views regarding the newspaper.
3. Devise a realistic timetable.
4. Specify how and by whom decisions will be made.
5. Make the design decisions.
6. Produce a prototype.
7. Evaluate and refine the prototype.
8. Produce a final prototype to be used as a guide in designing actual pages.
9. Put a new design into action, evaluate it, get reader reactions, and make necessary adjustments.
10. Continue evaluation, solicit reader and staff reactions.

Goal Setting for Newspaper Design

There isn't much point in jumping into a design program without first deciding what it is supposed to accomplish. Goals should be set, and these goals might be entirely different from one newspaper or one community to another.

For instance, one of the criticisms leveled at newspapers by the judges in an Inland Daily Press Association makeup contest was that some newspapers were printing sixteen or more stores on the front page. The judges ruled that the effect was too much clutter and decreased readability. The judges also noted that "the most annoying design element on many newspapers is promotions found at the top of the front page in dark, ugly boxes and in color." They pointed out that the devices were so powerful that "they easily pull the reader's eyes away from stories that are less graphically appealing but which should be read nevertheless."

On the other hand, when the *Orlando Sentinel* was redesigned, more stories and visual items were packed into page 1, the nameplate was underlined with a color bar and topped with a promotion in colorful high-tech deco style. And, in the first four months following its redesign, the sales were up 13.5 percent from the previous year.

The lesson for the designer is that goals should be set, and the design should help the newspaper achieve these goals. In the case of the *Sentinel,* the main goals of the redesign were to increase sales to tourists visiting the city, establish name recognition, and attract attention.

Each publication, then, should set its goals to fit its individual situation, not necessarily to win awards in contests.

However, a number of goals are valuable for all designers to consider. Study after study has shown that readers like a well-organized newspaper. They like to find information easily, and they like to find it in the same spot issue after issue. A basic objective of any redesign project might be to organize the content to achieve this goal.

Goals should include adherence to the general guidelines for good design, such as making the newspaper more visually attractive while building a consistent design theme throughout and designing with simplicity and restraint. That is, the design should never overwhelm the message. Graphics and design elements should not only be colorful but also should convey information to the reader.

A consistent award-winner and a newspaper that is recognized for its effective design is the *New York Times.* Yet this newspaper continues to use a traditional design for its main news section that might be regarded as outdated and old-fashioned. One reason the *New York Times,* regarded as *the* newspaper of record, receives acclaim for its graphics is that it exemplifies the basic premise of effective design. A newspaper's appearance should reflect its editorial philosophy and appeal to the audience it wishes to attract.

After sixteen months of work the *Press Democrat* of Santa Rosa, California, emerged in a completely new format. The design was greatly influenced by what readers said they wanted in their newspaper. The goal of the *Press Democrat* staff was to produce a newspaper that skillfully delivered the news.

One of the first steps taken was a readership survey. This was made by a Boston marketing firm, Urban and Associates. The firm did a telephone survey of 1,000 households in the *Press Democrat* circulation area. Results of the survey included the discovery that subscribers were reading the newspaper deeply and critically. They wanted hard news, but they also wanted good reporting that contained more than just the facts—they wanted stories that were interesting and insightful.

As Chris Urban, who conducted the survey, told the *Press Democrat* staff, there was a strong interest in news. At the same time, the lighter and more entertaining stories appealed to a growing readership of younger and more mobile individuals. But the light approach should be in the proper place and with the proper perspective. In other words, the serious news should be handled seriously, and the lighter feature stories could be made to be more fun to read.

Fig. 17-3 ■ The Santa Rose *Press Democrat* as it appeared before the redesign project. It had a modular look that designer Lou Silverstein found "clean but boring." (Courtesy *Press Democrat*)

Lou Silverstein, chief designer for the *New York Times,* worked with the *Press Democrat* staff on the new design. He is not an admirer of modular design, which was the approach used by the newspaper before the redesign. Silverstein sees modular as a way to cram news into little boxes. It creates the impression that everyone at the newspaper spends time making sure everything is neat. The result is a newspaper that looks clean but boring.

Fig. 17-4 ■ After redesign, the *Press Democrat* won the "best front page in California" award of the California Newspaper Publishers Association. Also, it has won five Society of Newspaper Design Awards of Excellence, plus a bronze medal. Reader reaction has been overwhelmingly positive. (Courtesy *Press Democrat*)

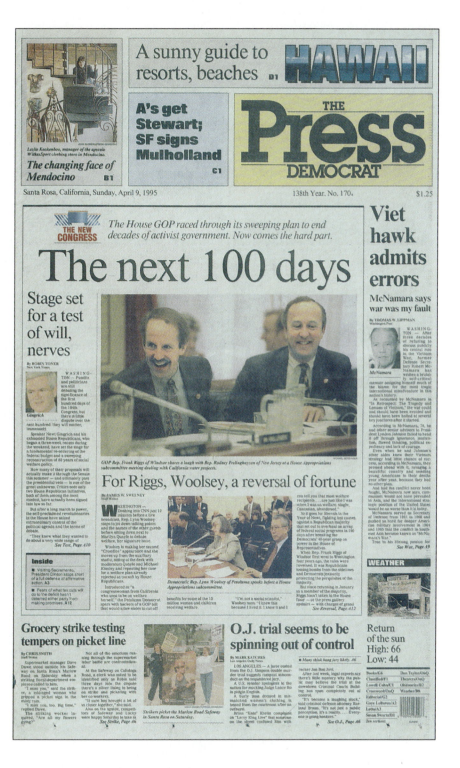

"My criteria for a well-designed news section is that it have a balance between newsiness, surprise, serendipity on the one hand, and on the other a feeling of organization and a demonstrated effort on the part of the editors to make things easy and clear, including the use of graphic tools," says Silverstein.

"Graphics should play an important part in the presentation of news just as every available tool should play an important part for an editor. Ideally, the best visual people in the organization should be involved as early as possible and as deeply as possible in the planning and then the design of important news pages . . . a sophisticated top editor will use the best visual talent in the most integrated way with his own journalistic talents," he adds.[3]

The look of the new *Press Democrat* is altogether different from its previous appearance. It has a more vertical thrust with more one-column heads and stories. The look is more unpredictable than with the modular approach. It is more exciting. At the same time, the whole package is better organized. Each edition is chock-full of material and does not look rigid.

Publisher Michael J. Parman says, "Reader response has been overwhelmingly in favor of our new look. We were perceived as being somewhat dull in appearance. Obviously, the wonderful design that Lou Silverstein gave us is anything but dull. We have had exceptional growth the past several years, and I have no doubts that the design has a great deal to do with that."[4]

Press Democrat circulation has increased from 73,000 to 98,000 since the change (Sunday circulation is 103,000), and this has outstripped the grown in population of the circulation area.

The newspaper won the "best front page in California" award from the California Newspaper Publishers Association in 1989. It won three Society of Newspaper Design Awards of Excellence in 1994 and two Society Awards of Excellence in 1993.

Making Design Decisions

Once goals have been set, the design or redesign of a publication can proceed. The design decision-making process can be organized along general and specific lines. First, let's consider some suggestions for the overall design and then the specifics, such as the front page, inside pages, section pages, and the editorial page.

Designers generally agree on these rules for good design:

1. The design must communicate clearly and economically with maximum legibility.

2. The design should create identity for the newspaper.

3. The design must communicate with a sense of proportion. That is, the breadth of the design should be controlled by the context of the news of the day.

4. The design must communicate in a style that is easily recognized.

5. The design must communicate with consistency. This consistency should be helpful to the readers in finding content in each edition.

6. The design must accomplish its goal with economy. This means changes in arrangement can be made quickly, and space and materials used with acceptable budgetary restraint.

Effective design can often be achieved if the designer will consider four steps: (1) Square off type masses. (2) Use plenty of white space. (3) Put life in the four corners of the page. (4) Keep it simple.

(a)

(b)

(c)

Fig. 17-5 ■ A more colorful *Christian Science Monitor* greeted the new year in January 1989. This was the third redesign of the newspaper in 13 years. Shown is (a) the *Monitor* in 1983 just before the second redesign; (b) the paper when it appeared in a new dress in the fall of 1983; and (c) the *Monitor* as it appears today. When the present redesign was implemented, the *Monitor* installed $1.8 million in electronic color prepress and communications equipment. The paper switched from 25-pound newsprint to 40-pound stock to achieve high print quality. It has been selected as one of the twenty best newspapers in the world by a research group at the School of Journalism, Columbia University—one of six U.S. papers to make the list.

Although some designers are moving away from the modular approach that was so popular in the 1970s and 1980s, it is still an approach of choice for many, and should be studied. In the modular approach a newspaper page consists of building blocks of pleasing rectangles. Type should be squared off so that each column of type in a rectangle ends at the same depth. The square off at the bottom of columns should be in a straight line to create harmonious rectangles. Type should not be allowed to zigzag across the pages. The rectangles, both vertical and horizontal, should be arranged to create a pleasing combination and an appealing page.

Pages need breathing room. White space used effectively can brighten a page—it is not wasted space but a necessary design element. It can help the reader by isolating and emphasizing elements and by indicating where one item ends and another begins. A crowded, jammed-together page should be avoided.

Judicious editing of reading matter can provide increased white space and increased readability. White space can also be added by adequate separation between columns, indenting heads, using a pica of white consistently between stories, and/or setting captions in a width narrower than the art they identify.

Any element on a page that does not help the reader can be called an ornament. Any type of decoration is an ornament. Ornaments should only be added to layouts if they perform a function, such as establishing identity for a publication or specific departments.

The four corners of a newspaper page have been called the hot spots. They are the contact and turning points as the eye scans the page. A strong element in each hot spot will help give a page movement and balance.

In making design decisions, the basic principles of design plus the precepts of legibility, readability, and suitability must be applied. In addition, the design should be flexible so changes can be made easily to avoid a rigid, day-after-day sameness.

It should be remembered that nothing lasts forever, and the design should be reevaluated from time to time. Changes should be made as conditions warrant, but they should only be made after careful evaluation and study.

Finally, it is important to communicate what is happening every step of the way with all staff members and solicit feedback. The final decision, however, should be made only by the person responsible for the design.

Once the design changes have been agreed on and everything is in order, it is time to see how these changes will look in a finished page. This can be done by creating a prototype. A prototype is a "dummy" page made on the computer or by pasteup. Headline types are used, illustrations are put in place, and simulated body matter is arranged on the page.

It is a good idea to photocopy the page. This copy will give a more "printed" look to the prototype and will help it appear realistic.

Prototypes are models of actual pages. During the design or redesign process many prototypes may have to be made before the final design is adopted.

New Nameplate
The paper's new "signature" is both traditional and modern. Derived from a hand-altered Garamond face, the nameplate sits flush left at the top of the front page.

News Summary
Key news stories are listed ine same place each day, providing readers with an at-a-glance overview of what is inside.

More Graphics
Although the paper was already using information-al graphics (all produced by hand), it is now running many more, produced on the Macintosh.

Front Page Index
This regular feature was moved from page two for easier access.

Refer Boxes
Important features inside of each day's paper are promoted at the top of the page, next to the name-plate.

New Head Face
The paper's head-line typeface, Rotation, an Adobe typefont, improves readab-nility and provides space for more characters per line.

Better Color
The Daily Herald's Koenig & Bauer offset presses provide better color reproduc-tion, allowing the paper the option of using more color throughout each issue.

More Spot Color
The decision to use more spot color pulls ele-ments of stories together.

Fig. 17-6 ■ The major design decisions that were made in a complete overhaul of the *Daily Herald,* Arlington, Heights, Illinois, are shown in this new front page for the newspaper. (Courtesy *Daily Herald*)

THE BODY TYPE

The tendency in newspaper design is to start with the front page and spend most of the time and effort with this small part of the whole package. While the importance of an attractive "display window" cannot be overlooked, the rest of the publication deserves equally serious planning.

Since the basic objective is to get the newspaper read, the first step in creating a design should be an examination of what is read most—the body type. Time spent on good design should not be wasted because the reader gives up on a story set in type that inhibits pleasant reading.

The criteria for selecting a proper body type are legibility and readability. Legibility is the visual perception of type, words, and sentences. Readability is the comprehension and understanding of the communication.

Body type should be legible, of course. The variables that make one typeface more legible than another include the serifs, the type size, and the letter design. The size of the typeface on the body, the leading, the set width, and column widths are also factors.

Studies have shown that serif type is preferred for newspaper body type. Serif types have more reader appeal, but this may be changing. Numerals are more legible when set in Sans Serif. Italics, obliques, and boldface types should not be used for body type in newspapers. Reverse type slows reading by almost 15 percent.

Typeset words are perceived not by letter but by shape, and this shape outline is lost when words are set in all caps. Type set in all caps slows reading speed, reduces legibility, and takes up to 30 percent more space.

Quite often the most frequent comment received when a new design is in place concerns the type used for reading matter. When the *Charleston Gazette* was redesigned the body type was increased from 9 to 9.5 points. Don Marsh, the editor of this West Virginia newspaper, reported in *Editor & Publisher,* "Although we've given up about 5 to 7 percent of our news space by using larger type, with our readers the change was the most popular aspect of our redesign."[5]

When the *St. Joseph* (Missouri) *Gazette* was redesigned, one change the readers seemed to like most was an extra ½ point of leading between the lines. The *Gazette* sets 9-point type on a 9.5-point base.

Body type should be examined for its legibility and its reproduction qualities. It should have a clean and open cut. When type is printed at high

Fig. 17-7 ■ Century, a popular reading matter typeface, as it was cast in foundry type (top) and as it was redesigned (bottom) by Tony Stan for International Typeface Corporation. The ITC version was designed for modern printing methods and digital typesetting. Note the more subtle letterfitting, larger *x* height, and shortened ascenders. The opening in the *c* has been enlarged, and some serifs have been selectively eliminated.

Fig. 17-8 ■ Which letter form would you select for the reading matter in your publication? The variations in these representative types seem slight when viewed individually but when compared they are striking. (The wording doesn't make sense since meaningful words might interfere with study of the letter forms.)

VENETIAN (Bembo)	Lorem ipsum dolor sit amet, consectetuer adipiscing elit, sed diam nonummy nibh euismod tincidunt ut laoreet dolore magna aliquam erat volutpat. Ut wisi enim ad minim veniam, quis nostrud exerci tation ullamcorper suscipit lobortis nisl ut aliquip ex ea commodo consequat. Duis autem vel eum iriure dolor in hendrerit in vulputate velit esse molestie consequat, vel illum dolore eu feugiat
OLD STYLE (Goudy)	Lorem ipsum dolor sit amet, consectetuer adipiscing elit, sed diam nonummy nibh euismod tincidunt ut laoreet dolore magna aliquam erat volutpat. Ut wisi enim ad minim veniam, quis nostrud exerci tation ullamcorper suscipit lobortis nisl ut aliquip ex ea commodo consequat. Duis autem vel eum iriure dolor in hendrerit in vulputate velit esse molestie consequat, vel illum
TRANSITIONAL (New Baskerville)	Lorem ipsum dolor sit amet, consectetuer adipiscing elit, sed diam nonummy nibh euismod tincidunt ut laoreet dolore magna aliquam erat volutpat. Ut wisi enim ad minim veniam, quis nostrud exerci tation ullamcorper suscipit lobortis nisl ut aliquip ex ea commodo consequat. Duis autem vel eum iriure dolor in hendrerit in vulputate velit
MODERN **(Bodoni)**	**Lorem ipsum dolor sit amet, consectetuer adipiscing elit, sed diam nonummy nibh euismod tincidunt ut laoreet dolore magna aliquam erat volutpat. Ut wisi enim ad minim veniam, quis nostrud exerci tation ullamcorper suscipit lobortis nisl ut aliquip ex ea commodo consequat. Duis autem vel eum iriure dolor in hendrerit in vulputate velit esse molestie**
EGYPTIAN, or SLAB SERIF (Lubalin Graph)	Lorem ipsum dolor sit amet, consectetuer adipiscing elit, sed diam nonummy nibh euismod tincidunt ut laoreet dolore magna aliquam erat volutpat. Ut wisi enim ad minim veniam, quis nostrud exerci tation ullamcorper suscipit lobortis nisl ut aliquip ex ea commodo consequat. Duis autem vel eum iriure
SANS SERIF (Franklin Gothic)	Lorem ipsum dolor sit amet, consectetuer adipiscing elit, sed diam nonummy nibh euismod tincidunt ut laoreet dolore magna aliquam erat volutpat. Ut wisi enim ad minim veniam, quis nostrud exerci tation ullamcorper suscipit lobortis nisl ut aliquip ex ea commodo consequat. Duis autem vel eum iriure dolor in hendrerit in vulputate velit esse molestie

speeds with thin ink on absorbent newsprint, the letters tend to spread and distort. The space between the ends of the strokes of the letter spread and distort. The space between the ends of the strokes of the letter *c*, for instance, should have an opening big enough so it won't appear to be an *o* when printed at a high speed.

The letter should be strong, or bold, enough to avoid a gray look. It should have sufficient contrast between thick and thin strokes to break monotony, but the thin strokes should not be so thin they tend to fade away.

Fig. 17-9 ■ Skillful use of layout and design techniques were used to create this impressive spread. A huge amount of complex material became attention-grabbing, interest-holding, and just plain understandable. This is visual communication at its best. (Reprinted with permission of Barton Memorial Hospital, © Coffee Communications, Inc.)

The typeface chosen for setting the great majority of words in a newspaper should have good proportions. The relationship of height to width should approximate the golden rectangle in proportion. The x-height should be ample enough to give full body but not so large that it interferes with the clear distinction of the ascenders and descenders of the letters. Time taken to select a body type that increases legibility will pay dividends in reader reaction.

THE NEWSPAPER "SHOW WINDOW"

First impressions are hard to change, and the first impression the reader will have of a newspaper is created by its front page and the design elements it contains. These elements include the nameplate (also called the *flag*) and any embellishments in the nameplate area, the headlines and cutlines, any standing heads such as those for the weather and index boxes, plus any other regular features on the page.

The *nameplate* is the newspaper's trademark. It should be legible, distinctive, attractive, and appropriate. As a general rule designers recommend that it should have harmony with the other types on the page. This usually means it should be of the same type family as the basic headlines or it should contrast well with them.

Fig. 17-10 ■ A stylebook and a design manual are important reference sources for a publication's staff. The precise specifications for handling a reverse kicker head are spelled out in this illustration from the typographic manual of the *Philadelphia Inquirer.*

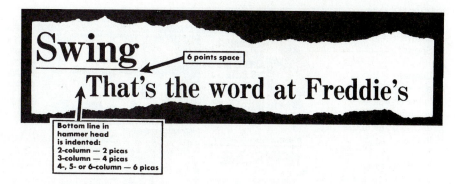

Many newspapers choose a Black Letter type for the nameplate because of the image created of a time-honored, respected institution. Black Letter contrasts well with most types chosen for headlines.

One of the first steps in planning a newspaper is to adopt a *stylebook* that incorporates correct usage regarding grammar, spelling, capitalization, and so on for handling various types of information. It is the newspaper's operating handbook. It is a good idea to create a *typography manual* as well.

The typography manual should include a *head schedule.* This is a listing, with examples, of all the sizes and styles of types to be used in headlines and their unit counts as well as their arrangements. The head schedule becomes a handy reference source and helps create a consistent, well-organized appearance.

Some newspapers have very elaborate typography manuals that are virtual textbooks of design. For the small newspaper, a simple manual can be created that includes samples of the sizes and styles of types and borders available as well as samples of cutline treatments and other typographic features of the publication. Duplicate copies can be made on a copying machine for each member of the staff.

The headline has several functions to perform. It can attract the reader, persuade the reader to consider a story, and help make the page attractive. It can help create identity and personality. The typeface and arrangement should help the headline accomplish its tasks.

Fig. 17-11 ■ (Left) Many newspapers are adopting a headline form that includes a short paragraph as a subhead rather than the traditional deck. When the *Los Angeles Times* was redesigned in late 1989 it devised a head similar to this one from the *Oregonian.* In its promotion of the redesign the *Times* said the form would give busy readers a quick summary of the stories. (Right) Note that the top deck of this head is in downstyle and the "nut graf" has a solid square instead of an open square as in the head at left. (Courtesy the *Oregonian*)

2 officials 'a-peel' tax distribution

☐ Road improvements are in danger, say Mayor Bud Clark and Portland Commissioner Earl Blumenauer

By GORDON OLIVER
of The Oregonian staff

Council approves housing project despite protests

■ Construction will start in May even though 300 area residents express disapproval. A greenbelt is included in revised plans.

By ANN RUDRUD
NEWS STAFF WRITER

Left ear
always just for Sports.

Leader
a 3- or 4-line brief in the Newsline column; "leaders" always come above the . . .

Newsline mug
(not shown) a photo of someone in the news.

Centerpiece
sometimes a big promo, but most often illustrates the cover story.

Silly little hole
a sometimes-awkward space forced by the page format.

Notch
usually a subhead or a liftout quote; sometimes the notch is a photo.

Ribbon
in color across top —and often the bottom—of all color pages, this ribbon of color helps to set the color balance on the presses.

USA Snapshots
a look at statistics, illustrated with a graphic, always in lower left corner.

Band-aid
usually a label; sometime a reefer

Right ear
always reefers for Life and sometimes also for Money

Strip
usually a story; sometimes it is a graphic.

Billboard
used to promote special packages inside.

Shoulder
or the off-lead story

Hot corner
always some form of color. On 1A, it's usually a "bright" or promo box.

Fig. 17-12 ■ The Impact of *USA TODAY* on newspaper design extends to the lexicon of the trade. Here are some design terms coined at the newspaper. (Courtesy *Design,* the Journal of the Society of Newspaper Design)

Usually the most attractive newspapers stick to one type family for best appearance and effective design in headlines. Another face that harmonizes with the basic family is sometimes chosen for contrast. Headline type is selected for legibility, personality, durability, range of services available in the family, and its unit count.

The guidelines below are helpful when placing elements on the front-page grid:

1. Study other newspapers, especially those that have been recognized for their outstanding design (see "Creative Communication" box in

Poles Say Holdouts Quit Mine

Associated Press

Fig. 17-13 ■ Typical flush left head with all words capitalized. Note treatment of source line with rules above and below. (Courtesy *Denver Post*)

this chapter). Spend some time on visualization. Try to form an idea of how the page should look when completed.

2. Make some thumbnail sketches of possible arrangements. Then select the sketch that most closely resembles the page arrangement you think is best.

3. Decide where the nameplate will be placed. Will it be a permanent fixture at the top of the page? Or will a "skyline" story, headline, or promotion device be placed above it? Will a *floating page* (a smaller version of the nameplate) be used? Often newspaper designers create several sizes of a nameplate in several column widths. These can be moved around the page. But if the flag floats, care should be taken not to lose it on the page and thus lose the newspaper's identity.

4. Decide on strong elements for each hot spot on the page. Usually the major elements are placed in the upper-left and upper-right quadrants. Tradition dictated that the lead story of the day be placed in the upper-right corner, but this is no longer necessary.

Fig. 17-14 ■ This downstyle head uses a hairline and 4-point rule with all-cap credit line. (Courtesy *Orlando Sentinel*)

181 feared dead in Spain jet crash

UNITED PRESS INTERNATIONAL

Fig. 17-15 ■ Head with kicker. Kickers are usually underlined. (Courtesy *Las Cruces Sun-News*)

Gas 'abuse' found

$100 million refund due

Fig. 17-16 ■ Reverse kicker. The kicker is larger than the following line in the head. (Courtesy *Philadelphia Inquirer*)

Swing
That's the word at Freddies's

Fig. 17-17 ■ Many newspapers are using a lighter face version of the type used in the top deck for a contrasting line. (Courtesy *Chicago Tribune*)

Pilots ignored warning, tape shows
26 passengers died on blazing jetliner June 2

Fig. 17-18 ■ A consistent style for a jump head is a part of the headline schedule for newspapers. (Courtesy *Christian Science Monitor*)

LANDMARK from preceding page

Fig. 17-19 ■ Some examples of typical newspaper captions. Caption (or cutline) styles for newspapers usually differ from those in other types of publications. A caption style should be designed and used throughout the newspaper. It should become a part of the newspaper's stylebook.

THIS IS ONE STYLE of caption that can be used in newspaper design. The first few words are set in caps and boldface.

THERE ARE MANY forms for captions. The point is, the designer should select one and stick with it except, perhaps, in layouts for special featuers or suppplements and so on.

This Is A Catchline

A catchline is a line similar to a headline that is placed between a photograph or other art and the caption. It is one style for handling the caption used in newspaper work.

This Is A Sideline   A sideline might be called a "mini-head" that is set on the side of the body of the caption. It is a style of caption that can be used in newspaper design.

Some newspaper designers will choose a typeface for the caption that is different from the style for the body type. This can make a pleasing contrast in the layout of the page.

---

5.   Consider placing strong elements in the two lower quadrants of the page as well as in the top ones. This will cover the hot spots and help to create a well-balanced page.

6.   Check to see if headlines fight each other, if heads "tombstone," or "butt." Tombstones are heads of identical form placed side by side. If they seem to confuse the reader they should be changed. If heads are side by side they should be distinctly different, in most cases.

7.   Check each design element on the page to see that it is performing a function. If not, consider eliminating it.

8.   Have the page exhibit the attributes of basic design principles—balance, harmony, proportion, unity, rhythm, and contrast.

THE INSIDE PAGES

➤ Since the change to optimum format, the design of inside pages has been in a state of turmoil. When the broadsheet (the full-size newspaper page) was changed from eight to six columns and the tabloid from five to four, the placement of advertisements changed from several basic patterns to confusion and often chaos. It was possible to find reading matter set in as many as four or five different widths on one page. The reader was faced with a hodgepodge that defied comfortable reading and the basic rules of legibility.

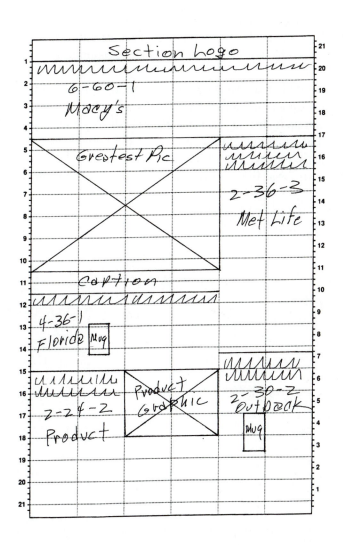

Fig. 17-20 ■ A rough dummy of the *Tampa Tribune* business page. Newspaper page dummies are usually made one-half scale on 8½ by 11 sheets. You can make dummy sheets quite easily and duplicate them. Each story has an identifying slug (a word or two) and a code to indicate headline size. The code 2-36-3 for the Met Life story means a headline two columns wide in 36-point type and three lines deep. The code 6-60-1 for the Macy's story means a one-line headline six columns wide in 60-point type.

Fig. 17-21 ■ Good design should extend from the front page to every page in the newspaper. This carefully designed business page is from the *Tampa Tribune*. We will use it to illustrate the first step in page design. Whether you use a computer or traditional methods, it will pay dividends to start by creating a thumbnail. (Courtesy *Tampa Tribune*)

The situation has improved, however, as most newspapers have adopted the *Standard Advertising Unit.* The SAU was devised by the American Newspaper Publishers Association in an attempt to bring standardization and order out of the chaos caused by the use of various column widths.

The SAU system starts with a 2 1/16-inch column with ⅛ inch between columns. Note the substitution of inches for points, picas, and agate lines. The full-page width contains six columns for advertisements. The ANPA suggests that only inches and fractions of inches be used to measure advertisements. It also recommends fifty-seven modular sizes for national advertisements but leaves size decisions for local advertisements up to the individual newspapers.

The new system has helped designers produce more attractive inside pages, and helped newspapers sell advertisements as well.

There are several standard patterns for placing advertisements on a page. A designer should adopt one of them and use it throughout the publication—except, perhaps, for special sections. But even there, if the section includes more than one page the pattern should be the same for all the pages.

The most common basic patterns include:

Fig. 17-22 ■ Some of the more popular inside page arrangements for placement of advertisements. The key to attractive inside pages is to adopt a consistent pattern and keep the top of the page, especially upper left-hand corner, open as much as possible for editorial display.

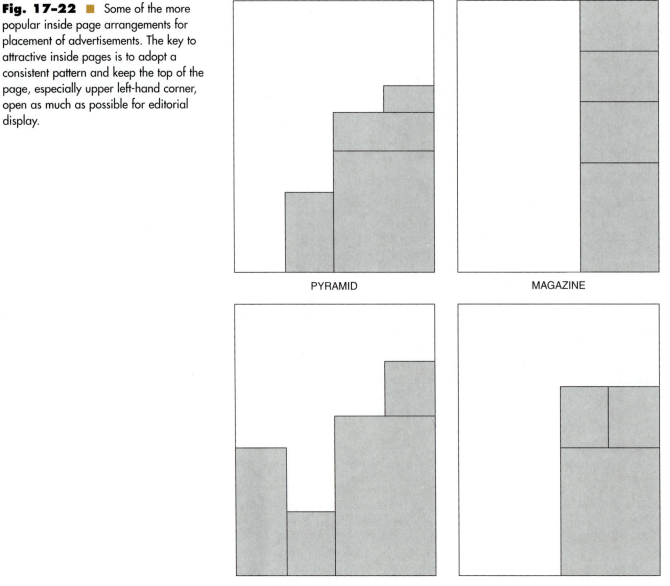

PYRAMID

MAGAZINE

WELL

MODULAR

■ *Pyramid:* Here the advertisements are built like varying sizes of building blocks from the base of the largest ad in the lower right-hand corner of the page. This leaves the hot spot or area of initial eye contact—the upper-left corner—open for editorial matter. This is actually a half-pyramid, and it is often called that.

■ *Magazine:* Here some columns are filled with advertisements and others are completely open for editorial display. This arrangement works well with modular layout and pagination.

■ *Well or double pyramid:* Here advertisements are placed on the inside and outside columns plus across the bottom of the page. This forms a sort of well that can be filled with editorial material.

Fig. 17-23 ■ The magazine approach to placement of advertisements was used here. Such an arrangement leaves full columns open for display of editorial matter. It also gives an orderly appearance to the page. (Courtesy *Carson Valley News*)

Fig. 17-24 ■ Often design efforts are concentrated on the front and section opener pages. This inside page illustrates effective design. The half-pyramid is built to the right. The largest advertisement serves as an anchor. A powerful illustration in the "hot spot" grabs the reader. The three multi-column heads do not compete, add weight to the editorial matter, and help balance the page. (Courtesy *The Bulletin*, Bend, OR)

■ *Modular:* Here advertisements are clustered to form rectangular modules on the page, another arrangement that works well with the pagination equipment coming on line in many newspapers.

Regardless of the pattern adopted, there are a few points to remember when planning inside pages for maximum effectiveness. The important top-

Fig. 17-25 ■ Too often we neglect the inside pages when considering newspaper design. The design of an effective total newspaper package should include every page. Dramatic design, such as in this section page from the *Anchorage Daily News,* will help create reader involvement "from cover to cover." (Courtesy *Anchorage Daily News*)

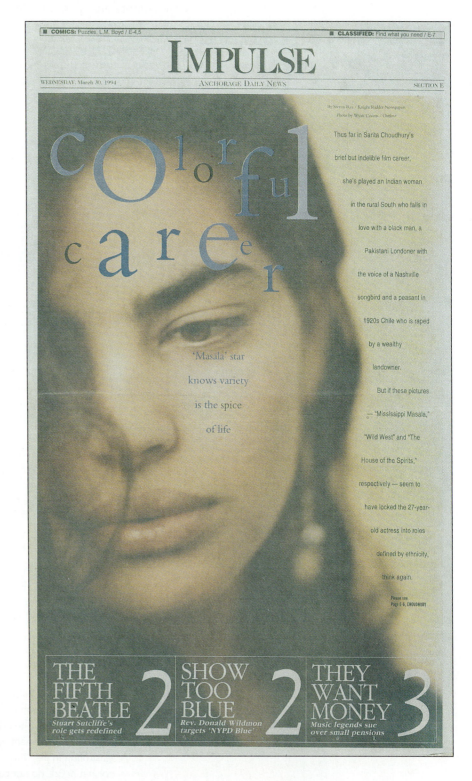

of-the-page areas should be kept open for the display of editorial material as much as possible. Advertisements should not be placed so high in the columns that little space is left for reading matter. There should be enough space above advertisements for a headline and arm of body type at least as deep as the headline. If the space left is smaller, the advertisements should be rearranged if at all possible.

There should be at least one "stopper" on each inside page. The attention-getter could be an illustration or a story with a strong headline. Some editors try to have an illustration on every inside page. When editorial art is placed on the page, however, it should not compete with advertising art. The two should not be placed side by side.

Care should especially be taken to harmonize editorial and advertising content. A story about an airline crash, for instance, should not be placed on the same page with an airline advertisement.

The best designed inside pages are pages that have no tombstones; no long, unbroken columns of body type; and no "naked" columns (tops of columns of body type without headlines, art, or rules).

Fig. 17-26 ◼ Many newspapers try to get a "stopper" on each inside page. This inside page of the award-winning *Washington Times* demonstrates several inside-page layout techniques. The page is effective despite the dominance of a strong advertisement. The art is a stopper and separates two top-of-the-page stories. A subhead with top and bottom rule separates long legs of grey type under the three-column head. A strong head below the top story in the lefthand column adds weight to the news section of the page. (Courtesy *Washington Times*)

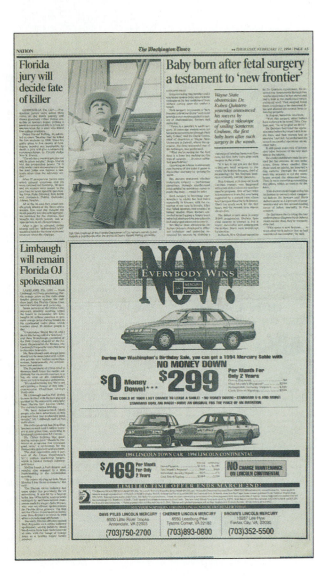

Fig. 17-27 ■ The front page of the new *Press Democrat,* Santa Rosa, California, Forum section. It was a new section added recently. Publisher Michael J. Parman notes that putting design and editorial punch in Forum has resulted in increased reader participation and less interest in "alternative" publications.

THE EDITORIAL AND SECTION PAGES

▶ The design of editorial and section pages should reflect the interests and content of that particular unit while preserving the flavor of the entire publication. Some ways this can be accomplished include using page logos that incorporate the publication's nameplate, using the same type family for headlines but in a different posture, and using the same headline form throughout the newspaper. For example, if downstyle, flush left is used in the main section, unity can be preserved if that form is used in all sections.

The Design of the Editorial Page

The editorial page should be distinctly different from the other pages. The readers should understand clearly that this is the page of opinion, the page where ideas clash. But while the page should be different, it should invite the reader by being lively and bright.

There is a trend toward eliminating the editorial page. However, those who believe taking positions is an important function of the media maintain that editorial pages should be improved, not eliminated. They point out that the key to developing a good editorial page is presenting well-written editorials that take strong stands on issues that are important to the readers.

The design of the editorial page can help make it a vital part of the publication. Some things that can be done to make it graphically different and interesting include:

- Eliminate column rules and use more white space between columns.
- Set body type in a larger size.
- Use larger size heads but in a slightly lighter weight than the main headlines.
- Design fewer columns to the page, with a wide measure, but keep within the readability range.
- Use graphics to add interest to the page. These could include cartoons, editorial pictures, charts, maps, or diagrams.

The editorial page can help a publication develop its distinctive personality, and it can be an attractive graphic feature that can increase reader interest.

The Design of Section Pages

Each section presents a specific challenge to the editor and designer. The design of each section should reflect its purpose and personality and be in harmony with the complete newspaper. Some sections that most frequently appear in newspapers are "Family Living," "Food," Sports," and "Business."

Features   The "Family Living" or "Life-Style" section is a recent development. It has taken the place of what was called the "Society" or "Women's" section. The scope and content of this section has been broadened and changed. Traditionally this section was given what was thought to be a "feminine" design treatment. Type styles were softened, and photo treatment was formal and subdued. The trend now is toward the use of magazine design techniques while maintaining the general design philosophy of the entire newspaper.

Fig. 17-28 ■ Ornamentation with a purpose. Section logos should give distinct identity to each section and help unify the entire newspaper package. The page one flag and section logos of the *News Sentinel*, Fort Wayne, Indiana, do a splendid job. Note the unity created by the selection of color. Note the rather subtle use of the rising sun for a morning newspaper. (Courtesy the *News Sentinel*)

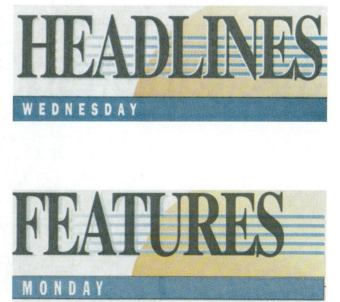

Fig. 17-29 ■ While many in the profession lament the apparent lack of interest in reading newspapers on the part of the younger set, the *St. Petersburg Times* has successfully appealed to this segment of the population with a lively section just for them. Note the use of color and creative design work. Ron Reason is the design editor of the *Times*. (Courtesy *St. Petersburg Times*)

Fig. 17-30 ■ This two-page spread from the Sunday edition of the *Toronto Sun* is a good example of dramatic design that helps the newspaper to create a total design package. Often too much time is spent on the front page and not enough for the rest of the newspaper. This spread was for the travel section. The *Sun* is in tabloid format. (Courtesy the *Sunday Sun*)

Food pages often were incorporated with the women's section in the past. Now many men are cooking enthusiasts, and feminine typographic treatment is no longer used. The designer should remember that these are working pages, that recipes and instructions should be presented in a clear and accurate style. It is also helpful if the arrangement makes the material easy to clip and file.

Sports   Sports pages are worlds unto themselves, and the sports staffs have operated as virtually separate entities on many newspapers. They have often had their own head schedules set in type of their own choosing regardless of whether it harmonized with the rest of the newspaper. In recent years a change has taken place, and the appeal of the sports page has been expanded as more sports, such as soccer, have become popular, more attention has been paid to women's sports, and more people have participated in recreational sports.

A number of newspapers produce a separate section on a regular basis aimed at participation sports such as bicycle riding, hiking, and fishing.

The typography of the sports pages should reflect the vibrant action-packed activities they record. At the same time, they should be in harmony with the rest of the newspaper. A bolder posture of the same type as used in the entire newspaper might give more life to the sports pages. If the newspaper head schedule is upper- and lowercase or it is downstyle, the sports page heads should use the same style. This helps present a unified package for the whole newspaper.

Sports news includes much statistical matter, box scores, standings, and summaries. The trend is to set this material in agate (5½ point) type and group it for all sports in a separate page or part of a page. This practice helps the orderly organization of sports information and enables the editor to set the type in the optimum line width for agate. The typographic appeal of the statistical matter can be improved with distinctive headings for each topic. Small sketches to identify each sport can also be incorporated with the headings.

Business   There must be a reason why the *Wall Street Journal* has the largest daily circulation in the United States. It has been the leader for a number of years, and it keeps getting stronger, nearing 2 million copies a day. Business news is big business. But it is more than business news that has made the *Wall Street Journal* a success. It features excellent writing, careful, accurate editing, and a broadening of its coverage.

Newspapers everywhere are recognizing the reader appeal of the business section. There was a time when business news was presented in staid, conservative—even dull—writing and layouts. As the interest in business news has grown, business pages have become more lively. Publishers now recognize that the techniques of effective visual communication should apply equally to the business pages as to the other sections of the newspaper.

Fig. 17-31 ■ Here is the circulation leader in the United States. This newspaper illustrates important points beyond the fact that business news is big business. While design can help communicate and make the package more attractive, it is no substitute for content the target audience wants and needs. Many visual communication students study the Wall Street Journal for its carefully written stories, and its consistency in makeup, accuracy and completeness. (Reprinted by permission of the *Wall Street Journal*, © Dow Jones & Company, Inc. All Rights Reserved Worldwide)

Fig. 17-32 ■ Good design isn't restricted to large metropolitan newspapers. In our over-communicated society the challenge is to make your newspaper attract its target audience and then get the audience to read it. The *Idaho Farm Bureau News* does an excellent job of it. Note the use of art and color plus the arrangement of the index to invite the reader inside. The "hot" red catches the eye and illuminates inside page numbers. (Courtesy *Idaho Farm Bureau News*, Rich Johnson, editor and publisher)

➤ **EFFECTIVE DESIGN CHECKLIST**

■ Make sure that all essential elements are included in folio lines and masthead.

■ Avoid setting type in unusually narrow measures. Studies show that 9.5 and 10 pica widths simply are not read.

■ Keep basic headline types within the same family. If another family is used, it should be used sparingly and for contrast.

■ Avoid jumping stories from one page to another. If stories are jumped from page 1, try to continue them all on a convenient page, such as the back page of the front section or page 2. Studies indicate that 80 percent of the readership is lost on most jumped stories.

■ Arrange advertisements so there is effective editorial display. Square off columns of advertising, and if the well or pyramid style is used, keep ads as low on the page as possible.

■ Avoid pictures (usually mug shots, called "pork chops") that are less than one column wide. Try to use mug shots that show what a person is like, rather than what that person looks like.

■ Don't run headlines too wide for the type size. A good rule is to keep headlines to thirty-two characters or less regardless of type size.

■ Try to have a "stopper"—art or a dominant head—on each page. Never separate a picture from the story it accompanies.

■ Eliminate barriers. But if long copy is broken with art or large subhead arrangements, make sure the reader can tell where the story continues.

■ After a page is designed, try to judge it from the reader's point of view. Is it easy to follow, interesting, attractive?

➤ **GRAPHICS IN ACTION**

1. A major project in newspaper design could be redesigning your hometown newspaper. Examine current copies of the newspaper and then outline a complete plan for redesign. Make prototype pages by cutting heads, art, and body copy from newspapers that use the styles you would like to adopt. Write justifications for the changes you make.

2. If newspapers did not exist and you decided that a daily printed medium of news and advertisements was needed, how would you design it? What form would it take? What would be its page size? How would the contents be presented? Explain your answers.

3. Obtain a copy of a newspaper. Assume you have inherited the ownership of this paper. Since you are interested in graphics, you take a long, hard look at the paper. How would you change the front page? Don't forget that this is a profitable business and you do not want to take a chance on the new design adversely affecting reader acceptance and thus circulation and advertising revenue.

4. Redesign an inside page of a newspaper. Examine the pattern of advertisement placement. If the pyramid or well is used, redesign to magazine or modular. Redesign the editorial content to make its display more effective.

5. Examine the prototype pages that professional designers have constructed on pages 000 and 000 of this book. Devise a prototype of a newspaper front page as you envision it for the 21st century. Consider its role in the age of the information superhighway.

NOTES

[1]*Design,* the Journal of the Society of Newspaper Design, no. 23, p. 4.
[2]Ibid.
[3]*Design,* the Journal of the Society of Newspaper Design, no. 19, p. 7.
[4]Interview with the author, January 18, 1994.
[5]Don March, *Editor & Publisher,* October 16, 1980, p. 15.

NEWSLETTERS

© Churchill & Klehr

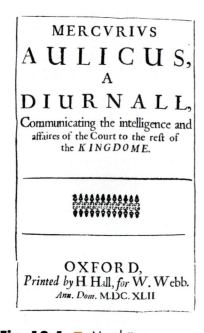

Fig. 18-1 ■ Newsletters were popular before newspapers came into existence. Many "newsletters" or news pamphlets were sold in Europe in the 1500s and 1600s.

18 Laser beams, word processors, editing terminals, cable television, videotext—these are all electronic miracles, and they are causing revolutionary changes in our communications systems. But no matter what the new technology may bring during the coming decades, one ancient form of communication is sure to survive—and prosper. The newsletter seems certain to keep its place in the communications mix.

Communicators agree that the success of an information program often rests on producing a medium for the information on a regular basis and supporting it with auxiliary tools to reinforce and repeat the message. For many organizations and businesses, the ideal tool for accomplishing this basic, regular communication is a *newsletter.*

The newsletter is not a new communications tool. It has been in existence for a long time. Researchers report that the Han dynasty in China published a daily newsletter in 200 B.C. The forerunners of the modern newspapers were leaflets and pamphlets—newsletters—which described an event or happenings from some other place. These were called diurnals, curantos, and mercuries, and they were printed and then sold in the streets. The first successful newspaper in America was called the *Boston News-Letter.*

The modern American commercial newsletter can be traced back to 1923 when Willard Kiplinger brought out the first issue of the *Kiplinger Washington Letter.* Today the newsletter is one of the fastest growing segments of the printing industry in the country. There are more than 100,000 newsletters being produced and distributed on a regular basis. They range from the small mimeographed parish or club sheet to elaborately designed and printed publications that are more closely related to magapapers or in-house magazines.

It is estimated that 3,000 to 5,000 of the 100,000 published newsletters are sent to paid subscribers who pay from one dollar to several thousand dollars a year to receive them. The newsletter with the largest circulation is the *Kiplinger Letter.* It has more than 600,000 paid subscribers.

The newsletter format is so popular and has such high reader interest that many magazines use its format for special-interest and updated information pages. Business and organizational publications have found that a page of upbeat information in newsletter style has high readership. We have included examples of such pages in this chapter.

Why are newsletters to popular?

They are liked by communicators and readers. Communicators find the newsletter an ideal communications link with various audiences. A special audience can be targeted easily and reached on a continuing, regular basis. Since the newsletter is brief and to the point, it can be aligned easily with the interests of the target audience. Identification with the interests of an audience is one of the criteria for effective communication.

Messages in a newsletter can be tailor-made for the situation, the time, the location, and the audience. The newsletter can have a personality, and it can come closer to one-on-one personal communication than most other forms of mass communication. Its chatty style can resemble a personal letter.

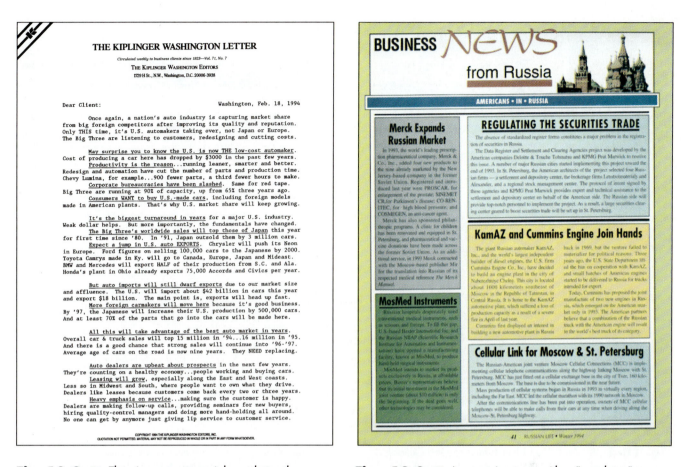

Fig. 18-2 ■ The pioneer commercial newsletter, the *Kiplinger Washington Letter,* was founded in 1923. It set the design style that has been known as the "classic" newsletter format. The fourth page of the classic newsletter concludes with an ending similar to a personal letter. (Reproduced by special permission of the Kiplinger Washington Editors, Inc.)

Fig. 18-3 ■ A magazine page with a "newsletter" approach. Note the moduclar design. Unity is achieved with the outside margin frame in color and the use of a sans serif head type plus all heads cetered. Contrast and variety are achieved with the use of color and the design of the nameplate (Courtesy RIA Novosti/ *Russian Life*)

In addition, the newsletter can accomplish its goals at a low cost because it can be produced very economically. It would be difficult to find a more cost-efficient method of effective printed communication.

Audiences like newsletters because they contain specialized information that cannot be found elsewhere. The newsletter usually condenses information from many sources. Often newsletter readers do not have access to all these sources or the time to peruse them. People like to receive information in brief, to-the-point writing.

A PUBLIC RELATIONS TOOL

The newsletter can be an effective public relations tool. It can be used to target specific publics with specific interests in an organization. Minnegasco is a public utility headquartered in Minneapolis which serves customers in Minnesota. It has won a number of awards for its excellent public relations programs. It publishes separate newsletters for different publics.

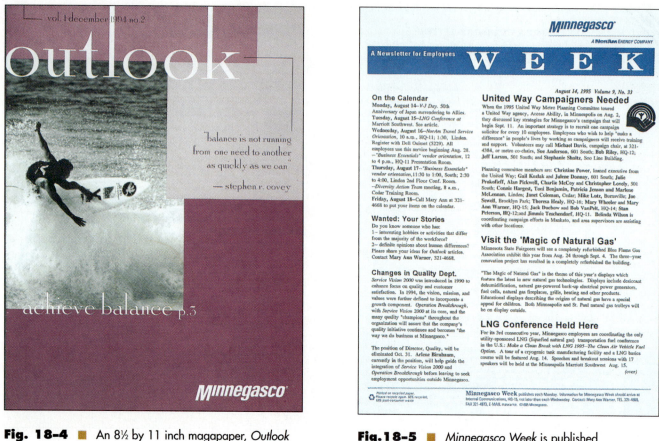

Fig. 18-4 ■ An 8½ by 11 inch magapaper, *Outlook* goes out to employees and retirees every other month.

Fig. 18-5 ■ *Minnegasco Week* is published electronically every Monday. It is circulated to all employees at their workstations via e-mail.

Outlook is an 8½ by 11 inch, 16-page bi-monthly newspaper that goes to employees and retirees. *Minnegasco Week* is a weekly newsletter that is circulated to all employees at their work locations. *In-Touch*, in a 6½ by 7 inch format, is included with bills that are sent to customers. *Link* goes out to all commercial and industrial customers.

Employee feedback obtained at face-to-face roundtable sessions was used to reshape Minnegasco's employee communications efforts. Employees discussed what worked and what didn't work for them regarding employee publications, videos, and face-to-face communications efforts. Based on this feedback, Minnegasco discontinued its monthly newsletter and created a new bimonthly magazine called *Outlook*.

The new publication features various viewpoints and perspectives on issues and events, instead of reporting "news." *Outlook* provides information about the outside world (Looking About) and about Minnegasco departments (Looking Within). It recognizes employee achievements (Looking at You) and offers workplace tips (Looking Out for You).

Minnegasco Week is the main source of company news items. It is published both in electronic and paper formats. The electronic version

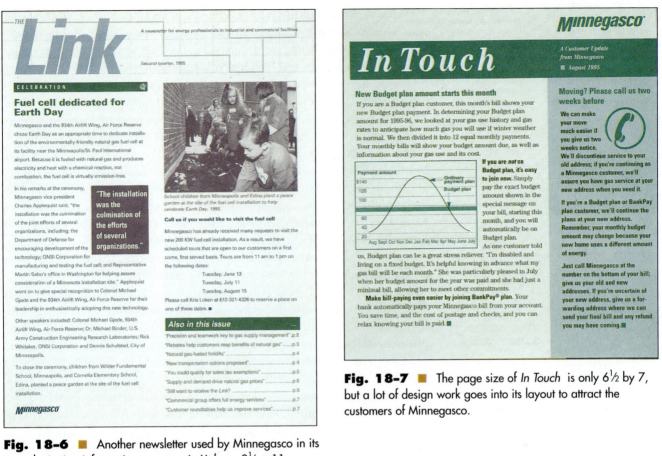

Fig. 18-6 ■ Another newsletter used by Minnegasco in its award-winning information program is *Link*, an 8½ ×11 newsletter that is distributed to commercial and industrial customers.

Fig. 18-7 ■ The page size of *In Touch* is only 6½ by 7, but a lot of design work goes into its layout to attract the customers of Minnegasco.

is sent to all employees every Monday via e-mail. Paper versions are sent only to those who don't have e-mail or upon request.[1]

DESIGNING THE NEWSLETTER

➤ The newsletter is a rather uncomplicated printed communication. It doesn't seem to offer much challenge to the editor or designer. But therein lies the problem. It is such a basic form of printed communication that it can be put together too easily. As a result, too many lose effectiveness because they look inept and amateurish. But they don't have to. Application of basic typographic and design principles can change an unattractive, ineffective newsletter into one that is an asset to its publishers.

As always, before the designer or editor begins to make decisions concerning the format and graphics of a newsletter, it is necessary to consider its purpose. A thorough understanding of the reasons the newsletter is being produced will help make its appearance appropriate to the subject matter and the audience.

A description of the planned contents and a definition of the audience should be written as a basic policy guide for editing and designing. Potential readers should be described according to such characteristics as their professions, age category, education, sex, beliefs, attitudes, interests, hobbies, and family situation, or whatever else is relevant.

Out of this preliminary research should come some ideas of how to develop the newsletter's personality. Each newsletter should have its own personality, look, and style. This helps it establish its niche in the communications spectrum. The goal should be to design a newsletter that will be welcomed as a letter from a friend each time it appears.

One way to spark ideas about a newsletter's contents and appearance might be to have a brainstorming session in which everyone concerned in the newsletter's production writes down single words that form the basis for a list of goals. Such words as attractive, important, reliable, timely, impressive, lively, and so on can trigger discussions about the goals, format, and style of the newsletter.

Consistency of style is important. A consistent style means each issue will look basically the same as all the others. Since the design elements of a newsletter are rather limited compared with many other printed communications, we may worry about producing a monotonous product. The page that we spend one or several hours on will only be seen for a few minutes by the reader. Still, many newsletters have been produced in the same basic design for years with great success.

This does not mean that the simple newsletter format cannot have sparkle and variety. Although a basic, consistent style is important in newsletter design, we should keep in mind that even the smallest change will become immediately apparent to the reader. A different size head type or a boxed item will stand out in a newsletter when it might be virtually unnoticed in a more complicated layout.

If an item is boxed or a few words are underlined or set in italic type, the design change will be so apparent to the reader that it will grab attention and send the signal that something of unusual importance is being presented. Changes in design elements should thus be made very carefully. If change is made continually, nothing will stand out and the newsletter will become a confusing design hodgepodge.

Remember, the design of the newsletter sends out signals to the reader. The design tells the audience the attitude of the publication, its approach to the subject matter, and which items are especially important. A feature that is always boxed, for instance, or set in the same typeface every issue tells the reader something about the contents of the feature. Readers will get in the habit of seeking this element for certain information.

The First Step: Selecting a Size

The first step in designing a newsletter is to settle on a size. Just as certain sizes have developed into the standard for newspapers and magazines, so has the 8½ by 11 page become the standard for newsletters. There are a number of reasons for this. The 8½ by 11 page is the same size as the standard business letter. This size is easy to file or to punch

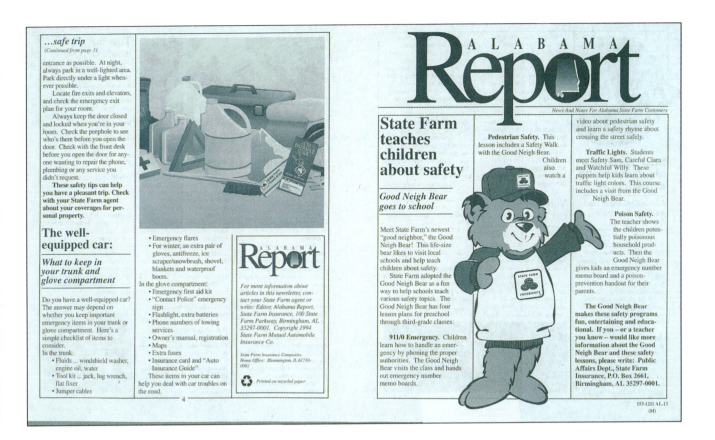

Fig. 18-8 ■ Quite often an 8½ by 14 sheet can be accommodated by office equipment; it makes a practical size for a newsletter. The State Farm Insurance Companies produce a number of newsletters in this format, with each tailored to a particular state. This is the *Alabama Report*. Note the number of design decisions and techniques illustrated here. Note the state map in the *o* of *Report* in the logo. The masthead is in the lower right on page 4. (Reprinted with permission of State Farm Insurance Company, One State Farm Plaza, Bloomington, IL 61710.)

and put into a binder. It folds easily to fit a number 10 (business size) envelope.

In addition, a four-page 8½ by 11 newsletter can be printed on an 11 by 17 sheet, two pages at a time, in most "quick print" or in-house printing facilities. The 11 by 17 (or 17 by 22) sheet is stocked by most shops and so is readily available. It is the standard sheet out of which business letterheads are cut.

Sometimes the method of printing or the equipment available will determine, or at least affect, the page size. If office or in-house duplicating equipment is used, the page size might be limited to a legal-size sheet that is 8½ by 14 inches. The legal-size sheet can be folded in half to create a four-page 7 by 8½-inch newsletter. A small organization or business might find this a workable size. It could also help the newsletter stand out from the more standard-size communications.

A newsletter produced by office equipment such as copying machines or ink-jet or laser printers could be an 8½ by 11 sheet folded in half. This would make four 5½ by 8½ pages.

Another possibility would be to fold an 8½ by 11 sheet to make six 3⅔ by 8½ pages. An accordion or gate fold could be used. If such a format is selected, many of the design techniques used in producing brochures could be employed as were discussed in Chapter 11.

Probably the best solution if printing capabilities are limited to 8½ by 11 or 8½ by 14 is to stick to one 8½ by 11 sheet printed on both sides. If more than one sheet is used, a method of binding the sheets together

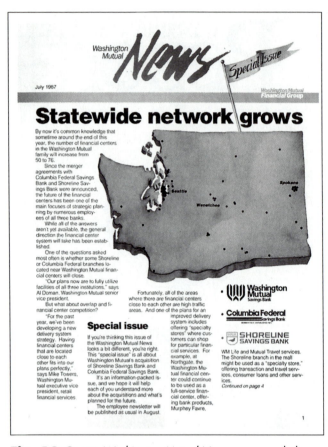

Fig. 18-9 ■ *Washington Mutual News* was awarded a four-star rating by evaluators for *Newsletter Design,* a publication of the Newsletter Clearinghouse. Shown here in an 8½ × 11 format, it was changed to a tabloid after extensive research.

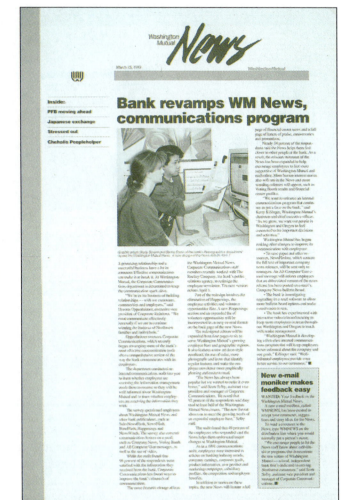

Fig. 18-10 ■ This is the *Washington Mutual News* as it appeared after its redesign to tabloid format. It continued in this format for six years and then, in 1993, another redesign was in order. "Our readers had tired of our old design," reports Terry J. Onustack, communications specialist, "and were looking for something different." Onustack and co-worker Roger Nyhus, with the help of an outside graphic artist, undertook the project.

will be needed. Sometimes sheets are held together with a single staple in the upper-left corner. This should be avoided as it is a flimsy device and the pages come apart easily. A solution is to leave a wider margin on the binding side of the page than on the outside and staple the newsletter in sidewire fashion, like a magazine.

Newsletters can be found in all shapes and sizes. Some, called *magaletters,* are actually more closely related to magazines or tabloid newspapers in format. Some, called *magapapers,* are a mix of newsletters, magazines, and tabloid newspapers. The designer of these hybrid publications can employ some of the design techniques of all three in planning such a publication.

Fig. 18-11 ■ "The *Washington Mutual News* remains one of the most popular communication tools for our firm since it became a tabloid," explains Terry Onustack. This is the new *Washington Mutual News.* It is published semimonthly. Color was added and the publication was expanded from four to six pages. All the writing for the *News* is done in Word for Windows, then transferred on disk to the in-house graphics department. Pages are laid out on Macintosh computers using Quark Express. Then, it is printed at a commercial plant. Current editor is Jennifer Maxwell-Muir.

Designing the "Classic" Newsletter

Let's begin our discussion of newsletter design by considering the "classic" or traditional newsletter format. This is an 11 by 17 sheet folded in half to produce four 8½ by 11 pages. More pages can be added, of course, but four 8½ by 11 pages seem an ideal size for the content and design of one issue of a newsletter. If there is so much material that it will not fit into a four-page issue, it may be time to consider more frequent publication.

> **WHY WASHINGTON?**

The largest publishing house in the world is located in Washington, D.C. It is the government printing office.

Washington has the largest concentration of journalists in the world, representing more than 2,600 newspapers and radio and television stations. There are 3,000 journalists who correspond for periodicals.

Yet Washington is called the cradle of newsletters. Why are so many newsletters published in a place that is saturated with information professionals?

One Washington newsletter publisher offers an answer: "My newsletter will be a profitable business as long as the government doesn't learn to write in plain English. I doubt if that will happen in my lifetime, if ever."

Characteristics of the classic newsletter format, developed for the 8½ by 11 page size include:

■ Type set one column to the page, in ragged right, to resemble, as closely as possible, a personal letter.

■ A short, punchy writing style in which obvious words are often left out and key sentences, phrases, and names are underlined.

■ A limited number of graphic elements designed with care and used consistently. Simplicity is stressed.

■ One style of type for the content; sometimes italic or boldface is used for limited emphasis.

■ Avoidance of a magazine look.

This classic newsletter format was developed by Kiplinger, and many newsletters follow it faithfully.

An example of effective use of the classic, or traditional, newsletter format is *Rotunda Review,* published by the Nebraska Farm Bureau Federation when its state legislature is in session. The *Rotunda Review* was developed by Susan Rodenburg in 1984. Its goal is to keep Farm Bureau leaders up-to-date on issues and activities involving their organization and the Nebraska legislature.[2]

The newsletter presents information in an easy-to-read and easy-to-understand style. Paragraphs are limited to no more than eight lines. All reporting is focused on the one goal of explaining how legislation will affect the readers—farmers and ranchers.

The logo of *Rotunda Review* incorporates the bronze statue located on top of Nebraska's state capitol in Lincoln. As readers are aware, the rotunda is the area just outside the legislative chambers where most lobbying takes place.

Since its inception, "*Rotunda Review* continues as a readily identifiable communications vehicle," says Douglas A. Gibson, Farm Bureau chief administrator. "Approximately 2,000 leaders receive it twice a month during the legislative session. For quick and easy reading it's one sheet, back-to-back, usually letter size. However, occasionally it's legal size. Paragraph length is eight lines."

Gibson notes that the *Rotunda Review* is printed on a special paper, which helps focus on "The Sower" in its logo.

"Because of new technology at Nebraska Farm Bureau, we are able to give *Rotunda Review* a crisper graphic look, while stopping short of a desktop-published appearance. We retain the use of ragged right typesetting as a means to simulate the immediacy conveyed by the old typewritten format."[3]

The Nebraska Farm Bureau also publishes a monthly tabloid-format newspaper that goes into more detail concerning issues as a part of its communications mix.

A traditional-format newsletter might be considered when there is a need for short-term communication such as during a campaign or event. Or it can be effective as a regular publication for a small organization or one with limited facilities.

Fig. 18-12 ■ An effective newsletter in the classic format published by the Nebraska Farm Bureau Federation to inform its members about actions of the legislature. The logo incorporates the bronze statue on top of Nebraska's state capitol. The "rotunda" of the title refers to the area where most of the lobbying takes place. The logo was designed by Susan Larson Rodenburg.

ROTUNDA REVIEW
A Report of Nebraska Legislative News

January 14, 1994

LEGISLATURE BEGINS WITH NEW SPEAKER AND NEW FACES
With the departure of Speaker Dennis Baack, the 93rd Legislature elected Senator Ron Withem of Papillion as the new speaker. Senator Withem defeated Senator George Coordsen of Hebron by a 25-24 vote on the opening day of the session. The speaker of the legislature is the body's top leader, setting the legislative agenda and acting as the main spokesman to the news media.

With Senator Withem taking the top post, the chairmanship of the Education Committee became open. Senator Ardyce Bohlke of Hastings defeated Senator David Bernard-Stevens of North Platte for the Education Committee Chair.

Three new senators, appointed by the Governor, also take their places in the Unicameral to fill vacancies created during the past year.

Senator Leo "Pat" Engel, an insurance agent from South Sioux City, has been appointed to represent District 17 following the resignation of former Senator Kurt Hohenstein of Dakota City. Senator Engel was also appointed to the serve on the Appropriations Committee.

Senator James Monen, a former Omaha judge, replaces Senator Tom Horgan to represent District 4. Horgan left the legislature to take a job in New Hampshire. Senator Monen will also serve on the Education and Natural Resources Committees.

Senator Jerry Matzke, an attorney from Sidney, fills the District 47 seat vacated by former Speaker Dennis Baack of Kimball. Baack resigned to become the executive director of the Nebraska Community College Association. Senator Matzke will serve on the Transportation and Health & Human Services Committees.

The second session of the 93rd Legislature (60-day session) is expected to end April 15. There are 343 bills carried over from last year and, to date, 250 new bills have been introduced. A copy of the state senators' addresses and telephone numbers is included with this mailing.

GOVERNOR'S INITIATIVES INCLUDE FERTILIZER TAX REPEAL
In his "State of the State" address on January 10, Governor Nelson announced that he is seeking repeal of the $4/ton fertilizer tax. Nelson proposes repeal of the tax effective October 1994, which would save farmers an estimated $3.8 million during the next legislative fiscal year, and $7.3 million annually thereafter. Senator Scott Moore of Seward has a vehicle for the repeal with LB 37, which is Moore's priority bill from last session calling for elimination of the tax.

Published by the Nebraska Farm Bureau Federation
P.O. Box 80299, 5225 S. 16th St., Lincoln, NE 68501   Phone 402-421-4400

The logo and masthead information can be printed in a large quantity, perhaps a full year's supply, and current information included and the required number printed for each issue. This method of production can help reduce costs.

Some designers have criticized the single-column page, saying that the column width is too wide for easy reading. However, since this is a standard for letters, people are used to it. If you prefer narrower line widths, an alternative is indenting the columns and placing the heads for items in the left-hand margin.

Even with one column, using wider margins and more space between paragraphs can help readability. If the margins are, say, 6 picas, the line width can be held to about forty-five characters.

There are two ways to handle a two-column page format. One is to vary the widths of the columns. The left-hand column can be 14 to 16

Fig. 18-13 ■ The single-column newsletter in an 8½ by 11 format can have a narrower and more readable column width if heads are placed on the side of the reading matter.

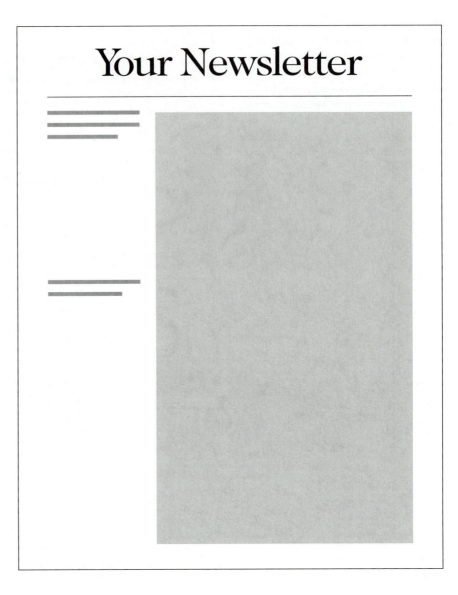

picas wide, for example, and the right-hand column 24 or 25 to 30 picas wide. The other, of course, is to plan two columns of equal size.

The two-column format has a number of advantages. It produces a more readable line width, and more words can be accommodated on a page compared with a single-column page. There is greater opportunity for creative design, and more variation and interest can be worked into the layouts. It is easier to use graphics such as charts and illustrations.

If a three-column format is adopted, the newsletter moves toward a magazine or miniature newspaper in appearance. But white space should be at least 1½ picas for 12 point or larger type and 1 pica for type 10 points or smaller.

Since the three-column format tends to look like a magazine in the eyes of readers, it might be judged as such. Since most newsletters are not produced with the extensive talent and mechanical resources of a large magazine, the newsletter will suffer by comparison.

Fig. 18-14 ■ Two possibilities for a two-column newsletter format. Two equal-width columns or one narrow and one wide can be used. Often an identifying slogan can add impact and memorability to the logo.

On the other hand, the three-column page gives the designer an opportunity to blend the best qualities of magazine design with those of the newsletter.

Along with deciding on the number of columns per page, we need to determine margin size. Page margins should be at least 3 picas all around. If the pages are to be punched for a binder, the margins should be wide enough to prevent the punch holes from obliterating some of the reading matter. As mentioned, if the newsletter is set in a single column, margins of 6 picas all around are not too much.

White space between columns should not be more than about 2 picas. Too much white space between columns can destroy unity by creating a wide white alley in the middle of the page. But white space should be at least 1½ picas wide for word processed copy and 1 pica for typeset copy if it is to do a neat job of column separation.

Some newsletters are designed with *rules for framing* the type spaces and separating the columns. Rules can be effective design devices, but they should be added to a page only if they serve a useful purpose. A rule across the top and bottom of each page, bled to the edge, can help unify the whole newsletter and be an identifying device. Thin lines under headings can add individuality to the newsletter.

Reading matter should be set ragged right if there is a chance that justifying the lines will create awkward spacing between words. Some

Your Newsletter

Your Newsletter

Fig. 18-15 ■ (Above, left) The newsletter with a three-column page approaches the magazine format. Magazine design techniques can be used. (Above, right) Some newsletters achieve orderly format and memorability plus quick identity with ruled borders around the pages and a symbol added to the logo

computer-generated copy using programs that are not sophisticated page layout or word-processing programs produce an unacceptable word spacing if the lines are justified. If the copy is set ragged right, the page will often look more organized if vertical hairline column rules are used. These rules should be centered between columns in at least 1 pica of white space. Be careful in selecting thicker rules between columns. If they are too thick they can create disunity and detract from the appearance of the page.

Rules and borders that are too heavy and too complex should be avoided. Such ornamentation usually succeeds in attracting attention to itself rather than enhancing the whole layout. Wide borders, if used, can be toned down by screening.

NEWSLETTER DESIGN DECISIONS

▶ Along with the basic format for the newsletter, a number of other graphic decisions must be made. These include the design of the nameplate or logo, headline treatment, constants such as masthead and folio lines, and heads for regular features, as well as the design of the body type.

Fig.18-16 ■ Once the number of columns have been determined, layout of a newsletter can be simplified by constructing grids. They can be done either on lightweight poster board or on the computer for repeated use. Here are typical grids for two-, three-, and four-column layouts.

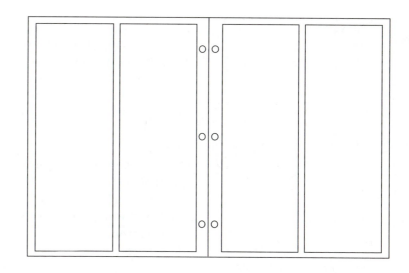

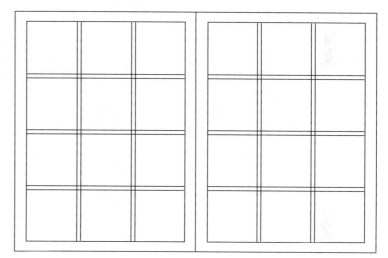

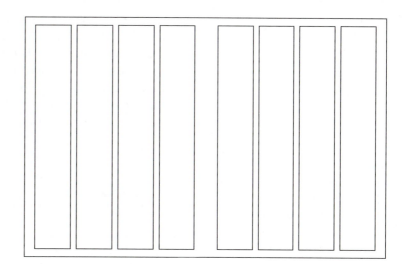

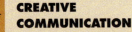

CREATIVE COMMUNICATION

"Fools rush in"—creativity can be foiled and the process can take longer if preparation and analysis of the problem are inadequate. Creative scientists who seek to solve problems spend considerable time analyzing the situation. In a famous example, Albert Einstein once spent seven years on intensive study and fact gathering. But then it only took him five weeks to write the resulting revolutionary paper on relativity. He was working full time as a clerk in a Swiss patent office as well.

Thorough preparation often can shorten the period spent on actual creativity. Thorough preparation might include assembling pertinent facts, asking questions and finding answers, and seeking out leads for possible solutions.

The Logo

The newsletter logo deserves serious consideration. In this discussion the term *nameplate* refers to the actual typeset name of the publication and *logo* to the whole treatment of the name plus any symbols or slogans. The logo creates the first impression, and it should identify the newsletter and its scope quickly but not overpower the other elements on the page. It should not occupy more than 20 percent of the page, in most situations.

The newsletter name should be imaginative—it should distinguish the newsletter from the thousands of others that are in circulation. Designers suggest avoiding use of a name that is dull and that cannot be expressed with some imaginative graphics. Such names as the initials of the organization with the word *newsletter* or *bulletin* tacked on the end can be deadly dull.

The logo design should help translate the title, and the type style used should be appropriate for the purpose of the newsletter. It should provide contrast with the headline type, but it should not dominate the page to the point that it overshadows the content. It should be distinctive so it will not be confused with the headline types.

Often a symbol or design can be incorporated with the name to create a distinctive logo. This logo can be made in different sizes to be used in the masthead, house ads, letterheads, envelopes, and so on. The more the logo is used, the better it can help create identity and recognition.

The logo should not be so large or strong that it interferes with the content of the newsletter. Designers say the logo plus the folio lines should not take up more than 2 inches at the top of page 1. However, as with most "rules," there might be situations where the exception is the most effective design device.

When Kiplinger created the name for the *Kiplinger Washington Letter*, he deliberately left the word *news* out because his plan was to write about the news rather than report it. Many newsletter publishers have adopted this personalized style. There are the *Granville Report* on stocks and the *Lundborg Letter* on oil, for instance.

A touch of distinction that can set a newsletter out of the ordinary is to print the logo in color. It is possible to do this inexpensively if arrangements are made with the printer to print a supply of blank paper for the newsletter when color is on the press. Then the body of the

Fig. 18-17 ■ Two logo approaches to avoid. All-capital letters in Black Letter, Script, or Miscellaneous typefaces most likely will be unattractive and unreadable. A logo in all-lowercase letters can cause confusion when used within reading matter or if it appears in articles in other publications.

YOUR NEWSLETTER

your newsletter

A service provided by the Dreyfus Family.   Fall 1993, Number 66

Fig. 18-18 ■ This is the nameplate of a newsletter sent to its customers by an investment firm. Note the use of minus leading and downstyle format. ("Letter from the Lion" is a registered service mark of Dreyfus Service Corporation. Reprinted with permission)

newsletter can be printed in black, or whatever, at a later date. Some newsletter producers have a year's supply of colored logos printed at one time at a considerable savings.

Other ways to add color and brighten the newsletter is to print a screened tint block across the top of the first page and surprint the logo over it. Or a rule that extends across the top or both the top and bottom of all pages can be printed in color. The logo can be printed from a reverse plate in color, too.

Some newsletter names are printed in all lowercase letters. But this design technique can cause problems. One newsletter is titled *communications briefings*. There is no problem when the title appears in the content of that newsletter because it is always set in italics. But if it were to appear in another publication, it could be confusing. Then there was the headline that appeared in a newspaper trade journal announcing "presstime staff changes." Readers had to know that "presstime" was the name of an association publication that elected to use a lowercase *p* for the first letter of its name. Readers should not have to stop and figure out an ambiguous or puzzling communication device.

Sometimes a slogan can be useful. It might be incorporated with the nameplate and, perhaps, a symbol to create an effective logo. Such phrases as "all about airplanes" or "your financial adviser" can help identify the newsletter and create memorability.

For a more detailed discussion of the planning that goes into the creation of a logo and ideas for its design, see Chapter 11.

The Folio Line

Newsletter design should make it easy for the reader to find out by whom, where, and when the newsletter is produced. A good practice is to include the volume number, issue number, and date in a folio line just below the logo. The name of the originator, address, telephone, and copyright information can be added in small type at the bottom of page 1. This information, plus staff members, subscription date, and so on, can be incorporated in a masthead at the bottom of page 4. This plan is standard practice for many four-page newsletters.

Repeating the name of the publication, page number, and date on every page is not necessary in a four-page newsletter. However, if the publication is filed or stored for future reference and a semiannual or annual index is issued, it might be worthwhile to consider a page-numbering system.

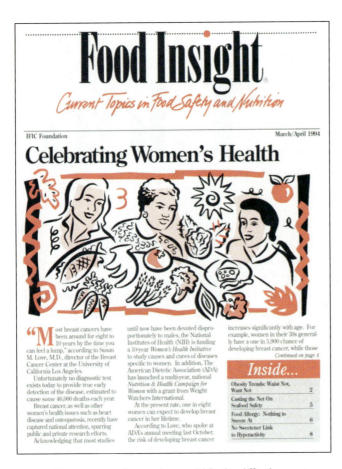

Fig. 18-19 ■ The reader would find it difficult to resist *Food Insight*. The dramatic art arouses interest and invites you to find out what it is all about. Note the contents box in the lower left. The logo tells the reader what the newsletter is all about and the explanation line expands on its purpose. (Courtesy International Food Information Council)

Fig. 18-20 ■ Often a basic newsletter format and content philosophy can be tailored for a number of audiences. *Visions* is a newsletter aimed at Saturn team members, retailers, and owners. A four-color shell (shown) is used for all three audiences. A two-color insert is added that is tailored for each public. This illustrates good application of design principles plus imaginative use of graphic and typographic techniques. (Courtesy Saturn Corporation)

One such system follows the style used by the printers of "mercuries" in England in the late sixteenth and early seventeenth centuries. The mercuries were series of news pamphlets of continuing accounts of affairs. The first pamphlet of a series might contain pages 1 through 4. The second issue would have pages 5 through 8, and so on until the series was completed. *National Geographic* follows this page-numbering system today.

In addition to their own system of filing, some newsletter publishers obtain an International Standard Serial Number (ISSN) and include it with the page 1 or masthead information. Anyone can obtain an International Serial Number at no cost. This number goes into a worldwide computer data bank, and libraries refer to it when subscribing to publications. Information concerning the number can be obtained from the National Serials Data Program (Library of Congress, Washington, DC 20540).

Fig. 18–21 ■ *Status Report* is a consistent award winner in newsletter contests. It is produced by the Insurance Institute for Highway Safety and goes to 15,000 readers who are members of target audiences concerned with highway safety. Heads and body type are in a condensed Cheltenham which is used throughout. Anne Fleming is director of communications and editor.

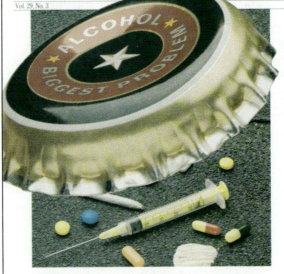

Headlines

Headline type for newsletters should harmonize but stand out from the body type. Since newsletter design stresses simplicity, an uncomplicated Sans Serif or clean modern Roman type will work well for headlines. The headlines should be kept small; usually 12 to 18 points are adequate. If the newsletter is set in Roman, a Sans Serif of the same size but in all capital letters can be effective.

Some newsletter designers simply set the heads in all capitals of the same type as the body or set the first few words in the first paragraph of an item in all capitals. Others do not use heads or capitals but simply underline the first few words of the first paragraph.

Regardless of the style selected for headline treatment, it should be consistent. If some headlines are set flush left, all should be flush left. If some are centered, all should be centered. The flush left is the simplest and quickest to use, and it can be given distinction by indenting it an

Fig. 18-22 ■ This is the front page of *Desktop for Profit*. Note the creative design of the logo (with all lower case letters), the "dfc" icon in the lower right, and the use of a unifying graphic to lead from the logo to the list of contents. The address area completes this excellent newsletter page. (This page and Fig. 18–24 reprinted with permission from the March, 1994 issue of *Desktop for Profit*. © 1994, National Association of Printers & Lithographers, Teaneck, NJ.)

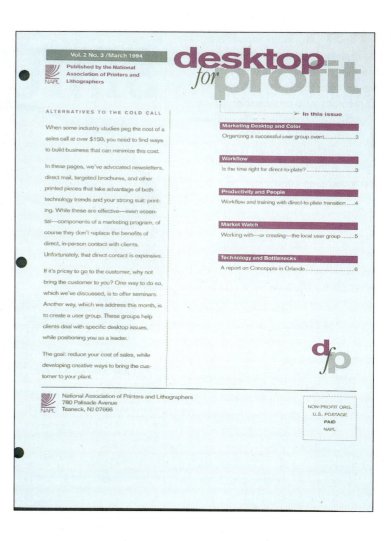

en or em instead of lining it up with the body type. This will let more light into the page. But no matter what style is adopted, allow ample white space around the heads to help them stand out.

Subheads

Since the newsletter thrives because it gives information quickly, most articles are short. When a long article is included, *subheads* should be used to break it up into short takes to enhance the punchy appearance of the newsletter. Subheads look best when set in the same type style, though in a smaller size, as the main heads.

Some designers do use a different type style for subheads, but one that harmonizes well with the main head type.

For example, they say there is nothing wrong with using a Sans Serif subhead with a Roman main head. But they do suggest that an old style Roman of one family will not mix well with an old style Roman of another family. The same basic principles of good type selection apply to newsletters as they do to all other printed communications.

Italics or lightface of the same family as used for the main head work well for subheads. One rule of thumb concerning subhead size is to make the subhead about half the size of the main head. If this practice

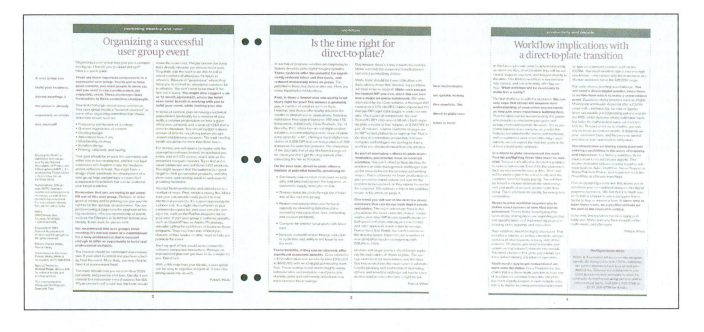

Fig. 18-23 ■ *Desktop for Profit* opens to three pages which fold to 8½ by 11. Page 4 is 8 by 11 so it will fold and not overlap the punch holes. Note that these holes, for filing the newsletter in a binder, do not obstruct the page layouts.

is used, the subhead should be checked to ensure that it is at least the same size as the body type. Subheads should be placed so they do not interfere with the story line of the article. They should be in natural breaks. Also, they should not confuse the reader by appearing to signal the start of an entirely different article.

Punch can also be added by using typographic devices to emphasize points in the body copy. But such use should be very limited.

Standing Heads

Newsletters often contain features that continue from one issue to the next. Many times these regular features are titled with heads such as "A Chat with the President" or "Front Office Notes" that never change. These standing heads can make a newsletter seem dull and static. You should plan a method of handling them so the material they identify comes alive.

A standing head can be supplemented with subheads, or, better yet, the identifying head can be used as a *kicker* (a head above the main head, usually underlined) so the subject head can be changed with each issue. An arrangement such as this can help:

<u>**A Chat with the President**</u>

Things are Looking Up: Membership Is Increasing

Quite often the organization of the newsletter can be improved by boxing constants, copy that does not change from issue to issue, such as the masthead information. Another way to handle the constants might be to surprint this information over a screen.

Fig. 18-24 ■ *Heart Health* is an award winner. The reason is obvious. This newsletter illustrates many of the attributes of excellent design. It is attention-grabbing, and it uses color and a light-hearted approach that will attract its target audience. Note the use of color and the clean, neat layout. (Courtesy Ariad Custom Publishing, Toronto)

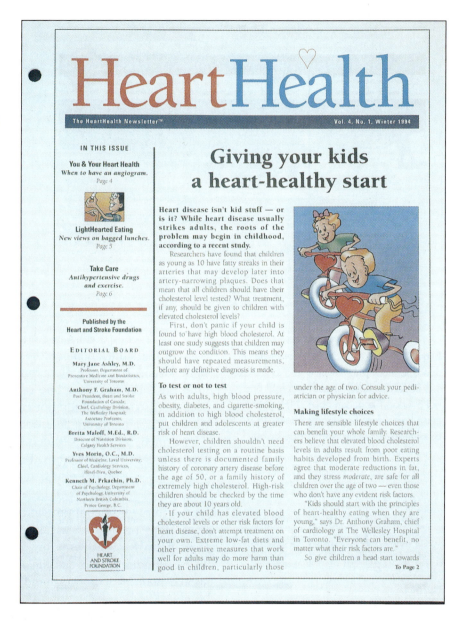

Things to Avoid

One newsletter designer summed up the shortcomings of too many newsletters:

- Small, difficult-to-read typefaces for reading matter.
- Crowded pages.
- Dull, static layouts with little accent or variety.
- Too much gingerbread in designs.
- Tiny photos that should have been enlarged for more impact.
- Group shots in which faces are hardly recognizable.
- Inconsistency in design.

Fig. 18-25 ■ An inside page of the award-winning *Heart Health*. The section heading is enhanced with the art of an apple. Other section heads receive similar treatment. The light-hearted art with excellent color choices enhances the page. The chart is attractive and legible with the use of black type on tan tones. (Courtesy Ariad Custom Publishing, Toronto)

AWARD-WINNING NEWSLETTERS

➤ Since 1972 the *Newsletter on Newsletters,* published by the Newsletter Clearinghouse, has conducted a competition held in conjunction with the International Newsletter Conference. Awards for overall excellence are made to newsletters that exhibit design, typographic, photographic, and printing quality. Judges for the competition are selected from the communications and graphics industry.

Comments made by judges in recent contests indicate that they do not like odd, unusual layouts. They pay particular attention to the designs of front pages and nameplates. (After all, the nameplate is the major design element of many newsletters.)

They applaud the use of color. They are impressed by newsletters that are printed on colored paper stock rather than white paper. They point out that color can be an important element in creating identification for a newsletter.

On the negative side, the judges criticize the use of nondescriptive names and initials for newsletter names. Such tags make it difficult to identify the newsletter quickly. If initials are used for a newsletter name, they should be followed quickly by a descriptive phrase.

The judges also criticize many newsletters for using small, difficult-to-read type. (We have recommended that no newsletter be set in less

Fig. a

Fig. b

Fig. 18-26 ■ Let's build a newsletter page.

We have been using a typical three-column grid, but we decide to move to a simple four-column grid. We make a prototype of the page as we visualize it (Fig. a). By dividing the page into a four, five, or six-column grid we gain flexibility. It also enhances the readability and visual stimulation of the page while still maintaining design consistency.

We've started with the top-of-the-page. In this instance we have combined our logo with masthead information and added the dateline. Our plan follows a logical order. The main story is emphasized, then the secondary story, and finally the contents items. We have added a pull quote to the lead story. Our finished page looks like this (Fig. b).

However, we believe this page needs more punch so we build on what we have set up. Aligning the headline with the masthead increases visual consistency and improves the directional flow of the main information. Echoing the reversed text of the dateline in the table of contents provides a friendly "opening" and "closing" of the page. It helps develop unity (Fig. c).

Now let's look more closely at the logo. It is just a humdrum condensed bold Sans Serif. We might try making "Irvine" in reverse (Fig. d). But we can do better than that. By changing

than 10-point type.) They found that type packed into a newsletter without heads for items or breathing space was difficult to read. White space should be used to get air into a newsletter page just as it is used for all types of printed communication. Packed pages are unappealing and tend to turn readers away.

An effective newsletter should be attractive and neat. Its design should be uncomplicated and consistent from issue to issue.

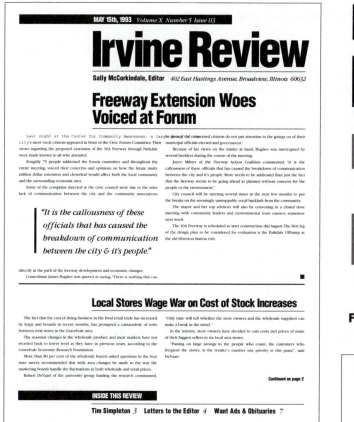

Fig. c

Fig. d

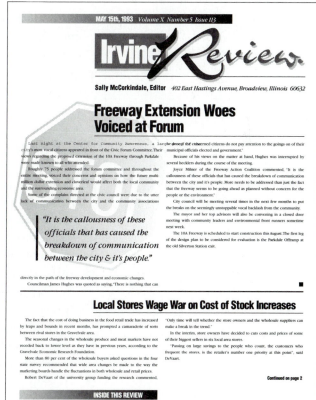

Fig. e

"Review" to a Script we can add interest. Then, we go back to the reverse block for "Irvine" and see how it looks in various gray scales. We'll select the gray scale we think looks best and add the resulting logo to the masthead. Our completed newsletter page layout then has interest and appeal (Fig. e).

We have avoided too much clutter that can result if we add too many graphics to the page. In selecting graphics we abide by the three S's—simple, subtle, and suitable. (© Image Club Graphics, 1-800-387-9193)

➤ **EFFECTIVE DESIGN CHECKLIST**

■ Consider using an initial letter at the start of each article. However, don't use initial letters if subheads are being used, as too many elements in a newsletter can create a typographic mishmash.

■ Use a different type style for cutlines, or a different size or weight of the same type family as the body type, to brighten the page. The cutlines should all be in the same style and used in the same form, however.

■ Use a distinctive style for handling bylines to add a touch of contrast. But use one style for all the bylines.

■ Set off a list of specific points in an article by numbers or appropriate small ornaments. Or indent the points an em or so to bring in additional white space to brighten the page.

■ Since so much printed material is produced on white paper, consider using colored stock and/or ink to make your newsletter stand out from the rest.

■ Word processed body copy will save space and look more like professional typesetting if reduced 10 percent.

■ Once the basic format is designed, stick with it and do not make format changes from issue to issue. Such changes can be costly and time consuming.

■ Study the effects of various screen percentages on the ink used. Often the effect of a second color can be obtained without the cost.

➤ **GRAPHICS IN ACTION**

1. Plan the format for a four-page 8½ by 11 newsletter about your favorite hobby. Begin by outlining the research you would do, including evaluation of the target audience. Then decide on the number of columns per page and design the logo, folio lines, and all the graphic and typographic elements. Explain what you did, and why.

2. Plan a newsletter to accompany a letter soliciting membership in an organization to which you belong. The letter will be sent to prospective members in a Number 10 envelope. The newsletter should give the prospective member some of the purposes and activities of your organization. Include appropriate art and design a distinctive logo.

3. Design a prototype for the front page of a newsletter for an organization to which you belong. Use either desktop publishing or traditional design tools, whichever are available to you.

4. Find a four-page newsletter that has a one-column page and redesign it to a two-column format. Be creative and consider using such innovations as pages boxed with rules, tint blocks for surprinting the logo, and screens of various designs for illustrations.

5. Select a section from a metropolitan Sunday newspaper (sports, business, travel, and so on) and plan a newsletter devoted to that area of interest. Write a prospectus for such a newsletter including the research that should be done and a description of the format and graphic elements the newsletter would contain.

NOTES

[1]Don H. Follett and Mary Ann Warner, Minnegasco. *Minnegasco News,* April 1989, p. 4.
[2]Letter from Susan Larson Rodenberg, *Rotunda Review* editor, to the author, May 25, 1989.
[3]Interview with Douglas A. Gibson, April 20, 1994.

CHAPTER 19

VISUAL COMMUNICATION IN THE NEW CENTURY

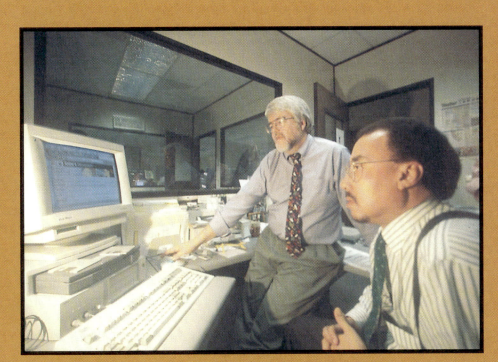

© Mark Richards, Photo Edit

19 Digital and fiber optics—those are the words of the future for visual communicators. Digital refers to the way images are assembled and transported on their trips from you to your target audience. Fiber optics holds the key to transportation along the information superhighway.

A dictionary definition of digital communications tells us it is "transmission of binary-coded data through a communication channel."[1] But what does that mean? It means the information you feed into a computer is changed into digits and processed. Printing presses are being developed that can receive these images from a computer and change them into pages to be printed. The process is referred to as c-t-p (computer to press).

Now, as to the highly-touted information superhighway, this is a means of employing fiber optic transmission lines to send digital information at incredible speeds from point A to point B. For instance, point A could be a library many miles from you and point B could be you.

The fiber optic line is made of a thread of glass no thicker than a hair. It is capable of two-way transmission of information and pictures so fast it can send the entire *Encyclopedia Britannica,* (all 43 million words of it) in two seconds. It would take copper telephone wires 50 hours to do the same thing. Those developing the system say the copper-wire transmission would not have the quality of the fiber optic product, either.[2]

Until the middle 1990s the information superhighway was a vision in the minds of futurists. However, Time-Warner made an initial step towards the reality of the superhighway when it put its Full Service Network to work in Orlando, Florida.

Initially, the network provided video on demand of more than 60 titles, such things as home shopping, video games, wireless two-way voice communications, video picture phone service, and two-way educational instruction. The idea was to learn about customer behavior regarding the service and apply these findings to an envisioned national network.[3]

CHANGES ARE COMING FASTER AND FASTER

➤ As the new technology rolls out change after change, it also brings more and more developments that will directly affect the visual communicator.

The printing industry is moving into the digital era with several innovations. These have great potential at the same time they place greater responsibility for the quality and effectiveness of the end product on the shoulders of the communicator. A trio of developments will eliminate more of the traditional production steps between the visual communicator and the finished product. In addition to computer-to-plate (also called direct-to-plate), computer-to-press production is coming to pass. In each instance, the person who creates a communication on the computer will be the person who guides that image through to the plate or the press.

Fig. 19-1 ■ It's coming—the whole world at your finger tips. Time Warner has put its Full Service Network to work in Orlando, Florida. If you are one of the "first families" to connect with the system you will see, above left, the carousel that will appear on your screen. You can rotate it to select a topic. In this case three topics are visible. The remote control unit is shown above, middle illustration. With it, you will be able to select a topic and then zero in on a specific item. If you are shopping for breakfast cereal, for instance, you can call up the variety available as shown on the right. It's not only coming, it's here. At right is the "first family" to go on line with equipment now available. (Courtesy Time Warner Cable)

Already, several large commercial printers have started to install computer-to-plate systems. R. R. Donnelley & Sons put systems on-line at two of its plants in the spring of 1994. A study of computer-to-plate was commissioned by the Printing Industries of America recently. The study "Bridging to a Digital Future" included the prediction that by the year 2000, 15 to 20 percent of commercial printing establishments will be using the new technology. It predicted that compter-to-plate would be expanded from short runs to magazines, yearbooks, directories, newspapers, and virtually all sorts of publications.[4]

More and more the computer is becoming the heart of a visual communications work area. Suppose someone arrived at your work station from another planet, looked at your computer, and, pointing, asked, "What is that?" How would you explain it to him or her (or it)?

Back in 1986 a popular encyclopedia defined a computer as "an electronic device that can receive a set of instructions, or program, and then carry out this program by performing calculations on numerical data or by compiling and correlating other forms of information.[5]

Today the computer has become much more than that. It is the vehicle that will allow you to cruise the information superhighway. The computer is becoming more than just a device that will "compute data." As its use has expanded and its capacity to store and handle data has expanded along with it, the need for greater and greater capacity is growing.

In the middle 1990s CD-ROM (Compact Disk Read Only Memory) technology entered the desktop publishing arena. CD-ROM offered the desktop publisher a number of advantages that appeared to spell the end of the era of diskettes. Its potentials are that:

■ Electromagnetic fields such as metal scanners cannot destroy data on the disk.

■ Compact disks can store up to 680 megabytes, 600 times as much as a 3½-inch disk.

■ The CD-ROM is read by a laser rather than a drive with a head that can scratch or gouge the disk.

■ The CD-ROM can be used cross-platform; it can be compatible with both MacIntosh and Personal Computers.[6]

ROBOTS AND SATELLITES

➤ Many of the technological advances of this computerized age are being adopted by the graphic arts industry. Robots and satellites are playing their part. Other new age equipment permits many of today's visual communicators to work from their "cocoons."

Although robots have been used in manufacturing for many years, they are just beginning to invade the graphic arts. These are not the robots we visualize as resembling humans with arms and legs and antennae that run around doing simple tasks. These are machines that are programmable to perform quite complex tasks and to relieve humans from the monotony of assembly-line work. Robots have been used to manufacture machinery, to load, handle parts, weld, drill, and die-cast.

In graphic arts they are being used in large printing plants for handling material from the press to the bindery. They load signatures of books and magazines from the bindery onto skids. They watch over perfect-binding machines and wrapping equipment as well as printed pieces as they pass through the bindery.

It is anticipated that in the future robots will be working in newspaper and magazine publishing plants handling paper, changing press plates, and sorting the printed product for distribution to delivery vehicles. Satellites have been used for some time by such publications as *USA Today,* the *Wall Street Journal,* and *Newsweek,* to mention just a few. *Vanity Fair* digitizes its pages and sends them via satellite from New Jersey to a printing plant in Illinois. There the digital information is received, decompressed, and made into film for plate making. Satellite transmission has given monthly magazines the tool to compete with the more frequently published weekly magazines.

Satellites and telephone lines are being used in a number of ways in addition to shortening the production cycle and making publishing

Fig. 19-2 ■ *Vanity Fair,* a monthly magazine, uses modern technology, including satellite transmission, to speed the production cycle. Each issue contains a late section that includes material prepared just days before the publication goes to press. (Courtesy *Vanity Fair,* © 1995 by The Conde Nast Publications Inc.)

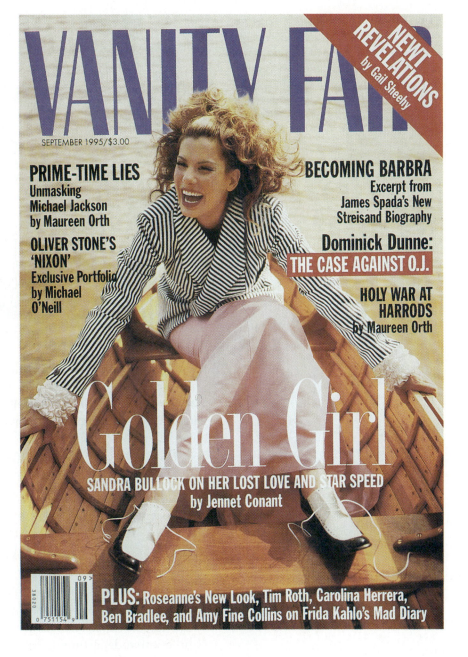

more timely. Advertising agencies have the capability to transmit advertisements directly to a publication. Electronic mail (E-Mail)—devised from the technologies of fax, computers, videotext, sound, and graphics—allows phone calls to become greeting cards, allows a keyboarded message to be digitally voiced, and permits single messages to be edited and distributed to many receivers. In 1989 E-Mail was a $415 million service industry. Predictions are that 60 billion messages will be buzzing around the world via E-Mail by the year 2000.[7]

Cocooning, the practice of working at home with the aid of electronic communications equipment, has come to the world of visual communications. One California designer has set up a special kind of desktop publishing and typesetting service in his home. Customers send

Fig. 19-3 ■ Modern technology has created cocooning—the growing trend of working at home or conducting businesses in the home. Here a designer works with computer, fax, and scanner at TP Design in Atlanta. The studio was established in the home of its owners. (Photography: Ernest Washington)

their work to him by fax over a toll-free number. The customer is promised type set in 24 hours; proofs are faxed back to the customer. The owner of this cocoon business says he has never met most of his clients in person, but they know each other well by E-Mail, phone, fax, and modem.[8]

What does all this portend for the future of desktop publishing? David Creamer, desktop publishing consultant, predicts these changes:[9]

■ *Editorial:* Typography as a separate job function will disappear and editors will need to learn more about basic typography. They will need to know how to use style sheets.

■ *Design:* Like editors, designers must also learn more about typography, along with several other aspects of production. Color is another area that designers will need to master.

■ *Production/prepress:* At the same time, editorial and design departments will experience downsizing due to desktop publishing. Most production departments will be completely eliminated.

TELEVISION GRAPHICS: A GROWING OPPORTUNITY

➤ The video display terminal is playing an increasingly important role in the work of editors and designers. But anyone who is investigating graphics in communications should consider it from one other aspect—its role in television.

Television graphics is a growing area of opportunity for designers. The medium offers challenges quite different from those of the print media. The more senses a message can stimulate, the more impact it can have. Television offers the opportunity to combine motion, sound, and color to create presentations that stimulate several senses.

While the basic principles of design, type selection, and the use of illustrations still hold for television, there are unique differences in their application.

First of all, graphics for television are viewed in a rectangular area that is in the ratio of 4:3. All design elements and art must be prepared with this in mind. Television screen sizes are measured on a diagonal line from one corner to another. Thus the actual viewing area of a 22-inch television set is 17.6 by 13.2 inches. A 26-inch set has a viewing area of 20.8 by 15.6 inches.

The designer concerned with preparing visuals for television also needs to know how these visuals are transmitted. A television picture is made up of a series of fine horizontal lines. The image is scanned much like a person's eyes scan a printed page while reading. An electronic beam traces the visual in a 525-line zigzag thirty times each second. As a result, it is difficult for television to transmit delicately drawn lines or fine shading. Typefaces with very thin strokes or serifs can be distorted or become virtually illegible when seen on the television screen. Spacing is also an important factor in type placement for television transmission. Lines and letters that are too close together can merge and become blurs.

The amount of the total picture that leaves the station to be seen on various receivers can vary depending on the types and sizes of the receivers used by the audience. The designer must be aware of this and allow for a "safety margin." This is a margin or frame around the visual to compensate for the loss of the full picture by some receivers. If a visual is made on a 12 by 9 card, for example, the actual design area should be only about 10 by 7 inches.

The designer must be aware of viewing conditions on the receiving end of the transmission, too. If the program is viewed in the home by a few people sitting 6 to 8 feet from the screen, the design elements should be quite different than if the program is educational and intended for viewing by a large audience in a classroom.

As a general guideline, designers believe that the minimum size for type in a graphic for television should be at least ⅕ of the total picture height. The type size used in a 12 by 9 layout should be at least 36 point if this guideline is followed.

The designer of graphics for television has to become skilled at working with a number of techniques that do not apply to design for the print media. Probably the most complex is the whole area of animation. Others are such devices as inlay, overlay, back projection, color separation overlay, and split-screen effects, to mention a few.

Inlay is a technique by which part of a television picture is cut out electronically and replaced by visuals from another source. Overlay is accomplished in a similar way. Foreground material from one camera is projected on top of background originating from another source.

Back projection involves showing an image of a photographic transparency on a translucent screen. Then a person or object in front of the screen is recorded by the television camera along with the image. Color separation overlay is another method of projecting graphics and art from two sources at the same time. Split-screen effects also enable

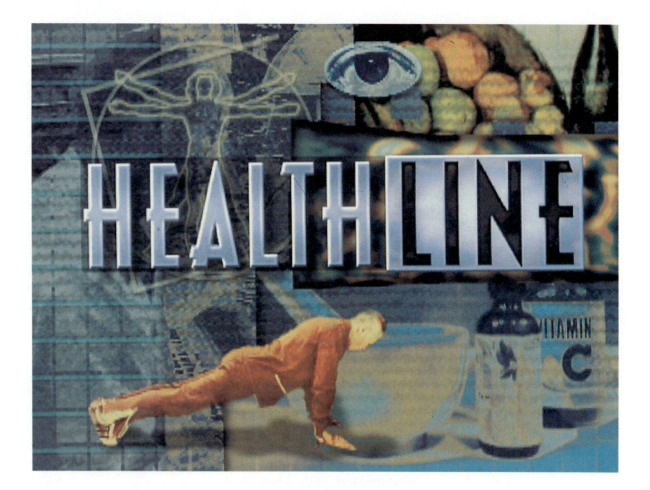

Fig. 19–4 ■ This dynamic image was produced for *Dateline NBC* and was nominated for a 1994 News & Documentary Emmy Award. It is an end frame of a segment animation for *Healthline,* which is part of the program. The type and storyboard were created using a Macintosh; image rendering and frame layout were done using Quantel Paintbox; and Quantel HAL and Harry were used to create the animation effects and digital compositing. (Design team: Ralph Famiglietta Jr., Guy Pepper, Bettina Ewing, Mary Devitt, Paul Bennett. Courtesy NBC, Broadcast Creative Services.)

the producer to project material from more than one source simultaneously.

All of these techniques require close coordination between the designer and the other staff members engaged in producing a television program. It is obviously helpful for the designer of graphics for the video screen to become familiar with all phases of television production.

The road to a successful career in television graphics leads the beginning designer through many complicated processes that require much study and practice. The starting place, however, is an introductory course in graphics that covers the same basic information and techniques needed for work in print media.

DOES PRINT HAVE A FUTURE?

➤ Most information during the past 70 years has been distributed by the broadcast and print media. Futurists, however, predict that by 2010 most information will be distributed by advanced forms of interactive telephony. Designers working on the information superhighway will have to create graphical interfaces for on-line digital products. These could include catalogs, video games, banking, shopping services—the list goes on and on.

Well, is that going to spell the demise of print media? Those in the printing business don't think so. "Print is a powerful and enduring medium that triggers interaction with other media," R. R. Donnelley & Sons told its stockholders in its 1993 annual report.

Although some print products will disappear, the giant printing company said for every new electronic medium, a related set of print products is developed.

"Consumers turn to print for browsing, for making decisions, for ideas about what they would like to try in electronic platforms," the Donnelley report continues. "For example, we print *CompuServe* magazine, which has a monthly circulation of 1.1 million members of CompuServe's on-line information service. Its publisher tells us that when the magazine arrives each month, user activity rises sharply for products mentioned."

It also notes that the release of movies based on books sparks a surge of popular books, resulting in reprints.

The newspaper industry may be struggling, but in 1993 a record of 800 new magazines were published in the United States. Moreover, an average of 50,000 new titles are produced by the book publishing industry each year. Book superstores are popping up around the country.

The Landoll story is an example of the American Dream coming alive in the printing industry. It should be an inspiration for all those with high hopes in the world of printed visual communications.

The story started in 1971 when James Landoll left a promising future with Ford Motor Company to realize his dream of owning his own business. He started a children's book business, and worked out of his home to secure customers. Landoll depended on commercial printers to supply his needs. The business developed until by 1979 he had nearly

Fig. 19-5 ■ A printing business started in a home in 1971 now has more than 160 employees working three shifts. Many of the press runs top 1 million copies. Here, bindery workers keep the line of books going in the Landoll plant. (Courtesy Landoll, Inc.)

Fig. 19-6 ■ Cover for a Landoll Afterschool Activity Book. The American dream was realized with a printing press. James Landoll started his business by working out of his home and today his company serves 35,000 accounts worldwide with their production of preschool workbooks, puzzle books, and a wide variety of other books. (Courtesy Landoll, Inc.)

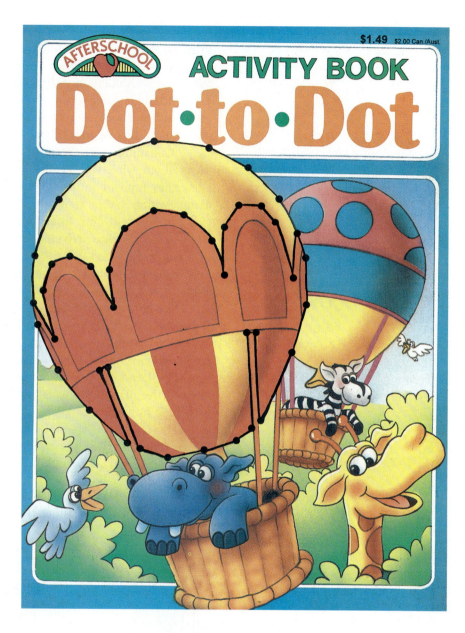

3,000 accounts. Landoll decided it was time to start his own printing plant.

Landoll started with used printing equipment that he had to learn to operate. He set up the plant in a small cement-block garage. His entire staff consisted of one person—himself.

The Landoll line now includes preschool workbooks, puzzle and crossword books, dictionaries, cookbooks, and illustrated classics for young people. The company is the largest employer in Ashland, Ohio, from where it serves 35,000 accounts worldwide. About 160 employees work in three shifts. Many of the press runs top 1 million copies of a single title.

Fig. 19-7 ■ Opportunities for visual communicators seem bright in the field of association and special-interest publications. Hundreds of magazines, brochures, newspapers and printed ephemera are produced by such organizations. Demand for these materials seems assured for years to come. One publication that has received recognition for its design is *Rural Living,* published by the Michigan Farm Bureau. (Courtesy Michigan Farm Bureau)

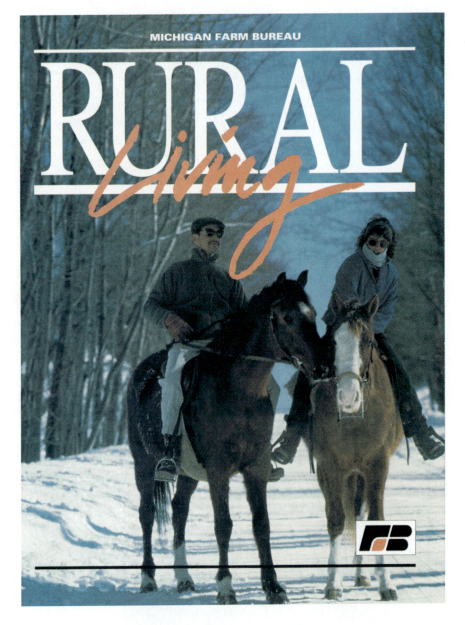

TRENDS IN CORPORATE GRAPHIC DESIGN

➤ The graphic designer who works in the corporate world will see increased use of sophisticated printed communications. Everything from letterheads to annual reports are being produced with a greater focus on type and graphics. In a world of information overload, corporations and their public relations professionals are turning more and more to graphic designers to produce printed material that is not only attractive but innovative and memorable as well.

In seeking to achieve the corporation's goals, the designer is planning communications that capture the attention and pull the reader into and through the entire message. Also, the designer seeks to reinforce the image the corporation wishes to create with the use of appropriate visuals.

Current trends in graphic design for corporations include:

- Increased use of the techniques of the graphic journalist to help explain information.
- More use of the tabloid format for employee publications. Many company newsletters are adopting this format; editors and designers like the opportunity for graphic display this larger page provides.
- Using more colorful art and concise copy for brochures.
- Using the annual report to build the company image and bolder and more expansive graphics to make it more interesting and colorful.
- Increased use of strong visual elements such as bold initial letters and brilliant color bars in layouts to give impact to points the company wishes to emphasize.

Fig. 19-8 ■ This two-page spread from the *Clark Memorandum,* an award-winning publication of the J. Reuben Clark Law School at Brigham Young University. It makes effective use of art, color, display type, and a bold initial letter to pull the reader into the story. (Courtesy *Clark Memorandum*)

A NEW EMPHASIS ON CREATIVITY

► Now that the new technology is in place and is being continually refined, designers are contemplating their future in this electronic age. Some observers predict less of a separation between art directors,

designers, editors, and production personnel. The designer will become more involved in the work of all those who create and produce communications, and the others will become more involved in the work of the designer.

As we have discussed in earlier chapters, creativity occurs when a person synthesizes existing information or knowledge and uses it in a new and useful way. To be creative in this world of information overload, graphic designers might need to develop skills that enable them to:

■ Eliminate useless information, or at least recognize the shallow nature of much of the information they receive.

■ Look behind the headlines, and beyond material designed to entertain, to obtain knowledge from solid sources.

■ Seek out information from as many sources as possible and not just from sources that reinforce preconceived beliefs.

■ Read widely, and not only read but also experience and participate in actions that relate to the graphic problem for which a solution is sought.

Fig. 19–9 ■ This two-page spread from *U&lc,* publication of the International Typeface Corporation, was created to illustrate the "anything goes" philosophy that represents one aspect of the cutting-edge approach to design. The approach has its advocates and its detractors. The question is, does the spread do its job—does it *communicate?* (Courtesy *U&lc*)

A VARIETY OF MEDIA

➤ As we cruise down the information superhighway we will become more selective in the messages we tap into. There will be an incredible number of messages and sources of information available to our target audiences. Competition for attention will increase. As a result, the visual communicator will be faced with a real challenge in devising effective programs of communication. Many and varied devices must be employed in the process.

An example of an effective communication mix, employing media not usually considered, was the successful program in which the American University and two hotels cooperated. The target audience was 1,600 sets of parents whose sons and daughters were incoming freshmen or transfer students to the university. The goal was to generate hotel business among parents of students.

The plan included:

■ The "Eagle Club" was formed to tie in with the school's mascot.

■ Letters with "gold" membership cards were sent to parents. These included a pitch to stay at the sponsoring hotels. Special discounts were offered.

■ On arrival, Eagle Club members were shown to their rooms, where they found VIP gift baskets containing a coffee mug, key tag, area map, and corkscrew and snacks.

■ Included were a T-shirt bearing the logos of the school and the hotel plus a welcoming letter.

■ A brief questionnaire on the promotion and the accommodations was included to provide feedback.

Did the effort work? "All our goals and expectations have been surpassed nearly tenfold," the promoters reported. In the month of the promotion $85,000 in additional room revenues were generated.

Note the number of graphics in Fig. 19–10 that were created by designers for the program.

PREPARING FOR THE FUTURE

➤ While the mounting explosion in technology may appear intimidating, it should not. It is providing opportunity, challenge, and reward—all the ingredients of an exciting and satisfying career. How can we parpare to take advantage of all that the future years will hold? Let's listen to the professionals.

Walter Bender, director of the electronic publishing group of the Massachusetts Institute of Technology media laboratory, says that "this industry (publishing) has an important role to play, but the end product is going to be a little bit different" in the future. Despite changes, though, Bender maintains, the industry still will need "someone to create the pictures and the copy . . . someone to organize and format the information."[10]

Fig. 19-10 ■ The visual communicator of the future, faced with intense competition, will need to develop graphic design skills in a wide variety of media. These are the pieces designed for the successful American University promotion. (Courtesy Promotional Products Association International)

Ron Mechler, of RE Design, suggests that there are three things visual communicators should learn: the history of design, how to design, and how to use the electronic tools.[11]

When it comes to using electronic publishing equipment, designer Gail Wiggins urges, "Do your thinking before you get on the machine. Do roughs. Learn how to think visually and to draw on visual references from every arena. Look at other designers' work, look at magazines, go to art museums. Develop excellent computer skills. Then be modest about your skill level."[12]

Graphic editor Jim Jennings holds both a master's in journalism and a doctorate in mass communications from Ohio University. He has won awards for photography and editing. He offers this advice to those aspiring to careers in visual communications: "I would hope that students would seek to find a balance between the technology of graphic design and the knowledge of a well-rounded liberal arts education."

He notes that "too often we are faced with the decision to hire wonderfully gifted technical people, individuals who can make a computer sing and dance, but who are totally unaware of the workings of the world around them. In this situation I would choose the individual capable of bringing a sense of context to the work before them. Computer skills can be quickly learned. Contextual thinking is harder to master."

When Jennings looks at an entry level person he wants someone who knows how to run a computer, but keeps the machine in perspective, remembering it is only a tool and should not force form over function.

"More important," Jennings points out, "I want someone who understands something of national and international affairs and is capable of putting current events into perspective . . . someone who is capable of analyzing a story and getting beyond the basics . . . someone capable of using design to assist the reader in understanding not only how something happened, but why."[13]

Fig. 19-11 ■ The newspaper of the future as envisioned by Michael Keegan, art director of the *Washington Post*. The pages would be 14 by 8.5 inches; each issue would be printed by facsimile in your home. The newspaper company would deliver a supply of fan-folded paper to your home once a month. The images would be delivered to your home printer by telephone or some sort of fiber optic lines. You would punch in a code whenever you wanted a copy of the paper. Keegan chose Century Old Style type for text and italic heads. The main head on the first page is Franklin Gothic condensed. (Courtesy American Press Institute)

The design would combine the best of newspaper and magazine techniques. Full color throughout, it would be printed in the subscriber's home on a facsimile machine. This would pass some of the cost of paper on to the subscriber (they would need to buy paper and printer for other household computer needs), and greatly reduce the cost of distribution. Newspapers would subsidize the cost of paper, which would be delivered independent of news deadlines.

14 x 8.5 inches, fan folded to as many pages as necessary.

An advertisement could bleed horizontally to as many pages as it chose to pay for.

Printing would be high speed, at least 300 dpi color. Concurrent printing on both sides of the sheet would make delivery via telephone fast and simple.

Color indexing starting on the front would carry throughout.

Focus on communication. Show an active interest in the content of your message—not just how it can be conveyed visually, but also why the message itself is important. That's the advice of Neal Pattison.

Pattison has been a reporter and editor at daily newspapers ranging in size from 3,500 to 400,000 circulation. He has taught at Gonzaga University and organized graphics workshops in conjunction with Washington State University.

Further reinforcing comments heard frequently from designers and graphics editors, Pattison says he would rather hire well-informed journalists with some graphic talent than gifted artists who want merely to decorate pages.

"I told you so," was the comment of designer David B. Gray, who teaches at the Rhode Island School of Design. He was responding to a request by the author for his views concerning careers in visual communications. When the first edition of this book was being written, Gray said, "There will be no careers in the publishing field that won't be touched by computers. More especially, the design field in particular will rely more and more on computers."

That was Gray's view in 1985. He recommended a strong background in the liberal arts. Design schools should spend more time on writing and journalism schools should spend more time on design, he said then.

Five years later, when asked again for his views, Gray said, "The same thing applies today as when I said it five years ago, only more so."

The professionals urged students who are considering careers working in visual communications to learn as much as possible about the principles and philosophies of the great movements or schools of design. These include classic revival, Art Nouveau, Art Deco, Bauhaus, Swiss design, and International (architectural) Style.

In addition, students should learn about the principles, philosophy, and richness of typographical design and develop an interest in all the graphic arts, especially photography. Students should study layouts in newspapers, magazines, and all sorts of printed and electronic images. The idea is to know not only the rudiments of design but, perhaps more important, what the designer is trying to accomplish.

Study of the principles of statistical and informational graphics is a must. And students are urged to learn to think of design and typography as absolutely integrated and interrelated with the processes of communication, not as decorative appendages. The goal of visual education today is to teach students to think, to explore, to question, to wonder, and to approach old problems with new solutions.

Finally, it is important to remember that, even with the new technology, visual communications are still "consumed" with a device that has not changed in the 500 years since Johann Gutenberg cast the first piece of movable type—the human eye.

THE FUTURE BELONGS TO THOSE WHO CREATE

▶ The future belongs to the creative visual communicator who has mastered electronic equipment. One of the pacesetters in electronic design today is Laurence Gartel. He has designed covers for national magazines and advertisements for many products; his work has been exhibited at the Smithsonian Institution and in many countries of the world.

"My interest in creating electronic images started in 1975, working with video artist Nam June Paik at Media Study/Buffalo," Gartel relates. "There we utilized 'primitive' one inch reel-to-reel video tape

Fig. 19–12 ◾ In creating this advertisement Laurence Gartel says, "I took one of my most famous Polaroid SX-70 murals and manipulated it in Adobe Photo shop and then used it as a background. A photograph was then taken of the Absolut bottle with my digital camera. Lastly, a halo was created around the bottle to make it glow. Final image output to film. " (Mural © 1982; Absolut Gartel © 1991 Gartel.)

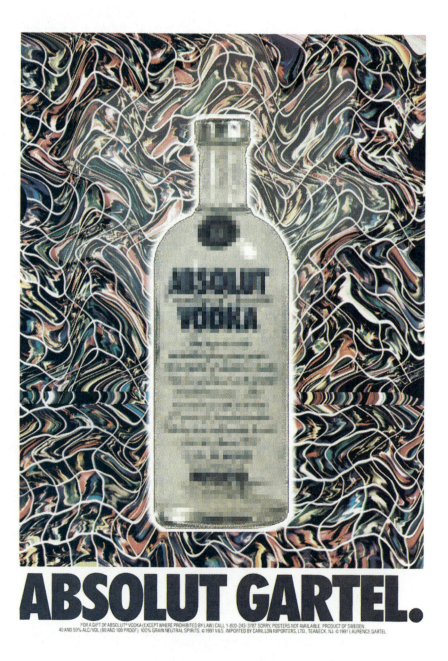

ABSOLUT GARTEL.

FOR A GIFT OF ABSOLUT® VODKA (EXCEPT WHERE PROHIBITED BY LAW) CALL 1-800-243-3787. SORRY, POSTERS NOT AVAILABLE. PRODUCT OF SWEDEN. 40 AND 50% ALC/VOL (80 AND 100 PROOF). 100% GRAIN NEUTRAL SPIRITS. ©1991 V&S. IMPORTED BY CARILLON IMPORTERS, LTD., TEANECK, N.J. ©1991 LAURENCE GARTEL.

Fig. 19-13 ■ This image by Laurence Gartel gives us a lesson in creativity. He photographed various scenes, people, and so on with a Canon Still-Video camera. Some of the older photos in the montage were taken by Gartel's family during trips to Florida in his childhood. They were scanned on a 1200 dpi scanner. All images were then assembled and manipulated in Adobe Photoshop. The final image was used on a poster for the Museum of Discovery and Science in Fort Lauderdale, Florida.("7-Up" © 1993 Laurence M. Gartel)

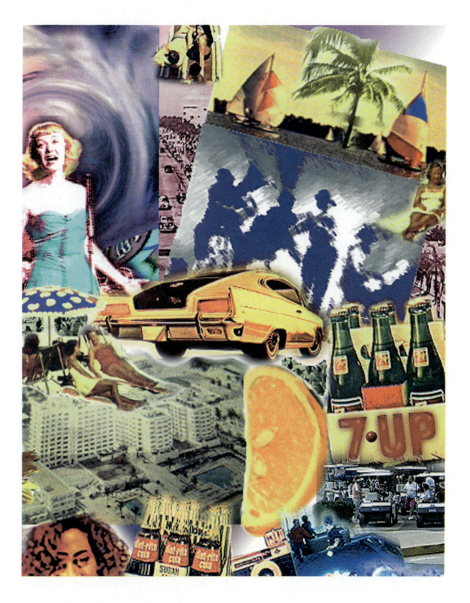

and 'portable' cameras that weighed 75 pounds." They were considered cutting-edge equipment at the time.

By 1978 Gartel saw electronic imaging as the future of our culture. "The advances in technology have changed at lightning speeds, so I have always attempted to work with the very latest 'state of the art' equipment."

"I have never put the emphasis on 'image resolution.'" This means, he explains, that the pixels in the picture do not get in the way of communicating ideas. Gartel points out that this might seem contradictory, but he cautions that photography gives creative license to bend, stretch, distort, or mutilate.

"Photography is the way you perceive and add to reality. Computers are an extension of photography, expanding and elaborating on a conventional process," Gartel explains. He believes computers release untapped creativity and a myriad of possibilities, some that would never have been considered without this new tool.

NOTES

[1]*Dictionary of Computer Terms* (New York: Barnes & Noble, 1993), p. 46.

[2]From *CBS News Sunday Morning,* January 16, 1994, transcript produced by Burrell's Information Service, Livingston, NJ).

[3]*Graphic Arts Monthly,* February 1994, p. 71.

[4]Ibid., pp. 47–48.

[5]*Funk & Wagnalls New Encyclopedia,* Volume 7, p. 74, 1986.

[6]*An Introduction to CD-ROM* (Pomona, CA: Autographics, Inc., 1993) pp. 1–3.

[7]"The Future of Print," *American Printer,* August 1986, p. 44.

[8]"Cocooning," *Electronic Publishing & Printing,* January/February 1989, p. 4.

[9]"Desktop Publishers in the Year 2000," *Journal of the Association of Desktop Publishers,* October 1993, p. 26–27.

[10]"Interesting Times," *PRE-,* May 1993, p. 32.

[11]"Desktop Publishers in the Year 2000," *Journal of the Association of Desktop Publishers,* October 1993, p. 40.

[12]Ibid., p. 38.

[13]Letter to the author, February 15, 1994.

A BASIC DESIGN LIBRARY

CONTENTS
- Books
- Sources for New Publications
- Periodicals

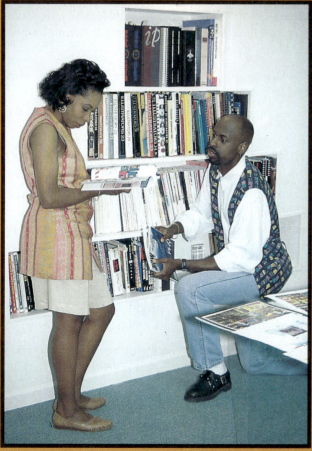

© 1994 Ernest Washington

It would be impossible and impractical to include a truly comprehensive list of publications in graphic design. However, the books and periodicals listed have been chosen to form a good, basic library for the graphics communicator.

➤ BOOKS

Adams, James L. *Conceptual Blockbusting*. Stanford, California: Stanford Alumni Association, 1974.

A concise, readable approach to creative problem solving with thought-provoking ideas of value to all who write or design.

American Institute of Graphic Arts. *Graphic Design: A Career Guide and Education Directory*. New York: American Institute of Graphic Arts, 1994.

Defines the practice and positions in the graphic design industry. Lists over 300 schools in the United States and Canada that offer four-year degrees in graphic design. Write to the Institute at 1059 Third Avenue, New York, NY 10021.

Arnold, Edmund C. *Designing the Total Newspaper*. New York: Harper & Row, 1981.

A comprehensive examination of all aspects of newspaper design by America's leading newspaper designer for many years.

Barnes & Noble. *Dictionary of Computer Terms*. New York: Barnes & Noble Books, 1993.

More than 3,000 definitions, symbols, and abbreviations in easy-to-understand explanations. The most comprehensive collection of computer terms anywhere. It is compact I keep it very close to my computer at all times.

Beach, Mark. *Editing Your Newsletter*. Portland, Oregon: Coast-to-Coast Books, 1982.

A guide to the writing, design, and production of newsletters. Excellent for beginners in newsletter production.

Beach, Mark and Ken Russon. *Papers for Printing: How to Choose the Right Paper at the Right Price for Any Printing Job*. Portland, Oregon: Coast-to-Coast Books, 1989.

This no-nonsense book describes classifications of paper, features and benefits of various stocks, selecting and specifying, and business considerations. Includes 40 samples of the most common papers specified by printing buyers.

Beaumont, Michael. *Type Design, Color, Character and Use*. Cincinnati: North Light Books, 1987.

A delightful, colorful, and profusely illustrated collection of typography from around the world.

Blum, Mike. *Understanding and Evaluating Desktop Publishing Systems*. San Luis Obispo, California: Graphic Services Publications, 1992.

An excellent overview of basic desktop publishing equipment. A good orientation booklet for the novice.

Bonura, Larry S. *Desktop Publisher's Dictionary*. Plano, Texas: Wordware Publishing, Inc., 1989.

A valuable addition to the professional library of anyone involved in graphics in this age of electronic publishing.

Bove, Tony. *The Art of Desktop Publishing*. New York: Bantam Books, 1987.

Probably the best introduction to desktop publishing for the novice. Very easy to understand.

Bovee, Courtland L. and William Arens. *Contemporary Advertising*. Homewood, Illinois: Richard D. Irwin, Inc, 1992.

A complete and readable basic advertising text. Helpful to anyone involved in advertising design and planning whether full time or occasionally.

Garcia, Mario R. *Contemporary Newspaper Design*. Englewood Cliffs, New Jersey: Prentice-Hall, 1984.

An outline of the basics of newspaper design, very contemporary, with many illustrations plus examples of redesign projects completed by the author.

Gottschall, Edward M. *Typographic Communications Today*. Cambridge, Massachusetts: MIT Press, 1989.

A handsomely produced critical review of 20th century typographic design. Over 900 images (half are in color) show influences on design and type, including examples from Japan, Finland, Brazil, Canada, and Czechoslovakia. A worthwhile reference.

Heller, Steven and Seymour Chwast. *Sourcebook of Visual Ideas*. New York: Van Nostrand Reinhold, 1989.

A collection of graphic solutions organized by category. It provides models, showing how others have solved common problems in fresh ways, while underscoring how personal style increases the effectiveness of an idea.

Hudson, Howard Penn. *Publishing Newsletters*. New York: Scribner's 1990.

This is considered the most complete guide to all aspects of newsletters, including editing and design.

International Paper Company. *Pocket Pal*. New York: International Paper, 1983.

A must for all those working with graphic arts. Write International Paper Company, 220 East 42nd Street, New York, NY 10017.

Kneller, George F. *The Art and Science of Creativity*. New York: Holt, Rinehart and Winston, 1965.

Easy reading, concise, and a good introduction to creativity.

Lem, Dean Phillip. *Graphics Master 4*. Los Angeles: Dean Lem Associates, 1986.

A workbook of planning aids, guides, and graphic tools for the design and production of printing; it also contains a line gauge and ruler, copy-fitting charts, and a photo sizing proportion scale.

Lindegren, Erik. *ABC of Lettering and Printing Typefaces*. New York: Greenwich House, 1982.

A collection of representatives typeface alphabets from the various races to use in selecting and tracing types.

Nelson, Roy Paul. *The Design of Advertising*. Dubuque, Iowa: Wm. C. Brown, 1989.

A comprehensive book on all aspects of advertising design and production with an overview of the basics of typography and graphics.

Nelson, Roy Paul. *Publication Design*. Dubuque, Iowa: Wm. C. Brown, 1991.

Emphasizes magazine and periodical design, and touches on newspapers and typography. It was originally published in 1972. Many illustrations.

Nesbitt, Alexander. *The History and Techniques of Lettering*. New York: Dover, 1957.

A classic by one of the leading students of letter forms and typography; it traces the development of letter forms and the basic races of types as well as their uses in typography and graphic design.

Parker, Roger C. *One Minute Designer*. Carmel, Indiana: Que Corporation. 1993.

A paperback choice full of ideas for desktop publishing. Very readable.

Rosen, Ben. *Type and Typography*. New York: Van Nostrand Reinhold, 1976.

A workbook for students of graphic design and all those who work with type. It contains more than 1,500 specimens and alphabets of text and display types.

Sanders, Norman. *Graphic Designer's Production Handbook*. New York: Hastings House, 1982.

A valuable, comprehensive reference work for anyone involved in the creation and production of printed communications. It explains with illustrations and diagrams such processes as overlays, keying, preparing for printing.

Sausmarez, Maurice de. *Basic Design: The Dynamics of Visual Form*. New York: Van Nostrand Reinhold, 1983.

A classic introduction to the basic elements and dynamics of design.

Tschichold, Jan. *Treasury of Alphabets and Lettering*. London: Omega Books, 1985.

An excellent treatise on the proper selection and arrangement of type. Contains many unique and historic alphabets.

V and M Typographical. *The Type Specimen Book*. New York: Van Nostrand Reinhold, 1974.

Complete alphabets of 544 different typefaces in more than 300 sizes.

Verbum. *The Desktop Color Book.* **Cardiff, California: Verbum, 1993.**
This is a splendid, well-written and well-illustrated book that gives a detailed, but very understandable explanation of desktop publishing and color. Should be in every desktop publisher's library. Write to Verbum, P.O. Box 189, Cardiff, CA 92007.

White, Jan V. *Mastering Graphics.* **New York: R. R. Bowker, 1983.**
A handy reference tool for those who edit or produce internal or external publications for businesses or organizations.

Wildbur, Peter. *Information Graphics.* **New York: Van Nostrand Reinhold, 1989.**
A survey of typographic, diagrammatic, and cartographic communication. Rather complex and not a beginners' book, but worthwhile as a reference.

➤ SOURCES FOR NEW PUBLICATIONS

In the fast-paced world of the information age, new books are being produced constantly. The following are sources for books on graphics and typography. Lists of current offerings are available.

Bacon's Publicity Checker
(In reference section of your library or write to them.)
Bacon's Information, Inc.
332 South Michigan Avenue
Chicago, IL 60604
Telephone: (312) 922–2400

Lists 50 or more publications concerning printing and graphic arts as well as nearly 300 magazines and newsletters concerning every aspect of computer applications and computer publishing and gives information about contents and location of each.

Desktop Publishing Institute
462 Old Boston St.
Topsfield, MA 01983
Home of the National Association of Desktop Publishers and publisher of the monthly *Desktop Publishers Journal.*

Dynamic Graphics, Inc.
6000 North Forest Park Drive
P.O. Box 1901
Peoria, IL 61656–1901
1–800–255–8800
Large selection of books and self-teaching videos.

Graphic Artist's Book Club
P.O. Box 12526
Cincinnati, OH 45212–0526

A "book-of-the-month" book club for graphic designers.

Graphic Arts Publishing, Inc.
3100 Bronson Hill Road
Livonia, NY 14487–9716
Telephone: 1–800–725–9476

Comprehensive catalog of the latest desktop publishing and graphics books.

Print Book Store
6400 Goldsboro Road
Bethesda, MD 20817

The Pointner Institute for Media Studies
801 Third Street, S
St. Petersburg, FL 33701

Contact Jo Cates, chief librarian, for a bibliography listing more than 150 books and periodicals covering all aspects of visual communication with addresses.

➤ PERIODICALS

Communication Arts—A bimonthly publication containing detailed reports on designers, illustrators, photographers, and art directors. *Communication Arts*, 410 Sherman Avenue, P.O. Box 10399, Palo Alto, CA 94303.

Communicators, The—A monthly publication of the International Association of Business Communicators that contains many articles and regular features on magazine design. IABC, 879 Market Street, Suite 940, San Francisco, CA 94102.

DESIGN—A quarterly journal of the professional society dedicated to improving newspapers through design; it provides information on newspapers undergoing design overhauls, computer graphics, trends. The Society of Newspaper Design, The Newspaper Center, Box 17290, Dulles International Airport, Washington, DC 20041.

Electronic Publishing—Published 18 times a year in newspaper format. Gives up-to-the-minute developments in the world of computer design. One of the best ways to keep up-to-date. Electronic Publishing and Typeworld, P.O. Box 2709, Tulsa, OK 74112.

Ninth Edition—An annual publication of the Society of Newspaper Design showing the winners in numerous categories of design. Issued yearly as First Edition, Second Edition, and so on. The Society of Newspaper Design, address above.

HOW—A bimonthly, profusely illustrated magazine emphasizing ideas and techniques in graphic design. Worthwhile but somewhat advanced for the neophite designer. HOW, Post Office Box 12575, Cincinnati, OH 45212–9927.

Newsletter on Newsletters, The—A twice-a-month newsletter for those who edit and produce newsletters; it contains a frequent "Graphics

Clinic" section. The Newsletter Clearinghouse, 44 West Market Street, P.O. Box 311, Rhinebeck, NY 12572.

Personal Publishing—A magazine for desktop publishers that monitors new products and emphasizes how to get the most out of your desktop programs. Personal Publishing, 191 South Gary Avenue, Carol Stream, IL 60188.

Print—A bimonthly, profusely illustrated design periodical; a source of new ideas and trends in design and typography. *Print,* 6400 Goldsboro Road NW, Washington, DC 20034.

Step-by-Step Electronic Design—A monthly newsletter for desktop publishers. *Step-by-Step Electronic Design,* 6000 N. Forest Park Drive, P.O. Box 1901, Peoria, IL 61656–9975.

Step-by-Step Graphics—As the title suggests, this is a practical, how-to-magazine in which designers and illustrators share their secrets and demonstrate how they work. Published seven times per year. *Step-by-Step Graphics,* 6000 North Forest Park Drive, P.O. Box 1901, Peoria, IL 61656–9975.

Technique—Subtitled "The How-To Guide to Successful Communications", this monthly magazine provides practical information on all aspects of print and electronic communications. It focuses on electronic design, and offers tips for using a wide range of software applications. Technique Subscriptions, P.O. Box 9164, Hyattsville, MD 20781–9164. 1–800–272–7377.

U&lc—A quarterly tabloid-size free magazine about typography; an excellent source of ideas. U&lc, International Typeface Corporation, 2 Hammarskjold Plaza, New York, NY 10017.

Publish!—A monthly magazine for desktop publishers that provides professional help in typography, graphics, page design and layout. Practical tips and how-to articles appear in every issue, as well as reviews of the latest technology. *Publish!,* Subscription Department, P.O. Box 51966, Boulder, CO 80321–1966.

TYPE SPECIMENS

72 POINT BERNHARD MODERN BOLD

ABCDEFGHI JKLMNOPQR STUVWXYZ

abcdefghijklm nopqrstuvwxyz

1234567890

36 POINT BERNHARD MODERN BOLD

ABCDEFGHIJKLMNOPQRSTU VWXYZ
abcdefghijklmnopqrstuvwxyz
1234567890

36 POINT BERNHARD MODERN BOLD ITALIC

ABCDEFGHIJKLMNOPQRSTU VWXYZ
abcdefghijklmnopqrstuvwxyz
1234567890$

24 POINT BERNHARD MODERN BOLD

ABCDEFGHIJKLMNOPQRSTUVWXYZ
abcdefghijklmnopqrstuvwxyz
1234567890$&

24 POINT BERNHARD MODERN BOLD ITALIC

ABCDEFGHIJKLMNOPQRSTUVWXYZ
abcdefghijklmnopqrstuvwxyz
1234567890$&

72 POINT BODONI BOLD

ABCDEFGHIJ
KLMNOPQR
STUVWXYZ
abcdefghijklm
nopqrstuvwxyz
1234567890$

36 POINT BODONI BOLD

ABCDEFGHIJKLMNOPQRSTUV WXYZ
abcdefghijklmnopqrstuvwxyz
1234567890$&

36 POINT BODONI BOLD ITALIC

ABCDEFGHIJKLMNOPQRSTUV WXYZ
abcdefghijklmnopqrstuvwxyz
1234567890$&

24 POINT BODONI BOLD

ABCDEFGHIJKLMNOPQRSTUVWXYZ
abcdefghijklm nopqrstuvwxyz
1234567890$&

24 POINT BODONI BOLD ITALIC

ABCDEFGHIJK LMNOPQRSTUVWXYZ
abcdefghijklm nopqrstuvwxyz
1234567890$&

72 POINT CASLON OLD STYLE

ABCDEFGHIJ
KLMNOPQRS
TUVWXYZ
abcdefghijklmn
opqrstuvwxyz
1234567890&$

36 POINT CASLON OLD STYLE

ABCDEFGHIJKLMNOPQRSTUV WXYZ

abcdefghijklmnopqrstuvwxyz

1234567890&$

36 POINT CASLON OLD STYLE ITALIC

ABCDEFGHIJKLMNOPQRS TUVWXYZ

abcdefghijklmnopqrstuvwxyz ABCD EGJKLMNPQRT 1234567890

24 POINT CASLON OLD STYLE

ABCDEFGHIJKLMNOPQRSTUVWXYZ

abcdefghijklmnopqrstuvwxyz

1234567890

24 POINT CASLON OLD STYLE ITALIC

ABCDEFGHIJKLMNOPQRSTUVWXYZ
abcdefghijklmnopqrstuvwxyz ABCDEGJK LMNP R TUY& 1234567890&$

72 POINT CENTURY EXPANDED BOLD

ABCDEFGHIJ
KLMNOPQRS
TUVWXYZ
abcdefghijklmn
opqrstuvwxyz
1234567890

36 POINT CENTURY EXPANDED BOLD

ABCDEFGHIJKLMNOPQRST UVWXYZ
abcdefghijklmnopqrstuvwxyz
1234567890

36 POINT CENTURY EXPANDED BOLD ITALIC

ABCDEFGHIJKLMNOPQRST UVWXYZ
abcdefghijklmnopqrstuvwxyz
1234567890

24 POINT CENTURY EXPANDED BOLD

ABCDEFGHIJKLMNOPQRSTUVWXYZ
abcdefghijklmnopqrstuvwxyz
1234567890

24 POINT CENTURY EXPANDED BOLD ITALIC

ABCDEFGHIJKLMNOPQRSTUVWXYZ
abcdefghijklmnopqrstuvwxyz
1234567890

72 POINT GARAMOND BOLD

ABCDEFGHIJ
KLMNOPQ
RSTUVWXYZ
abcdefghijklm
nopqrstuvwxyz
1234567890$&

36 POINT GARAMOND BOLD

ABCDEFGHIJKLMNOPQRSTUV WXYZ

abcdefghijklmnopqrstuvwxyz

1234567890$&

36 POINT GARAMOND BOLD ITALIC

ABCDEFGHIJKLMNOPQRSTUV WXYZ

abcdefghijklmnopqrstuvwxyz

1234567890$&

24 POINT GARAMOND BOLD

ABCDEFGHIJKLMNOPQRSTUVWXYZ
abcdefghijklmnopqrstuvwxyz
1234567890$&

24 POINT GARAMOND BOLD ITALIC

ABCDEFGHIJKL MNOPQRSTUVWXYZ
abcdefghijklmnopqrstuvwxyz
1234567890$&

72 POINT GOUDY BOLD

ABCDEFGHIJK
LMNOPQRSTU
VWXYZ
abcdefghijklmnop
qrstuvwxyz
1234567890

36 POINT GOUDY BOLD

ABCDEFGHIJKLMNOPQRST UVWXYZ
abcdefghijklmnopqrstuvwxyz
1234567890

36 POINT GOUDY BOLD ITALIC

ABCDEFGHIJKLMNOPQRST UVWXYZ
abcdefghijklmnopqrstuvwxyz
1234567890

24 POINT GOUDY BOLD

ABCDEFGHIJKLMNOPQRSTUVWXYZ
abcdefghijklmnopqrstuvwxyz
1234567890

24 POINT GOUDY BOLD ITALIC

ABCDEFGHIJKLMNOPQRSTUVWXYZ
abcdefghijklmnopqrstuvwxyz
1234567890

72 POINT PALATINO SEMIBOLD

ABCDEFGHIJK
LMNOPQRST
UVWXYZ
abcdefghijklmn
opqrstuvwxyz
1234567890
1234567890

36 POINT PALATINO SEMIBOLD

ABCDEFGHIJKLMNOPQRSTU VWXYZ

abcdefghijklmnopqrstuvwxyz
1234567890   1234567890

36 POINT PALATINO SEMIBOLD ITALIC

ABCDEFGHIJKLMNOPQRSTU VWXYZ

abcdefghijklmnopqrstuvwxyz
1234567890

24 POINT PALATINO SEMIBOLD

ABCDEFGHIJKLMNOPQRSTUVWXYZ
abcdefghijklmnopqrstuvwxyz
1234567890 1234567890

24 POINT PALATINO SEMIBOLD ITALIC

ABCDEFGHIJKLMNOPQRSTUVWXYZ
abcdefghijklmnopqrstuvwxyz
1234567890

72 POINT TIMES NEW ROMAN BOLD

ABCDEFGHIJ KLMNOPQRS TUVWXYZ& abcdefghijklmno pqrstuvwxyz 1234567890$

36 POINT TIMES NEW ROMAN BOLD

ABCDEFGHIJKLMNOPQRST UVWXYZ& abcdefghijklmnopqrstuvwxyz 1234567890$

36 POINT TIMES NEW ROMAN BOLD ITALIC

ABCDEFGHIJKLMNOPQRST UVWXYZ& abcdefghijklmnopqrstuvwxyz 1234567890$

24 POINT TIMES NEW ROMAN BOLD

ABCDEFGHIJKLMNOPQRSTUVWXYZ& abcdefghijklmnopqrstuvwxyz 1234567890$

24 POINT TIMES NEW ROMAN BOLD ITALIC

ABCDEFGHIJKLMNOPQRSTUVWXYZ& abcdefghijklmnopqrstuvwxyz 1234567890$

60 POINT WEISS

ABCDEFGHIJKLM
NOPQRSTUV
WXYZ&
abcdefghijklmnopqr
stuvwxyz
1234567890$

36 POINT WEISS

ABCDEFGHIJKLMNOPQRST
UVWXYZ&
abcdefghijklmnopqrstuvwxyz
1234567890$

72 POINT FRANKLIN GOTHIC BOLD

ABCDEFGHIJK
LMNOPQRSTU
VWXYZ
abcdefghijklmno
pqrstuvwxyz
12345

36 POINT FRANKLIN GOTHIC BOLD

ABCDEFGHIJKLMNOPQRST UVWXYZ
abcdefghijklmnopqrstuvwxyz
1234567890$&

36 POINT FRANKLIN GOTHIC BOLD ITALIC

ABCDEFGHIJKLMNOPQRST UVWXYZ
abcdefghijklmnopqrstuvwx yz 1234567890$&

24 POINT FRANKLIN GOTHIC BOLD

ABCDEFGHIJKLMNOPQRSTUVWXYZ
abcdefghijklmnopqrstuvwxyz
1234567890$&

24 POINT FRANKLIN GOTHIC BOLD ITALIC

ABCDEFGHIJKLMNOPQRSTUVWXYZ
abcdefghijklmnopqrstuvwxyz
1234567890$&

60 POINT FUTURA DEMIBOLD

ABCDEFGHIJKLMNO
PQRSTUTUVWXYZ
abcdefghijklmnopqrst
uvwxyz 1234567890

36 POINT FUTURA DEMIBOLD

ABCDEFGHIJKLMNOPQRSTUVWXY
Z abcdefghijklmnopqrstuvwxyz&
1234567890

36 POINT FUTURA DEMIBOLD ITALIC

ABCDEFGHIJKLMNOPQRSTUVWXY
Z abcdefghijklmnopqrstuvwxyz&
1234567890

60 POINT FUTURA LIGHT

ABCDEFGHIJKLMNOP QRSTUVWXYZ abcdefghijklmnopqrstuv wxyz& 1234567890

36 POINT FUTURA LIGHT

ABCDEFGHIJKLMNOPQRSTUVWXYZ
abcdefghijklmnopqrstuvwxyz&
1234567890

36 POINT FUTURA LIGHT ITALIC

ABCDEFGHIJKLMNOPQRSTUVWXYZ
abcdefghijklmnopqrstuvwxyz&
1234567890

72 POINT HELVETICA BOLD

ABCDEFGHIJKL
MNOPQRSTUV
WXYZ
abcdefghijklmno
pqrstuvwxyz&
1234567890

36 POINT HELVETICA BOLD

ABCDEFGHIJKLMNOPQRSTUV WXYZ
abcdefghijklmnopqrstuvwxyz& 1234567890

36 POINT HELVETICA BOLD ITALIC

ABCDEFGHIJKLMNOPQRSTUV WXYZ
abcdefghijklmnopqrstuvwxyz& 1234567890

24 POINT HELVETICA BOLD

ABCDEFGHIJKLMNOPQRSTUVWXYZ
abcdefghijklmnopqrstuvwxyz&
1234567890

24 POINT HELVETICA BOLD ITALIC

ABCDEFGHIJKLMNOPQRSTUVWXYZ
abcdefghijklmnopqrstuvwxyz&
1234567890

60 POINT HELVETICA

ABCDEFGHIJKLMN
OPQRSTUVWXYZ
abcdefghijklmnopqrst
uvwxyz 1234567890

36 POINT HELVETICA

ABCDEFGHIJKLMNOPQRS
TUVWXYZ
abcdefghijklmnopqrstuvwxyz&
1234567890

36 POINT HELVETICA ITALIC

ABCDEFGHIJKLMNOPQRS
TUVWXYZ
abcdefghijklmnopqrstuvwxyz&
1234567890

60 POINT HELVETICA LIGHT

ABCDEFGHIJKLMN
OPQRSTUVWXYZ
abcdefghijklmnopqrst
uvwxyz&1234567890

36 POINT HELVETICA LIGHT

ABCDEFGHIJKLMNOPQRST
UVWXYZ
abcdefghijklmnopqrstuvwxyz&
1234567890

36 POINT HELVETICA LIGHT ITALIC

ABCDEFGHIJKLMNOPQRST
UVWXYZ
abcdefghijklmnopqrstuvwxyz&
1234567890

72 POINT HELVETICA EXTRA BOLD

ABCDEFGHIJ
KLMNOPQRS
TUVWXYZ
abcdefghijklm
nopqrstuvwx
yz1234567890

36 POINT HELVETICA EXTRA BOLD

ABCDEFGHIJKLMNOPQ
RSTUVWXYZ
abcdefghijklmnopqrstuv
wxyz& 1234567890

60 POINT OPTIMA

ABCDEFGHIJKLMN OPQRSTUVWXYZ abcdefghijklmnopqrs tuvwxyz&1234567890

36 POINT OPTIMA

ABCDEFGHIJKLMNOPQRST UVWXYZ abcdefghijklmnopqrstuvwxyz& 1234567890

36 POINT OPTIMA ITALIC

ABCDEFGHIJKLMNOPQRST VWXYZ abcdefghijklmnopqrstuvwxyz& 1234567890

72 POINT UNIVERS 75

ABCDEFGHIJK
LMNOPQRS
TUVWXYZ
abcdefghijklmn
opqrstuvwxyz
1234567890

36 POINT UNIVERS 75

**ABCDEFGHIJKLMNOPQR
STUVWXYZ
abcdefghijklmnopqrstuvwxyz&
1234567890**

60 POINT UNIVERS 55

ABCDEFGHIJKLMN OPQRSTUVWXYZ abcdefghijklmnopqrs tuvwxyz& 1234567890

36 POINT UNIVERS 55

ABCDEFGHIJKLMNOPQRSTU
VWXYZ
abcdefghijklmnopqrstuvwxyz&
1234567890

36 POINT UNIVERS 56

ABCDEFGHIJKLMNOPQRSTU
VWXYZ
abcdefghijklmnopqrstuvwxyz&
1234567890

60 POINT UNIVERS 45

ABCDEFGHIJKLMN
OPQRSTUVWXYZ
abcdefghijklmnopqrst
uvwxyz&
1234567890

36 POINT UNIVERS 45

ABCDEFGHIJKLMNOPQRSTUV
WXYZ
abcdefghijklmnopqrstuvwxyz&
1234567890

36 POINT UNIVERS 46

ABCDEFGHIJKLMNOPQRSTUV
WXYZ
abcdefghijklmnopqrstuvwxyz&
1234567890

72 POINT STYMIE BOLD

ABCDEFGHIJK
LMNOPQRST
UVWXYZ
abcdefghijklm
nopqrstuvwxyz
1234567890

36 POINT STYMIE BOLD

ABCDEFGHIJKLMNOPQRST UVWXYZ
abcdefghijklmnopqrstuvwxyz
1234567890

36 POINT STYMIE BOLD ITALIC

ABCDEFGHIJKLMNOPQRST UVWXYZ
abcdefghijklmnopqrstuvwxyz
1234567890

24 POINT STYMIE BOLD

ABCDEFGHIJKLMNOPQRSTUVWXYZ
abcdefghijklmnopqrstuvwxyz&
1234567890

24 POINT STYMIE BOLD ITALIC

ABCDEFGHIJKLMNOPQRSTUVWXYZ
abcdefghijklmnopqrstuvwxyz&
1234567890

36 POINT STYMIE LIGHT

ABCDEFGHIJKLMNOPQRST UVWXYZ
abcdefghijklmnopqrstuvwxyz&
1234567890

36 POINT STYMIE LIGHT ITALIC

ABCDEFGHIJKLMNOPQRST UVWXYZ
abcdefghijklmnopqrstuvwxyz&
1234567890

24 POINT STYMIE MEDIUM

ABCDEFGHIJKLMNOPQRSTUVWXYZ
abcdefghijklmnopqrstuvwxyz&
1234567890

24 POINT STYMIE MEDIUM ITALIC

ABCDEFGHIJKLMNOPQRSTUVWXYZ
abcdefghijklmnopqrstuvwxyz&
1234567890

48 POINT STYMIE EXTRA BOLD

AABCDEFGHIJKL MNOPQRSTUVW XYZ aabcdefghijklmnop qrstuvwxyz 1234567890

36 POINT STYMIE EXTRA BOLD

AABCDEFGHIJKLMNOP QRSTUVWXYZ aabcdefghijklmnopqrstu vwxyz 1234567890

48 POINT STYMIE OPEN

ABCDEFGHIJKL
MNOPQRSTUV
WXYZ&
1234567890$

36 POINT STYMIE OPEN

ABCDEFGHIJKLMNOP
QRSTUVWXYZ&
1234567890$

24 POINT STYMIE OPEN

ABCDEFGHIJKLMNOPQRSTUV
WXYZ&
1234567890$

24 POINT GOLD RUSH

ABCDEFGHIJKLMNOPQ
RSTUVWXYZ
1234567890$&

36 POINT HELLENIC WIDE

ABCDEFGHIJ
KLMNOPQRS
TUVWXYZ
abcdefghijklm
nopqrstuvwxyz
1234567890

ABCDEFGHIJKLM
NOPQRSTUVW
XYZ abcdefghijk
lmnopqrstuvwxyz
1234567890$&

48 POINT P. T. BARNUM

ABCDEFGHIJKLMNOPQRST
UVWXYZ
abcdefghijklmnopqrstuvw
xyz 1234567890$&

36 POINT LUBALIN GRAPH LIGHT

ABCDEFGHIJKLMNOPQRSTU
VWXYZ
abcdefghijklmnopqrstuvwxyz
1234567890

36 POINT LUBALIN GRAPH BOOK

ABCDEFGHIJKLMNOPQRSTU
VWXYZ
abcdefghijklmnopqrstuvwxyz
1234567890

36 POINT LUBALIN GRAPH BOLD

ABCDEFGHIJKLMNOPQRS
TUVWXYZ
abcdefghijklmnopqrstuvw
vwxyz&
1234567890

48 POINT TOWER

ABCDEFGHIJKLMNOPQRSTUV
WXYZ
abcdefghijklmnopqrstuvwxyz
1234567890

36 POINT TOWER

ABCDEFGHIJKLMNOPQRSTUVWXYZ
abcdefghijklmnopqrstuvwxyz
1234567890

36 POINT TRYLON

ABCDEFGHIJKLMNOPQRSTUVWXYZ&
abcdefghijklmnopqrstuvwxyz
1234567890$

SCRIPT AND CURSIVE TYPES

---

48 POINT BERNHARD TANGO

ABCDEFGHIJKLMNOPQ
RSTUVWXYZ
abcdefghijklmnopqrstuvwxyz
1234567890

---

48 POINT CORONET BOLD

ABCDEFGHIJKLMNO
PQRSTUVWXYZ&
abcdefghijklmnopqrstuvwxyz
1234567890$

72 POINT BRUSH

ABCDEFGHIJ
KLMNOP2R
STUVWXY3
abcdefghijklmnopqrst
uvwxyz1234567890

36 POINT BRUSH

ABCDEFGHIJKLMNOP2
RSTUVWXY3
abcdefghijklmnopqrstuvwxyz
1234567890$$&

60 POINT LYDIAN CURSIVE

ABCDEFGHIJKLMN
OPQRSTUVWXYZ
abcdeefghijklmnopqrstuv
wxyz
1234567890

36 POINT LYDIAN CURSIVE

ABCDEFGHIJKLMNOPQRSTUVW
XYZ
abcdeefghijklmnopqrstuvwxyz
1234567890

48 POINT LEGEND

$ABCDEFGHIJKLMNOP$

$QRSTUVWXYZ$

abcdefghijklmnopqrstuvwxyz

1234567890

36 POINT LIBERTY

$ABCDEFGHIJKLMNOPQ$

$RSTUVWXYZ$

abcdefghijklmnopqrstuvwxyz

1234567890

48 POINT MISTRAL

ABCDEFGHIJKLMNOPQRSTU
VWXYZ&
abcdefghijklmnopqrstuvwxyz
1234567890$

48 POINT STRADIVARIUS

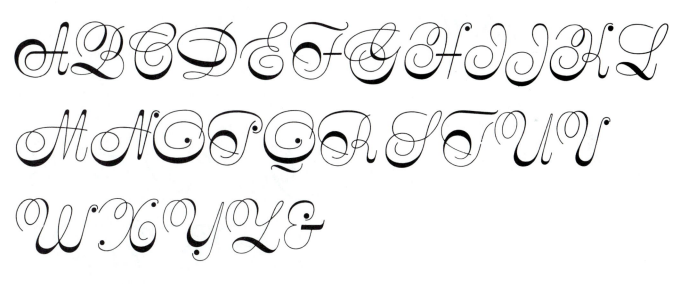

ABCDEFGHIJKL
MNOPQRSTUV
WXYZ&

abcdefghijklmnopqrstuvwxyz

1234567890$

48 POINT SHELLEY ALLEGRO SCRIPT

ABCDEFGHIJK
LMNOPQRSTUVW
XYZ

abcdefghijklmnopqrstuvwxyz

1234567890$

---

48 POINT SHELLEY VOLANTE SCRIPT

ABCDEFGHIJK
LMNOPQRSTUV
WXYZ

abcdefghijklmnopqrstuvwxyz

1234567890$

BLACK LETTER TYPES

72 POINT AMERICAN TEXT

ABCDEFGHIJKLM
NOPQRSTUVWXYZ
abcdefghijklmnopqrstuvw
xyz 1234567890

36 POINT AMERICAN TEXT

ABCDEFGHIJKLMNOPQRSTUVWXYZ
abcdefghijklmnopqrstuvwxyz.-:;,ˇ!?$&
1234567890

60 POINT CASTLE

𝔄𝔅ℭ𝔇𝔉𝔊ℌ𝔍𝔎

𝔏𝔐𝔑𝔒𝔓𝔔ℜ𝔖𝔗

𝔘𝔙𝔚𝔛𝔜𝔷

abcdfghijklmnop

qrstuvwxyz

1234567890$

60 POINT CLOISTER BLACK

ABCDEFGHIJK
LMNOPQ
RSTUVWXYZ&
abcdefghijklmnopqrstu
vwxyz 1234567890$

36 POINT CLOISTER BLACK

ABCDEFGHIJKLMNOPQ
RSTUVWXYZ&
abcdefghijklmnopqrstuvwxyz
1234567890$

72 POINT GOUDY TEXT

ABCDEFGHIJ
KLMNOPQ
RSTUVWXYZ
abcdefghijklmnopqrstu
vwxyz 1234567890$

36 POINT GOUDY TEXT

ABCDEFGHIJKLMNOPQR
STUVWXYZ&
abcdefghijklmnopqrstuvwxyz
1234567890$

MISCELLANEOUS AND NOVELTY TYPES

36 POINT AMELIA

ABCDEFGHIJKKLMNOPQRSTUVWXYZ
abcdef ghijklmnopqrstuvwxyz
1234567890&!?$

36 POINT GALLIA

ABCDEFGHIJKLMN
OPQRSTUVWXYZ&
1234567890$
AERST

36 POINT KISMET

ABCDEFGHIJKLMNOPQRSTUVW
XYZ
abcdefghijklmnopqrstuvluwxxyz
1234567890&$?

36 POINT PAISLEY ONE

ABCDEFGHIJKLMNOPQR
STUVWXYZ
abcdefghijklmnopqrstuvwxyz
1234567890$

36 POINT PAISLEY TWO

ABCDEFGHIJKLMNOPQR
STUVWXYZ
abcdefghijklmnopqrstuvwxyz
1234567890$

36 POINT PAISLEY TWO ALTERNATE

ABCDEFGHIJKLMNOPQR
STUVWXYZ
abcdefghijklmnopqrstuvwxyz
1234567890$

60 POINT POSTER ROMAN BOLD

ABCDEFGHIJKL
MNOPQRSTU
VWXYZ&
abcdefghijklmnopq
rstuvwxyz
1234567890$

36 POINT POSTER ROMAN BOLD

ABCDEFGHIJKLMNOPQRST
UVWXYZ&
abcdefghijklmnopqrstuvwxyz
1234567890$

---

36 POINT PRISMA

ABCDEFGHIJKLMNOPQR
STUVWXYZ&
1234567890$

---

36 POINT ROMANTIQUE

ABCDEFGHIJKLMN
OPQRSTUVWXYZ&
1234567890

---

36 POINT SMOKE

ABCDEFGHIJKLMNOPQRSTUVWXYZ
abcdefghijklmnopqrstuvwxyz
1234567890&!?$

---

36 POINT STENCIL

ABCDEFGHIJKLMN
OPQRSTUVWXYZ&
1234567890$

48 POINT STUDIO

ABCDEFGHIJKLMNOPQ RSTUVWXYZ& abcdefghijklmnopqrstu vwxyz 1234567890$

36 POINT STUDIO

ABCDEFGHIJKLMNOPQRSTU VWXYZ& abcdefghijklmnopqrstuvwxyz 1234567890$

GLOSSARY

A

Access To retrieve information from a storage device (internal memory, disk, tape). Access time is the time it takes to retrieve the stored data.

Accordian fold Two or more parallel folds with adjacent folds in opposite directions.

Achromatic The absence of color; black, gray, or white.

Agate This is 5½-point type. There are fourteen agate lines in 1 inch. The term is used to measure advertisements and can be used to designate tabular and classified matter in newspapers.

Alignment The positioning of letters so all have a common baseline; it also refers to the even placement of lines of type or art.

Alphabet length The width of lowercase (usually) characters when lined up *a* through *z*.

Ampersand The symbol used for *and* (&).

Antique A coarse and uneven paper finish.

Ascender The letter stroke that extends above the x height of a lowercase character.

B

Bank One line of a multiline headline.

Banner A large multicolumn headline, usually extending across the top of page 1 in a newspaper.

Base alignment The positioning of characters so the bottom of the x height lines up evenly on a horizontal line; in phototypesetting this alignment is used for the even positioning of different type styles on a common line.

Ben Day The regular pattern of dots or lines used to add tonal variation to line art.

Bezier curves Curved lines that are used in computer illustration for drawing and type rendering. These points set the shape of a curve.

bf The designation for setting type in boldface.

Bidirectional printer A printing device that speeds hard copy production by printing left to right and then right to left and so on until the printout is completed.

Bit Binary digiT. This is the single digit of a binary number; 10 is composed of two bits. Also the smallest unit of information making up the digital or dot image of a character or graphic; small parts of a letter; just little dots.

Bit-map graphic A graphic image document formed by a series of dots, with a specific number of dots per inch. Also called a "paint-type" graphic.

Black Letter A race or group of type characterized by its resemblance to medieval northern European manuscript characters.

Bleed To run art to the edge of the page.

Blind embossing Embossing (see below) without printing.

Block A group of words, characters, or digits forming a single unit in a computerized system.

Block letter A letterform without serifs (the finishing stroke at the end of a letter), in the Sans Serif type group.

Blueline Copy composed of blue lines on a white background.

Blurb Copy written with a sales angle, usually in brief paragraphs.

Body type "Reading matter" type as differentiated from display or headline type.

Boldface Characters of normal form but heavier strokes.

Bond paper Paper with a hard, smooth finish for ruling, typing, and pen writing.

Boot Getting your computer going; getting it started up and into the program you're going to use.

Border A frame around the type, art, or complete layout in either plane lines or an ornamental design.

Bowl the interior part of a letter in a circle form such as in a *b, c, d,* or *o.*

Box A border or rule that frames type.

Bracketed serif A serif (see below) connected to the character stem with a curved area at the connecting angle.

Break of the book The allocation of space for articles, features, and all material printed in the magazine.

Broadsheet A standard-size newspaper page as contrasted to the small tabloid size.

Brownline A brown-line image on a white background.

Bullet A round, solid ornament resembling a large period: •.

Byte A number of binary digits, or bits, needed to encode one character such as a letter, punctuation mark, number, or symbol.

C

Calender The process in papermaking that creates the amount of smoothness in the paper.

C&lc The symbols for setting type in which the first character of each word is capitals.

Camera ready The completed image from which a printing plate is made.

Canned format The specifications for composition and/or makeup of type

501

kept on magnetic or paper tape for repeated use to command a typesetter.

Capitals Large characters, the original form of Latin characters.

Caption The term used in magazine layout for the explanatory matter accompanying art; usually called a *cutline* in newspaper editing and layout.

Card A printed circuit board; computer systems are made up these boards.

Cast off To determine the space a type-written manuscript will occupy when set in type.

Catchline A line of display type between a picture and cutline.

Cathode ray tube (CRT) An electronic tube used to project images on a screen; it is also called a *visual display unit;* a television picture tube.

CEPS Abbreviation for color electronic prepress system, a high-end computer system that is used to correct colors and assemble images into final pages.

Clipboard A temporary holding place for material, in the computer. You can store text, graphics, or a group selection on a clipboard for later use.

Cloning Pixel manipulation used in image processing to add or remove detail in a picture.

Colophon The data about design, type styles, and production of a book; usually found at the end of the book.

Combination plate Halftone and line art on a single printing plate.

Composing room The area of a printing plant where type is set and arranged for plate making or printing.

Comprehensive A completed, detailed layout ready for making a plate; also called a *comp.*

Computer graphics Any charts, diagrams, drawings, and/or art composed on a computer.

Condensed type A vertically compressed character.

Constants The typographic and graphic elements in a publication that don't change from issue to issue.

Continuous tone Any art, such as a photograph or painting, which contains black and white and the variations of grays between the two.

Contract proof A color proof that printer and client agree is exactly how the printed product will appear.

Copy Information to be printed or reproduced.

Copy block A segment of body type or reading matter in a layout.

Copy fitting Determining the area a certain amount of copy will occupy when set in type.

Crop To eliminate unwanted material or change the dimensions of art.

Cropping L The two right angles used to frame art to determine where it should be cropped.

Cursive A form of type that resembles handwriting.

Cursor A spot of light on a video screen that the user manipulates to indicate where changes in copy are to be made.

Cut A piece of art ready for printing; originally referred to as a mounted engraving used in letterpress printing.

Cutline The descriptive or identifying information printed with art—a caption.

Cutoff rule The dividing rule between elements, usually used in newspaper format.

Cyan A vivid blue color used in process (full color) color printing.

Cylinder press A printing press in which the form to be printed is flat and the impression is made on paper clamped on a cylinder that is rolled over the form.

D

Daisy wheel A metal or plastic disk with typewriter characters on spokes redialing from its center. It is about 3 inches in diameter. Hard copy printers can be equipped with more than one daisy wheel to mix faces. On typewriters, the wheel can produce type with differential spacing.

Dash A small horizontal rule in layouts; also a punctuation mark.

Data base A collection of information that is organized and stored so that an application program can access individual items.

Debugging Correcting errors in programs.

Deck One unit of a headline set in a single type size and style.

Densitometer A tool used to measure the density (darkness) of visual images and check colors and to control color processes.

Descender A stroke of a lowercase letter that extends below the x height.

Digital computer A device used to manipulate data and perform calculations; most work on the binary number system (the number system based on powers of 2 rather than powers of 10).

Digitized type A form of type produced photographically by computer instructions created by patterns of black and white spots similar to the way television images are produced.

Dingbat A typographic ornament.

Diskette A flexible plastic recording medium, also called floppy disks or flexible disks.

Double pyramid The placement of advertisements on a page or facing pages to form a center "well" for editorial material.

Double truck A single advertisement that occupies two facing pages.

Download To transfer data from one electronic device to another. You could download information from one computer to another with a modem, for instance, or you could download information from a hard disk to a floppy disk.

Downloadable fonts Fonts that you can buy separately and install so as to expand the variety of fonts available on your printer.

Downstyle A form of headline in which only the first word and proper nouns are capitalized.

dpi Dots per inch.

DTP Desktop publishing

Dummy A "blueprint" or pattern, usually half size for newspaper pages, used as a guide in making finished layout or pasteup.

Duotone A technique for color printing in which two plates are made from a black and white photo and printed in different colors to produce a single image.

E

Ear The editorial matter alongside the nameplate (the name of the publication) on page 1.

Em A unit of space equal to the square of the type size being used.

Embossing The process of impressing an image in relief to achieve a raised surface over printing. Embossing on blank paper is called *blind embossing.*

En A unit of space that is the vertical half of an em.

Extended A form of type in which the normal character structure is widened.

F

Face The style of a type, such as boldface.

Family A major division of typefaces.

File A collection of stored information with matching formats, the computer version of filing cabinets.

Finder The file that manages all the other files; the finder is like an index; it saves, names, renames, and deletes things in a file.

Flag Synonymous with *nameplate;* the name of the publication in a distinctive design.

Flexography Printing from relief plates usually made of rubber as in letterpress but using a water-base ink rather than paste ink.

Floating flag A flag set in narrow width and displayed in a position other than the top of a page.

Flush left Type set even on the left margin and uneven on the right margin.

Flush right Type set with uneven lines on the left and even lines on the right margin.

Folio lines Originally the page numbers, but usually now the line giving date, volume, and number; or page number, name of publication, and date in small type on the inside pages.

Font All the characters and punctuation marks of one size and style of type.

Font downloader A device used in computer imaging to send digital font information from a computer to an output device.

Footer One or more lines of text that appear at the bottom of every page, similar to folio lines or running feet.

Form All the typographic elements used in a particular printed piece arranged to be placed on a printing press.

Format The general appearance of a printed piece, including the page size and number of columns per page.

Foundry type Printing type made of individual characters cast from molten metal.

Frame A newspaper makeup pattern in which the left and right outside columns are each filled with a single story.

Function code A computer code that controls the machine's operations other than the output of typographic characters.

Functional typography A philosophy of design in which every element used does an efficient and necessary job.

G

Galley A three-sided metal tray used to hold type; the term also refers to long strips of printed photographic or cold type ready to be proofread and used to make pasteups.

Galley proof The impression of type used for making corrections.

Gigabyte A thousand megabytes or one billion bytes.

Gothic A group, or race, of monotonal types that have no serifs; also called *Sans Serif.*

Gravure An intaglio (see below) printing method that uses recessed plates.

Grid In graphic design, a pattern of horizontal and vertical guidelines for making layouts or dummies; in typesetting, an image carrier (a piece of film containing the characters) for a font of type for phototypesetting.

Grotesk The European name for Gothic type.

Gutter The margin of the page at the point of binding, or the inside page margin.

H

Hairline The thinnest rule used in printing, or the thinnest stroke in a letter form.

Halftone A printing plate made by photographing an image through a screen so that the image is reproduced in dots.

Hanging indent A headline style in which the first line is full width and succeeding lines are indented the same amount from the left margin.

Hanging punctuation Punctuation set outside the margins of justified text. Some designers consider this to be aesthetically superior to setting puctuation within the line length.

Hard copy Printed or typed copy, usually the printout from a computer or word processor or similar device.

Hardware The actual equipment that makes up a computer system (see also *software*).

Head An abbreviation for headline.

Header Same as footer, but at the top of each page; like a running head.

Headletter The type used for headlines.

Headline The title of an article or news story.

Headline schedule A chart showing all the styles and sizes of headlines used by a publication.

Highlight The lightest portion of a half-tone photograph; the area having the smallest dots or no dots at all.

Horizontal makeup An arrangement of story units across columns rather than vertically.

Hot metal Type, borders, and rules made of molten metal cast in molds.

Hue A color, or the quality that distinguishes colors in the visible spectrum.

H&J Hyphenation and justification; there are programs that will do the hyphenation of text for you following a standard dictionary.

I

Icon A small graphic image that identifies a tool, file, or command displayed on a computer screen.

Imagesetter A typesetter connected to the desktop publishing work station that records art as well as type. There are two main types of imagesetters—flatbed and drum.

Imposition An arrangement of pages for printing so they will appear in proper order for folding.

Impression cylinder A printing press unit that presses paper on an inked form to make the print.

Initial The first letter in a word set in a larger or more decorative face, usually used at the beginning of an article, section, or paragraph.

Ink-jet printing A method of placing characters on paper by spraying a mist of ink through tiny holes in the patterns of the characters.

Inline A style of type in which a white line runs down the main stroke of the letter.

Insert Reference lines inserted in the body of an article; also called a *refer* or *sandwich*.

Intaglio A printing method in which the image is carved into, or recessed, in the plate; also called *gravure*.

Inverted pyramid A headline style in which each centered line is narrower than its predecessor; term is also used for a newswriting form.

Italic A form of Roman type design that slants to the right.

J

Jaggies The ragged edges of an image that are produced when a digital or circular line is scanned into a system. Jaggies are caused by lack of resolution; some say they resemble stair steps.

Jim dash A small rule—usually used to separate decks in a headline or title.

Jump head A headline on the part of a story continued from another page.

Justify Setting type so the left and right margins are even.

K

Kerning Placing two adjacent characters so that part of one is positioned within the space of the other; kerning may be controlled by the keyboard operator or programmed into the computer.

Keylining A process of using an overlay in a layout to indicate color separations, reverses, outlines, or other special effects.

Kicker A small headline, usually underlined, above a main headline.

Kilobyte 1,024 bytes or 1K; a 3½ inch floppy disk holds 800 kilobytes (800K) or about 400 double-spaced typewritten pages (a rough estimate).

L

Layout A diagram or plan, drawing, or sketch used as a guide in arranging elements for printing.

lc The abbreviation for lowercase.

lca The abbreviation for lowercase alphabet.

Lead The space between lines of type, usually 2 points (pronounced "led").

Leaders The dots or dashes often used in tabular matter.

Letterpress A printing method that uses raised images.

Letterspace The space added to the normal spacing between the letters in a word.

Ligature Two or more characters joined to make a single unit.

Lightface Characters with strokes that have less weight than normal.

Light pen An electronic stylus used to position elements or indicate changes in copy on a CRT.

Line art A piece of art or a plate in black and white, not continuous tones.

Line conversion A line printing plate made from a continuous tone original by eliminating the halftone screen.

Linen paper A paper made from linen or having a finish resembling linen cloth.

Lines per inch (lpi) Rating of halftone screens. Lines per inch represent rows of halftone dots per linear inch. A 150-line screen would consist of 150 rows by 150 rows of halftone dots per inch.

Lithography A flat-surface printing method based on the principle that oil and water are mutually repellent.

Logo Abbreviation for logotype.

Logotype A distinctive type arrangement used for the name of a publication, business, or organization.

Lowercase The small letters of the alphabet.

M

Magenta Also called *process red;* it is a purplish red color and is used in process (or full) color printing.

Magnetic ink An ink that contains ferrous (iron) material that can be sensed magnetically.

Makeup The art of arranging elements on a page for printing.

Markup The process of writing instructions on a layout for the size and styles of types and the other elements desired by the designer.

Masthead The area in a publication that lists the staff, date of publication, and other pertinent information.

Matrix (mat) The brass mold from which type is cast (or molded) in the hot metal process.

Measure The width of the lines being set.

Mechanical A pasteup ready for plate making.

Mechanical separation Copy prepared by a designer with each individual color in a separate section.

Megabyte (MB) One million bytes of information or 1,048,567 bytes.

Menu A list of commands that appears when you point to and press the menu title in the menu bar.

Menu bar The area at the top of a computer screen by which the user can access the actual pull-down menus.

Mezzotint A screen used for creating a crayon drawing effect on a printing plate.

Middletone Tonal values of a picture midway between the highlight and shadow. Sometimes called midtone.

Minimum line length The shortest width of lines of type of acceptable readability.

Minuscules Small characters.

Minus leading The elimination of space between lines; a technique possible with photographic or electronic typesetting.

Minus letterspacing Reducing the normal space between characters; a technique possible with photographic or electronic typesetting.

Miter To cut a rule or border at a 45-degree angle for making corners on a box.

Mixing Combining more than one style or size of type on the same line.

Mnemonics Ancient memory-aiding devices; also used to refer to abbreviations of complex terms used in encoding computer instructions.

Mock-up A full-size, experimental layout for study and evaluation.

Modem A telecommunications device that translates computer signals into electronic signals that can be sent over a telephone line; a way to get information from one computer to another or from your computer to a print shop and so on.

Modular makeup The arrangement of elements in rectangular units on a page, also called *Mondrian*.

Moiré A distracting pattern that results when a previously screened halftone is screened again and printed.

Mondrian makeup The arrangement of elements into rectangles of various sizes and shapes, also called *modular*.

Monospaced type A typeface where each character occupies the same amount of horizontal space.

Monotonal Typefaces with strokes of equal thickness.

Montage A composite picture, usually made of two or more combined photographs.

Mortise An area cut out of a piece of art for the insertion of type or other art.

Mug shot A head and shoulders photograph.

N

Nameplate The name of a publication set in a distinctive type form, also called *flag*.

Newsprint A low-quality paper mainly used for printing handbills and newspapers.

Notch mortise A rectangle cut from a corner of a rectangular illustration.

Novelty A category of type that is usually ornamental in design and does not display any strong characteristics of one of the basic races or species.

O

Object-oriented graphic An illustration created in an object-oriented, or draw-type application. An object-oriented graphic is created with geometric elements. Also called a "draw-type" graphic.

Oblique Letters that slant to the right, usually Sans Serif or Square Serif; Roman slanted letters are called *italics*.

OCR (optical character recognition) A device that electronically reads and encodes printed or typewritten material.

Offset A printing process in which the image is transferred from a printing plate to a rubber blanket to paper.

Old style A Roman typeface subdivision characterized by bracketed serifs and little difference between the thick and thin strokes.

Opaque Something that blocks light; in paper a lack of show-through.

Optical center A point about 10 percent above the mathematical center of a page or area.

Optimum format A format in which the width of the type columns is within the range of maximum readability.

Optimum line length The line width at which reading is easiest and fastest.

Ornament A decorative typographic device.

Orphan In typeset copy, a single word or a short line left at the bottom of a column or page (see widow).

Outline A type design in which the letter is traced or outlined by lines on the outside of the strokes and the inside of the letter is blank.

Overlay A sheet of transparent plastic or paper placed over a piece of art or a layout on which instructions are written and areas to be printed in color are drawn.

Overline A display type heading placed above a picture.

Overprint To print over an area that has already been printed.

Overset Body matter that exceeds the allotted space.

Oxford rule Parallel heavy and light lines.

P

Page description language (PDL) Software that describes an entire page including all its elements. PostScript is a popular page description language for computer publishing.

Pagination The process of arranging pages for printing; a computer-generated page layout; and/or the numbering of the pages of a book.

Parallel fold Two or more folds in the same direction.

Pasteup The process of fixing type and other elements on a grid for plate making; a *mechanical*.

Pebbling Embossing paper in its manufacture to create a ripple effect.

Perfect binding A method of binding that uses flexible glue rather than stitching.

Photocomposition Phototypesetting by film or paper.

Photoengraving A printing plate with a raised surface.

Photolithography An offset printing process that uses a plate made by a photographic process.

Phototypesetter A device that sets type by a photographic process; letter images are recorded on light-sensitive film or photographic paper that is then developed and printed.

Pi To mix type; individual metal characters that have been mixed up by accident.

Pica A 12-point unit of measurement.

Pixel (picture element) The smallest part of a graphic that can be controlled through a program. You could think of it as a building block used to construct type and images. The resolution of text and graphics on your screen depends on the density of your screen's pixels.

Planography A printing process that uses a plate with a flat surface; offset lithography is a planographic process.

Plate A printing surface.

Platen press A machine in which paper is held on a flat surface and pressed against the form for printing.

PMT (photo mechanical transfer) A positive print that is ready for pasteup.

Point A unit of measurement approximately 1/72 of an inch.

Pork chop A small head shot of a person, usually half a column wide.

Poster makeup An arrangement of a newspaper's front page that usually consists of large art and a few headlines to attract attention.

Prescreen   A halftone positive print that can be combined with line copy in pasteup, thus eliminating the need to strip in a screened negative with a line copy negative.

Primary color   The colors red, yellow, and blue, which combine to make all other hues.

Primary optical center   The spot where a reader's eye usually first lights on a page, the upper left quadrant.

Process color   Printing the three primary colors in combination to produce all colors; full color.

Production department   The mechanical department of a printing plant.

Proof   A preliminary print of set type or a comprehensive, used to detect errors before the final printing.

Prototype   A mock-up; a model that is the pattern for the final product.

Pyramid   An arrangement of advertisements on a page to form a stepped half pyramid.

Q

Quad   A unit of space in setting type.

Quad left, quad middle, quad right Commands that instruct a typesetting machine to put space in lines.

Quadrant makeup   A plan for a page in which each quarter is given a strong design element.

R

Race   The basic division of type styles, sometimes called *species;* type groups.

Ragged right   Type set unjustified (uneven) at the right margins.

Ragged left   The opposite of ragged right.

RAM   Random access memory; the temporary memory inside the computer that allows you to find stored text and graphics.

Readability   The characteristic of type and/or its arrangement that makes it easy to read.

Readout   The headline or unit of a headline between a banner head and the story; also used to refer to devices for breaking up body matter such as

quotes (called quote-outs or pulled quotes) set in display type and embellished with typographic devices.

Recto   In book or pamphlet design, the odd-numbered, right-hand pages.

Register   To line up color printing plates so the multiple impressions will create an accurate reproduction of the original.

Relief printing   Printing from a raised surface; letterpress.

Repro (reproduction proof)   The final image used for pasteup and plate making.

Resolution   The number of dots per inch (dpi) used to represent a character or graphic image. The higher the resolution the more dots per inch and the clearer the image looks.

Reverse   A printing area in which the background is black and the image is white.

Reverse kicker   A headline form in which the kicker is larger than the primary headlines.

Reverse leading   The technique of operating a phototypesetting device so superior figures or mixed display type can be added to the line.

Rivers   Vertical strips of white space in areas of type created by excessive space between words; also called "rivers of white."

Roman   A basic race or species of type in which the characters have serifs and variations in the widths of their strokes.

ROP (run of press)   Color or other matter that isn't given a specific special position in the publication.

Rotary press   A press that uses a curved plate to print on a continuous roll of paper.

Rotogravure   A recessed-image (intaglio) printing process on a continuous roll of paper.

Rough   A sketchy dummy or layout to show the placement of elements.

Rule   An element that prints a continuous line or lines usually used to frame type, art, or a layout.

Run-in head   A headline that is part of the first line of the text.

Running foot   A line at the bottom of a book page that indicates the book, chapter, or section title, and/or the

page number.

Running head   A line at the top of a book page that contains the same information as a running foot.

S

Saddle stitch   A binding method for magazines or pamphlets that uses a wire stitch on the centerfold.

Sandwich   A short notice placed within the body of an article.

Sans Serif   A race or species of type without serifs (the finishing strokes on characters) usually containing monotonal letter strokes.

Scale   To size art to certain enlarged or reduced dimensions.

Scanner   A hardware device that reads information from a photograph, image, or text, converting it into a bit-map graphic.

Score   To crease paper on a line to facilitate folding.

Screen   A device, available in various densities used to reduce continuous tone art to a halftone plate.

Script   A typeface that resembles handwriting.

Scroll   To move a story up or down on a video display terminal screen, usually for editing purposes.

Secondary color   A hue (color) produced by mixing two primary colors.

Section logo   A typographic device used to identify a section of a publication.

Series   A basic subdivision of a type family; it has family characteristics but an individual posture; all the sizes of that particular posture of a family.

Serif   The finishing stroke at the end of a primary stroke of a character.

Set solid   Type set with no leading between the lines.

Shade   A darker hue obtained by adding black to a color.

Shaded   Type that gives a gray instead of solid black imprint.

Sideline   An arrangement with short display lines to the left of the cutlines.

Sidestitch (sidewire stitching)   A binding in which the staple is placed on the side rather than on the spine as in saddle stitch.

Signature   A group of pages printed on a single sheet.

Silhouette   Art in which the background has been removed.

Sinkage   A point below the top margin of a page where chapter openings or other material is set.

Skyline   A headline or story at the top of the first page of a publication, above the nameplate.

Slug   A unit of space, usually between lines of type and usually 6 or 12 points thick; a line of cast hot type; an identifying line on copy.

Small cap   A capital letter for a font of type smaller than the regular capital letter.

Software   The instructions or programs that cause a computer to operate and perform desired functions.

Sorts   Characters that are obtainable but not ordinarily included in a font of type, such as mathematical signs and special punctuation and accent marks.

Species   A basic division of type; a race of type.

Spine   The midpoint area between the front and back covers of a book or magazine; the center point of the outside cover.

Spot color   One hue (color) in addition to black, usually in a headline, display line, border, or ornament.

Square Serif   A typeface characterized by monotonal strokes and heavy, squared serifs; also called *Egyptian, Slab Serif.*

Standing head   A headline that remains the same from one issue of a publication to another.

Stepped head   An arrangement of display type in which the top line is flush left, the middle line (if used) is centered, and the third line is flush right, and all the lines are less than full width to create a stair step effect.

Stereotyping   The process of casting a printing form from molten metal by using a mold (called a *mat*) or paper, usually in a curved form, to create a curved printing plate for a rotary press.

Stet   A term meaning "do not change," used in proofreading.

Stick-on letters   Alphabet characters printed on paper, usually self-adhesive,

for cold type composition.

Straight matter   Reading matter; body type; the text material in a book.

Streamer   A banner headline.

Strike-on   Type produced by a typewriter or other percussion keyboard device that impacts character forms directly on paper.

Stripping   Combining halftone and line negatives to create a comprehensive negative for printing plates that contain line and screened art.

Subhead   A display line that is auxiliary to the main headline or used to break up masses of body type.

Sunken initial   An initial inset in reading matter.

Surprint   Something printed over art.

Swash   A letter decorated with an elongated stroke, usually decorative.

Symmetrical   An arrangement of elements in formal balance.

T

Tabloid   A newspaper format usually about half the size of a broadsheet or approximately 11 by 15 inches.

Tabular matter   Statistics arranged in table or columnar form, such as stock market reports, financial statements, and so on.

Terminal   A device in a communications network or system where information can be entered, removed, or displayed for viewing and arranging.

Text   The Black Letter race or species of type.

Text   Reading matter.

Text wrap   To run text around an illustration on a page layout. Some programs have an automatic text-wrap feature that will shorten lines of text when a graphic is encountered; in other systems you need to change the length of lines to go around a graphic.

Thumbnail   A small preliminary sketch of a possible arrangement of elements; also the term for a portrait that is less than a column wide and inset in reading matter.

Tint   A value of color created by adding white to a hue (color).

Tint block   An area on a printed page

produced in a tint, usually with type or art surprinted on it.

Tombstone   Identical side-by-side headlines that compete for attention.

Tone   Shading or tinting a printing element.

Transfer letter   A letter for printing obtained by rubbing from a master sheet onto the layout sheet.

Transitional   A subdivision of the Roman type race with characteristics of both old style and modern Romans.

Type   The characters from which printing is done.

Typeface   The distinctive design of an alphabet of letters and related characters.

Typo   An error in set type.

Typography   The use and arrangement of elements for printing.

U

U&lc   The designation for setting type in capital and lowercase letters where it is appropriate.

Unit   A fraction of an em; in a 36-unit phototypesetting system, for instance, an em would have 36 units; more units allows more latitude in programming space between letters and words in designating character widths.

Unit count   A method of determining whether display type will fit a given area.

Uppercase (uc)   Capital letters.

V

Value   Synonym for tone, or the relative tint or shade of a printing element.

Velox   A black and white print of a half-tone photograph.

Video display terminal (VDT)   A device and screen for arranging elements.

Verso   The even-numbered, left-hand pages.

Vertical justification   Automatic adjustment of leading or the space between lines, in very small amounts so columns on a page can all be made the same depth.

Vignette   An illustration in which the margins appear to fade into the background.

W

Watermark A design, name, and/or logotype impressed on paper during manufacture.

Waxer A device for coating the back of layout parts with melted wax to attach them to a grid or layout sheet.

Web A wide strip or roll of paper that travels through a press for printing.

Weight The comparative thickness of strokes of letters.

Well The arrangement of advertisements on the right and left sides of a page so editorial matter can be placed between.

Widow A short line at the top of a column that completes a paragraph from the bottom of the preceding column; also used to refer to a very short final line of a paragraph.

Wrong font (wf) A type character set in a different family or series from the rest of the specified set matter.

WYSIWYG An acronym for "what you see is what you get."

X

x height The distance between the baseline and meanline of type; the height of a lowercase letter excluding the ascender and descender.

Z

Zipatone A transparent sheet containing dot or line patterns that provides a tonal effect similar to that provided by Ben Day.

INDEX